Entrepreneurial
Activity and the
Development of
Swedish Industry,
1919-1939

THE AMERICAN ECONOMIC ASSOCIATION
TRANSLATION SERIES

WALRAS: *Elements of Pure Economics,* trans. by W. Jaffe

CHAYANOV: *The Theory of Peasant Economy,* ed. by D. Thorner, B. Kerblay, and R. E. F. Smith

DAHMÉN: *Entrepreneurial Activity and the Development of Swedish Industry, 1919–1939,* trans. by Axel Leijonhufvud

CAMERON: *Essays in French Economic History,* ed. by Rondo Cameron, assisted by Franklin F. Mendels and Judith P. Ward

TUGAN-BARANOVSKY: *The Russian Factory in the 19th Century,* trans. by Arthur and Claora Levin, under the supervision of Gregory Grossman

The participation of the American Economic Association in the preparation and publication of this volume consisted of the planning of the "Translation Series," and the selection of this title for the third volume with the hope of obtaining a wide distribution of an important economic classic among English-speaking scholars.

ERIK DAHMÉN

Entrepreneurial Activity and the Development of Swedish Industry, 1919-1939

TRANSLATED BY

Axel Leijonhufvud

Associate Professor
Department of Economics
University of California, Los Angeles

1970
Published for
THE AMERICAN ECONOMIC ASSOCIATION
By
RICHARD D. IRWIN, INC.   HOMEWOOD, ILLINOIS
IRWIN-DORSEY LIMITED, GEORGETOWN, ONTARIO

First Printing, September 1970

Library of Congress Catalog Card No. 73–118184

Printed in the United States of America

Translator's Foreword

This English edition of Professor Erik Dahmén's *Svensk Industriell Företagarverksamhet: Kausalanalys av den industriella utvecklingen 1919–1939*, Uppsala: Almquist & Wicksell, 1950, comprises only Volume I of the work. Volume II of the original edition consists primarily of the data collected and tabulated by Dahmén as a basis for the analysis here translated; in addition to the tables, it also includes appendices discussing the methods used in gathering and interpreting new data, the quality of the data drawn from existing statistical sources, and other related matters.

Omission of Volume II means that the translation gives an entirely inadequate reflection of the magnitude of the empirical work that was undertaken by Professor Dahmén. It was judged, however, that it is primarily his methods and approach, together with the study's demonstration of the kind of results to which the approach leads, that would be of interest to a wider audience of American economists. The second volume, on the other hand, would be of interest mainly to the small number of economists with a research interest in Swedish economic history—who, presumably, would be able to go directly to the original Swedish edition. These considerations would apply also to a number of passages of varying length in Volume I. Except for the deletion (by the author) of a couple of footnotes, and one or two instances where a brief passage from the text has been moved down into the footnotes, this volume has, however, been translated without any changes in its content. Even references to the appendices and tables of the "missing" Volume II have been left as they stand since their purpose is to document the statements made in the text.

The work on this translation has had to be done in the intervals between more immediately pressing duties. It has taken a long time to complete. Professor Bert Hoselitz, as Chairman of the Translations Committee of the American Economic Association, and Professor Dahmén have both shown me a great deal of patience. I am most grateful to them. The translation has benefitted substantially from the careful reading given it by my good friends, Professor Robert Eagly of The University of

Massachusetts. I owe great gratitude to Mrs. Birgitta Swedenborg for her assistance with the tables, figures and other matters, to Miss Margaret Calvo for cheerful help with the typing of the several drafts that the translation has gone through, and to Mr. Lars Jonung and Mrs. Christina Ros-Jonung for compiling the indexes.

Los Angeles   Axel Leijonhufvud
August, 1970

Preface

This study is Part One of my doctoral dissertation.[1] It was first published in Swedish in 1950 only a couple of months after the death of Joseph A. Schumpeter, who was my main source of inspiration in undertaking the study. Schumpeter had, ever since my first years as a student of history and economics, greatly influenced my thinking, and his writings guided me both in my selection of and approach to the subject matter of my dissertation. Most important for me was his path-breaking work of 1911, *Theorie der Wirtschaftlichen Entwicklung*. Here Schumpeter succeeded in integrating the dynamics of technology and business enterprise into the body of economic theory. Thus, with this work, he greatly advanced the prospects of applying economic theory more profitably in historical research.

I believe it is fair to say that Schumpeter had bad luck with this work. Its translation into English in 1934 was most untimely. The depression, and later on the War, muted its reception. Economists were then mainly concerned with short-run problems. In the middle Forties, when I began the work on my dissertation, it was becoming increasingly apparent that, in the years to come, problems of technological progress and economic development would become more urgent. Yet the problems of short-run instability still held the stage in economic debate and research. The digestion and testing of the ideas of Keynes absorbed much of the intellectual energy of economists. Thus, when I started my work, no one had made any systematic attempt to use and develop Schumpeterian concepts in development studies or in historical research. Schumpeter's own *Business Cycles* (1939) was only in part an exception to this. It concentrated too much on the business cycle and, on the whole, lacked sufficient underpinnings of what I would call "grassroots research."

The suggestion some years ago to translate my book raised the question of a possible revision. However, in view of the subsequent development

---

[1] The second part containing the statistical source material has not been translated.

ix

of economic theory and debate, I felt that a revision would be too difficult a task. Furthermore, when viewing my study as a contribution to Swedish economic history, what is called for is not a revision of my book but rather a continuation of the work that this book initiated.

Stockholm   ERIK DAHMÉN

November 1969

From the Author's Preface
to the Swedish Edition

The present work may be regarded as a primarily historical and statistical description of Swedish industrial development during a very eventful period. Its main emphasis is not on theoretical analysis. Nor is it intended as a contribution to the current economic-political debate. In deciding on the plan of the book, however, it has been my ambition to leave the doors open, as far as possible, for further theoretical analysis as well as for considerations of an economic-political nature. Thus, I have attempted to place the work, from the very outset, within a wider frame of reference by briefly discussing some methodological problems relevant to the scientific study of economic development. I have furthermore done my best to account explicitly for the most important issues and concepts in order to achieve a treatment that is both systematic and historical and, at the same time, relevant to the theoretical and economic-political questions that are not discussed in any detail here. I am conscious that my concepts and analytical apparatus may be irritating to many readers. I do believe, however, that the mode of analysis has scientific advantages that an entirely descriptive chronicle would lack and, also, that it provides an essentially more lifelike picture of the development process. I hope, therefore, that even these readers will come to benefit from getting the material presented in this form. Without a framework of this sort, the basic outlines of the development process become difficult to perceive and the distinction between essentials and inessentials difficult to draw; most of all it becomes difficult to retain in one's mind the content of the historical and statistical description for any length of time.

A study of industrial entrepreneurship must, in one way or another, be a part of any analysis of economic and social development. At the same time, however, it is self-evident that such a study must leave out many exceedingly important aspects of the socioeconomic development and leave an even greater number of questions unanswered, despite the fact that they often are relevant to entrepreneurial activity. In my opinion, there is still the advantage in focusing attention on entrepreneurship that it raises some fruitful questions concerning the general history of Sweden in the interwar period where traditional business cycle theory has failed to do so. Frequently, these questions pertain to areas where several social sciences overlap but where little research has been done. In restricting myself to certain specific aspects of socioeconomic development, I have relied on the validity of Professor Erik Lindahl's view, as expressed in his 1939 inaugural lecture in Lund:

If the treatment of the problems, that pertain to the economic development of Sweden since the 1860's, is to yield any really new and valuable results, it seems desirable that researchers devote themselves less to general surveys and more to an intensive treatment of various special problems. Thus it would seem appropriate, in each specific case, to concentrate on some particular aspect of the development process in question, and to leave its other aspects to other researchers.

Although this study has been limited to entrepreneurial activity in manufacturing, the treatment is in many instances somewhat cursory, of some aspects even lapidary. When beginning to plan this work in the spring of 1946, I hesitated for quite some time between concentrating heavily on a few industries or letting the study include a larger number. The advantages of the first alternative were obvious. The analysis could have gone into more detail and it would have been possible, in particular, to give more life to the portrayal of the individuals behind entrepreneurial activity. On the other hand, however, it seemed worthwhile to put the main emphasis on a comparative study of many industries which might contribute in several respects to a better understanding of the development process. Having chosen the latter alternative, I gradually became convinced that the study would gain, in essential respects, from the inclusion of an even greater number of industries than I had initially begun to work with. The inevitable consequence of thus broadening the analysis has been some limitation of its depth. In making this choice, I have, however, attempted to formulate the issues and present the results in such a manner that it should not be too difficult for others, who wish to do so, to relate their work to mine and, perhaps, to pursue it further. In this connection it should be pointed out that the great amount and rich variety of primary data, that has been filed at *Industriens Utredningsinstitut*, certainly could serve as a basis for further in-depth studies of entrepreneurial activity in Swedish manufacturing industries. I have to a large extent seen it as my task to provide a formulation of the relevant issues and a general framework for such studies.

Stockholm   Erik Dahmén
March 1, 1950

Contents

LIST OF FIGURES. xvii

LIST OF TABLES AND MAPS. xviii

PART I
Introduction

1. THE STUDY OF ECONOMIC DEVELOPMENT: CRITICAL AND CON-
STRUCTIVE PREMISES 3

A. Critical Premises. B. Constructive Premises.

2. SOME DATA ON ECONOMIC PROGRESS BEFORE WORLD WAR I. . 13

A. Stages of Sweden's Industrialization. B. Innovations, the Formation of New Firms, Employment, and Production.

3. INTERWAR ECONOMIC DEVELOPMENT OF SWEDEN IN ITS INTER-
NATIONAL CONTEXT 24

A. The Situation at the End of World War I and Developments
during 1919–20. B. The Deflation and Reconversion Crisis of
1920–21. C. The Revival and Prosperity of the Twenties. D. The
Economic Crisis and Depression, 1929-31. A New Era in Economic
Policy. E. The Revival and Prosperity of the Thirties.

4. THE ANALYSIS OF INDUSTRIAL TRANSFORMATION: ITS CONCEPTS
AND PROBLEMS. 44

The Two Components of Transformation. The Concept of Innovation. Principles of Transformation Analysis. Demand-Pull and
Supply-Push in Expansionary Processes. The Meaning of Stagnating and Regressive Processes—"Malinvestment." The Analysis
of Transformation and Its Relation to Business Cycle Theory.
Some Concepts of "Structure." The Transformation Process and
the Formation, Development, and Discontinuation of Firms.

PART II
Transformation of Industrial Production in the Interwar Period

5. SOME FEATURES OF THE INDUSTRIAL TRANSFORMATION PROCESS
    BEFORE WORLD WAR I   61

    A. The Entrepreneurs. B. Structural Tensions and Structural
    Balance in the Development Process. C. The Cumulative Indus-
    trialization Process. D. Business Cycles and the Formation of New
    Firms.

6. THE STATISTICAL MATERIAL AND A SUMMARY ANALYSIS . .   88

    A. Data on Progressive, Stagnating, and Regressive Industries, and
    on Rates of Return in Different Industries. B. Issues and Concepts
    of the Analysis. C. Summary Analysis.

7. ANALYSIS OF PROGRESSIVE INDUSTRIES   126

    Engineering Industries. The Cement Industry. The Concrete and
    Lightweight Concrete Industry. Woodworking Industries. The
    Pulp Industry. The Paper and Cardboard Industry. The Paper
    and Cardboard Processing Industry. Confectionery Industry.
    Mineral Water and Soft Drinks. The Canning Industry. Cotton
    Manufacturing. Ready-Made Clothing. The Hosiery Industry.
    Light Chemicals.

8. ANALYSIS OF STAGNATING AND PROGRESSIVE INDUSTRIES . . .   158

    The Iron and Steel Works. The Chinaware and Ceramics Industry.
    The Glassworks. The Woolen Industry. Gloves, Leather, and Fur
    Products. The Margarine Industry.

9. ANALYSIS OF STAGNATING INDUSTRIES   172

    The Brickworks. The Lumber Mill Industry. The Tanneries and
    the Leather Shoe Manufacturing Industry.

PART III
Formation, Development, and Disappearance of Industrial Firms in the Interwar Period

10. GENERAL SURVEY OF RATES OF FORMATION AND DISAPPEARANCE
     OF FIRMS   181

     A. Issues, Concepts, and the Empirical Data. B. The Statistical
     Picture. C. The Formation, Development, and Disappearance of
     Firms in Relation to the Transformation of Production and Profit-
     ability: Preliminary Analysis.

11. CYCLICAL ASPECTS 208
    A. The Questions. B. The Data.

12. ANALYSIS OF INDUSTRIES WITH HIGH RATES OF ENTRY . . . 228
    The Engineering Industries: *Four Categories of New Enterprises.*
    Subcontracting Firms. New Final Goods Producers Engaging in
    Parallel Competition. Firms Pioneering with Product Innovations.
    Cyclical Variations in Entry Rates. The Degree of Product Special-
    ization. Collusive Practices in Restraint of Competition. Firm
    Mortality and Its Cyclical Variation. Concrete Products and
    Lightweight Concrete. The Woodworking Industries. Paper and
    Cardboard Processing Industry. The Oleomargarine Industry. The
    Confectionery Industry. The Canning Industry. Mineral Water
    and Soft Drinks. The Clothing and Hosiery Industries. Gloves,
    Leather, and Fur Products. The Leather Shoe Industry. Paints and
    Varnishes. Oils, Soft Soap, Soap, Perfumes, and Cosmetics.

13. ANALYSIS OF INDUSTRIES WITH LITTLE ENTRY 309
    Iron and Steel Mills. The Cement Industry. Porcelain and Ceram-
    ics Industry. The Glassworks. The Brickyards. The Forest
    Industries: *The Lumber Mills. The Pulp Industry. The Paper and*
    Cardboard Industry. Cotton and Woolen Manufacture. The
    Tanneries.

14. THE FINANCING OF NEW ENTERPRISES 345
    A. Problems and Data. B. Results and Analysis.

15. THE GEOGRAPHICAL ASPECTS: SOME BRIEF REMARKS . . . 363
    A. The Questions and the Data. B. Results and Analysis.

PART IV
Conclusions

16. SYSTEMATIC SUMMARY AND CONCLUDING REMARKS 385
    A. Systematic Summary: *The Interwar Period—An Era of Indus-*
    trial Metamorphosis. Consequences of World War I and Impulses
    from the United States. The First Stage of the Industrial Trans-
    formation. The Second Phase of the Industrial Transformation.
    Characteristics of the Formation, Development, and Disappearance
    of Firms. B. The Industrial Transformation and the Problem of
    Business Fluctuations. Some Methodological Comments and Con-
    clusions in the Light of the Results of the Causal Analysis.

Indexes

INDEX OF NAMES 431

INDEX OF FIRMS 433

INDEX OF SUBJECTS 435

List of Figures

1. Mean Population in Age Groups 15–65 and National Income and Investment in 1929 Swedish Crowns per Capita (Age Groups 15–65) for the Period 1861–1939. 14

2. Distribution of Labor Force by Industry Groups, 1860–1913. 20

3. Output of Major Products, 1846–1913. 21–22

4. Distribution of Labor Force by Industry Groups, 1919–39. . 25

5. National Income, Imports, and Exports in Current Swedish Crowns, 1919–39 26

6. The Labor Market, 1919–39. 27

7. Residential Construction, 1914–39. 31

8. The Composition of Imports, 1930–37. 42

9. Economic Fluctuations in Sweden, 1860–1913. 76

10. International Economic Fluctuations, 1850–1913. 77

11. Number of New Firms Started, 1850–1909. 83

12. Major Features of the Industrial Transformation Process 1913–39 95–116

13. Output and Exports of Pulp, 1919–39. 140

14. Output and Exports of Paper and Cardboard, 1919–39. . . 144

15. The Steel Market, 1913–39. 162

16. The Formation of Firms, 1919–39. 210

17. Discontinuation of Firms, 1919–39. 211

18. Number of Workers in Firms of Different Categories, 1919–39 212–220

19. Number of Plants, 1919–39. 222

20. Concentration of Engineering Industries in 1919 and 1939. . 230

21. Capacity of Sulphate Pulp Mills in 1919 and 1939. . . . 332

22. Capacity of Sulphite Pulp Mills in 1919 and 1939. . . . 333

23. Capacity of Mechanical Pulp Mills in 1919 and 1939. . . . 334

24. Capacity of Paper and Cardboard Mills in 1919 and 1939. . 336

25. Number of Persons in Each Income Class in 1912, 1920, and 1930 358

26. Total Incomes in Each Income Class in 1912, 1920, and 1930. 358

List of Tables and Maps

TABLES

1. Average Annual Net Growth of Population in Age Groups 15–65. 32
2. Number of New Firms Started, 1850–1909. 78–80
3. Reported Profits as Percent of Net Worth. 94
4. Survey of the Transformation of Production in the Interwar Period 122
5. Survey of the Formation and Disappearance of Firms in the Interwar Period 191–192
6. Initial Size of Enterprise and Development Types. . . . 195
7. Survey of Process Types and Formation of Enterprises. . . 201
8. Mortality of Firms of Different Size Classes. 209
9. Survey of Engineering Firms Founded by Workers, Foremen, etc. 238
10. Engineering Firms Grouped According to Development Type and Status in 1939 or When Discontinued. . . . 241
11. Specialization of Engineering Firms. 251
12. Specialization of Engineering Firms in 1939. 251
13a. Building Joineries Grouped According to Type of Development and Degree of Specialization. 264
13b. Building Joineries Grouped According to Value of Output and Degree of Specialization. 264
14. Survey of Joineries Established by Workers, Foremen, etc. . 267
15. Survey of Clothing and Textile Manufacturing, Firms Established by Workers, Foremen, etc. 291
16. Mortality of Lumber Mills in Norrland. 327
17. The Financing of Firm Formation. Survey of All Sources Used 348
18. The Financing of Firm Formation. Number of Firms with Only a Single Source of Funds. 349
19. The Financing of Firm Formation. Survey of Most Important Sources for Firms Utilizing More than One. 352

20. The Financing of Firm Formation. Survey of Only Source or Most Important Source of Funds, Grouped According to Previous Occupation of Founder.   353

21. Total Population and Employment in Industry and Crafts, 1920, 1930, and 1940.   367

22a. Number of Firms in 1919 Grouped According to Geographical Location and Size of Work Force.   375

22b. Mortality between 1919 and 1939 among Firms in Operation in 1919 Grouped According to Geographical Location and Size of Work Force.   376

23a. Number of Enterprises Newly Established 1919–1939 Grouped by Geographical Location and Size of Work Force.   376

23b. Mortality of Enterprises Established 1919–39 Grouped by Geographical Location and Size of Work Force.   377

24. Number of Firms in 1939 Grouped According to Geographical Location and Size of Work Force.   377

MAPS

1. The Furniture Industry in 1939.   371

2. Building Joineries in 1939.   372

Part I

Introduction

1 The Study of Economic Development: Critical and Constructive Premises

A. Critical Premises

The study of economic development has followed three major paths. In business cycle theory, important aspects of the periodicity of economic activity in the industrial era have been analyzed, in part by the construction of formal, dynamic models. In empirical business cycle research, a great amount of statistical material has been collected and organized, particularly on the interwar period between 1919 and 1939. We now have a number of time series on production, construction activity, employment, international trade, prices, money supply, financial markets, and so on. Econometrics—the newest branch of inductive business cycle research—has made great advances, especially where combined with an interest in deductive theory.

Economic historical research, which began as a reaction against classical theory, has unearthed and critically examined the sources of vast amounts of empirical material. While economic historians have been successful in shedding light on the economic events of the industrial revolution and earlier periods, the same interest has not been devoted to 20th century developments. Despite the very considerable advances in knowledge made in the three areas mentioned, some topics have not been too well covered. Certain aspects of economic development have received remarkably little attention.

It is not easy to present a comprehensive picture of the state of business cycle research. In the realm of pure theory we have had a proliferation of models, and inductive business cycle research is similarly difficult to survey. It is sufficient for our present purposes to sketch some common characteristics. This sketch, however, ignores certain distinctive lines of thought in business cycle research. These will be commented upon in Section B below.

Haberler, for example, in his League of Nations work, *Prosperity and Depression,* brings out three important features of the cyclical process: (1) Both boom and depression have usually involved a cumulative process of at least two years' duration. The mechanism of this process has been pretty thoroughly described, and there have been many different, complementary explanations. To explain how a boom or a depression, once started, feeds upon itself no longer poses any substantial problems. (2) The longer the duration of a boom (or depression), the more sensitive the economic process becomes to disturbances and "shocks" (or to an improvement) in some part of the economy. This is also well understood. Furthermore, (3) it has been demonstrated why, given certain assumptions, an expansionary process sooner or later must turn into contraction and vice versa. Thus it is not difficult to explain why the industrial era has experienced business fluctuations. Alternating good and bad times have been inherent in modern industrialism. It should be emphasized, too, that specialists in this area agree on many crucial issues. The substantial accomplishments of econometric research deserve much of the credit for this consensus.

One should not conclude, however, that cyclical fluctuations no longer present problems to economists. Nor should one conclude that there are no problems with respect to the process of economic development proper. We do not as yet have an adequate grasp of the *economic transformation* process, that is, the introduction of new commodities, new technology, and new markets, and how these innovations struggle with, and win out over, older commodities and methods. It should be noted that such a transformation may well take place without any concurrent variations whatsoever in the aggregates that primarily interest the business cycle specialist, such as employment, investment, national income, and so on. Similarly, in studies spanning several cycles, little attention has been devoted to analyzing the *trend*, except for certain gross statistical aggregates that do not necessarily reveal much about the transformation process.

There is a close connection between business cycle research in its traditional form and modern theories of monetary and fiscal policy. The critical premise under discussion may be clarified by contrasting these theories with the problems of economic transformation as they are conceived here. There have been significant advances in theories of monetary and fiscal policy, and the possibilities of achieving, say, "full employment" by politically directed economic means have improved. Modern national income analysis deals mainly with the following categories: demand, national income, interest rates, liquidity, savings, investment, exports, imports, and employment. It is said, for example, that if a depression is to be avoided, investment must be large enough to equal total savings at the rate of national income which corresponds to full employment. Such analysis can be heuristically helpful. It can also be useful in planning economic policy. But it does not touch on the transformation aspect of economic development.

A study of the usual concepts of business cycle research reveals, at least in part, their limited applicability to the economic development process. By and large, these theoretical concepts comprise such categories as the sum of all production of capital goods or consumption goods, total consumption, total savings, the level of wages, and so forth. The following statements are typical: "When the demand for goods in money terms (the money flow) grows, production will increase and prices go up." "A deficiency of savings brings about the crisis." "Changes in the demand for final goods tend to give rise to much stronger fluctuations in the demand for the capital goods used in their production." "Depressions are caused by too small a part of incomes being spent on consumption goods." "When the propensity to save goes up, but the propensity to invest stays the same, national income will fall until savings equal investment."

With such aggregative concepts as instruments, and with empirical research being directed toward the corresponding total categories, it is obvious that attention has been primarily concentrated on those general aspects of the development process that have been emphasized as being characteristic of most business cycle research. The driving forces behind the investments, behind the technical and economic deliberations, behind the new commodities and the new production methods, etc., are not matters ordinarily within the purview of such aggregative analysis. Rather it has become customary to regard the transformation process as exogenously given.

The interdependence of theory and empirical research in the business cycle field has contributed to this state of affairs. Empirical work has been relatively constrained to the concepts of theory, while at the same time theory has been limited by the fact that empirical results appear in the form of aggregates of the type indicated. This is one reason why it has been rather difficult to achieve cooperation between business cycle researchers and those who have studied the development process from a purely historical perspective.

From the point of view of *economic historical research*, the aggregative concepts which business cycle theory has borrowed primarily from monetary and capital theory are rather alien. The result has been a certain skeptical attitude toward theory in general. In addition, the mathematical character of econometrics has made it by and large an unknown territory to the historians. Thus historians have not to any great extent sought close interaction with business cycle researchers with their concentration on theoretical problems and model building. Moves in this direction have been difficult because business cycle theory and the accompanying empirical research led to questions of cyclical policy rather early. This tended to preserve the gulf between the business cycle economists and the historians. We cannot at this point delve into the reasons why business cycle research developed this way instead of evolving out of economic historical research or why an early, close connection was not established.

One may note that economics had its origin in natural law doctrines and evolved into "political economy." Cyclic fluctuations came to be generally regarded as "disturbances" in an economic system where the goal was maintenance of equilibrium. It should be pointed out, finally, that a controversy between classical economic theory in general and the so-called Historical School in Germany had already arisen in the middle of the 19th century before business cycle research had evolved as a distinct field.

The transformation process has been a primary object of study for the historians and of secondary importance for business cycle specialists. The consequence of this development has been that the transformation process has received little systematic theoretical attention. This, in turn, has indubitably reduced the prospects of reaching a real understanding of the economic transformation process. Economic historical research has not been able satisfactorily to complement the basic approach of business cycle theory to the study of economic development. But neither has the latter approach contributed a fully appropriate theoretical framework in support of economic historical research. Thus there is a gap, or at least little apparent cooperation, between macrotheorists and econometricians on the one hand and historians on the other—as can be seen by a glance at the shelves of any social science library.

With this discussion as background, the first working hypothesis of the present study can be stated. It is that an analysis of actual, historical processes, starting from explicit issues suggested by theory (i.e., *causal analysis*), is the approach most likely to lead to coordination of economic business cycle research and economic history. A second, and related, working hypothesis is that such coordination is appropriate if the desired objective is to cover those areas which previous research in economic development has to a certain extent disregarded.

The transformation process can certainly be systematically studied by means of a conceptual apparatus having no explicit connection with the usual aggregative framework of business cycle theory. Indeed, such an approach might well take its place alongside current business cycle research. But it is evident, also, that macroeconomic study of cyclical fluctuations, in itself of great importance, could be made more penetrating if it were based on an analysis of the transformation process. The more economic transformation is studied in terms of causal analysis, the more realistic the premises upon which business cycle theory is based will become. At the same time, the econometricians, so far mostly preoccupied with the traditional questions of business cycle theory, would be furnished with new materials and new problems.

These working hypotheses have one particularly important principle in common. The first aspect of this principle is that *theory* should be systematically oriented toward actual historical processes. A theory which is independent, in the sense of having no such specific historical orientation, may be of great value—indeed, it may be quite indispensable in certain areas of economic research. But experience indicates that the prospects of its leading to an analysis of the transformation process are relatively dark.

The second aspect of the principle is that the *empirical* study of development should proceed with the help of a systematically constructed and coherent analytical framework. This framework should contain explicit questions, thus providing the guidelines for delimiting the empirical work and for selecting the relevant data. There is no reason why economic historical research should not be pursued with a larger kit of theoretical tools than is the present practice; nor is there any reason why it should not be directed toward the analysis of repetitive phenomena (i.e., essentially similar, although superficially different, processes).

A mainly descriptive chronicle may, of course, still fulfill the very important function of making public previously unknown information. If, however, one desires a really analytical elucidation of the transformation process, the descriptive method must be judged deficient on the basis of past performance. What, then, are the constructive premises for the desired analysis?

B. Constructive Premises

Three contributions to the subject of economic development which do not fit the categories of business cycle research or economic history discussed so far have been of particular importance to the constructive basis of the present work: (1) the issues which Thorstein Veblen raised at the turn of the century; (2) the related methodological views of Johan Åkerman; (3) and most importantly, Joseph Schumpeter's approach to the development problem.

Veblen outlined his criticism of the then ruling economic doctrines in a couple of essays first published between 1898 and 1900.[1] The strengths and weaknesses of neoclassical theory are particularly evident in the sys-

---

[1] The essays first appeared in the *Quarterly Journal of Economics*, Vols. XII–XIV, and were later partly reprinted under the heading "Why is economics not an evolutionary science?" in Veblen's *The Place of Science in Modern Civilization and Other Essays* (New York, 1919).

tem of Alfred Marshall. His is a taxonomic theory: a mapping of static models of price formation, a classification of microeconomic decision problems with occasional application to macroeconomic issues. Unfortunately, Veblen says, it is not an analysis of actual processes in a calendar time context, nor of causal forces and changing institutions. According to Veblen, the concern is too much with the result of the development process and not enough with the development process itself. Economic science thus resembles the system of Linnaeus more than it does that of Darwin.

There is an obvious affinity between Veblen's argument and Åkerman's methodological views. In his *On the Rhythm of Economic Life*, Åkerman's approach was in certain respects quite Veblenian. The agreement with Veblen's basic position is most clearly evident in a later book, written for a wider audience, *Economic Progress and Economic Crises*, in which Åkerman called for the development of a "temporal economic theory."[2] In later years, he developed the deeper methodological issues involved, and in his *Economic Theory* formulated what he terms the "fundamental dualism" between choice-theoretical and causal analysis.[3] The central role given to the causal analysis and the stress put on the contrast between choice-theoretical models and the causal analysis of actual temporal development processes stem from a fundamental position shared by both authors.

The emphasis on causal analysis and the demonstration of its basic principles constitute the *general* orientation of the present work. The most important influence on the *specific* direction taken has come from the approach developed by Schumpeter in his *Theory of Economic Development*.[4]

Veblen's ideas reappear also in Schumpeter's work. But in this case it is hardly the general concept sketched above that has been most important, for Schumpeter has been influenced by certain specific ideas advanced in Veblen's *Theory of Business Enterprise*.[5] The importance given to the role of entrepreneurship in the discussion of economic development (as, for example, the clear distinction between "machine process" and "business enterprise"), as well as the dynamic approach to problems, all adumbrate Schumpeter's ideas of "entrepreneurial activity" and "new combinations in production" and his skeptical attitude toward aggregative analysis. Schumpeter, however, has posed the issues more rigorously and precisely, and therefore his theoretical structure has an instrumental value for the causal analysis far greater than Veblen's.

---

[2] J. Åkerman, *Om det ekonomiska livets rytmik* (Stockholm, 1928), and *Ekonomiskt framåtskridande och ekonomiska kriser* (Stockholm, 1931).

[3] Åkerman, *Ekonomisk teori* (Lund, 1939), Vol. I, and (Lund, 1943), Vol. II.

[4] J. Schumpeter, *Theorie der wirtschaftlichen Entwicklung* (Jena, 1911).

[5] T. Veblen, *Theory of Business Enterprise* (New York, 1904).

Since the Schumpeterian system provides the most immediate source of constructive premises for the present work, it requires special attention. This does not entail any lengthy presentation: the fundamental conception is simple.

For our purposes, it is unnecessary to distinguish between Schumpeter's *Theory of Economic Development* and his later *Business Cycles*.[6] The analysis presented in the latter work is more thorough, but the formulation of the central problem remains essentially the same—at least in those respects that are of most interest in the present context.

In order to clarify the implications of his argument, Schumpeter starts with a description of a hypothetical, *stationary circular flow,* an economic process which continually repeats itself within a framework of unchanged production functions. Although this model is used as a theoretical tool to bring the later emphasized changes into bold relief, Schumpeter does not regard the circular flow altogether as a fiction. Many actual processes have the character of stages in such a circular flow.

Next, in his line of reasoning, the circular flow is disturbed by changes in the production functions. New methods of production and new commodities emerge—new factor combinations supersede older ones.[7] These new combinations, or rather innovations, are brought about by the entrepreneur. This specific function—not to be confused with that of the inventor or engineer nor with that of the owner or financier—makes the entrepreneur a driving rather than a preconditioning force in the development process.[8] The special character of entrepreneurial activity

---

[6] J. Schumpeter, *Business Cycles* (New York and London, 1939), Vols. I and II.

[7] "New combinations" is not really a very felicitous term, however, since, taken literally, it would refer to *all* changes including those that take place *within the framework of unaltered production functions.* Such adjustments frequently occur as a consequence of changes in relative prices (cf. Schumpeter, *op. cit.,* Vol. I, p. 87, fn. 2). To be of use in causal analysis, Schumpeter's concepts must be defined more precisely than done in his *Business Cycles,* where the discussion hardly is completely satisfactory in this regard. We will have occasion to return to this issue below. For the moment it is sufficient to paraphrase Schumpeter since the objective is only to sketch the main outlines of his argument.

[8] This, of course, does not mean that investors, engineers, owners, or financiers never play the role of entrepreneurs. Individuals can naturally combine entrepreneurial activity with other activities. Nor, of course, does this statement about the role of the entrepreneur have any normative significance. Cf. Schumpeter, *op. cit.,* Vol. I, pp. 84 ff., where Schumpeter develops the invention-innovation distinction and discusses the three roles of entrepreneur, owner, and financier. Schumpeter's treatment of these conceptual problems can hardly be improved upon, and for present purposes it is sufficient just to refer to it. It must be pointed out, however, that, whereas Schumpeter's decision to reserve the term "entrepreneur" for those who carry out innovations does serve the cause of conceptual clarity, the result is alien to popular usage, and it will not be possible to adhere strictly to his terminology in the casual analysis attempted here. The present study will use "entrepreneur" and "entrepreneurial activity" in the more general, everyday senses of the terms. To do so need not mean that one fudges the distinctions between the different entrepreneurial functions.

is clearly apparent when set against the background of the stationary flow, where no such changes take place.

According to the third step of the argument, these "new combinations" set *adjustment processes* in motion. Competition for the factors of production, for instance, may lead initially to an upward pressure on prices—the possibilities of creating credit are decisive here—and to rejection of older factor combinations. Generally speaking, the whole system is forced to adjust to the innovations.

These three connected elements constitute the core of what is usually considered Schumpeter's theory of business cycles. They are also the tools Schumpeter himself uses in his *Business Cycles* to reconstruct actual processes. The theory had been developed, however, in the earlier work of 1911. The more exhaustive and detailed presentation in *Business Cycles* contains basically only one fundamental addition to the original scheme.

The process which the innovations set in motion has certain "secondary" effects which bring about larger disturbances than the innovations themselves could cause. Schumpeter speaks in terms of a primary and a secondary wave, and he notes that the latter might well be the more noticeable and quantitatively the more significant despite being secondary in the causal sense.[9] In the primary wave the upper turning point is not an equilibrium position. Schumpeter considers this position, or rather equilibrium neighborhood, to lie around the lower turning point. The turning points of the secondary wave are both disequilibrium positions. In the primary process the change from contraction to expansion is caused by the innovations. The primary wave is not self-generating—whereas this is the rule with the secondary process.

It is important to note that in Schumpeter's conception of a primary process, cyclical fluctuations do not depend on the occurrence of certain new combinations which, when completed, are revealed as "malinvestments" and therefore have to be weeded out. In the primary process, new combinations emerge as elements in the development process and force the system to adjust; no older combinations need be revealed as mistakes. Even if no mistakes at all were committed, such an adjustment process could become necessary and the theoretical formulation would still retain its relevance.[10] The fact that the manufacture of tile stoves entirely disappeared with the advent of modern central heating, for example, does not imply that a mistake was made at the time when the production of tile stoves was first begun.

---

[9] Cf. Schumpeter, *op. cit.*, Vol. I, pp. 145 ff.

[10] Cf. Schumpeter, *op. cit.*, p. 140. This, of course, says nothing about the malinvestment theory *per se*. The entire problem of the role that partial, "strategic" malinvestments and the consequent excess capacity may play in shaping economic development and creating cycles falls quite naturally within the purview of the study of development from the standpoint of economic transformation.

It is also important to emphasize that the Schumpeterian system should not be classified simply as a business cycle theory on a par with the others. The fact that Schumpeter himself puts the explanation of *cyclical fluctuations* in the foreground should not be misinterpreted. This is simply another matter altogether, and besides, there is nothing unreasonable about it. For present purposes, however, it is not very important whether or not his analysis implies the presence of cyclical fluctuations in the development process.[11] Even though this question is of some interest and deserves discussion, the essential point is the way in which Schumpeter has posed the problem.[12]

The decisive consideration is that Schumpeter does not work with the kind of aggregates usual in business cycle research and that, consequently, he finds it easier to pose the questions relevant to the transformation process. These questions do not supplant but rather complement other business cycle theories. The Schumpeterian approach in all its simplicity offers promising avenues toward a systematic and theoretical analysis of economic transformation, an analysis closely related to actual historical processes. It presents a somewhat different approach to the analysis of economic development problems; although almost always ignored, this fact cannot be emphasized strongly enough.

. . .

A study of economic development issues based on the ideas discussed in this introduction may be more or less ambitious in scope. One possibility is to aim at reconstruction of the entire economic process in a single country in order to obtain an analysis of the multiplicity of factors that fall within this frame of reference. Such an approach would strive for a balanced picture of the relative importance of different factors. The main emphasis then is on the total picture of the historical process which the analysis can provide and less on any particular, more detailed, investigation.

---

[11] For present purposes, therefore, there is no reason to enter into a discussion of the entire complex of problems that Schumpeter deals with in detail in his *Business Cycles*. We may just note that Schumpeter sees no reason to expect that the actual process should exhibit a single, typical wave pattern or even two or three such superimposed patterns (cf. Schumpeter, *op. cit.*, Vol. I, p. 69). In the historical part of the study, however, he finds it convenient, given the approximate pattern of actual developments, to base his analysis on a "three-cycle schema."

[12] Schumpeter is, of course, quite conscious of the distinctiveness of his approach but emphasizes at the same time (and rightly so) that it is so simple in principle as to be almost trivial: ". . . it should never be forgotten that at the outset all we need to say to anyone who doubts is: Look around you!" (*op. cit.*, Vol. I, p. 87). But, as already mentioned, his own attention is entirely focused on the business cycle problem and not on the transformation problem for its own sake.

A study can, on the other hand, also be planned as an analysis with a more limited objective, e.g., certain elements of the total process can be singled out. The other elements are then touched upon only to the extent absolutely necessary. With this approach there is no claim of presenting a balanced picture of the relative importance of the different factors in the total process.

The latter alternative has been chosen for the present work. The objective is delimited with respect to time and space as well as issues. First, the time period studied is mainly the *interwar period* (i.e., the years 1919–39) and the study involves *Sweden* only. The discussion of the first half-century of Swedish industrialism should be considered only as providing a background to the main task. Paucity of data has also made the analysis of this period rather sketchy and tentative in nature. Second, the problems under study concern only developments in the *industrial sector*. Third, *the main theme is the analysis of the industrial transformation process in conjunction with an analysis of the formation, evolution, and discontinuation of firms.* In contrast to Schumpeter's work, business cycle aspects of the development process play a secondary role.

The immediate task is to outline the background of interwar industrial developments. The following two chapters are therefore devoted to (*a*) a very brief account of some of the main features of economic progress in Sweden before World War I, and (*b*) a somewhat more detailed, but still very cursory, survey of Sweden's general economic development in the interwar period as seen in its international setting. Both chapters utilize data which are by and large easily available; hence, no claim is made for originality. The fourth chapter is devoted to a discussion of the general approach taken to the analysis of economic transformation, and of its central issues and concepts. This discussion draws heavily upon the critical and constructive premises of Chapter 1 and the historical account presented in Chapters 2 and 3.

2 Some Data on Economic Progress before World War I

A. Stages of Sweden's Industrialization

At the middle of the 19th century the population of Sweden was almost 3.5 million. About 80 percent of the people earned their livelihood in the agricultural sector, while only 10 percent were engaged in industrial types of employment or in the crafts. The communications network was extremely primitive. There were no railroads and only a few highways. Factory production for sale outside local markets was confined mainly to the steel, lumber, and textile industries. The steel and lumber industries were located in rural areas. The urban population, which accounted for around 10 percent of the total, was only to a very small degree occupied in industrial employment. Except for government agencies, urban life was almost completely dominated by commerce and craft activities; in the latter instance production was for a local market and utilized little if any machine equipment.

At the outbreak of World War I, 60 years later, Sweden's population had grown to 5.7 million despite a net emigration of 1.2 million people. Of the total, 1.8 million, or more than 30 percent, earned their livelihood in manufacturing and crafts. The country owned a railway network with a total track length of 8,700 miles, and the volume of both internal and external trade had multiplied several times. National and local autarky had to a large extent been supplanted by division of labor and specialization. The banking and credit system had undergone revolutionary changes. Although the steel and lumber industries, the primary carriers of the rapid industrialization movement, were still rurally based, the character of urban life had changed considerably.

The development of the textile industries, of an engineering industry

13

independent of the old ironworks, and of a whole range of consumption goods industries accounted for the rise in urban industrial employment. At the outbreak of World War I, 26 percent of the population lived in the cities and was by and large, directly or indirectly, dependent on the new industries and on commerce. The urban commerce which had developed in conjunction with the new factory industries was in many respects different in nature from that at the middle of the 19th century. Finally, Swedish national income had multiplied several times even when measured on a per capita basis (Cf. Figure 1).

FIGURE 1

Mean Population in Age Groups 15–65 and National Income and Investment in 1929 Swedish Crowns per Capita (Age Groups 15–65) for the Period 1861–1939 (Index 1929 = 100)

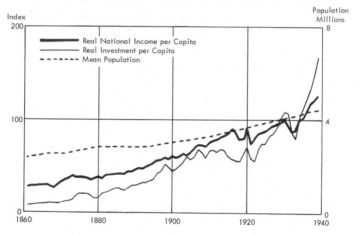

SOURCES: *Wages, Cost of Living and National Income in Sweden 1860–1930:* Vol. II, G. Bagge, E. Lundberg, I. Svennilson, *Wages in Sweden 1860–1930*, Part II, Table 190; Vol. III, E. Lindahl, E. Dahlgren, K. Kock, *National Income of Sweden*, Part I, Table 52 and Table 53 and Part II, Table 64; *Statistisk Årsbok; Svensk Tidskrift 1941*, p. 593; *1941 års statsverksproposition*, appendix 1, p. 4; *Undersökningar rörande det samlade skattetrycket i Sverige och utlandet* (SOU, 1936, No. 18, pp. 213 and 214); *Kommersiella Meddelanden: Ekonomisk översikt*.

The economic structure of Sweden had thus undergone a radical transformation, although this transformation was not without roots in the past. A study of the growth of the Swedish economy, focusing on innovations, enterprise formation, employment, and production, yields a picture of greater continuity in development than would perhaps be expected.[1] The fact remains, however, that in comparison with preceding

---

[1] T. Gårdlund, *Industrialismens samhälle* (Stockholm, 1942), p. 60, makes the point very well: "In scrutinizing popular conceptions about historical epochs, one is often struck by the fact that the phenomena regarded as characteristic of the epoch can be traced back far earlier and became of great importance only far later than is generally claimed."

years the development just after the middle of the century took on a wholly different rate of change and became considerably more revolutionary in character.

Almost every division of a process into stages must do violence to the continuity of development. Bearing this in mind, one could perhaps characterize the 1850's and 1860's as the first stage of Sweden's industrialization. Particularly in the case of the great basic capital goods and export industries, we find in these years the beginnings of most of the developments that in later decades grew to vast proportions. Naturally the beginnings were often modest indeed, and in many cases they were of less importance quantitatively than as symptoms of what was to come.

In certain areas, the beginnings of a modern industry were present in the first half of the 19th century; this was true of the iron and lumber industries and to a certain extent the engineering industry. But progress was not nearly as rapid as in the decades immediately following 1850. It would be difficult to justify a claim that the 1830's or 1840's, for example, saw the beginnings of most of the industrial developments that took place in the latter half of the century. It cannot be denied that the industrialization of Sweden got off to a late and relatively slow start.

If one is to continue with the attempt at dividing the industrial development of Sweden into stages, the mid-1890's would mark the beginning of a new stage. Following the exceptionally rapid industrialization of the early 1870's, the structural transformation of the economy continued at a more moderate but still quite rapid pace into the mid-1890's, when another hectic surge of industrialization started. The general price level had fallen considerably in the interim, and the number of recession years was greater than the number of boom years. The industrialization of more and more sectors of the economy as well as the modernization of agriculture nonetheless brought a rising standard of living to practically all social groups. This occurred despite the very high rate of population growth which was primarily a result of the falling death rates.

Difficulties in many areas of industrial activity as well as agriculture led to a steady strengthening of protectionist forces. Agriculture suffered particularly because of the mounting competition from transocean countries. The decision to raise tariffs substantially in most areas was reached in 1888. Yet, this year cannot be regarded as marking the beginning of the new industrialization stage. This stage began rather in the mid-1890's. Nothing indicates that the new surge of industrialization was crucially dependent upon the tariff increases. Yet the year 1888 remains a historical milestone.

The new stage, 1895–1914, was characterized by developments in three areas: (1) the exceptionally important "take-off" of iron ore and pulp exports, (2) the rapid electrification of the country and the first big spurt of growth in the electrical engineering industry, and (3) the continued, strong expansion of the other engineering industries. But the rapid industrialization of a large number of consumer goods industries was also an important feature of this stage. Thus the fact that the growth of the lumber industry ceased around the turn of the century and the era of railroad construction reached its end did not cause the economy to lose momentum.

The increased size of manufacturing firms, as a result both of larger plants and the emergence of multiplant companies, was another element of strength. The declining trend of prices was reversed and the price level rose from the mid-1890's on; most years of the 1895–1914 period must be considered as boom years. Living standards continued to rise at a pace which was apparently substantially the same—and for the agricultural population probably even a bit faster—as in the preceding period.

The last decade of the 19th century signaled a new stage in other respects as well. The old social structure had started to fade with the development of communications and industry, and a new structure now began to emerge. Both sides of the labor market organized themselves, and the political parties achieved their modern form with the first emergence of parliamentarianism and an increasingly democratic social life in general. The years between the mid-nineties and the outbreak of World War I were the founding period of Sweden's modern "organized society."

Cartel agreements became more common, although as a rule they did not become strong enough to eliminate competition altogether. Finally, during this period, Sweden passed two important milestones in its economic history, curiously enough at about the same time. Between 1910 and 1914 the previously high rate of capital imports began to decrease and ceased completely just before the outbreak of World War I. At the same time, the birth rate, and even the total number of births, started to fall, thereby marking the beginning of a demographically new era.

A preliminary survey of innovations, enterprise formation, employment, and production in the industrial sectors during the first half-century of industrialism will show that the indicated periods were reasonably chosen.

B. Innovations, the Formation of New Firms, Employment, and Production[2]

Steam engines began to be utilized in the iron ore mines for the pumping of water and hoisting of ore after the middle of the century, but waterwheels and horses were still dominant in the early 1870's. The innovation of steam had not yet been generally accepted. By the turn of the

---

[2] With regard to the innovations, Gårdlund, *op. cit.*, is the best source.

century, however, the changeover had been largely completed. Rail transportation, introduced into the mines in the 1860's, followed a similar pattern.

In the steel mills, the Bessemer process had first come into use in 1858, but the puddling process still dominated completely in the 1870's and started to disappear only after the turn of the century with the rapid acceptance of the open hearth process. The movement toward concentration in the operation of the hearths and their continual operation throughout the year started in the 1860's but became general only later.

In the area of steel manufacturing, production in Eskilstuna began gradually to shift after 1850 from the small craft shops to the larger, mechanized factories. The great era of progress for this industry did not begin until the 1870's, however.

A heavy engineering industry of limited scale but independent of the old ironworks had by the middle of the century existed for several decades. It had a rather special character, however. Often established in connection with railroad or canal projects, it produced mainly individual items to order for local or regional markets. The first signs of change appeared around 1850. A certain degree of specialization, and resulting mass production, was introduced with the epoch-making first milling machine—a prerequisite of large-scale production. Markets no longer remained purely local or regional.

But specialization did not become the general rule until the last years of the 19th or the first decade of the 20th century and did not proceed very far even in this later period. Besides the milling machine, one finds a number of other significant innovations in productive techniques before 1870, but these did not become widespread. From the 1840's onward, more and more signs of the coming industrialization appear, but quantitatively, the great surge of growth came only in the last decades of the century and especially after 1895.

In lumber milling, the 1850's and 1860's were typical pioneer decades. The period saw the first steam saws introduced and also the development of big joint-stock companies, particularly in the northern provinces. These companies began to acquire their own forests, a policy that became much more common after 1870 and was generally prevalent after 1895. Water-driven sawmills appear to have grown in number at about the same rate as the steam mills up to 1870, but they were closed down by the thousands in the following decades. The task of clearing the rivers and constructing the channels for floating logs to the coastal mills began before 1860, but the era of great investment in the floating ways did not come until the 1870's and 1880's.

Sweden's first planing mill was built in the late 1860's and was in operation by 1870. A string of other planing mills followed with a big breakthrough for the industry around 1890. The trend away from rough-sawn lumber and toward smaller size roundwood and boards can also be traced back to the late 1860's, but it did not become quantitatively important until later. More examples could be given, but the development of this industry can be summarized briefly: The foundation for most of the modern lumber mill industry was laid in the decades before 1870, but the industry's era of extraordinarily rapid absolute growth belongs to the following decades, while the period since the turn of the century has been one of stagnation.

The years before 1870 were marked by raw material shortages for the rag-paper mills and a general scarcity of paper; they also represent the first period of innovation in the Swedish pulp industry. The first plant for the production of mechanical pulp was erected in 1857. The chemical method of making pulp was introduced in the early 1870's, after several years of technical experimentation. Thus the construction in 1871 of a mill for the production of sulphate pulp marks the introduction of this innovation in Sweden; the production of sulphite pulp dates from 1874 or perhaps somewhat earlier.[3] In the case of both mechanical and chemical pulp, widespread adoption did not come until the last two decades of the 19th century; in terms of total output the period after 1895 is by far the most significant. After the turn of the century, the drive to modernize older mills also became quite general.

Mechanization in the paper industry had begun already in the 1830's, and after 1850 many mills procured paper machines, especially those specializing in fine-grade paper. But mechanization became general only when wood pulp and cellulose came to dominate as raw materials. As late as 1870, for example, there were only about a dozen machine mills in the industry. The development of the paper industry after 1895 closely parallels that of the pulp industry.

Fundamental innovations were introduced in a number of other industries in the decades before 1870. But the general dissemination of these innovations and the consequent stage of revolutionary growth and high rates of entry took place only after this year. In the case of the consumption goods industries in particular, one would judge the 1870's and 1880's rather than the 1850–70 period to be the initiating stage. In absolute terms most of these industries achieved rapid growth only after 1895.

Basic innovations occurred in, or even before, the early 1870's in several other industries as well. In textiles, for instance, innovations of the 1850's and 1860's already heralded the demise of home production. Other examples are offered by the glove, glass and ceramics, building joinery, sugar, brewing, flour and bakery, matches, and industrial fertilizer industries. In a number of other industries the corresponding stage belongs to the

---

[3] Cf. Lundén, *Till frågan om sulfitfabrikationens uppkomst och utveckling* (Gothenburg, 1927).

period 1870–90, and in these industries, rates of output of a new order of magnitude occurred mainly after 1895. Examples are: furniture, leather and shoes, rubber products, hosiery and clothing, stone, bricks and cement, several food products, and chemicals.

Available statistical data on Swedish industrial development in the 19th century are both incomplete and unreliable. This is true for data on the number of firms as well as on employment and production. Satisfactory statistics for most industries date only from 1896, although certain earlier figures exist that may be used if only a very rough sketch of development is required.[4]

The number of firms at mid-century was about 2,000; by the late sixties the number was about 2,200; and at the end of the eighties it was 3,200. In the mid-nineties the number was in excess of 5,000. The "number of firms" is here defined as "number of industrial plants," and the data for the period before 1895 do not include either ironworks and mines (which were counted separately) or the lumber mills (for which data were not collected at all). There are other grave weaknesses in the statistical material, and the data provide information only on the total number of plants at different times and not on the rate of entry of new firms. But evidently the number of new entrants did not begin its rapid rise until after 1870. The large number of new firms after this year is especially striking since, in contrast to the preceding period, the total number of firms in many industries started to decline as new, big enterprises displaced smaller and older ones. As to the number of iron ore mines and steel mills, reasonably reliable estimates are lacking for the earlier period. The number probably did not grow, however, as concentration of production was an especially prominent feature of developments in this sector.[5]

The data on the number of firms from 1896 on are far more reliable,[6] and it is possible to get a clearer picture of the size distribution of firms.[7] The official count in 1896 for the number of firms (including mines, steel mills, and lumber mills) was 7,550. By 1912—the last year for which fully comparable data exist—the number had grown to almost 9,400.

---

[4] For the early industry statistics the following official sources are the most important: *Underdånigt betänkande angående Sveriges ekonomiska och finansiella utveckling under åren 1834–1860* (Stockholm, 1863); *Tullkomiténs underdåniga betänkande af år 1882, I-II* (Stockholm 1882); "Statistisk översikt av det svenska näringslivets utveckling aren 1870–1915," *Statistiska Meddelanden*, Serie A, Band III:1 (Kommerskollegium, Stockholm, 1919). Cf. K. Key-Åberg, "Sveriges industristatistik," *Statsvetenskaplig tidskrift* (1898), p. 189, and the commentary in Gardlund, *op. cit.*, p. 451.

[5] Cf. Gårdlund, *op. cit.*, and A. Montgomery, *Industrialismens genombrott i Sverige* (rev. ed., Stockholm, 1947).

[6] As a rule, the statistics include all firms with a value of output per year in excess of 10,000 Swedish crowns.

[7] N. Wohlin, *Driftkoncentrationen i svensk fabriksindustri* (Stockholm, 1915).

In the interim, however, considerable concentration of production had occurred in many industries. While small firms with 10 workers or less composed 63 percent of all firms in 1896, in 1912 the proportion was 55 percent. Their share of the work force had at the same time decreased from 8.8 percent to 7.2 percent. The largest firms—those with more than 500 workers—were 0.4 percent of the total in 1896 but 0.6 percent in 1912, while their share of the work force increased from 11.9 to 15.5 percent. This tendency was evident in most industries. In mining, textiles and clothing, leather and hair, rubber products, matches, and tobacco products, the number of firms fell while the work force increased.

FIGURE 2
Distribution of Labor Force by Industry
Groups, 1860–1913

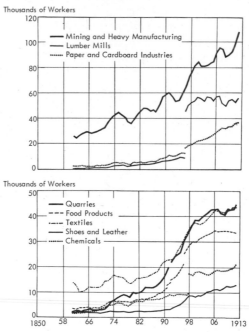

SOURCE: *Wages, Cost of Living and National Income in Sweden 1860–1930:* Vol. II, G. Bagge, E. Lundberg, I. Svennilson, *Wages in Sweden 1860–1930*, Part II, Table 187.

The number of workers in "factories" (i.e., excluding mines and steel mills) amounted to somewhat less than 15,000 in the 1830's and to somewhat more than 20,000 at mid-century. At the end of the sixties the number had passed 50,000. The growth of the industrial work force continued at an accelerated pace in the 1880's and 1890's. The figure recorded for 1895 is 140,000. But these figures fail to give a correct picture

FIGURE 3
Output of Major Products, 1846–1913

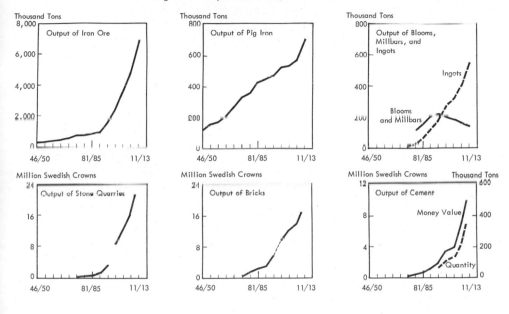

FIGURE 3 (Continued)

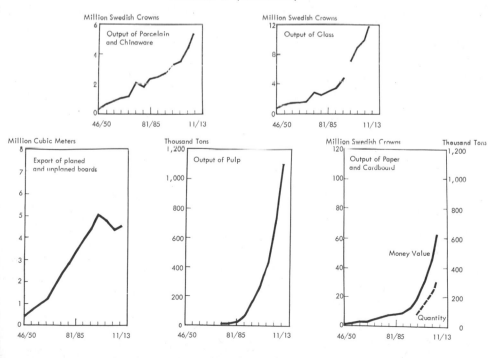

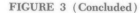

FIGURE 3 (Concluded)

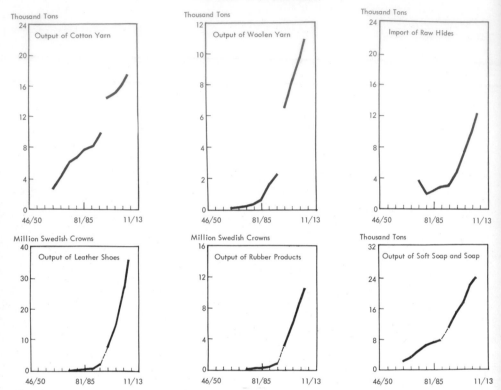

Source: *Statistisk översikt av det svenska näringslivets utveckling åren 1870–1915.*

of the speed of this development. Some of the manufacturing industries that existed in the middle of the century and undoubtedly expanded very rapidly are missing from the statistics up to 1895. This is the case with the lumber mills, for example. In addition, wholly new industries were established but were not included in the official statistics. In 1896, when mines, steel mills, lumber mills, and these new industries are included, the industrial work force totaled 238,000. At the outbreak of World War I the number was 360,000. This development is shown in Figure 2 for a number of broad industry groups for which data from decades prior to 1896 are available. The break in some of the series is due to a lack of comparability between the figures given before and after 1896.

Figure 3 gives a survey of some of the available output series. Those shown are fairly reliable; the prominent gaps are due to the uncertain value of the statistical material. Here, also, the break in some series is due to insufficiently comparable data. In certain cases where the output data are too uncertain, import or export data have been used. This was done when the latter series appeared to be relatively reliable and dealt with the dominant raw material or finished product of an industry. No logarithmic scales have been used, although these do present certain technical advantages in charts of this type. In the present context it is important to make the absolute expansion more noticeable than the relative (i.e., rate of) expansion.[8]

---

[8] The relative (percentage rate of) expansion is best discussed in connection with the innovations. Whatever may be gained from using logarithmic scales can just as easily be accomplished by verbal description while the disadvantages of the logarithmic scale are obvious. It seems better simply to mention that the innovations, say, in the pulp industry occurred in a certain period, and then to follow the development of output totals, than to present a logarithmic diagram. Such a diagram will show a fantastic rate of expansion during this initial, innovatory stage when the totals were often insignificant and show slower growth for the subsequent period when increments to total output grew to vast magnitude.

3 Interwar Economic Development of Sweden in Its International Context

Surveying the economic development of Sweden after World War I, it is apparent that the industrial expansion continued at a very rapid pace while the economy became progressively more diversified (Cf. Figures 1, 4, and 5). The whole era bears the imprint of the definitive breakthrough of electricity and the automobile—new technologies with vast implications for the development of both economy and society. Both the number of firms and the volume of production grew very rapidly. It is characteristic, however, that the work force increased relatively slowly in most of the larger industries. The interwar years were not only a period of rapidly growing output, they were also a time of labor-saving mechanization.

Agriculture also developed rapidly, despite the loss of a large part of the rural population to urban areas and urban industries. Living standards apparently improved at about the same pace as before the war. A more precise estimate cannot be made. Differences in the rate of growth of per capita income of a fraction of 1 percent must be disregarded; the margin of error in the data is too great and the data are moreover not sufficiently comparable over long stretches of time. The same objections apply to other comparisons of this type.

In the late 1930's, the population of Sweden had reached 6.4 million despite a considerable decline in the birth rate in the interwar period. Of the total population, 2.3 million, or about 36 percent, earned their livelihood in industry or crafts. The railroad network had been completed with a total track length of almost 10,600 miles. The highway network had undergone a period of extraordinary development. The volume of trade, especially internal, but also external, was far greater than ever before. Local autarky was all but eliminated, and the Swedish social structure had changed considerably in this short interwar period.

Although industrial growth in the 1920's and 1930's had been concentrated in rural areas and smaller urban communities in a manner characteristic of Sweden, its varied nature together with the expansion of commerce and services, had led to strong population growth in the cities

FIGURE 4
Distribution of Labor Force by
Industry Groups, 1919–30

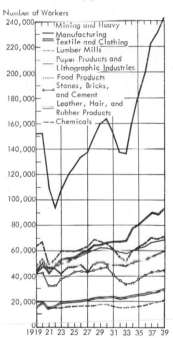

SOURCE: *Industristatistiken* (IS).

and larger towns. This represented a continuation of the trend begun between 1895 and 1914. At the outbreak of World War I, 26 percent of the population lived in urban areas. The proportion had grown to 37 percent at the outbreak of World War II. Also, life in the rural areas and small towns had a far more urban character at the latter date than previously.

The interwar period may not exhibit any features distinguishing it sharply from earlier periods. The gigantic transformation of the economy continued largely along the path established before World War I. But a closer look reveals a new phase in the development process. World

War I created great dislocations in the world economy. These had profound consequences for Sweden, both in the short run and in the long run. The first postwar crisis of 1920–21 was a result of these dislocations. This was true, also, of other difficulties that persisted far into the 1920's.

It is important to realize, however, that many of the consequences of World War I did not come to the surface in the decade of the twenties.

FIGURE 5
National Income, Imports, and Exports in Current
Swedish Crowns, 1919–39

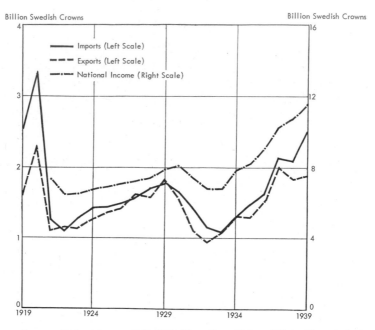

Sources: National Income: 1921–1929: *Wages, Cost of Living and National Income in Sweden 1860–1930*, Vol. III; E. Lindahl, E. Dahlgren, K. Kock, *National Income of Sweden, 1861–1930*, Part I, Table 48. National Income 1930–1939: *Svensk Tidskrift*, 1941, p. 593. Exports and Imports: *Handelsstatistiken (HS)*.

The problems inherited from the war were both political (hence indirectly economic) and economic in nature. In the early 1930's they became acute once more and contributed greatly to a general and deep depression which also affected Sweden. Several countries experienced a change of economic-political systems at this time. The year 1931 can be regarded—also for Sweden—as marking the end of a largely liberal economic era and the beginning of an era in many respects quite different.

This is a very rough outline of the interwar development. Since the analysis of industrial transformation is to be focused on this period, it is necessary to go into somewhat more detail on the outward events of the general evolution.

FIGURE 6
The Labor Market, 1919–39

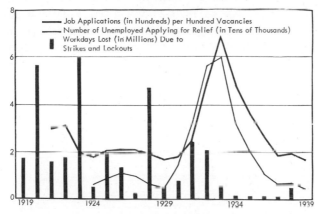

SOURCES: Job applications per hundred vacancies: *Sociala Meddelanden.*
Number of unemployed applying for relief: *Sociala Meddelanden.* Workdays lost:
Arbetsinställelser och kollektivavtal samt förlikningsmännens verksamhet.

A. The Situation at the End of World War I and Developments during 1919–20

Prices in international commodity markets started to fall immediately following the armistice in November of 1918. These price movements spread rapidly to Sweden. The immediate future was regarded with great uncertainty in most quarters of the Swedish economy. Westward exports got off to a very sluggish start and initially the situation in the export sector was consequently dominated by the loss of central European markets. Imports, on the other hand, were able to expand while at the same time defense orders stopped altogether. As a consequence many wartime enterprises, producing a great many *ersatz* commodities or defense materials, were forced to close down. The months after the armistice to the middle of 1919 saw the end of war demands without any general start on the postwar upswing.

The situation changed during the second half of 1919. International prices now started to climb. Exports grew and import possibilities improved still more. In the domestic market a reconstruction boom began, based on more optimistic forecasts. A survey of the main factors[1] behind the upswing reveals, however, that the basis for the boom was weak.

---

[1] For a more detailed study of these factors and underlying causal relationships, cf., e.g., Eli F. Heckscher (ed.), *Bidrag till Sveriges ekonomiska och sociala historia under och efter världskriget* (Stockholm, 1926); A. Östlind, *Svensk samhällsekonomi 1914–1922* (Stockholm, 1945); and A. Montgomery, *Svensk ekonomisk historia 1913–1939* (Stockholm, 1946).

In some areas these more or less concealed weaknesses prevailed; in other areas they induced expansion but carried at the same time the seeds of strongly depressive forces. It is significant that the trade press quite generally painted the cyclical situation as very uncertain.

The favorable situation for pulp and paper exports constituted the primary basis for the expansion. Lumber mills and engineering industries also experienced rather lively foreign demand. Here, however, the basis of the expansion was less reliable, depending primarily on reconstruction demands in the countries that had participated in the war and less on favorable long-run market conditions. In the home market, inventories that had been depleted during the war years created the basis for a typical postwar expansion. The preconditions for such an expansion were also present because, among other things, imports could continue on a large scale. An import surplus developed with respect to both raw materials and consumption goods. This import surplus could be financed out of the large claims that had accumulated through export surpluses and freight earnings during the war years.

Market conditions in the Swedish steel industry were one weakness. In many countries to which Sweden had exported in earlier years, the steel industry had developed tremendously with regard to both quality and quantity of output and now offered the Swedish mills strong competition. The situation was similar though less accentuated in the engineering industries. Both industries had other difficulties too. The war had led to expansion of capacity in excess of short-run peacetime needs in most capital goods industries. The postwar upswing built largely on imports. To a great extent it was consumption-stimulated and exhibited the typical characteristics of an inventory accumulation boom. Residential construction, in particular, but apparently also investment in manufacturing, remained at a low level.

Another characteristic of the period was the rapid rise of the wage level which occurred at a time when working hours were cut approximately 15 percent as the eight-hour day became law. Wages had started to climb toward the end of the war as a result of the deterioration in the overall supply situation and of the inequalities that had developed in real wages.[2] Since economic policy put few obstacles in the way of an inflationary expansion, the rising wage level did not in general present industry with insuperable difficulties. The resistance to wage increases was generally rather weak in those areas where conditions for a favorable development of profits existed, particularly the consumption goods industries and the industries exporting forest products.[3]

_____
[2] Östlind, *op. cit.*, pp. 452 ff.
[3] Östlind, *op. cit.*, pp. 388 ff.

In other sectors wage demands encountered stronger opposition, often resulting in conflict. To the extent that wage increases were granted, losses resulted which contributed to a considerable watering down of industrial equity. The Swedish economy became overstrained despite the fact that both production and imports could be expanded in most areas and despite the shrinking government demands on the productive resources of the country once the war had ended. The result was rapid inflation. The balance of trade turned negative, and as the prohibition on gold exports was continued, exchange rates rose.

The inflation caused speculation in both securities and commodities. This in turn gave added impetus to the inflation. Speculative inventories in several consumer durable goods were built up. There was considerable speculation on the stock exchange. Equity in many corporations was watered down through stock splits, insufficient depreciation allowances, write-ups of assets in plant and inventory, and in many cases through distribution policies which were entirely too liberal. Finally, the activities of the holding companies should be recalled. In some cases, these were no doubt prompted by an economically motivated striving for concentration and integration, but in many instances they were built on literally fraudulent illusions.[4]

B.   The Deflation and Reconversion Crisis of 1920–21

The international inflation began to show signs of reaching a turning point in the early spring of 1920. As in Sweden, it had been a boom characterized by inventory accumulation and speculation but without a firm foundation in either residential construction, investments in plant and equipment, or innovations. During the spring and summer, the signs of a cyclical turning point became clear in Sweden also and monetary policy became restrictive. Industry spokesmen complained about dear money and high fuel prices, about stagnating or weakening demand, and about falling prices.

The autumn months of 1920 saw the development of an economic crisis along largely traditional lines, although reaction against earlier speculative excesses was an unusually strong element. The rate of bankruptcies rose rapidly. Several banks were in difficulties due to too liberal loan policies. Through the fall of 1920 and the ensuing winter, unemployment grew rapidly as production was cut back and many firms closed down.

The general decline of wages was an important element in the situation. These wage cuts appeared imperative to all the firms that were hard hit by falling prices, decreasing sales, and liquidity troubles. To workers

---

[4] Östlind, *op. cit.*, pp. 590 ff.

and their organizations wage cuts appeared a lesser evil than an even more drastic rise in unemployment. The wage reductions did not generally bring any decrease in real wages, however, since costs of living were falling very rapidly also. Indeed, real wages in many areas rose in 1921–22. The cost reductions made possible in manufacturing by the fall in wages were accompanied by other cost reductions due not only to lower prices on raw materials and fuels but also to intensified mechanization and modernization of production. But in general, industry undoubtedly experienced a time of low returns and weak liquidity. The wage cuts and the improvement in productivity could not generally keep pace with the decline of output prices.

The year of 1921 was thus a period of depression in most parts of the Swedish economy. Idle capacity, unemployment, production for inventory, low returns, and weak liquidity were the distinguishing features of the situation. It was noteworthy, however, that many industries in the field of nondurable consumer goods—which naturally had not participated in the inventory speculation—were not much affected.[5] Conditions were at their worst in sectors that had already shown themselves weak at the end of the war, particularly steel and engineering, but also in those home-market industries where demand dried up in anticipation of a further fall in prices.

The difficulties of competing with countries that had experienced strong economic expansion during the war, and whose currencies in many cases had been drastically depreciated, were really brought home in this period.[6] The lumber industry also faced stagnating or contracting markets because reconstruction needs in Europe had been largely met and, in addition, a certain amount of inventory accumulation had occured in the foreign markets. The pulp and paper industries were relatively less affected, although earlier inventory purchases were noticeable even here. Agriculture, finally, was hard hit. Farm values had been very much inflated, and indebtedness had often risen at the same pace. Market conditions were anything but favorable due to the competition from overseas countries.

C. The Revival and Prosperity of the Twenties

The deep international reconversion and deflation depression (outside Germany and Austria, where inflation accelerated in 1923) was rather short-lived. The fall of prices virtually came to a halt after about 18 months, and in most countries unemployment reached its peak during

[5] Östlind, op. cit., p. 418.
[6] Cf. "Utlåtande med förslag till förordning om åtgärder till skydd mot så kallad valutadumping," Tull- och Traktatkommitténs utredningar och betänkanden, X (Stockholm, 1922).

FIGURE 7
Residential Construction, 1914–39

SOURCES: A. 1914–23: *Wages, Cost of Living and National Income in Sweden, 1860–1930,* Vol. III: E. Lindahl, K. Kock, E. Dahlgren, *J A6 National Income of Sweden 1861–1930,* Part II, p. 340.
    B. 1924–36: *Sociala Meddelanden,* 1937, No. 7.
    C. 1937–39: G. Ekdahl and J. Gustavsson, *Byggnadsverksamhet och bostadsbehov,* p. 31. Series adjusted upward to correspond to the 1936 level of series B.

the winter of 1921–22. A growing demand for both lumber products and textiles was felt in Sweden in the course of 1921, and when producers' inventories began to decline, output increased. Price developments for lumber were unfavorable, however. Exports could be increased only through price reductions. Also, in areas other than lumber and textiles, conditions for a revival were created simply by the earlier abnormal inventories beginning to run down.

The modernization* efforts, in combination with the falling wage level, also led to a gradual improvement in returns. But profits remained relatively low in many areas for several years, and liquidity positions were very strained for a prolonged period as industry was saddled with heavy indebtedness. The definitive liquidation of most wartime enterprises constituted a purge that contributed to a more optimistic business attitude. The supply of housing fell noticeably short of demand at the prevailing levels of rents; in addition, there were in all probability large investment needs in the manufacturing sector. The growth in construction activity which began in 1921 and 1922 and accelerated markedly in 1923 was one important element in the revival (Figure 7). The stabilization of the dollar exchange rate—which took place in the fall of 1922 even though the gold standard was not formally reintroduced until April,

---

* *Translator's note:* There is no perfect counterpart in American usage to the British (or Swedish) "rationalization," meaning "mechanization," "automation," or "reorganization"—or all of them at once. "Modernization" has been chosen here since it conveys the desired sense of a break with long-accepted, traditional methods.

1924—as well as the repeated reductions of the discount rate and a firmer conduct of monetary policy in general, were other important factors.

It is generally agreed, however, that the first strong impulses toward a more lasting revival came somewhat later with the increase in the foreign demand for pulp and paper, iron ore, and engineering products. This growth in foreign demand was connected with the end of the deflation and reconversion crisis in most countries. The expansionary influence of the American upswing on the Swedish economy was especially great. One reason for this was that a large proportion of Swedish pulp exports went to the United States. The U.S. upswing was based primarily on developments in construction, the automobile industry, consumer durables, electric utilities, and on extensive modernization efforts.

Even in those cases where progress abroad was less rapid, as for example in Great Britain or in Germany, the Swedish economy was stimulated because of the particularly favorable position of Swedish export products. Total exports seem to have grown somewhat faster than national income (Figure 5). Developments abroad had favorable consequences for Sweden also in that prices fell on many important raw materials and fuels which Sweden had to import. The barter terms of trade developed favorably and contributed to a trade-balance surplus. Growing freight earnings were also very important in this connection; the Swedish merchant marine expanded rapidly at this time. Finally, it should be recalled that Sweden in the 1920's was a capital-exporting country. The engineering industry in particular was moving part of its activities abroad, and several countries obtained long-term loans with the help of the Kreuger interests.

TABLE 1

Average Annual Net Growth of Population in Age Groups 15–65

Period	Number of Men	Number of Women	Total
1920–29	19,400	17,800	37,200
1930–39	23,200	18,800	42,000
Entire interwar period	21,300	18,300	39,600

SOURCE: Population census data for 1920, 1930, and 1940.

Apart from the role of foreign trade, the speed of economic progress after the deflation crisis was over should be attributed also to *demographic developments* which gave the Swedish economy large additions to the labor force. The yearly increment in the number of men in productive age groups (i.e., 15–65) was considerable (Table 1). Industry was able to absorb whatever it needed out of these increases. The need for labor in manufacturing increased relatively slowly, however, a fact which undoubtedly should be attributed to the rapid rise in production per man-hour caused by extensive modernization. The strongly expanding distribution sector, the service industries, and government administration had on the other hand great need for additional labor and were able to offer relatively good wages. In this respect the agricultural sector could not compete with urban employment opportunities, and it was therefore unable to retain its natural population growth in rural employment.

The high rate of *construction* activity—already important at the beginning of the upswing—certainly contributed to making the basis of the expansion less uncertain than had been the case with the inventory accumulation and speculation of 1919 and 1920. Several factors contributed to the construction boom: the high rate of expansion in the export industries, pent-up demands from the war which were not satisfied until the late 1920's, and demographic developments, including the high rate of formation of new households. The growth of home-market industries likewise played a role. The interaction of these factors was a conspicuous and characteristic feature. The rapid *motorization* and nationwide *electrification* were also extremely important factors both directly and indirectly—directly through the multitude of small enterprises that both created, indirectly through the revolution in transportation that they brought about.

Even a cursory glance reveals certain conspicuous features of the *technical* and *organizational innovations* that were created and/or utilized by *industrial entrepreneurs*. The industrial evolution of this decade will, however, be the focus of interest in the main portion of the present work; in this context it suffices to recall that the process was dominated by the modernization of production methods in almost all areas and by a number of new or "young" commodities rather than by the exploitation of new natural resources. The whole industrial sector showed a very rapid growth, qualitatively as well as quantitatively, in return per man-hour.[7]

Compared with the industrial expansion (Figure 4), the development of agriculture looked less favorable. Production measured in so-called harvest units increased relatively little. Farm earnings were not good. The relatively slow increase in wages was one symptom. After the cessation of general wage inflation in 1924, money wages for farmhands showed almost no change during the rest of the 1920's, while a corresponding worker's wage—some 70 percent above the farmhand's at the outset of the period—increased by about 10 percent.

---

[7] Cf. I. Svennilson, "Industriarbetets växande avkastning i belysning av svenska erfarenheter," in *Studier i ekonomi och historia, tillägnade Eli F. Heckscher* (Uppsala, 1944).

D. The Economic Crisis and Depression, 1929–31. A New Era in Economic Policy

International economic developments took an unfavorable turn at the end of the 1920's, and within a year and a half most countries were in the grip of a deep depression. It is not necessary in the present context to analyze the complex causes underlying the great world depression; these have already been covered in many foreign and Swedish works.[8] Some special features should be noted, however.

It has often been pointed out that the depression of 1929–33 was to a considerable extent a second peace crisis. Many of its most important causes are found in the events surrounding the war or were direct or indirect consequences of the war. Every serious description and analysis of that depression has revealed its roots in an "accelerated disparity in the interaction of driving forces and, as a consequence, a progressively greater incongruence between the political factors, production, monetary conditions, and the international and national flows of purchasing power."[9] These studies have revealed also how this disparity originated in the war or increased noticeably during that period.

Great maladjustments prevailed in production. The curtailment of international trade during the war caused many countries to establish wholly new industries or to expand existing ones. The international division of labor was disrupted. As trade was gradually freed, grave difficulties arose. Tendencies toward "overproduction" were evident in many areas. In certain cases these tendencies were not very noticeable immediately after the war; reconstruction needs put great demands on industries that harbored excess capacity in the longer run.

But pressures grew along with progressive completion of reconstruction through the twenties. The creation or expansion of new industries in overseas countries was not allowed to lead to contraction of the corresponding, former export industries in other countries, however; neither were the new industries abroad allowed to contract. Thus adjustment to the expansion of agriculture that had taken place both in the partly blockaded Europe and in overseas countries was prevented after the war. The decisive factors in this case derived from government economic policies and the structure of the private sector itself. In both areas sluggishness in adjusting production to the new conditions appeared greater than before the war. In many cases the delay was extreme—attempts were often made to continue an activity as long as possible, with the

---

[8] The latest and most comprehensive description and analysis in Swedish are found in E. Lundberg, "Det svenska näringslivets konjunkturkänslighet," *Meddelanden från Konjunkturinstitutet, Serie B:5* (Stockholm, 1945).

[9] J. Åkerman, *Ekonomisk teori*, Vol. II, p. 574.

help of tariff protection, subsidies, cartels, and production for stockpiling, even when it was ill-suited to the new conditions. Whole industries were "conserved," and even the least efficient production units were often kept alive, even though only the most efficient had any chance of meeting the competition in the long run.[10]

The significance of these rigidities for the course of the world depression can hardly be exaggerated. The intensity of the depression was to a great extent accounted for by the fact that the need for adjustments was especially great as a consequence of the war-induced dislocations in the world economy and that, finally, these adjustments had to be made within the short span of only a few years. It should be added, however, that the need for adjustment was connected not only with wartime dislocations, but also with the more normal process of development. In many areas, moreover, the sluggishness in adjustment to such normal developments had also been very marked during the 1920's.

Increased obstacles to free international migration accentuated disparities and the sluggishness of adjustments in the area of production. The cuts in U.S. immigration quotas led to population pressures in many parts of Europe. These pressures, in turn, led many countries to adopt policies to stimulate agriculture. Generally speaking, better conditions for the international mobility of labor than those existing in the 1920's would have made adjustment easier. The effects of the war on the postwar economy were thus evident in this area also.

One maladjustment in the world economy of the 1920's which caused more discussion than others had to do with exchange policies and international capital movements. These difficulties were particularly attributable to World War I and its political consequences. Erik Lundberg has summed up the situation as follows:

An intimate connection prevailed during this period between the payments of war indemnities and war loans on the one hand and the movements of capital and gold on the other. In addition, equilibrium was conditional on the relations between exchange rates and cost-levels and price-levels in the different countries. The United States had as a consequence of the war acquired a dominating creditor position. But the U. S. economy was at the

---

[10] It is hardly necessary in the present context to illustrate these disparities and rigidities in any detail. A reading of the works that have sought to describe developments before and during the Great Depression will yield an abundance of such illustrations. The League of Nations–sponsored study by Ohlin is very rewarding in this respect. (Cf. B. Ohlin, *Den världsekonomiska depressionen jämte efterskrift om läget oktober–november 1931*, Swedish Ed., Stockholm, 1931.) Ohlin's analysis of the situation of the great raw material-producing industries and agriculture is particularly interesting. The brief survey by J. W. F. Rowe, "Produktionsreglering inom världens stapelvaruindustrier," *Svenska Handelsbankens Index*, X, No. 4 (Stockholm, 1935), is also very instructive. Reference should also be made to Schumpeter, *Business Cycles*, Vol. II.

same time structured so as to create a considerable export surplus—in itself a rather natural situation in view of the rich resources of the country in relation to the rest of the world. The willingness to receive a flow of imports corresponding to the income on capital from abroad did not exist, however. Balance could be achieved only through the considerable American capital exports that took place during the greater part of the 1920's. Thus, equilibrium in international payments came, in the last analysis, to hinge on such an unstable factor as the American capital market. Complete balance was, however, not to be reached in this way. The gold inflow to New York and Paris revealed a continuing lack of balance leading to difficulties for those countries which were forced to dispose of the gold. The fixation of exchange rates through the reintroduction of the gold standard made adjustment toward a stable international equilibrium still more difficult. . . . The return to the gold standard in the 1920's seems to have created predominantly deflationary pressures. Higher price levels than in the prewar period led to a shortage of gold in the 1920's—this despite measures to economize on gold through adoption of a gold exchange standard and retirement of the gold coinage. The uneven distribution of the gold stock among countries was important in this connection. The basic reasons why the gold standard refused to operate in the prewar manner stemmed, however, from the fundamental changes that had taken place in the structure and mode of operation of the international economy. It was partly a question of a war-induced amplification of prewar tendencies. The increased rigidity of prices and wages and the reduced mobility of productive factors were of great importance.[11]

The more the world economy of the 1920's is studied in detail, the more light can be shed on the crisis and depression between 1929 and 1933. It would seem evident, however, that the present sketch has brought out the most important causes. This still does not explain, of course, why the crisis and depression arrived in just these years, but this does not pose a serious problem. It cannot be disputed that the whole process of crisis and depression was triggered by the American stock market crash—a setback which in and of itself need not have had grave consequences.[12]

Sweden became seriously affected by the international crisis, especially from the end of 1930 on.[13] Exports had been affected already before that date, however (Figure 5). Thus the value of exports decreased between 1929 and 1930, and not just as a result of falling prices. During 1931 a general decline in industrial employment and national income occurred (Fig-

---

[11] Lundberg, op. cit., pp. 11–12.
[12] Lundberg, op. cit., pp. 12–13.
[13] Cf. Lundberg, op. cit.; A. Montgomery, Hur Sverige övervann depressionen 1930–33 (Stockholm, 1938), and idem, Svensk ekonomisk historia 1913–39. Cf. also J. Åkerman, Det ekonomiska läget 1928–32, in the series of pamphlets sponsored by Sveriges Industriförbund (Stockholm, 1928–32), and D. Hammarskjöld, Konjunkturspridningen, Statens Offentliga Utredningar (Public Reports of the Government), SOU 1933 No. 29 (Stockholm, 1933).

ures 4 and 5). The effects of the further decline of exports spread rapidly, affecting price-formation and income-formation as well as the labor market.[14]

It should be remembered that *stagnation* in employment was enough to create rapidly growing unemployment because of the large number of persons in productive age groups that entered the labor market each year (Table 1). This explains at least one third of the unemployment during the years 1931–33. The necessity of reducing production in export industries, together with the stagnation of sales in domestic markets, accounted almost completely for the remainder of the unemployment total in these years.

A preliminary survey gives no indication of any strong contractionary effects on the home-market industries other than those emanating from the export sector. It is significant, for example, that investment activity remained high as late as 1931 (Figure 1). Residential construction continued on an extensive scale, and domestic consumption remained at a high level despite the decline of exports and the effects of this decline on income. The main origin of the crisis and depression is thus to be found in the export markets; this does not mean, of course, that weaknesses in home-market industries were not important in the total cyclical picture. It is the task of the following transformation analysis to throw some light on this question.

It should be noted that imports showed no tendency to contract in step with exports (Figure 5). In 1931 imports did fall, but not far enough to avoid serious pressures on the balance of payments and thus on the reserve position. This unfavorable development had been postponed by short-term capital movements to Sweden in the first years of the depression. When these funds started to flow out again in the late summer of 1931 and when, in addition, the English situation rapidly deteriorated to culminate in the crisis in which Great Britain went off gold, Sweden, too, had to leave the gold standard.

This step was taken on September 27, while at the same time interest rates were sharply raised. After this event, the Swedish *krona* was clearly undervalued in relation to most foreign currencies except the pound. This led, at least in the short run, to improved conditions for the export sector and to a curtailment of imports. It thereby provided greater scope for the expansionary economic policy that was introduced in Sweden in 1932, with cuts in interest rates, an expansionary fiscal policy, public works, and thorough support for agriculture among the most important measures tried.

---

[14] Cf. e.g., the econometric study undertaken by E. Ruist and I. Svennilson, *Den norrländska skogsnäringens konjunkturkänslighet under mellankrigperioden*, Industriens utredningsinstitut (IUI) (Stockholm, 1938).

This general support of the private sector was stepped up still more in the summer of 1933, when the pound also was fixed at a level which undervalued the Swedish *krona*. Monetary policy was committed to low interest rates, even over the long run.[15] Discount rates had fallen to 2½ percent by December, 1933, and remained there for the rest of the inter-war period. Some rather insignificant tariff increases were made, mostly about the time the *krona* was devalued, in part later on during the 1930's. For industrial production these were of decidedly secondary importance in comparison with the devaluation. For the agricultural sector, the direct intervention in production, distribution, and price formation was most important.

Events abroad as well as in Sweden during 1931 marked a dividing line between two epochs. They marked the end of a largely liberal economic policy and the beginning of a new era of increased economic planning, leading among other things to the partial breakdown of the multilateral international system. Governments became active in most areas of the economy to a far larger extent than formerly, although for the industrial sector at least there could hardly be any talk about central planning. Political objectives, in any case, achieved importance in all areas of economic policy and thus influenced economic developments in different sectors and industries.

The outstanding feature of economic development after 1931, therefore, was the lack of synchronization of cycles between countries. A second prominent feature was the striving for autarky in most countries, particularly with respect to food production. This contributed toward growing monopolistic tendencies in private sectors and tended to create a certain "hothouse atmosphere" in many sectors of the economy. Even a superficial study will show that these strivings toward national self-sufficiency curtailed international trade. Although the volume of trade increased substantially after 1933 (when it was exceedingly low), it did not regain the 1929 level during the 1930's. Indeed, it did not even reach the mid-twenties' level.

The maladjustments discussed in connection with the 1920's accounted for the intensity of the depression. Considering world economic developments after 1931 against this background, one must conclude that relatively little was done to correct the situation. In fact, it can be asserted that some of these maladjustments were maintained by new and more radical means than had been used in late 1920's. Governments intervened to a far greater extent than formerly, and the war-induced dislocations in world trade were made permanent through the extension of the boundaries of economic political action.

---

[15] For a short survey of the role of monetary and exchange-rate policy, cf. B. Kragh, *Svensk penningpolitik 1914–1942* (Malmö, 1943).

Quite apart from its various long-run consequences, this development had considerable logic to it in view of the fact that, for a variety of reasons, no willingness existed to submit to a more fundamental adjustment. This was the choice that had to be made in the early 1930's—either adjustment had to be accepted, in which case one had to try to ease the process as far as possible with the help of various palliative measures during the transitional years, or the need for adjustment had to be prevented from exerting itself. The latter choice implied that free market forces must be made ineffective, and that the multilateral trade system be broken up and replaced with a system of bilateral treaties, combined with more or less thorough exchange controls. Although attempts were often made to suggest that the first alternative was the one chosen, the second was the one actually followed under more or less strong pressures from political interests. Unfortunately, there was no planned coordination of the various measures with regard to their long run effects.[16] This was the most significant aspect of the worldwide change in political and economic systems that took place in the 1930's.

E. The Revival and Prosperity of the Thirties

The international situation in 1932 was characterized by massive unemployment in most countries on a scale not experienced up to that time. In this year, however, certain signs of better times began to appear (for example, in Great Britain) within the general framework of the new economic policies. Typically, however, the improvement was confined to the home-market industries. Only later on was there any strong impulses from growing exports.

The United States showed a certain measure of recovery in 1933, the year in which the dollar was devalued relative to gold and the New Deal initiated. In those countries that did not leave the gold standard the cyclical situation remained bad. One example of this was France. Not even when the upswing in Great Britain and the United States was well under way—albeit with continuingly high unemployment— were the so-called gold countries pulled into it. In Germany the economic situation was dominated from 1933 on by government-directed rearmament and a more systematic striving for autarky than anywhere else.

In 1936 and the spring of 1937, the situation in the United States was one of monetary ease, but there was also evidence of a number of bottlenecks in industrial production. At the same time unemployment was far from being absorbed. Despite the incomplete recovery from the Great Depression, a speculative upswing developed with some inflationary

---

[16] Cf. the last section of my paper, "Ekonomisk strukturanalys," *Ekonomisk Tidskrift* (1942), No. 3.

features. On some commodities in particular, prices rose very rapidly. One causal factor was undoubtedly speculative inventory accumulation, making the situation in certain respects reminiscent of the first postwar boom.[17] In neither period was the American upswing based on lively construction or investment activity or on important innovations.[18]

The turning point in the spring of 1937 also showed some similarities to the turning point in the spring of 1920. This time, however, there was no strong cumulative deflation. The speculative inventory accumulation changed into a crisis dominated by inventory liquidation accompanied by rapidly falling prices. Employment and production fell rapidly. The setback in the United States had effects in most other countries where corresponding recession phenomena appeared, although on a less serious scale. France and the other countries that had clung to the gold standard as long as possible were an exception.

After giving up this policy in 1936, these countries experienced a strong rise of prices but, despite this, no immediate improvement in business activity. While the effects were hardly directly expansionary, the cessation of the strong downward pressure on prices, which had been the consequence of remaining on the gold standard while most other countries devalued, brought a gradual easing of the situation.[19] Germany continued to be a special case. The striving for autarky had been so strong that the country was to a certain extent isolated from the international cyclical developments. But its economy was dominated above all by the intensified armament effort.

Following the Munich crisis [in 1938], economic developments not only in Germany but in most other countries were increasingly dominated by the arms race and measures for economic and military preparedness. In the final years of the decade, the "normal" business cycle became almost totally submerged in these "abnormal" developments.

The year 1932 represented a cyclical trough in Sweden also (Figures 4, 5, and 6). The devaluation of the *krona* in the fall of 1931 thus did not have any immediately visible effects. Devaluation relative to the pound was not undertaken until 1933, however, and monetary policy remained restrictive into the summer of 1932 because of fears of inflationary developments. Swedish exports of iron ore and wood products experienced their normal seasonal low in the winter. The Ivar Kreuger crash occurred in the spring of 1932 and had adverse effects, not the least of which were psychological. The cyclical situation abroad in the winter and spring of 1931–32 was unfavorable also and gave little impetus to a Swedish recovery.

---

[17] Lundberg, *op. cit.*

[18] In this connection, cf. also Schumpeter, *Business Cycles*, Vol. II. pp. 1011 ff.

[19] On this, cf. esp., A. Montgomery, *Svensk ekonomisk historia 1913–1939*, pp. 301–2.

The situation was still uncertain in the first quarter of 1933, but tendencies toward improvement in some export markets had been noticeable (Figures 4, 5, and 6). In the second quarter the improvement became obvious, and it is rather generally agreed that the impulses primarily came from exports.[20] Even though at first the increase in exports came from inventories, soon it began to affect incomes and thus the home-market industries. Signs of improvement were evident here, too, in 1933. At the end of 1933, no doubts remained that the trend was decidedly upward for most sectors of the economy. In 1934 the previous highs of 1930 were in many cases reached or surpassed. Sweden was at that time further on the way to recovery than most countries.

The continued upswing until the partial recession of 1937, which was basically induced by events in the United States, gave evidence that the Swedish economy was moving into a previously uncharted phase of development.[21] To be sure exports continued to grow, and this stimulated recovery of the home market to a high degree. The growth in exports was considerably more rapid than the growth of total world trade. Sweden was in a favored position for several reasons. Most important was the fact that she had traditionally had a large import surplus in trade with Germany, the country which most consistently pursued bilateralism and was very anxious also to obtain the Swedish export products. Another reason was that the attempts to curtail imports in Great Britain had relatively little effect on Sweden.[22]

But there was a marked difference compared to the development in the 1920's (Figure 5). In view of price developments, the growth of exports was considerably weaker than during the upswing from 1922 to 1929. Despite this relatively limited increase of total exports, the Swedish economy, judging by national income, expanded at a more rapid pace than during the 1920's. Home markets, in other words, developed at a considerably higher rate than before. Domestic expansionary forces were particularly active, and in certain respects they counteracted the less favorable developments which Swedish exports encountered as a consequence of the tendency toward national autarky abroad and of the economic situation in several of Sweden's traditional customer countries.

Demographic developments were, as in the previous decade, an important factor in the rapid expansion of domestic markets during the 1930's.

[20] Cf., e.g., Lundberg, *op. cit.*, and *idem*, "Konjunkturläget hösten 1937," *Meddelanden från Konjunkturinstitutet*, Serie A:1 (Stockholm, 1938). Also K. Kock, *Konjunkturuppsvingets förlopp och orsaker 1932–1934*, SOU (1935) No. 16 and A. Montgomery, *Hur Sverige övervann depressionen 1930–1933*.

[21] Cf. esp., I. Svennilson, "Strukturella inslag i de senare årens ekonomiska utveckling," *Meddelanden från Konjunkturinstitutet*, Serie B:1 (Stockholm, 1939), which presents a fairly detailed analysis of these trends in the development process.

[22] I. Gerhard, *Problem rörande Sveriges utrikeshandel 1936–1938*, Gothenburg, 1948, p. 174.

The yearly influx of persons into productive age groups was even greater after 1930 than before (see Table 1). This increase was somewhat less for women than for men, but a greater proportion of women took employment outside the home. These increments to the labor force were absorbed in industrial employment to a greater extent than formerly. Their importance was evident in at least two respects. First, they constituted a continued shift of the demographic structure in a favorable direction, and second, they increased mobility in the labor market.

Beside these demographic factors, lively *construction activity* played an extraordinarily important role in the general industrial growth of domestic markets in the 1930's. This was in part due to the demographic developments just mentioned. Here, too, there was an increase over the 1920's after the strike year of 1933 had passed. The interrelationship between expansion in construction activity and in home-market industries generally was even more evident in this period. The continuing *motorization* and *electrification* of the country were again prominent features in the overall development picture.

FIGURE 8
The Composition of Imports, 1930–37

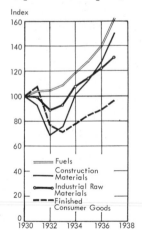

SOURCE: I. Svennilson, "Strukturella inslag i Sveriges ekonomiska utveckling under senare år," *Meddelanden från Konjunkturinstitutet*, Series B:1.

Two other factors were apparently of very great importance to the expansion of the home-market industries in this decade. One was the change in competitive position vis-à-vis foreign countries due to the *exchange rate policy* of 1931 and 1933. The other was the reorientation of *monetary policy*. Imports, for example, reflect the importance of these factors (Figure 5). The composition of imports shifted markedly from final consumption goods to raw materials and fuels (Figure 8).[23] This shift—in part a result of the changed competitive situation—was important because it contributed to a favorable development in the balance of payments, despite the modest growth of exports.

In turn, this development facilitated the low interest policy which characterized the latter half of the thirties and lent further strength to the expansion of domestic markets. On the other hand, the tariff protection, which was relatively modest in real terms even to begin with, shrank as the price level started to rise from the low of 1932. It should above all be recalled that the devaluation of the *krona* became progressively less important as other countries devalued their currencies. At the end of the decade, however, the krona was still depreciated by some 10 percent relative to the currencies of the most important sources of imports.[24]

The changed competitive position vis-à-vis foreign countries was perhaps most evident in the agricultural sector. As already noted, however, the specific farm policies appear to have been more important than the general exchange and monetary policies. Beginning in 1932, governmental farm policy provided almost complete protection against foreign competition and promoted strong monopoly tendencies in the domestic trade in agricultural produce. The effects were obvious. They included a certain redistribution of national income that favored the farm population to the detriment of the rest of the population.

In this connection one may also recall the export of agricultural products which took place—at a loss for the economy as a whole—in order to firm up prices in the home market. The large increase between 1929 and 1939 in the average yearly wages of farmhands compared with workers in industry—15 percent versus 12 percent—is in contrast to the trend during the 1920's.

By and large, *technical* and *organizational* progress in industry followed the same paths as in the previous decade and was at least equally strong. It was, however, more a question of routine progress on a broad front in the mechanization of production and distribution than of new and revolutionary lines of development. Compared with the previous decade, industrial productivity increased at an even more rapid pace. The development process had many special features some of which were very conspicuous. The discussion of them must wait, however, until the main parts of the study have been developed. Before turning to the empirical analysis of the industrial transformation, we must first discuss some of its methodological problems.

---

[23] Cf. esp., Svennilson, *op. cit.*

[24] Svennilson, *op. cit.* Svennilson has calculated a special devaluation index for the period 1931–37.

4 The Analysis of Industrial Transformation: Its Concepts and Problems

The Two Components of Transformation. The Concept of Innovation

The transformation process has two components, or sides, one *positive* and one *negative*. The positive side refers to the introduction of innovations and the negative side to the liquidation of old factor combinations or, better, to the old combinations which are no longer being considered for new investment. Both the positive and the negative components can be further subdivided according to whether they pertain to *production* and *distribution methods* or to *goods* and *services*. Change of technique and of product may sometimes be merely two aspects of the same event; in other cases they may be entirely unrelated.

The concept of "new production technique," or *process innovation*, may be stated more precisely as follows:[1] Take the production function

$$y = f(x_1, x_2)$$

where y is a product and x_1 and x_2 are two different factors of production known to businessmen at a certain time. For example, one of the latter may stand for a certain type of machine and the other for a certain kind of labor input. In a case like this, the introduction of a new factor (x_3)—a new type of machine, say—always implies a process innovation. The original production function can be expressed as a system of isoquants. The addition of another production factor will then change the

---

[1] The example illustrates the case of a "new distribution method" as well, since distribution may be counted among the factors of production.

form of the isoquants—for example from a to b in Diagram 1. The change implies that the input of factor x_1 for any given input of x_2 may be lessened without any reduction in output. The addition of x_3, as a partial substitute for x_1, signifies a process innovation.[2]

DIAGRAM 1

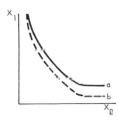

One should note, however, that the introduction of x_3 must not be a result of a change in the relative prices of x_1 and x_3. The possibility of using x_3 to advantage must have been previously unknown, or x_3 would have appeared in the original production function. It is difficult, of course, to draw the dividing line between known and unknown alternatives. This difficulty, however, will play a very minor role in the applied analysis to follow. We will adhere to the more obvious cases and avoid the borderline ones. In addition, combinations not previously utilized ordinarily appear in conjunction with other new elements, which must be regarded as innovations. Hence this difficulty will be of limited significance in the applied analysis.

A movement along the isoquants, in contrast to a change in their form, does not constitute an innovation. Such a movement may be induced by changing relative factor prices and must be considered part of the daily routine of management.[3] It is possible, of course, to argue that the isoquants may not be known in their entirety, and that an extension of the known area and the introduction of a new combination outside the previously known area should be regarded as an innovation. But, obviously, the discovery of the possibility of adding a new factor of production signifies something essentially more novel than the discovery of new possibilities of varying the proportions of known factors. Theoretically, the difference between a change in the form of the isoquants and a movement along the isoquants is perfectly clear.

The meaning of the chosen definitions may be made more concrete by considering an example. A manufacturing plant may have the alternatives

---

[2] For simplicity we disregard the need for a three-dimensional system of coordinates when x_3 is added.

[3] Cf. Schumpeter, *Business Cycles*, Vol. I, p. 88.

of using coal, pulverized coal, coke, or refuse for generating steam. It is part of the daily routine to adjust the use of different fuels to changes in their relative prices. Such adjustments can never be regarded as innovative. Even if pulverized coal, for instance, had never been used prior to a given date, its introduction does not constitute an innovation if the possibility of using it was previously known but not resorted to—because of the high price of pulverized coal, for example. If, on the other hand, a completely new fuel enters the market and is substituted for coke, say, because of a more favorable relationship between caloric content and price, then we are dealing with an innovation.

The conscious avoidance of dubious borderline cases in the following analysis also circumvents many of the difficulties involved in defining the concept of "commodity" or "product" as well as "new commodity" and "product innovation." This question will receive more detailed attention in the introduction to Chapter 6, where we will also differentiate between the concepts of "process innovation" and "product innovation."

Principles of Transformation Analysis

It is theoretically possible that all industrial development during a certain period would constitute transformation in the above sense. All relevant events would cause changes in the structure of industrial production, that is, in the composition of output.[4] At the other extreme, it is possible that no transformation would take place at all. The analysis of the interwar period attempted in the present study will focus on the creation and dissemination of new processes and products—and the disappearance of old ones—while, at the same time, relating these events to other changes of a different nature. The study will thus attempt to shed light upon the occasionally dramatic, but often less spectacular, struggle between the new and the old and upon the role of this struggle in the development process. In this context, one may refer to the difficulties of a firm as being due to pressures emanating from the negative component of the transformation, or development, process. The implication then would be that the output of the firm consists of products that are being superseded by other, novel commodities or that the production methods of the firm are too costly in relation to the newer and better methods of other firms. One may refer, also, to a product or a process as being "on the negative side of the development process." These expressions have terminological advantages

---

[4] We will avoid using the term "structural change" in referring to this transformation. The dichotomy of "structural change" vs. "cyclical change" has come to be used in so many different ways in both popular and scientific literature that it is undesirable to increase the terminological confusion further. In this study, the concept of "structure" will be used only in certain specialized senses that do not risk conflicts with everyday usage.

that may excuse a certain laxness in relation to the strict definition of the negative component of transformation.

Demand-Pull and Supply-Push in Expansionary Processes

The next extension of the analytical framework consists of a differentiation of various types of development processes in the industrial development of the interwar period A preliminary grouping of the material involves differentiating *progressive, stagnating,* and *regressive* industries. With regard to progressive industries, we will further distinguish between *demand-pull* and *supply-push* processes.

Consider an industry producing a single, homogeneous product which has only one use—in construction, say. Suppose, further, that the product cannot substitute for (or be substituted for by) other construction materials. Suppose, also, that production functions in the industry are unchangeable, that the rate of production precisely equals the rate of consumption and, finally, that no price changes or other attempts to alter the rate of sales are made. If, in such a situation, construction activity begins to increase from a certain date on, which under the given set of assumptions may happen for any number of reasons except actions taken by the industry itself, then we have a case of *demand-pull.*

The higher rate of construction activity in this period requires increased production in the industry in question. The *driving force,* from the point of view of the industry, is the increase in consumption which is independent of any measures taken by the industry. If we relax the assumption that no possibilities exist in construction technology of substituting different inputs for each other, then demand-pull growth may occur even without increased construction activity. But it should be considered a case of demand-pull expansion only when the industry's product is substituted for other inputs without any initiative by the industry itself. Conversely, it is possible that increased construction activity will not be associated with any demand-pull for this industry. This would happen if other construction materials were used instead—for example as a result of a lowering of their prices or an improvement in their quality.

If, in the original situation, instead of construction increasing for exogenous reasons, we assume that the increase is due to the product being offered at a lower price by the industry, then we have a case of *supply-push expansion.* If, further, the assumption of an unchanged product is relaxed, supply-push expansion may be due to the introduction by the industry of an improved or wholly new product which facilitates construction or supersedes other construction materials. Supply-push expansion may also be brought about by advertising. Both supply-push and demand-pull elements are equally easy to detect in any study of progressive industries. The problem is that usually both are present at the same time and may show outwardly very similar patterns of development.

In order to clarify further the distinction between the different types of processes, consider the following hypothetical examples. In Period I, all the original assumptions hold and everything proceeds in a stationary circular flow. In Period II, a combined product-innovation and process-innovation takes place in the industry. Throughout the period, knowledge of the product spreads among building contractors. At the same time, construction goes on as before in many quarters and total construction activity is unchanged. By the end of the period, the new product is generally known and has superseded the older type of construction material completely. Period II thus spans a supply-push process. In Period III, no increase in the output of the new product can take place without an increase in construction; only demand-pull growth is possible and it may result, for example, from an exogenous increase in construction.

The relation of this analytical framework to the concept of innovation is obvious. One should take note, however, of the possibility that supply-push expansion can take place without any *contemporaneous* initiative on the part of the industry, whether it be in the form of innovations, price reductions, improvements in quality, advertising, or some other measures. The process may have been initiated before the beginning of the interwar period. A "young" rather than a new product could be the source of the supply-push. Finally, this analytical method may be used not only in the study of a whole industry or of one of its several branches, but also in the study of an individual firm in the industry.

The objective in each such case is to trace and analyze the driving forces behind a certain actual process and to see how these forces affect the course of the process in different respects. In the first stage of a causal analysis, one's objectives cannot be more ambitious than that. But by proceeding in this fashion and spotlighting one area at a time, one can expect that a more integrated picture of interwar economic development will emerge when the analytical results are finally pooled.

The Meaning of Stagnating and Regressive Processes— "Malinvestment"

Consider again the case of an industry in a situation of stationary circular flow. A regressive process may occur at the end of Period I simply because of a reduction in demand which might stem, for example, from a decline in construction activity. The decline in construction, in turn, may have resulted from many different causes, including noneconomic ones. In Period II, a regressive process will ensue in the construction material industry in question, even though measures taken by the industry itself have not contributed in any way to the regression.[5] A reduction in demand also may be caused by the adoption of *new methods* in construction which reduce the need for the product in question. Another possibility would be the introduction of new processes in the corresponding industry abroad which lead to price reductions, making importation profitable. Process innovations in one segment of the domestic industry may, in analogous fashion, lead to regression for other segments of the industry. *New products* as well as new processes may lead to a reduction in demand. In the case of both new methods and new commodities we may talk about "pressures from the negative side of the development process."

A third case of regressive process may, however, stem directly from actions taken by the industry. The industry may have used a factor combination that made the product appear too expensive, with the result either that customers were lost or that the output was sold at a loss. Many different kinds of such measures can be imagined. One is the strategic *malinvestment*. The term malinvestment is applicable when mistakes have been made, the consequences of which are revealed independently of the struggle between new and old in the economy. Such a malinvestment may lead to a regressive process. In general, however, malinvestments are present in all types of processes. It is of some importance, therefore, that the malinvestment concept be differentiated.

First, we have additions to capacity which are underutilized and unprofitable in the short run and therefore appear to be malinvestments, although they may be both fully utilized and profitable in the longer run. Justification of the investment may depend, for example, simply on expansion of capacity in some other industry; meanwhile, because of the difficulty of surveying the situation and of appraising the prospects correctly, the investment may appear to be a mistake. When, however, temporary underutilization of capacity rather than too low a capacity in the other industry is the cause of inadequate returns, this would not be termed malinvestment according to the current definition.

Another excluded case occurs when low returns are due to a projected sales volume not yet achieved by a product. This yields, at least theoretically, a relatively clear distinction between a general situation of "cyclically" low returns and one of more "structurally" low returns caused by malinvestment. It is also clear that malinvestments should not be confused with inadequate returns when these appear as a normal concomitant of an industrial transformation process and are generally regarded as such.

---

[5] Here and in what follows, changing the initial assumption of "stationary circular flow" to "balanced expansion" will permit substituting the term "stagnating" for "regressive."

Second, we have investments which in the long run, and with full knowledge of the future, appear to be malinvestments in the given sense of low earnings and, perhaps, underutilization. It is often difficult to distinguish between actual and apparent malinvestment. One reason for this is that, in both cases, the book value of the capital assets is often reduced. After such a reduction in value, when the loss is written off at once, the investment may lose all appearance of being a mistake—at least until the question of reinvesting arises.

The Analysis of Transformation and Its Relation to Business Cycle Theory.   Some Concepts of "Structure"

A study of driving forces behind progressive, stagnating, and regressive processes must, as already suggested, lead to a study of the interrelationships among these forces. Supply-push in one market may lead to demand-pull growth in another area, and to stagnation or regression in still others. "Tensions" in the development process may also arise, as when innovations occur at a single stage of production or distribution. These tensions, in turn, may serve as driving forces. This may be the case with certain types of malinvestments, for example. Such a study, and the analysis of malinvestments in particular, may open up new approaches not only to the analysis of transformation per se, but in *linking it with the traditional issues of business cycle research.*

Reference to the general investment concept of business cycle theory introduces a crucial factor in the cyclical process into the discussion and raises problems central to business cycle theory and policy. What role in shaping investment activity did the negative and positive components of transformation play in the interwar period? What investments were part of a supply-push or a demand-pull process? Did the negative component of transformation play an active or passive role in the recession periods? To what extent did unemployment arise directly through the negative component of transformation, and to what extent was it a result of a decline in demand with no direct, or even indirect, connection with the transformation process? What role did different types of malinvestments play?

Theoretically, it is quite conceivable that a depression might arise due to a decline of investment not at all connected with pressures from the negative side of the development process. It is possible, for instance, for a decline to be induced by a rise in interest rates or other increases in construction costs. On the other hand, it is quite conceivable for a decline in investment to be caused by the introduction of a new product which all at once renders an older product noncompetitive and the corresponding capital assets obsolete.

In connection with these questions, it may be helpful to investigate the extent to which current returns—measured as net profits in percent of net worth—determined investment. It should be noted that there is no a priori reason to expect profitability in a given sector to have been a decisive factor. First impressions regarding the importance of these observed profit rates may be misleading because the net worth figures taken from the balance sheets of old firms may fall considerably below the amount on which a new investment would be required to earn a return. Similarly, a low profit rate may be misleading for the opposite reason. One does not have an a priori reason to expect profitability to be a decisive factor, even when using a concept of profitability based exclusively on expectations. Full mobility of capital cannot be counted on. In addition, the possibility of quite different investment motives must be recognized.

A study of the driving forces and their interrelationships within the framework of an analysis of industrial transformation of the type described brings us to what could be called the general analysis of structure. This becomes of particular interest when the analysis of transformation is combined with a study of cyclical problems. The study of changes in the general social structure is not an objective of this work. An analysis of industrial transformation in a more restrictive sense, however, can use to advantage some particularly important concepts of structure other than that of productive structure. Those factors on which the analysis of structure focuses may be treated, of course, without explicit use of a special conceptual apparatus. Such an apparatus may contribute, however, toward the desired rigor and systematic framework of a causal analysis.

In the first place, it is of essential importance to stress the *economic-political structure*, which has undergone many shifts in the era of industrialism. The economic-political structure refers to the relationship between national and local governments and the private sector. An important consideration in this connection is how the principles directing the use of governmental powers affect the transformation process. The question is how national or local governments shape the framework for the transformation process or, perhaps, more directly take part in the process—for example, through letting "the public good" modify "purely economic" motives, and so forth. A hint of this has already been given in Chapter 3, where the general features of interwar development were sketched.

It is important to obtain a concept that covers not only the configuration of public versus private influence but also the influence of different social groups on the economic development process and on economic policies. *The social structure in the sociological sense*, therefore, enters as an important factor. It must be assumed that the development process it vitally affected by those social groups which hold strategic power positions and also by the characteristics of these groups: their income levels, education, and so forth. Another factor that could be vitally important is the *group structure of the labor market and the economy generally*— the dependence of the individual agents on the respective organized groups, as well as the interdependence of the groups.[6]

Finally, the concept of *industry structure* should be mentioned. This term refers to the size distribution of firms in an industry. The structure of an industry in this sense may be static or dynamic, stable or unstable. A static structure refers to a situation in which the smaller enterprises generally are not growing or expected to join the ranks of the larger firms in the industry. In a dynamic industry structure, most of the small firms may simply be young firms on their way to becoming big. In an unstable structure, a certain category of firms, for example, might be threatened with extinction due to pressure from the negative side of the development process, and their demise would lead to a changed industrial structure.

The Transformation Process and the Formation, Development, and Discontinuation of Firms

In the following, we will attempt to make the analysis of transformation more penetrating, primarily by a closer study of *enterprises and entrepreneurial activity.* This will also serve to clarify the importance of various structural concepts. A realistic approach requires that the role of the human factor be recognized. *The main task therefore will be to study the formation, development, and discontinuation of Swedish industrial firms in the interwar period.*

This topic deserves a systematic study since in the field of economic development the task has so far never been tackled from a general economic point of view.[7] Thus a need exists for integrating, for example,

---

[6] Cf. Sune Carlsson, *Företagsledning och företagsledare* (Stockholm, 1945), pp. 13–29.

[7] Some systematic studies of discontinuations have been made, however. For Sweden, cf., e.g., *Rationaliseringsutredningens betänkande*, SOU (1913, Nos. 13 and 14). But these studies have been concerned with special problems, such as unemployment, and have consequently focused on discontinuations of production in the purely technical sense rather than on the failure of firms in the economic sense (cf. chap. 10, pp. 183 ff.). Thus all discontinuations lasting for at least one year have been recorded even when this has not been associated with the bankruptcy of the firm and when operations have later been resumed in the same manner as previously. Nor have the reasons for these discontinuations been the subject of detailed investigations. In addition, existing studies have dealt only with firms with at least 10 workers.

In the United States some primarily statistical studies of the formation and discontinuation of firms have been made mostly on the basis of material gathered by Dun and Bradstreet. This material, however, has the general disadvantage that it provides very little opportunity for a differentiation of the concepts of formation

the approach developed in Marshall's pioneering work with the problems of economic development, and for doing this within a wider framework of causal analysis. Marshall's theory of the "turnover" of firms is very stimulating, but his propositions on the possibilities open to small firms to (*a*) join the ranks of the large firms, (*b*) start on a relatively large scale, (*c*) capture the markets of older firms, and so forth, do not have sufficient foundation in a systematic causal analysis. The same can be said for his notion of "the representative firm."[8]

Schumpeter has expressed the need for more light on these topics in a way that is very much to the point:

Quantitative information about the life span of individual firms and analysis explanatory of their careers and their age distribution are among our most urgent desiderata. They would be important for many other purposes besides the study of business fluctuations, and throw a flood of light on the structure and working of capitalism, now obscured by so much empty phraseology and preconceptions of a pseudotheoretical nature.[9]

He presumes that innovations as a rule are carried out by new firms and, also, that new firms generally carry out innovations.[10] Schumpeter's definition of the concept of "firm" is not always consistent, but this affects his analysis relatively little.

A corollary to this proposition in Schumpeter's system is the idea that as firms grow older they gradually lose their ability to innovate and that this eventually leads to their demise. Schumpeter is very explicit, however, on the point that this need not be the case even though, so far, it has been true under capitalism.

What in Marshall and Schumpeter remains in the most part a subject of mere conjectures will be one of the main objects of analysis in the present study. This will bring us at least a step closer to a better integra-

---

and discontinuation of firms because the data have been gathered almost entirely on the basis of purely formal criteria (cf. chap. 10 below). The most interesting of existing studies is A. Oxenfeldt, *New Firms and Free Enterprise* (Washington, 1943). Oxenfeldt has attempted to illuminate the whole problem-complex in this area. Here also, however, the weakness is that the analysis must remain basically deductive. As the author himself emphasizes, the material does not permit a detailed causal analysis. Above all, it has proved impossible to relate the study of the firms to an analysis of the transformation of production (cf. p. 58 below). Oxenfeldt does, however, provide valuable compilations of statistical data relevant to several issues. We will have occasion, therefore, to refer to his work repeatedly in what follows.

[8] J. Steindl's essay, *Small and Big Business. Economic Problems of the Size of Firms* (Oxford, 1945), provides a good, concise summary of Marshall's central ideas in this area. Steindl also utilizes certain empirical data to discuss the realism of Marshall's assumptions. The opportunities for new firms to threaten the position of older firms are, according to Steindl, smaller than Marshall imagined. Cf. A. Marshall, *Principles of Economics* (5th ed., London, 1907), pp. 377–78.

[9] J. A. Schumpeter, *Business Cycles*, Vol. I, p. 95n.

[10] Schumpeter, *op. cit.*, Vol. I, p. 94.

tion of the areas of transformation analysis and business cycle analysis than has traditionally been achieved. On the basis of the analytical framework already sketched, the primary problems can be formulated as follows:

How did the industrial transformation generally—and its particular "cyclical manifestations"—take place under the institutional and structural conditions of interwar Sweden? How did it take place, that is, in a society based essentially on private enterprise, without much government planning or direction, but where the economic policy pursued from 1931 onward belonged, at least in part, to an economic-political structure other than that of earlier industrial periods? How smoothly or how sluggishly did the transformation take place? What roles were played in the transformation process and in the formation, development, and discontinuation of firms by the social structure, by the educational level of different groups, by their incomes and power positions, or by the group structure of the economy?

An important question in this context concerns the *form that competition* takes in different industries. In the first place, of course, formation of new firms may be prevented, or in any case hampered, by *organized control of entry*. This control may be exercised either by governmental agencies, or by individual firms or combinations of firms. The most effective method used seems to be that of barring the entrant from access to certain suppliers or customers that cooperate with the "controlling" firms. Another alternative is to *purchase the firm in order to close it down*. The primary motive is often to limit competition. The government may contribute to such a policy in different ways. It is possible, also, that firms that participate in organized curtailment of competition, although otherwise not viable, may be kept alive through cooperation or governmental assistance.

There are several other ways in which the mode of competition in an industry can affect the establishment and discontinuation of firms, even in the absence of organized attempts either to control entry or to support existing firms. A price war of sufficient duration to eliminate new competitors may be started—or threatened—when the market is dominated by one firm (monopoly), two (duopoly), or a few firms (oligopoly), or by a cartel. It is possible also that "outside" firms may close down when merely threatened with such a price war. On the other hand, such outside firms, which in other circumstances might have been forced out of the market, may also coexist with a market-dominating firm.

Organized curtailment of competition may thus restrict the rate of entry. It is just possible, however, that it will *stimulate the establishment of new firms*. Attention has often been called to the fact that small firms frequently spring up "in the shadow" of the big companies which by and large dominate a market. These small firms may thrive, for example, by holding their prices somewhat below those of their dominating competitor but on a higher and, to the small firm, more profitable level than a more competitive market would have allowed.

Hence, older firms can sometimes stay in business and new firms spring up outside cartels. Typically, this will be the situation when the cartel does not consider it worth the cost and trouble involved in forcing these firms out of the market—as long as they remain small. The risk of failure and collapse of the cartel may for that matter be considerable. The small independent firms on their side may not wish to become large and really serious competitors. They may be well aware of the potential strength that can be mobilized by the big company or the big cartel to defeat an attempt in this direction.

From these brief comments, it is evident that a big company, an organized cartel, or other organization may affect the formation, development, and discontinuation of firms in essentially different ways under different circumstances. A causal analysis has a significant subject of inquiry here. It should be stated from the beginning, however, that the possibilities of achieving a really satisfactory clarification of this problem are very circumscribed. Any attempt to judge what the course of development would have been in the absence of restrictive practices meets, of course, with great methodological difficulties. In addition, an investigation of restrictive practices, even in just a single market, would be a major research task in itself. This is particularly true of the latter half of the 1930's when such practices were particularly abundant. Furthermore, such an investigation would be impossible in many cases at such a late date; many of the original organizers of a cartel, or other knowledgeable individuals, would be dead or no longer able or willing to recall events.

In order to achieve success, as far as possible, in answering the questions that have been raised, the investigation must proceed in stages; at each stage new questions may arise. To begin with, what is an operational definition of formation of firms, of discontinuation of firms? The point is open to dispute, but a choice must be made with reference to the problem under study. It then becomes possible to chart the *quantitative role of firm turnover variables in* different industries. How many firms were established or dissolved in the period, and what quantitative role did they play for the course of production and employment?

Another area of study will be the industrial structures—the size distributions of firms and the production structures of the different industries. The latter refers to such variables as the number of different products in the industry and their distribution among the firms in the industry, and the extent to which firms specialize or market many products.

The next stage in the study of entrepreneurial activity in the interwar period will be an investigation of the *variations over time* in the firm-turnover variables. Were more firms established in boom periods than in recession periods? Was firm "mortality" greater in depression than in boom years? Which firms showed the greatest fluctuations in employment and output from one period to another? This stage of the investigation is not of direct interest to transformation analysis. It is of considerable indirect interest, however, because it may raise new problems relating to the driving forces underlying entrepreneurial activity.

The connection with the issues of business cycle research is obvious and may be formulated as follows: What role have the new and the old firms, respectively, played in investment (defined as an aggregate with known cyclical effects)? How much have the variations in employment been influenced directly or indirectly by the formation, development, and discontinuation of firms? To what extent were malinvestments connected with the formation of new firms or with the expansion of older firms?

If answers to the more fundamental questions are to be found, the study of the quantitative role of entrepreneurial activity, its surface features, and its variations over time must lead to a closer scrutiny of the character of entrepreneurial activity—particularly the establishment and discontinuation of enterprises. The primary task will be to find information on these related questions: *To what extent did new products and new production processes (innovations) originate in new and old firms, respectively? To what extent have the new and the old firms introduced new products and new processes? What role did the establishment of new firms play in the transformation process in general?* This will involve combining the results of the transformation analysis with a study of the individual firms.

Such an analysis of the dynamic industrial process leads to a more detailed analysis of the new and old firms from other viewpoints. For example: To what extent did the negative component of the transformation process lead to dissolution of firms? To what extent was the actual mortality rate due to this negative component, and to what extent was it due, for example, to strategic malinvestments? Another important problem concerns the relation between discontinuation of firms and the efforts at concentration.

Related problems concern the extent to which the new, old, and defunct firms had the same markets and produced the same commodities. To what extent did the new firms complement the older ones, and to what extent did they compete with them? What was the influence of firm-turnover variables on the degree of concentration and specialization in production?

But the relationships between the organization of production and marketing, on the one hand, and the firm-turnover variables, on the other, are not the only subject of interest here. The conditions of entrepreneurial activity—and thereby the driving forces—can be understood only when the *historical, sociological, financial,* and *geographical* aspects are considered also.

The historical aspects concern the origin of new firms. Origin data are fundamental to an understanding of the determinants of the formation of new firms because they bring to the fore the question of the recruitment of new entrepreneurs. To what extent did new firms evolve from craft production in some defined sense? To what extent were they started in connection with already existing wholesale or retail establishments, formed by older manufacturing firms as subsidiaries, or founded by private individuals in a manner unrelated to the types of origin already enumerated? The historical aspect also brings out the question of the motives behind the establishment of new firms.

The relevant *sociological* questions are closely connected with the historical questions just mentioned. They focus above all on the *earlier career of founders,* on their *education* and *age,* on the sociological groups to which they belonged, and on their personal circumstances in general at the time of the establishment of the new firm.

The study of the *financial* aspects has two main objectives: to increase our knowledge of the *initial financing of the new firms,* and the *financing of the continued development of the firm.* Both aspects must be expected to influence the scale and character of entrepreneurial activity in the different industries. Some of the specific questions to which answers would be particularly helpful are: What were the capital requirements in different industries, both in connection with the establishment of new firms and with their further development? In how many cases was the entrepreneur's own capital important at the start, or later? In how many cases was the initial capital, or capital for expansion, obtained through sale of shares? How often was capital obtained from firms contracting for the new firm's output? In how many cases were loans obtained? What forms of borrowing were important in the latter situation?

With regard to the *geographical* aspects, finally, one is primarily interested in the *localization of new enterprises* and *inter-local comparisons of the development of firms.* Questions that may be raised here, will in turn, demand a closer analysis in order to be answered. To the extent, however, that the analysis has provided answers to previous questions, the answers to these geographical questions will probably already be at hand. If, for example, some information on the historical aspects has been obtained, and some of the relations between the formation of firms and the structure of production and distribution have been clarified, this should shed some light on the localization of new establishments.

The next chapter deals with the transformation process in the first half-century of Swedish industrialism. It represents a preliminary attempt to analyze some of the questions raised. The discussion provides an introduction to the main task—the analysis of the period after 1919. This introduction is very schematical and hypothetical, however and the analysis cannot be carried through in the systematic manner intended for the interwar period. It relies for the most part on the existing literature. It is worth noting that, on almost every decisive point, this literature fails to provide the necessary foundation for a more thorough analysis.

Part II

Transformation of Industrial Production in the Interwar Period

5 Some Features of the Industrial Transformation Process before World War I

A. The Entrepreneurs

The new industries evolved from the old guild-organized crafts only in exceptional cases.[1] This characteristic feature of Swedish economic development prior to World War I emerges very clearly from a study

---

[1] In the strict sense of the term "handicraft" would refer to production without any assistance from machines. Such a restrictive definition is no longer very useful, however, since almost all of the activities that are now referred to as crafts in everyday usage would then be categorized as industry. A more common definition does not focus on the presence or absence of machinery. Instead, one calls it a craft when the output is produced piece by piece. Such production may very well utilize numerous machines even if, more commonly, handicraft in the literal sense still dominates. Such a definition, however, will not fit in all contexts either, principally because various mixed forms are quite common. A third definition refers to the marketing of the product. If the firm produces to the order of customers in a local market, the operation is referred to as handicraft, whereas production for stock of more or less standardized items intended for a larger market is referred to as industry. Nor is this definition without its difficulties. Segments of the modern industry—according to accepted everyday usage—would fall under crafts by this definition.

The best way to solve the problem, apparently, is to avoid commitment to a general definition. It seems more appropriate to use different definitions in different contexts depending on the industry being treated, the question being asked and the time period being studied. In the present context, handicraft may be defined as a type of operation in which production is almost completely manual and on a piecemeal basis. In discussing the early stages of industrialization, a definition relating to the marketing of the product is inappropriate, since what is regularly referred to as industry in everyday usage in those days frequently had very little in common with modern industry as far as marketing is concerned. An example would be the early mechanical engineering shops. At the same time some activities that were without hesitation referred to as handicraft were really industrial in nature, for example, steel manufacturing in Eskilstuna.

61

of innovations and of the formation of new firms as factors in the development process. Master craftsmen were seldom involved in the industrialization process during its first 50 years. Nor were their employees among the innovators or enterprise founders, at least not to any significant extent. This was true in those areas where a completely new industry evolved, as for example the pulp industry. But it was also true for the markets of such traditional crafts as those of the blacksmith, the plater, the shoemaker, the tailor, and the cabinetmaker, where the new manufacturing enterprises were also founded by others than the master craftsmen or their apprentices.

A development from craft production to industrial production that was not accompanied by the formation of new firms was therefore rare. The most conspicuous exceptions were the Eskilstuna manufacturers. The tanneries were to a certain extent an exception also. In the former case, however, the putting-out system played a considerable role in the development of "industrial" enterprises. Another characteristic feature was the frequent failure of the new industry to eliminate the old crafts, or even to change their basic character. The number of people employed in the crafts has been estimated as 76,000 in 1861 and as 166,000 in 1910.[2] While these figures are very uncertain, they do show a strong increase.

Although master craftsmen or their employees rarely started new manufacturing firms or converted their shops into such firms, there were many cases of strong connections between the crafts and the new industrial firms. Crafts or cottage industries were sometimes forerunners of the new industries. Though shoemakers, for example, seldom founded shoe factories, the new shoe manufacturers often acquired their skilled workers from the craft. Much the same was true of the textile industry, particularly around Borås. The first furniture factories hired apprentices, who had moved out from the cities, to great advantage. Such instances should be distinguished, however, from what we have called "evolution out of a craft."

The historical connection between commerce and the new manufacturing firms is a conspicuous feature in almost all industries. The first engineering firms that were independent of the old iron works were usually founded by merchants. The same applies to the big new lumber mills, the pulp mills, and to the construction joineries and furniture factories, which originally were mainly located in the cities. When the manufacture of furniture started to spread to rural areas in the 1890's, most of the enterprise founders were farmers or farm boys with some skill in cabinetmaking. They often received assistance from the urban

---

[2] *Wages, Cost of Living and National Income in Sweden, 1860–1930*, Vol. III: E. Lindahl, K. Kock, E. Dahlgren, *National Income of Sweden, 1861–1930* (London, 1937), Part II, pp. 210–11.

furniture merchants, who were in general only recently established at the time, but not from the master cabinetmakers, who were few in number. The pioneering textile firms had close connections with the wholesalers and jobbers in the industry. Similarly, the ready-to-wear clothing industry had its origin in the wholesale or retail trade. The great majority of the new shoe factories were started by wholesalers or jobbers. The chemical industry was largely founded by wholesale or retail merchants, and so on.

In the early decades of industrialization the number of founders seems to have been considerably smaller than the number of firms established. Twenty or so names appear in connection with at least a hundred of the new firms during this period; a relatively small group of individuals founded the pioneering firms. Everything indicates that the basis for the recruitment of entrepreneurs was rather narrow. One reason must certainly have been the comparative absence from it of master craftsmen and apprentices. Another explanation, however, lies in the relatively small number of people with significant capital at their disposal. Also of importance was the low level of education, according to present standards, and the frequent lack of close contacts with foreign countries. Early manufacturing efforts were not only associated with a few individuals, but were in great measure associated with the educated upper class and upper middle class.

The prominent, although far from dominant, foreign element among the founders of new firms should also be mentioned. The emergence of the first modern Swedish industries was often dependent on foreign inspiration. It was not just purely technical stimuli that were important but the fact that the Swedish enterprise founders usually had either traveled abroad or in some other way established close contacts with foreign, particularly English, businessmen and industrialists. The foreign contribution to the *financing* of the expanding Swedish industry before World War I was mostly of indirect importance; the construction of the railroads was primarily financed with foreign capital, leaving Swedish capital resources for domestic industry.[3] In the introductory industrialization phase, capital came mainly from a few merchant houses and from rich individuals of the upper middle or upper class. The government also contributed to some extent through the credit institution called the "Manufacturers' Discount." In only a relatively few cases was financing obtained from a large number of small contributors, as for example by stock subscription.

Corporations were not normally founded to tap small savings but to gain limited liability. The corporate form often came long after the estab-

---

[3] The financing has been studied especially by T. Gårdlund. Cf. his *Svensk industrifinansiering under genombrottsskedet 1830–1913* (Stockholm, 1947).

lishment of the firm. The development of the business was apparently financed largely by plowing back profits and through further contributions from the same sources utilized at the time of the firm's formation. After 1870, when the preceding decade's innovations in the banking and credit system were rapidly growing in importance, the old merchant houses began to lose their dominant position both as distributors and suppliers to the large manufacturing firms and as financiers. They were generally superseded in the first function by industry itself and by wholesalers of more modern type, and in the latter function by the banks.

It is apparent that the Swedish social structure with its narrow recruitment base for entrepreneurs and the scarcity of risk capital contributed to the relatively late, and slow, start of Swedish industrialization. There are other explanations, however. One that is often mentioned is the legislation, which up to the middle of the 19th century restricted private economic initiative, both in domestic and foreign trade. Undoubtedly the ascendancy of economic liberalism created a change in the economic-political structure that was of great importance to the industrialization of the Swedish economy. English free trade and, within Sweden, the school reform of 1846 and the constitutional reform of 1864, as well as the trade treaty with France in 1865, signaled the breakthrough of economic liberalism. The best examples of its importance to industrialization are found in the steel and lumber mill industries.[4] This influence should not be overemphasized, however. Thus the repeal of the regulations hardly had any decisive influence on the development of domestic commerce and production; it played a more important role in foreign trade, particularly for the lumber mills. The pressure of foreign and domestic economic forces had in many cases made the old economic legislation ineffectual long before its formal repeal. Earlier annulment would probably not have led to any significant acceleration of the industrialization process. The same may be said of foreign trade; it was the growing need for wood products, for example, that swept away the English tariffs on them. In any case it should not be assumed that the late breakthrough of economic liberalism in Sweden was the lone cause of the late and slow start on its industrialization.

B. Structural Tensions and Structural Balance in the Development Process

Limited markets undoubtedly slowed down Swedish industrial development. In order to deal with this problem it is necessary to distinguish

---

[4] Cf. esp. Eli F. Heckscher, *Svenskt arbete och liv från medeltiden till nutiden* (Stockholm, 1941), and A. Montgomery, *Industrialismens genombrott i Sverige.*

between, on the one hand, the introduction of an innovation and its dissemination, and on the other hand, the total Swedish market and a local or regional domestic market.[5]

If it is to be concluded that the introduction of an innovation was hindered because of the limited extent of the Swedish market, the innovation must have required a higher rate of sales than the market could absorb at a profitable price. This appears to have been the case for several branches of the capital goods industry during the initial stage of the industrialization process.[6] Their growth in many cases required a development of Swedish industry on a relatively broad front. This simply because, as long as they could not compete in export markets, Swedish industry was *the* customer of the capital goods industry.

Similar problems of "balance," which retard development, are encountered later on. In the early 1900's, for example, a certain equilibrium seems to have been reached between the engineering, textile, and wood-using industries and those industries supplying their machinery. On the other hand, the electrical engineering industry, the youngest of the capital goods industries, encountered a typical balance problem. ASEA, for example, faced a problem that threatened to be the end of the whole corporation. The firm finally solved it after several years, but only by engaging directly or through subsidiaries in the electrification task and by helping to create an industry requiring large electric power plants.[7] Only by completing a whole electric *"development block"* could a successful electrical engineering industry be established. A pioneering firm in another area, Skånska Cement AB, was another typical example. Some 20 years earlier, general ignorance of the uses of cement had created difficulties for this company. It therefore became imperative for its management to generate innovations in, and development of, a concrete products industry, and to engage in construction contracting where cement would be an important material.[8] The analogy with the problems of ASEA at the turn of the century is obvious.

In those cases where consumption was great enough to support a single firm profitably, the introduction of an innovation could not be blocked by the small size of the market. An innovating firm ought to be able to eliminate older ones through successful competition. To the extent that this did not happen, there must be some reason other than the extent

---

[5] At present we do not need to make distinctions between different types of innovation, although such distinctions will become necessary later. Cf. chap. 6.

[6] Cf. Gårdlund, *Industrialismens samhälle;* Montgomery, *op. cit.;* and A. Malcolm, *Factiska bevis att fabriks-och industriväsendet inom Sverige ej är lika tacksamt som i andra länder* (Linköping, 1870).

[7] Cf. J. Åkerman, *ASEA 1833–1933: Ett elektriskt halvsekel* (Västerås, 1933).

[8] Cf. K. Kock, *Skånska Cementaktiebolaget 1871–1931* (Uppsala, 1932), esp. pp. 41 and 179 ff.

of the total market.[9] Dissemination of the innovation could, on the other hand, still meet with economic obstacles; the total Swedish market was often too small for a number of innovating firms, although it could support one such firm or perhaps many of the older type. In such cases, "malinvestments" and tendencies toward overproduction would often occur. This was one reason for the weak financial position of several branches of the Swedish engineering industry, even after the market had become broad enough to support one profitable firm. Many other factors played their part—the lack of skilled workers being one.[10]

Old firms and obsolete activities often continued to operate in the shadow of the innovator-firms even when the latter showed low returns. The explanation seems ot be that as long as the old plants—and their owners—were not run down, they could continue to compete without depreciation allowances or reinvestments. By covering only their variable costs, they exerted pressure on the profit margins of the innovating firms. In other cases, the old activities would yield acceptable returns and the innovating firms good returns. This raises the question of why the number of innovating firms did not grow, or why the existing ones did not expand so that the rate of return was reduced. One reason could have been that more firms could not be started due to a lack of entrepreneurs, or financiers, willing to take the risk, or that existing firms either could not or would not expand to the point of eliminating all the older firms in the industry.[11] In any case, organized curtailment of competition did not play a role in this period.

When tendencies to overproduction exist and malinvestments occur, or when, for one reason or another, other factors inhibiting adjustment are present, there is a problem of development balance. "Structural tensions" of this kind would either cause economic difficulties for the innovating firms or lead to an increase in their number and/or further expansion of those already established. The latter situation would particularly affect the older firms. The process would continue until a more balanced industry structure was achieved through a progressive expansion of the market and/or the elimination of some of the firms, reducing structural tension. The early industrialization process frequently encountered obstacles of this sort which it took time to surmount. But these structural tensions and incomplete development blocks were at the same time driving forces in the development process.

---

[9] In analyzing the interwar period, we will devote special attention to this problem.

[10] Gårdlund, *op. cit.*, and *idem, Bolinders—en svensk verkstad* (Stockholm, 1945).

[11] In analyzing the interwar period, we will illustrate and discuss the various factors which may cause firms to cease to grow even though market conditions per se would permit further expansion. These factors have been of great importance in shaping the structure of industries. The question of the profit margins of innovating firms will also be discussed in the same context.

A capital goods industry would often be dependent on the expansion of one or more other specific industries. This was, of course, less frequently the case in the consumption goods industries where growth primarily followed that of the economy in general. For these industries, moreover, the extent of the *total* Swedish market was seldom an important retarding factor with respect to the *introduction* of innovations. The structure of production in the old consumption goods industries was rarely such that a single firm, or a few firms, supplied the entire Swedish market with the same product. Conditions were simply different from those in the capital goods industries. While Swedish production of textile machinery would be difficult to absorb if even a single firm entered into it, it could hardly be said that the market (e.g., before 1870) was unable to absorb the output of an "industrial" firm manufacturing clothing, shoes, or furniture at a profitable price.

On the other hand, the introduction and especially the *dissemination* of innovations sometimes encountered considerable difficulties because of the limited extent of *local or regional* markets. As long as the communications system remained relatively underdeveloped, firms in many industries could not sell outside their own local areas. Steam flour mills and bakeries, for example, were built only in the larger population centers during the initial stage of the industrialization process. Smaller centers could not offer a potential consumption volume sufficient to make the investment profitable. The same was true of the mechanized construction joinery and furniture factories. It is significant that steam saws were first introduced in those lumber mills that produced for a large export market. Only much later did they become profitable inland, where only a local demand could be counted upon. Even where the limitations of the local or regional market did not constitute an obstacle for a single innovating firm, the innovations were not always generally disseminated. As was the case with some commodities which could be produced for national distribution, tendencies to overproduction sometimes developed also in local or regional markets when too many firms tried to exploit an innovation.

A study of the industrial breakthrough in Sweden shows that the problem of development balance was particularly important in *communications*. The railway network could not be expanded rapidly in many areas simply because it was not profitable to be too far in advance of general industrial growth. Freight earnings would be insufficient until industry reached a certain size. Developments in the province of Småland are a good example. The first railroads were built here for the transport of lumber mill products, but the network did not become profitable and could not be expanded until the wood-processing industry had developed further.[12]

---

[12] Cf. O. Gasslander, "Halland och de moderna kommunikationerna," in *Halland, en bok om hembygden*, publ. by Hallands nation i Lund (Lund, 1938).

Examples could be taken also from the Bergslagen provinces and from Skåne, where several railroads were built initially to meet the needs of agriculture. Another example, not involving railroads, is offered by the early history of the lumber mill and pulp industries in Norrland. Here market conditions and production techniques were often such that almost any expansion rate could have been sustained; the necessity to clear the rivers and extend the floating channels was the retarding factor. Admittedly there were also some other hindrances—a lack of experts in erecting pulp plants seems to have been one—but the transportation of raw materials was probably particularly important. As in the previous cases, the expansion of entire "development blocks" of this sort was frequently a condition for the profitable operation of the individual components of the block.

In the discussion so far, insufficient purchasing power in local, regional, or national markets has in several instances been the strategic factor behind the retardation of innovations and/or their dissemination. This factor should not be overemphasized, however. Innovations have almost always created their own market to some extent; indeed they have very often created it completely. Lower price and/or better quality make the commodities desirable and bring them within reach of more people than before. The innovation may even *create* a need which previously either did not exist or did not manifest itself concretely. Actually, not many pure cases of insufficient demand are to be found in the earlier industrialization period. Nor are there many pure examples of supply-push development processes. It is possible, however, to characterize different processes as approximating one or the other pure type. In the beginning, ready-made clothes were by no means cheaper than those that were tailormade or home-sewn. They could not capture the market until changed conditions had, in particular, discouraged home production and created a strong demand from entirely new socioeconomic strata. Transport conditions were also such that distribution over a wider market was impossible. The early furniture, construction joinery, and shoe industries encountered similar obstacles.

Many other cases come closer to the supply-push type. The industries which began to produce machines to replace manual work, or consumer durables such as kerosene stoves and sewing machines, to a large extent created their own markets; even here, of course, a demand-pull element enters with the expansion of the economy in general. Thus there are good reasons for asserting that the first few decades of Swedish industrial development did not create favorable conditions for the growth of the former group of industries. With reference to the latter group, such a statement would be less justified. A closer study of the development processes of different industries, focusing on the theoretical issues developed in Chapter 4, would perhaps be of interest. But for the first 50 years of the industrialization process in Sweden it is almost impossible to do so; the task demands source material of a completely different scale and reliability from what now exists. The issues in question will be assigned a central role in the analysis of the interwar period in order to throw light on the formation, development, and discontinuation of firms.

Structural tensions in technological or organizational development constitute a problem of economic development balance which is superficially similar to, and often difficult in practice to distinguish from, those already discussed. Completion of a development block would often require that technological and organizational knowledge in different areas be brought to the same level. These balance problems are often fascinating objects for closer study. It is remarkable how little attention they have received in economics, despite that both as driving forces and as sources of great economic difficulties they may well have been more important than the previously mentioned, more noted balance problems.

Examples can be found even within individual firms with some measure of vertical integration. For one reason or another, bottlenecks could sometimes not be avoided through purchases of raw materials or intermediate products from other producers. At other times, the distributive structure of the industry would be so inflexible that an adequate sales volume for an intermediate product could not be achieved outside the firm, or else other conditions (e.g., in transportation), would have the same effect. A technical improvement in an intermediate process often could not become an innovation as long as such improvements had not been made in one or more other stages of production and balance thus achieved. The situation was in principle the same also in many cases where the different stages of the production process were divided between different firms. In such cases, there could either be an obstacle to the introduction of the innovation or an obstacle to its dissemination. Examples are to be found particularly in the history of the Swedish metal industries. Modern steelmaking processes often could not be profitably introduced because the blast furnace technology was not on a level where it was possible to feed the Bessemer converters or open hearths with enough sufficiently cheap pig iron.

This structural tension dissolved amazingly soon, however, as smelting technology made enormous advances, particularly under the pressure of this structural imbalance.[13] Another troublesome obstacle to the concentration of furnace operations which this required, namely inadequate transportation facilities, was overcome with the advent of the railroads. When a steel mill either could not or would not expand its own blast

---

[13] Cf. C. Sahlin, "Den basiska martinprocessens införande i Sverige," *Jernkontorets Annaler*, Vol. 124, No. 10 (Stockholm, 1940).

furnace capacity, the railroads made possible pig iron purchases from other producers and the scrapping of the mill's own furnaces. What has been said about blast furnaces applies also to the mines. These structural tensions in the relationship between steelmaking, smelting, and mining technologies were not the only ones, however. In the 1860's and 1870's the "steel block" was incomplete in relation to the steel manufacturing and engineering industries. This was at least in part due to technical and organizational factors, but market factors were also important.

A contemporary account is very informative:

Bessemer conversion has been in use in Sweden ever since its invention, but even as late as 1871 only 189,000 centners Bessemer metal were produced, and although this process must be regarded as especially suitable for us, because on the one hand most Swedish iron ores lend themselves well to it, and on the other hand the fuel consumption for the metal produced with this process is only half that for Lancashire iron, it is still only during the last few years that the Bessemer conversion has won more general recognition among us. The main reason herefor is without doubt to be found in the circumstance that this method requires such expensive contrivances and as a consequence is ill-suited for small works with inconsiderable production; but the situation referred to certainly also depends on the fact that the Bessemer process is not really suited to the production of bar iron, but should be followed by the further manufacturing and refinement of the produced ingots into finished product. The latter circumstance should of course not become a real obstacle to the adoption of the Bessemer process; a considerable expansion of the Swedish iron industry can only be made possible in such a way that, in addition to bar iron, of which world market demand in normal years is rather limited, also something else is produced; the fact is, however, that Sweden up until the last few years has hardly sold any iron abroad in other form than that of bar iron or acid steel, and it is therefore necessary to work up a wholly new market at the same time as one converts to the Bessemer process, which of course renders its adoption more difficult.[14]

The dissolution of the tension between conversion and smelting technique was largely a matter of deliberate efforts by the steel mills; this was also partly the case when the tension was dissolved between the steel mills on the one hand and the heavy manufacturing and engineering industry on the other. The steel mills were increasingly forced into the production of rolled steel and other heavy manufacturing, especially from the late seventies onward. The Swedish mills had to concentrate as far as possible on high-quality products, which meant in turn that individual sales organizations had to be built up.[15]

---

[14] R. Åkerman, *Några ord om jernhandteringens ståndpunkt i Sverige vid början af år 1873* (Stockholm, 1873), p. 26.

[15] Cf. *Ett svenskt jernverk, Sandviken och dess utveckling 1862–1937* (Uppsala, 1937). Also: Gust. Ekman, "Framtidsutsikterna för Sveriges järnhantering," *Affärsvärlden, 1901–26, Första kvartseklets festskrift* (Stockholm, 1926).

A study of the economic difficulties, leading to change of ownership, dissolution of firms, or financial reconstructions, brings out—as has already been repeatedly indicated—the effects on the industrialization process of these problems of development balance. Many such difficulties could certainly be explained by inadequate liquidity and/or inadequate returns as a consequence of incomplete development blocks and by the related scarcity of entrepreneurs and of credit. The necessity of developing complete blocks not only prevented numerous projects from being undertaken but also hampered projects already underway. Many large fortunes were probably sacrificed on incomplete development blocks. A closer study of this problem seems a tempting task, although it cannot be undertaken here. A typical example is found in the large British losses on the ore deposits and the ore railroad in Upper Norrland in the 1880's. Other examples could be taken from railroad enterprises farther south, from the pulp mills which frequently were unable to solve their energy problem, and so on.[16]

Even if this issue cannot be studied further in the present context, we will return to it later in discussing the cyclical aspects of the development process. It should be noted, however, that firms that were overexpanded in relation to other components of their development block—and therefore appeared to be in some degree malinvestments—often were purchased cheaply by persons or firms capable of completing, or at least continuing, the expansion of the development block. These firms would often, for this very reason, be more valuable to such investors than to other individuals or corporations which lacked the liquidity and/or the imagination to grasp the requirements and possibilities of the development block. Many of the great Swedish financial houses derive their origin and

---

[16] Given the problems of maintaining "balance" in the development process, it seems almost strange that the tendencies toward overproduction and malinvestment were not stronger than they actually were (cf. the following section on the problem of cyclical "stability" in development). Part of the explanation may be that the technical stimuli toward innovations in different stages of production often followed each other in such rapid succession that the problems were solved without too serious difficulties. This would especially have been the case so long as the Swedish merchant houses could still supply the capital or so long as foreign capital was attracted to Sweden. The various advances in blast furnace and oxidation technology, for example, "meshed" together surprisingly well, and the large capital requirements of the steel industry were met relatively well.

In addition, one should probably also adduce the fact that the dissemination of innovations in those parts of the development blocks that "were ahead" of the others went relatively slowly. Consequently, firms that would have tended to become malinvestments, at least over the short run, were never formed. The inhibiting factor was simply the very narrow basis for the recruitment of both entrepreneurs and skilled labor. Had the blooming mill innovations been more rapidly disseminated than was actually the case, the tendencies toward overproduction might perhaps have been stronger while at the same time those steel mills that did not adopt the innovations in question would have had more serious difficulties. If the ready-made clothing firms had multiplied more rapidly than was actually the case, this industry might perhaps have had to face transitory overproduction problems, while the tailors presumably would have found it more difficult to survive.

growth from a series of such takeovers. These sometimes exceptionally profitable "mergers" represented, whether intentionally or not, a state in the completion of a development block (i.e., a solution to a problem of development balance).

The often rather long intervals between a full-fledged technical invention and an innovation, as well as between an innovation and its general dissemination, might depend not only on a lack of adequate markets and/or technical balance, but also on wage trends. The introduction of a certain new machine would sometimes not be profitable as long as wages stayed below a certain level. In situations of this kind, the mechanization of a branch of industry would largely depend on developments in other parts of the economy (i.e., a more extensive and rapid development in quite different branches or industries would raise the general wage level and thus stimulate mechanization). Rapid expansion of an important industry could thus by way of the labor market induce new technical advances in other industries or lead to their practical application, i.e., cause the mobilization of latent innovations. The latter phenomenon is of special interest in the Swedish case. Together with the one previously discussed, it may help to explain why foreign technical advances were not widely adopted in Sweden as soon as they became known. The textile industry, where wages remained very low for a long time, may be an example, although the phenomenon was less marked in Sweden than in England.[17]

C. The Cumulative Industrialization Process

The above discussion may help to explain an industrialization process which in the beginning was relatively slow, hesitant, and marked by

---

[17] The development of the British textile industry provides several interesting illustrations of "structual tensions" of various kinds. Once the "flying shuttle" had come into use in the 1730's, there emerged an acute shortage of yarn. This induced a number of inventions and innovations in spinning shortly after 1750. These were so radical in nature that the weaving technology fell behind in its turn. As long as this technology did not catch up with that in spinning, the spinneries were plagued with serious overproduction problems. The invention of the mechanical loom toward the end of the century finally created the preconditions for balance among the different stages of production in the textile industry.

The immediate consequence, however, was that the wages of weavers were forced down by the threat of a general adoption of the mechanical loom. Wage rates were forced down to such an extent, in fact, that the introduction of this loom proceeded at a remarkably slow pace. One of the reasons for this was probably that the textile industry had developed so far in advance of other industries that the weavers did not have many other industrial occupations to transfer to. When, following the end of the Napoleonic wars, other industries also developed rapidly, the weavers became better able to resist the downward pressure on their wages. Through this effect on wages, the growth of other industries contributed to the finally fairly rapid introduction of the mechanical loom. Cf. F. Mantoux, *The Industrial Revolution in the 18th Century* (English ed., London, 1931).

many reverses. But it may also explain why this slow start turned into a very rapid, cumulative industrialization. The typical picture of a sluggish initial development turning suddenly into a very rapid process, is to be expected—it is implied in the characteristic features of the dynamics of industrialization that we have discussed. In addition, technical and organizational advances in one area are as a rule applicable in other areas.

The progressive widening of the recruitment base for both skilled workers and entrepreneurs constituted a first cumulative element. Each new industrial firm not only trained many engineers, salesmen, and skilled workers, but also many future enterprise founders. At the same time newly established schools began to offer technical education. Study of the formation of firms in the final decades of the 19th century provides a different picture of the recruitment of founders than at mid-century.[18] While merchants still dominated in the 1880's and 1890's, one finds a considerably larger number of technical people than before among the enterprise founders. Particularly in the rapidly expanding engineering industries, numerous founders of firms had earlier been employed in a technical capacity in the older machine shops.

Some of the cumulative elements in the development process are self-evident and do not deserve detailed comment. It is clear, for example, that improved communication with foreign countries, resulting in closer foreign contacts, was one such element, even disregarding its importance for the recruitment of enterprise founders. The same may be said of the cumulative element inherent in the demand-pull created by a growing and progressively more diversified economy, and of the developments in other industries which the capital goods sector engendered by providing technical resources on a completely new level and scale. Similarly, communication developments created new obvious opportunities for industrial growth in many areas. These elements have been more or less thoroughly described by all authors who have dealt with the great transformation of the Swedish economy.[19] The dissemination of innovations throughout the banking and credit system also helped to accelerate industrial developments,[20] often by making it possible to complete whole development blocks where liquidity problems had previously created difficulties.

While the role of the development blocks should not be overempha-

[18] Cf. Gårdlund, *Industrialismens samhälle.*

[19] Cf., e.g., Eli F. Heckscher, *Till belysning af järnvägarnas betydelse för Sveriges ekonomiska utveckling* (Stockholm, 1907); *idem, Svenskt arbete och liv;* Montgomery, *op. cit.;* and Gårdlund, *Industrialismens samhälle.*

[20] One phenomenon, which would well deserve a special study, is the rise of real estate values. This rise provided increased opportunities for a credit expansion based on mortgage collateral. The continued industrialization and urbanization, to which this credit expansion contributed, led in their turn to further increases in real estate values, etc.

sized in the present context, neither should their cumulative elements be ignored. Rapid expansion required growth in a combination of components as well as technical advances. These requirements were sometimes hard to meet in an initial stage when the development blocks often could not be completed because certain preconditions were not fulfilled. The latter might concern enterpreneurial skill (i.e., the ability to think in "blocks"), or capital and liquidity conditions (i.e., the ability to finance whole "blocks"). But when the preconditions were finally fulfilled, there ensued a cumulative expansion which often yielded high profits.

Just as the inadequate floating channels had to some extent held back the forest industries through the greater part of the 1880's, so the completion of an extensive water route system in the period made possible a rather sudden breakthrough for the industry, both with respect to the establishment of new firms and the development of older firms. Many other development blocks show a similar pattern. Development would often be slow as long as a technical component was missing. But when the "missing link" had been found, or had been copied from foreign models, a cumulative expansion followed. Not only the new but also several *earlier* advances would come to fruition at the same time; the consequence would be large profits, not economic difficulties.

A relatively slow and evenly progressing industrialization process appears improbable in the long run. At an advanced stage of industrial development, it may indeed be expected that the process will be in a different stage in different sectors of the economy, giving the aggregate process an appearance of relatively steady progress. But in the initial stage, one would expect a sudden acceleration into a cumulative process from a slow start. Swedish development in the first 50 years of industrialism should be regarded in this light. The difficulties of the 1870's and 1880's, even if sometimes exaggerated,[21] were in part a result of the many incomplete development blocks which then existed; the rest of the pre-World War I period brought their completion.[22]

Finally, attention should be given to the role of wage developments. The mobilization of technical advances already made was another cumula-

---

[21] One should remember that many of the contemporary accounts probably tended to exaggerate these difficulties since they appeared at the time when the tariff question was to be decided. It is perhaps always the case, for that matter, that those directly exposed to the pressure of negative development effects are prone to advertise their predicament and to make their voices heard as widely as possible. Periods of extensive economic transformation are likely, therefore, to be remembered by the general public as "bad times." Cf. H. Palme, *De hårda tiderna. En statistisk undersökning* (Stockholm, 1895).

[22] This should be emphasized, e.g., in discussing the significance of the tariffs instituted in 1888 and 1892 for the extraordinarily rapid development from the mid-nineties to the outbreak of World War I. Although such a discussion falls outside the framework of this study, it may be pointed out that, whereas these tariffs unquestionably played an important role in several sectors of industry, the

tive element. These technical advances would often not lead to innovations, or at least not to their general dissemination, because of prevailing low wages. The growth of a whole range of new industries in Sweden in the earlier part of the period not only caused technical advances and innovations but also mobilized a multitude of latent innovations in the older industries. It would require a considerably more detailed investigation, however, to weigh the importance of this cumulative element in relation to that of other such elements.

The cumulative factors have been discussed exclusively from the long-run point of view. Our primary interest has been in the factors influencing Swedish industrialization through its first 50 years. Several of these factors have, however, been especially evident in boom years. Some have long been recognized in business cycle theory; therefore they have been mentioned, but without detailed discussion. When we turn to the cyclical problems of development, it will not be necessary to dwell on factors that are the center of interest in aggregative analysis. Instead, attention will be focused on problems of development balance.

Since the following discussion concentrates on the issues posed in the preceding chapters, it is important to stress that these fundamental limitations are intentional. The fact that a number of more or less important issues of business cycle theory is left out altogether, or only mentioned in passing, should not be interpreted as a denial of their importance, but simply as a consequence of the particular objectives of the present work.

D. Business Cycles and the Formation of New Firms

Certain periods of the first half-century of Swedish industrialization have always been considered as times of cyclical depression. This has been particularly true with the beginning and end of the 1860's, the last years of the 1870's, the mid-1880's, as well as the years 1891–93, 1901–3, and 1908–9. Some easily available time series give a picture of the cyclical developments of the period (see Figure 2, Chapter 2 and Figure 9 below).

The cyclical swings have been remarkably moderate, judging by these indicators.[23] Only once, in 1878, did taxable income fall considerably

---

main features of the development process would surely have been the same even had these tariffs not been enacted. With regard to the problem of the effects of the tariffs, the main source is the sequence of studies published by Tull- och traktatkommittén.

[23] Unfortunately, we have no time series whatever on unemployment. To a modest extent the series on employment in manufacturing permits some inferences about the extent of unemployment or—given the emigration or reflux of industrial labor to agriculture in bad years—rather about the tendency to unemployment in manufacturing. In using this series, however, it should be realized that the data do not reflect the probably quite significant variations in hours worked.

below the level in the year immediately preceding the previous high. While the margin of error may be fairly large, and population growth also caused an upward trend—although for the period 1875–95 this was counteracted by a falling price trend—this fact still seems worthy of note. The work force declined appreciably only in 1878–79 and 1908–9, and then not to any considerable extent. A closer study of different

FIGURE 9
Economic Fluctuations in Sweden,
1860–1913

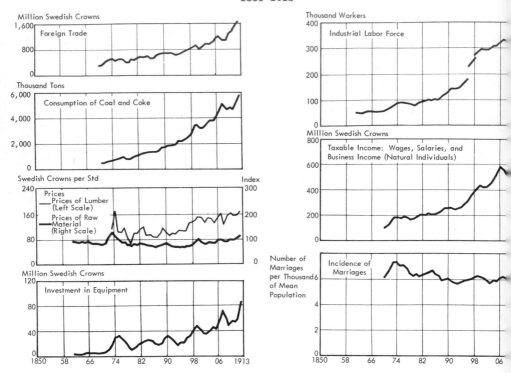

SOURCES: Foreign trade, consumption of coal and coke, prices of lumber, taxable income, incidence of marriages: *Statistisk översikt av det svenska näringslivets utveckling åren 1870–1915*, Table 345. Industrial labor force and price index of raw materials: *Wages, Cost of Living and National Income in Sweden 1860–1930*, Vol. II, G. Bagge, E. Lundberg, I. Svennilson, *Wages in Sweden 1860 1930*, Part II, Tables 187 and 190; Investment in equipment: *Wages, Cost of Living and National Income in Sweden 1860–1930*, Vol. III, E. Lindahl, E. Dahlgren, K. Kock, *National Income of Sweden, 1861–1930*, Part I, Table 53.

industries reveals only one depression, which can be called general, namely, the one in the late 1870's. Even in that case, some industries were relatively unaffected.

Swedish business cycle indicators (reproduced in Figure 9) show a generally parallel development with the time series over cyclical movements in other countries (Figure 10). Closer study reveals, however, that the upper turning points abroad as a rule preceded those in Sweden. In 1873, 1883, and 1890 this lead shows up in the annual as well as monthly data. This does not imply, of course, that the nature of the Swedish development process did not have much to do with bringing these downturns about, but further analysis of this problem cannot be provided for the period in question. The following discussion will point out certain important data concerning the formation of new firms as well as certain facts which are usually emphasized in historical literature,

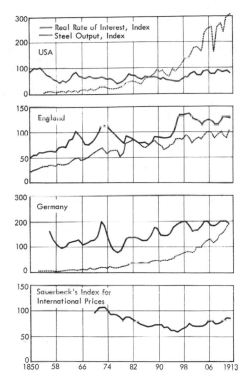

FIGURE 10
International Economic Fluctuations,
1850 1013

SOURCES: Real rate of interest and steel output: J. Åkerman, *Ekonomisk teori*, Vol. II, pp. 605-15.
Sauerbeck's index: *Statistisk översikt av det svenska näringslivets utveckling åren 1870–1915*, Table 345.

although without reference to statistical data. Unfortunately, it has not been possible to make any reliable investigation of the discontinuation of firms or of the negative aspects of the development process. This is the main reason why this period cannot be analyzed more thoroughly. It has been necessary to rely exclusively on the rather inadequate historical literature.

Data for estimating the extent of *firm formation* have been unavailable in large part or have otherwise been in such form that dates could not be reliably ascertained. The summary provided in Table 2 and Figure

TABLE 2
Number of New Firms Started, 1850–1909

Year	Steel Mills	Engineering Industries	Pulp Industry and Paper Mills	Matches	Total Capital Goods and Export Industries*	Textile and Clothing	Leather, Hair, and Rubber Products	Glass Works	Other Home-Market Industries†	Total Consumer Goods and Domestic Market Industries	Total Industry
1850	—	—	—	1	2	3	1	2	5	11	13
1851	—	1	—	1	2	—	—	—	2	2	4
1852	—	1	—	1	2	3	1	—	3	7	9
1853	—	1	—	—	1	1	1	—	1	3	4
1854	—	2	—	—	4	3	2	1	5	11	15
1855	—	—	—	2	2	3	1	—	4	8	10
1856	2	4	—	2	8	5	3	1	1	10	18
1857	1	4	1	3	8	—	—	—	8	8	16
1858	1	—	—	3	4	2	1	1	3	7	11
1859	—	3	—	3	6	—	—	1	2	3	9
1860	1	5	1	5	12	2	2	—	6	10	22
1861	—	1	—	3	4	1	1	—	3	5	9
1862	1	5	1	—	7	4	—	4	6	14	21
1863	—	3	—	3	6	3	—	2	1	6	12
1864	2	2	—	—	4	4	1	—	6	11	15
1865	—	1	2	2	2	1	4	—	7	12	14
1866	—	3	2	2	5	4	1	—	2	6	11
1867	—	3	1	2	6	2	1	—	7	10	16
1868	2	7	6	4	19	3	—	1	13	17	36
1869	—	2	2	6	10	4	2	—	—	6	16

Year											
1870	25	12	6	1	2	3	13	4	5	4	—
1871	22	7	3	1	2	1	15	6	6	1	1
1872	48	19	9	2	3	5	29	4	20	4	—
1873	26	16	7	2	3	4	10	6	—	4	—
1874	45	24	8	5	3	8	21	10	2	5	2
1875	23	15	7	2	2	2	8	5	1	2	—
1876	35	25	13	1	5	6	10	4	2	3	1
1877	21	9	3	1	1	4	12	5	—	7	—
1878	28	15	7	—	2	6	13	2	1	8	1
1879	16	9	3	1	2	3	7	—	2	5	—
1880	32	19	3	1	6	4	13	1	4	8	—
1881	25	16	3	1	2	5	9	2	2	3	1
1882	34	17	9	—	1	7	17	3	5	8	—
1883	23	8	—	—	2	3	15	—	7	7	1
1884	21	10	—	—	1	2	11	2	3	5	—
1885	23	18	11	—	1	9	5	—	2	2	—
1886	16	4	—	—	1	2	12	1	7	4	—
1887	32	20	—	3	10	4	12	—	9	3	—
1888	51	29	1	1	7	10	22	—	17	2	2
1889	68	24	8	1	4	11	44	—	33	9	1
1890	32	20	4	4	8	3	12	—	4	7	1
1891	23	21	3	1	3	9	2	1	1	—	—
1892	28	18	5	1	5	3	10	—	4	5	1
1893	31	21	6	1	5	9	10	—	3	6	—
1894	41	27	5	2	7	9	14	—	7	5	1
1895	42	29	6	4	4	15	13	—	9	3	1
1896	48	39	14	5	6	14	9	—	4	3	1
1897	54	36	8	5	10	13	18	—	5	4	5
1898	67	46	12	4	10	20	21	1	6	8	3
1899	52	33	12	1	10	10	19	—	9	7	1

TABLE 2 (Concluded)

Year	Steel Mills	Engineering Industries	Pulp Industry and Paper Mills	Matches	Total Capital Goods and Export Industries*	Textile and Clothing	Leather, Hair, and Rubber Products	Glass Works	Other Home-Market Industries†	Total Consumer Goods and Domestic Market Industries	Total Industry
1900	3	10	8	—	22	8	8	1	11	28	50
1901	3	8	7	—	18	16	5	1	4	26	44
1902	3	7	2	—	14	11	5	—	7	23	37
1903	2	6	8	—	17	6	5	1	8	20	37
1904	2	9	5	1	19	8	12	—	8	28	47
1905	2	12	8	2	24	12	11	2	5	30	54
1906	2	11	9	—	22	9	6	5	3	23	45
1907	3	15	10	1	31	14	18	1	5	38	69
1908	3	7	3	—	13	8	6	1	6	21	34
1909	2	3	5	—	10	12	10	—	6	28	38

* Including a number of brick yards, and firms producing cement and concrete.
† Including joineries.

11 relies mainly on formation data obtained from firms still operating at the end of the period under study (i.e., immediately before World War I).[24] To a lesser extent the data also concern firms which disappeared during the period 1900–1910. The material is thus incomplete: it does not contain all firms in existence at the outbreak of World War I, and a more serious defect, it does not normally contain firms that disappeared before 1910. The data from the pulp, paper, match, and glass industries are the main exceptions to this rule. In these areas it has been possible to obtain a practically complete mapping of the formation of new firms.

The summary concerns, first, a number of individual industries and a catch-all group (containing primarily joinery and furniture, chemical, and food processing industries), and second, a summation for all the industries involved. The material has also been subdivided schematically into two groups: (*a*) capital goods and export industries and (*b*) consumer goods and home market industries. All the larger industries are represented except the lumber mill industry, for which data on year of founding usually are unobtainable.

Cyclical variations in the formation rate are quite evident after the initial stage had passed. From the eighties onward, Sweden was linked with the fluctuations of the major industrialized countries.[25] Four peaks

---

[24] Data on the year of construction for different factories have been gathered from various handbooks and industry studies. While not complete, the data probably cover a relatively high proportion of those firms that survived up to the outbreak of World War I and were not of too small a size as of that date.

The following sources have been utilized: *Svenska industrien, 1911–1912* and *1918–1919*, publ. by Carl Sjögren (Stockholm, 1911 and 1918), respectively; *Svensk industrikalender 1918*; *Sveriges handel och industri i ord och bild* (Arboga, 1916); *Sveriges industri, dess stormän och befrämjare*, text by Herm. A. Ring (Stockholm, 1900[?]); *Sveriges äldsta företag*, ed. by Carl Forsstrand (Stockholm, 1923); *Svenska industrier, Industrilexikon över Västergötlands och Göteborgs och Bohus läns industriella utveckling med biografier över industriernas ledande män* (Göteborg, 1945); *Sveriges bergshantering år 1913. Specialundersökning av Kommerskollegium*, Stockholm 1917; *Textil- och beklädnadsindustrien. Specialundersökning av Kommerskollegium* (Stockholm, 1914); *Läder-, hår- och gummivaruindustrien. Specialundersökning av Kommerskollegium* (Stockholm, 1915); L. Bjerning, *Skånes jord- och stenindustri* (Hälsingborg, 1947); Unpublished data concerning the dates of construction of pulp mills, collected by E. Bosæus, principally from *Nordisk Papperskalender*, published by H. Brusewitz AB (Göteborg); Unpublished data concerning the dates of construction of glassworks, collected by Edv. Strömberg; *Svenska Pappersbruksföreningen 1923–1948, Minnesskrift vid 50-årsjubileet* (Stockholm, 1948); G. Cederschiöld och E. v. Feilitzen, *Den svenska tändsticksindustriens historia* (Stockholm, 1945). Cf. also the corporate histories listed in the bibliography of the Swedish edition.

[25] The picture up through the 1870's is remarkable: almost regular, fairly clearly marked two-year cycles that undeniably bring the "hog cycle" theory to mind. Although this pattern is found in several of the industry branches involved, it seems too daring to hypothesize that the pattern prior to the time that Sweden began to conform to the periodicity of the international cyclical movements can be explained in this way, i.e., that a relatively large number of entrants in one year scared away many potential entrants in the next, etc. The possibility of some source of systematic error in the data cannot be excluded, but there is nothing specific to indicate that this is the problem.

are prominent, namely 1872, 1889, 1898, and 1907.[26] The first and last are evidently common to all the main industrial groups. Developments in capital goods and export industries have generally paralleled those in consumer goods and home-market industries. The fluctuations are, however, somewhat stronger for the former than for the latter group, at least in the 19th century. It is conspicuous that the peak years are not simultaneous with the peak of the boom in Sweden, as indicated, for example, by the investment curve in Figure 9. Instead, they come one or two years earlier. With respect to 1872, it should be remembered that this was the last good year before the international crisis of 1873. The same can to some extent be said of 1889. In this case, however, one might equally well have expected the peak in 1890, since the international situation was far from uniform. Part of the explanation for the peak in Swedish firm formation in 1889 lies in special circumstances in the pulp industry, and to some extent also in the victory of protectionism in 1888, but there are also indications that developments abroad affected the rate of firm formation in Sweden before they affected the cyclical situation in general. Thus it is interesting to observe that the general recession hardly reached Sweden until 1891. If the rate of formation of new firms was actually closely dependent on the international business situation, the next peak should have occurred in 1899 instead of 1898. But the decline in firm formation between 1898 and 1899 was rather moderate. In contrast to the difference between peak year and surrounding years in the other three cases, the decline may fall within the margin of error. The year 1907 was a peak in both the Swedish and the foreign cycles and was a peak for the formation of new firms in Sweden. The explanation of this simultaneity may be that the turning point arrived only in late fall, whereas in 1873 and 1900 the turning points came in the spring.

The development picture suggests a strong international dependence with respect to establishment of new firms as soon as Swedish industrialization had reached its quantitative breakthrough phase (after 1870). The speed of reaction seems to have been considerable. It is hardly surprising

---

[26] There is some question whether the data on construction are sufficiently accurate for the dating of these peak years to be entirely reliable. The best answer seems to be that the actual peak years in any case cannot very well have been later than those reported here. It seems all but certain that, in those cases where the date reported does not refer to the year in which construction was begun, it refers instead either to the year in which construction was completed or to the year in which the main part of the construction period fell (even though this may not have been the year in which construction began). It is unlikely that a later year has been the one reported. Had the data been collected exclusively with reference to reported dates for the formation of the firm or corporation, the error would probably have been in the other direction, since the decision to start a firm sometimes antedated the initiation of construction by some length of time.

that it is greater than for investment; the completion of started projects must always create a certain lag in the latter variable.

Existing business cycle histories and the data presented here do not warrant the claim that the Swedish economy, by nature, fluctuated strongly during the first half-century of industrialism. Even disregarding the indicators in this study, there is sufficient reason to assert that the economy's susceptibility to fluctuations was rather low. The burden of proof must rest on those who would argue the opposite. Crises and depressions were rather moderate. The economy seems to have been capable of considerable resistance to external cyclical events, despite the already great importance of the export sector and the role played by foreign

FIGURE 11
Number of New Firms Started, 1850–1909

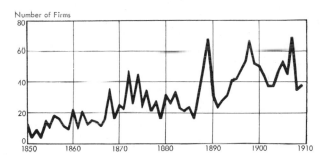

capital in the transformation of the Swedish economy.[27] The Swedish economy's propensity for cyclical behavior was relatively low, quite apart from the fact that unemployment tendencies in industry usually led both to emigration and to a return flow of labor to farming. In this connection one should also note the frequency with which dissolution of firms was immediately followed by formation of new firms so that the social effects were mitigated. Many lumber mills, and especially iron works, were turned into pulp mills.[28] There were difficulties, on the other hand, due to chronic pressure from the negative effects of the development process, particularly during certain periods.

One question that cannot be answered satisfactorily is the extent to

[27] Although, in quantitative terms, foreign capital did not play a dominant role in the development of Swedish industry—cf. Gårdlund, *Svensk industrifinansiering*—it seems reasonable to suppose that its marginal importance may have been larger in certain critical situations. Cf. the review of Gårdlund, *op. cit.*, by I. Svennilson in *Ekonomisk Tidskrift* (1947), No. 4.

[28] E. Bosæus, "När järnet och cellulosan möttes." *Med hammare och fackla*, XV (Stockholm, 1946). More than half of the steel mills that closed down, Bosæus notes, were converted to production of either mechanical or chemical pulp.

which booms have been characterized by innovations and dissemination of innovations which lead to more extensive discontinuation of firms in a following crisis and depression, or to other adjustments, reorganizations of production, etc. In other words, to what extent, has the interplay of the positive and negative components of the development process created business fluctuations?

Primary data bearing on this question that are available and could be processed at reasonable cost are quite inadequate, and the printed sources are seldom sufficiently informative. The literature suggests, however, a rapid dissemination of innovations in years of prosperity, when the international economic boom spread to Sweden through a rise in exports. This induced the establishment of new firms, while at the same time the dissemination of previously introduced Swedish innovations contributed to the upswing. It is also fairly clear from many historical accounts that the recessions brought great difficulties for many industries and branches, especially those which were made less viable by the transformation process. It is evident that not only were foreign innovations behind this negative transformation component, leading to difficult competitive conditions for the Swedish economy, but that Swedish innovations contributed as well. But this hardly warrants the conclusion that the negative component of the development process played an active role in bringing about the recession rather than merely being especially conspicuous and accentuated during the recession. Only in two decades, the 1870's and 1880's, is the picture clear enough to make possible a more positive statement. These periods would in all probability have been characterized by economic difficulties in a number of areas even if there had been no depressionary influences from abroad. It is evident that the economy experienced a "conversion and adjustment crisis" with liquidation of bad investments going on in several industries. All accounts of the process suggest that this was the case.

The difficulties of the agricultural sector, due to negative development effects, exerted a depressionary influence on industry by strongly dampening the demand-pull. The structural crisis in agriculture, in other words, led to recessionary tendencies in industry. The structural crisis element is, however, equally prominent in the crafts and in industry itself. The late 1870's were a period of fundamental conversion crisis for the steel industry. The great advances in steelmaking both at home and abroad, whether initially profitable in the Swedish plants or not, shook the domestic iron industry to its foundations. A number of old ironworks were either forced to close down or to undergo financial reorganization after a sometimes lengthy period of "throwing good money after bad." Those older ironworks which never acquired a railroad connection experienced particularly serious difficulties.

Similarly, the steam sawmills made existence difficult for the old water-powered mills and many of the latter had to close down. Typically, innovative firms in the superphosphate, match, brick, and tannery industries began to capture the markets of a number of old firms.[29] Successive tariff reductions in the 1850's, 1860's, and 1870's also had their effects, for example on the tanneries.[30] The introduction of steam engines in more and more plants in the Eskilstuna industry caused symptoms of depression in the other firms.[31] In many branches the old local crafts experienced hard times in competition with new manufacturers.[32]

Malinvestments, as far as can be judged, were at fault in many areas. In certain cases, these were "strategic" (i.e., based on speculative mistakes or miscalculations). In several railroad enterprises, for example, the entrepreneurs had underestimated construction costs. Other instances of malinvestment may be found in the context of incomplete development blocks—an altogether different consideration. Difficulties of this type have already been discussed, to some extent, in connection with the problems of development balance. Some steel mills, for example, that adopted the new blooming processes, ran into difficulties because the demand from the not-yet-expanded heavy manufacturing and engineering industry was insufficient to compensate for the decline of prices on all kinds of steel mill products induced by innovations abroad.

A striking illustration of the balance problems arising out of the dynamics of industrialism is afforded by the paper industry. Here an overproduction of paper occurred in connection with a rapid dissemination of the industry's innovations because innovations and expansion in the printing industry lagged behind. Before the advent of wood pulp the problem had been exactly the reverse.[33] A great many mechanical pulp mills were in great difficulties until they achieved forward integration by operating their own paper and cardboard plants, thus completing a development block.[34] The best examples are to be found, however, in the area of communications. Many railroad companies, particularly in the south of Sweden, had liquidity problems, not only because they had not had time to complete the whole network, but because the industries needed to make the railroads profitable had not yet developed far enough. One may also recall, once again, the case of the steel industry,

[29] T. Althin, *Stockholms Superfosfatfabriks AB 1871–1946* (Stockholm, 1946). G. Andreasson, "Tändsticksindustrien i Sverige," *Ymer* (1946), No. 4 (Stockholm, 1946). *Läder-, hår- och gummivaruindustrien. Specialundersökning av Kommerskollegium* (Stockholm, 1915).

[30] Cf. "En kritisk tid för svensk bottenlädertillverkning," *Sveriges läder- och skoindustri* (1925), p. 324.

[31] K. Hellberg, *Järnets och smedernas Eskilstuna*, Vol. II, (Katrineholm, 1938).

[32] Many illustrative examples of this can be found in *Tullkomiténs underdåniga betänkande åf ar 1882*, Vols. I–II (Stockholm, 1882).

[33] T. Althin, *Papyrus 1895–1945* (Mölndal, 1945).

[34] Cf. E. Bosæus, *Utvecklingen av produktion och teknik i svensk massaindustri 1857–1939* (Uppsala, 1949). Also, *Molæ Chartariæ Suecanæ* (Stockholm, 1923).

where the concentration movement was held back because the railroads were not completed.

The rather weak business situation during the years 1883–87 should be regarded partly as a continuation of the situation in the late 1870's and can, therefore, to some extent be characterized in the same way. This is particularly true as agriculture experienced hard times, again due to agricultural growth in transocean countries and to faster ocean transportation. Several industries apparently still had a high rate of firm mortality with small firms being forced out by innovating firms. This was still the case, for example, in the steel industry, in iron and steel manufacturing, and in the lumber mill, match, brick, and tanning industries. In other words, there was clear evidence of the negative effects of the economic transformation process.

It can hardly be argued that the recessions that started with the setbacks of 1891, 1900, and 1907 had the same conversion and adjustment character. The negative transformation component is, of course, encountered in all industries and branches in which old firms and old activities were superceded by the new, but it does not appear to have been particularly accentuated in the recessions, and one cannot attribute to it a decisive role. It was hardly decisive even in the steel industry, where the introduction of the basic open hearth method at home and abroad brought particularly severe difficulties for those mills that were unable to convert to production of specialized quality products. Even when competition from the big new mills in Norrland, utilizing important innovations, forced a large number of small mechanical pulp mills to close down, particularly in the provinces of Värmland and Småland, their disappearance seems neither to have had any active depressionary impact nor to have been concentrated around the cyclical troughs. The situation was similar for the tanneries, for the shoe-making craft shops, for the tile-stove makers, for the fish-guano factories, and so forth, which also were on the negative side of the transformation process.[35]

The hard times do not seem to have been closely connected with problems of incomplete development blocks either. Such cases were evident, of course, in certain areas—in the electrical engineering industry in the first years of the 20th century, for example. The lumber mill industry experienced its first sales difficulties at the same time also and found it necessary to buy its own forests and to invest in pulp mills to obtain a better balance in the utilization of the raw material base. The problems of this industry were, however, probably due more to strategic malinvestments that had to be weeded out. The exceptionally

---

[35] Cf. "Partiskomakeri och partihandel i Närike," *Sveriges läder- och skoindustri* (1926), p. 164. In shoe manufacturing, the job shop system was swept away within just a few years in the late 1890's—i.e., during a period of "general" prosperity.

lively development period which the pulp industry experienced in the late eighties led to a number of malinvestments due to technological inadequacies.[36]

But, in general, the fluctuations after 1890 do not seem quite comparable to the first two depressions in this respect either. To a certain extent this was due to the initial "Klondike-period" having passed. In part it was a result of the development of sounder criteria for the extension of credit and the investment of capital.

The most plausible explanation appears to be that the crises and depressions that began in the nineties basically originated abroad and reached Sweden by way of foreign trade and the money and capital markets— they were "trade and money crises" and were to a considerable extent psychological in nature. They can, with a certain justification, be regarded as external disturbances. This should not be taken to mean that they impinged on an economic equilibrium or a harmonious development process. In each instance, there were weak points in the Swedish economy— sometimes many, sometimes few. These weaknesses, results of the struggle between the old and the new, of incomplete development blocks and of strategic malinvestments, were made acute by the international disturbances and thus became a source of difficulties.

---

[36] Cf. Bosæus. *op. cit.*

6 The Statistical Material and a Summary Analysis

A. Data on Progressive, Stagnating, and Regressive Industries, and on Rates of Return in Different Industries

An analysis of the industrial transformation process does not demand a fixed classification of the industrial firms into different groups.[1] Rather, it is expedient to adjust this classification to fit various issues. Appendix 2 (Swedish edn.) presents a summary of the principles used in the preliminary processing and classification of the raw data.[2] As a second step in the analysis, the present chapter combines this first statistical grouping with a classification into the categories of *progressive, stagnating,* and *regressive* industries, in accordance with the theoretical discussion in Chapter 4.[3]

---

[1] The problem of where to draw the line between "handicraft" and "industry" may be put aside for the moment with reference to our earlier discussion (Chap. 5, p. 61, n.) and to the futher discussion below (cf. Chap. 10, p. 186 and also Appendix 1 of the Swedish edn.).

[2] In many cases it has been impossible to obtain "pure" industries. Numerous plants are engaged in the production of several, quite dissimilar products and it is not always possible to distribute the total work force according to these products. The main criterion used has therefore necessarily been to put the plants and thereby their workers in the various industries on the basis of whatever product is the predominant one. This schematic procedure should be kept in mind in connection with the following analysis. In certain cases it has proved necessary, or in any case desirable, to attempt to differentiate the data through various approximative calculations so as to obtain "pure" industry categories. This has especially been the case from Chap. 10 onward.

[3] These concepts must not be interpreted in such a literal way that "progressive" necessarily is taken to mean that the industry comes to be operated in a more

A *progressive* industry, generally speaking, is successful in the competition for the purchasing power of the investor and consumer. More precisely, an industry is progressive when an increase in output is observed between two cyclically comparable periods. "Comparable" years may sometimes be difficult to select, but averages over two or more years may be used. Even though not all traces of arbitrariness will be removed in this way, this method gives reasonable results for all practical purposes. In the present study, the base periods used for comparison are, as a rule,[4] chosen in the following manner: the average for the years 1913, 1919, and 1920 is compared with the average for 1920, 1929, and 1930 and for 1937, 1938, and 1939; at the same time, the average for 1921 and 1922 is compared with the average for 1931, 1932, and 1933.

There are two exceptions to the main principle. First, an increase in output should not warrant the classification "progressive," regardless of how small it is. Thus an industry is not considered progressive if the increase in output is less than 10 percent per business cycle. Second, an industry with a growth of output of less than 15 percent is still labeled "stagnating" whenever the increase in the preceding period, i.e., from 1896–1900 to 1910–13, amounted to 50 percent or more. Similarly, if an industry advanced at this last-mentioned rate from 1913 to 1929 but by less than 15 percent in the 1930's it is also considered "stagnating" during the latter decade. It has not been possible to arrange the statistical material from the pre-World War I period in such a way as to make it fully comparable with the series used for the interwar period. The former comparison may therefore at times be somewhat unreliable. But this has been of little or no practical consequence since the margins of error are rather moderate.

An industry is considered *regressive* when it experiences an intercyclical decline in output of 10 percent or more. When the output trend stays within the limits of ± 10 percent, the industry is considered as *stagnating*. As indicated above, certain cases of output increases in the 10 to 15 percent range will also be put in this category.

The arbitrariness of these definitions is evident. But a priori they do not defy common sense and thus should be judged by their results. Experimenting with various divergent definitions will show that those used are reasonable. The results obtained do not vary significantly as long as the definitions applied are not radically different from those used here.

The most difficult problems are not with definitions but with the measurement of output. A completely satisfactory measure for a whole industry is seldom obtainable. There are, of course, the output-volume

---

rational fashion or on any count "progresses" in the everyday sense of the word. The same comment applies, *mutatis mutandis*, to the term "regressive."

[4] Exceptions have been made only in certain cases where these years provide strikingly "abnormal" observations, e.g., due to raw material shortages or strikes.

estimates made since 1913 by the Bureau of Commerce.[5] These estimates are, however, frequently rather meaningless, since the transformation of production has made it impossible to compare conditions at two widely separated dates in this way. But other indexes, such as the size of the work force or the value of sales, will often be even more unreliable. Labor-saving rationalizations, or quality changes not reflected in prices quoted, may have been of dominating importance. In addition, it is frequently difficult to avoid double counting in estimating the aggregate value of sales.[6] Such double counting cannot be avoided in all cases.

The only solution to this dilemma, which stems only in part from technical statistical difficulties, seems to be to use the series on number of workers, supplemented as far as possible with the series on the volume of output of individual commodities, or groups of commodities, in the various industries. In certain cases, all the criteria will point in the same direction, and the classification will raise no difficulties; in other cases, they may point in opposite directions. The work force may decline, for instance, while the output of important products increases. While it is necessary to let one or the other be decisive, such an example illustrates the sometimes dubious meaning of the classification. The paper industry, for example, may be classified without hesitation; the leather shoe industry is a more questionable case.

In accordance with the principles laid down in Chapter 4, the grouping of industries as progressive, stagnating, and regressive is complemented with an investigation of their *profitability*. It has not been necessary to make this latter study very detailed. The primary objective has been a comparison of progressive, stagnating, and regressive industries during the different phases of the interwar period. A secondary objective has been to determine if there have been any conspicuous and lasting differences in rates of return among firms in the same industry. The task has been facilitated because smaller differences need not be taken into account in such a context and also because changes from year to year may be largely ignored. The balance sheets of the firms often give only a very unreliable basis for a more detailed study; but lasting divergences in rates of returns or intercyclical shifts of their level, as well as such divergences and shifts between individual firms in the same industry, are usually significant.[7]

---

[5] For the criteria, etc., cf. "Arbetslöshetens omfattning, karaktär och orsaker," *Arbetslöshetsutredningens betänkande*, Vol. I, *Statens offentliga utredningar* (SOU) (1931, No. 20), pp. 515 ff., and *Kommersiella Meddelanden* (KM) (1938, No. 2), p. 219.

[6] Note that this double counting will affect also those output calculations that are based on time series for output values and price indexes.

[7] For the concepts of "rate of return" or "profitability" (*räntabilitet*) and "profit" (*vinst*), cf., e.g., *Vinster, utdelningar, skatter, löner m. m. inom industrien 1946–1949*, Industriens utredningsinstitut (IUI) (Stockholm, 1949).

Profitability has been measured by relating reported net profits to own capital. Own capital has in this connection been defined as paid-in capital and earned surpluses, i.e., primarily the contingency fund, earmarked funds, this year's reported earnings, and the previous year's profit and loss. In addition the "financing" or "leverage position," i.e., the relation between own and borrowed capital, was computed as an aid in judging the financial position of the various companies and industries. Thus "financing" in the present context does not refer to the financing of the actual capital investments made during the year or period in question. This latter concept is something altogether different, requiring a different computation.[8] As a further aid, "taxable income" has been obtained for a large number of firms and related to own capital. The Swedish Tax Catalog has been used in this connection. The ratio of taxable income to own capital is often a better indicator of the profitability of a firm than reported profits. Since negative amounts are not taxed, however, this measure is less useful when applied to an entire industry. On the industry level, it can only be compared with the reported profits' measure if the firms that experienced losses are excluded from the latter.

A special problem with all profitability investigations is that, frequently, large capital losses have been written off in connection with financial reconstructions without ever having been reported as losses in the profit-and-loss statements. Such losses should be averaged over a number of years, during some of which the firm may even have reported positive profits. Very often, however, it is impossible to determine the number of years for which they should be averaged, and as a consequence it has been impossible to take this factor into account. Such capital losses have not been included in the estimates made in this study. This means that the estimates of profitability probably are misleading, particularly for certain industries and especially for the 1920's when many financial reconstructions occurred. The profitability estimates for the industries concerned have been marked with an asterisk in the tables to indicate that the values are no doubt too high.

It has not been possible to make these estimates for all the industries studied or, of course, for all the firms otherwise included in the study. Many firms were not incorporated, and to obtain and prepare the relevant balance sheet data would have required far too extensive investigations even for many of the corporations. The estimates, therefore, are limited primarily to industries comparatively well represented in *Aktieägarnas Uppslagsbok* (*AU*), a stock-owner encyclopedia. For industries inadequately represented in this encyclopedia, some complementary data have been obtained from the files of the Swedish Patent Bureau. Many smaller firms not included in *AU* have thus been represented in the study.

It has been considered unnecessary to cover all of the interwar years

---

[8] Estimates for this variable cannot be obtained through a summation of credit and debit items in the same way as for the study of "financing" in the sense that is relevant in our present context. Cf. "Finansieringen av industriens investeringar 1939–1944," in *Inkomster och investeringar inom industrien 1937–1944*, IUI (Stockholm, 1945).

in the investigation. As a rule, only the years in the early and late 1920's and 1930's have been studied. For purposes of comparison, the prewar years 1911–13 have also been analyzed. In the latter case, as well as for the early 1920's the studies of the Nationalization Committee have been utilized. The Committee's figures have been revised to the extent of recomputing the profitability estimates to agree with the definition of profitability used in the present study.[9] Despite this revision, it has not been possible to obtain results fully comparable with those for later periods because the samples of firms have not been identical. But this uncertainty factor has seldom been large enough to really invalidate a comparison between results expressed in percentage figures.

Intertemporal comparisons generally encounter this difficulty, of course, and it appears again when, after 1927, new firms enter the investigation or old firms disappear. But it is obviously impossible to restrict oneself to those firms that existed throughout the entire period studied. The results will be reported, therefore, both with and without the new firms and the subsequently discontinued firms.

The biggest problem besides the measurement of profitability itself has been to make the necessarily limited samples as representative as possible for the different industries. In Appendix 3 [of the Swedish edition], the number of workers in firms included in the investigation is expressed as a percentage of the total number of workers in the industry in question. Evidently these percentages are not normally large enough to ensure the validity of the conclusions on profitability in the various industries. The sample is of necessity biased since in general only large or middle-sized firms, i.e., firms with more than 50 workers, are represented. The percentages in question have therefore been termed "coverage percent" instead of "sample size."[10] In most cases they are large enough for the sample to be representative *for the large and middle-sized firms.*

An estimate of standard deviation for this category of firms would, of course, have been desirable. But this would have required a great amount of laborious computation, which could hardly be justified, since it is improbable that the margins of error would be larger than those temporal or interindustrial differences *which the analysis focuses upon.* Had the purpose been to discover lesser differences of this kind, a computation of the standard error would have been necessary.

It has unfortunately been impossible to judge the extent to which the general picture of profitability that emerges is representative of *all the firms* in the various industries. It has been impossible, also, to estimate standard deviations because of the bias in the sample. The results have, however, been computed first for the *AU* sample, and these have then been compared with the results for a larger sample having a relatively greater proportion of firms with comparatively few workers. Although this enlargement of the sample often resulted in a rather considerable increase in the coverage percent-

---

[9] Thus the study made by the Nationalization Committee does not include last year's profit in the firm's capital and surplus as is done in the present work.
[10] Cf. Appendix 1 of the Swedish edition.

age, only in exceptional cases did it affect the profitability picture to such an extent that preliminary analytical conclusions had to be changed. This would seem to indicate, therefore, that the picture really is usually quite representative, not only for the larger or middle-sized firms but for the respective industries in their entirety. This is especially true in industries with a relatively homogeneous structure, in the sense that the larger firms are not too different in character from the smaller firms. It cannot be asserted with the same confidence in the case of industries with a very heterogeneous structure.

With respect to the coverage percentages, it should be noted, finally, that the denominator is not the *total* number of workers employed in an industry. In the case of the "pure cellulose" industry, for example, the coverage percentage given is the number of workers in the firms studied as a percent of the number of workers in firms *almost exclusively engaged in the production of cellulose.*

Appendix 3 [Swedish edition] comments in detail on the investigation of rates of return.

The interwar transformation of industrial production in Sweden is illustrated to some extent in Figure 12. The series on which the diagrams are based are reported in Appendices 2 and 9 [Swedish edition]. The figures have been arranged in four groups. The first group encompasses industries classed as progressive in both the 1920's and the 1930's. The second group involves industries that were stagnating or regressive in the 1920's but progressive in the 1930's. A third group contains industries that progressed in the 1920's but stagnated or regressed in the 1930's; and the fourth group, finally, includes industries that were stagnating or regressive throughout the interwar period.

A short summary of the results of the profitability investigation is given in Table 3. Appendix 3 [Swedish edition] contains a more detailed report.

B. Issues and Concepts of the Analysis

As a third step in the analysis, the statistical picture given in Figure 12, in Table 3, and in Appendix 3 [Swedish edition] will be studied along the principal lines laid down in Chapter 4. Three major issues provide the points of departure for this inquiry: (1) Did progress in the various industries depend upon active supply-push associated with new products and/or processes or did it depend upon demand-pull? (2) Were the cases of stagnating or regressive development caused by the negative effects of the development process? (3) What light do the answers to these two questions throw on the observed profitability of different industries?

Such an analysis raises, in turn, new questions which we will attempt to answer in Chapter 10. The analysis provided in Chapters 7 to 9 will,

TABLE 3
Reported Profits as Percent of Net Worth
(selected years)

Industry	Code	1911	1912	1913	1923	1924	1925	1927	1928	1929	1931	1932	1933	1936	1937	1938
Steel mills	110	4.9	6.2	8.7	8.9	0.3*	-0.1	3.6*	4.6	7.2	2.0	0.1	2.9	7.7	9.6	8.3
Steel manufacturing	131 + 133	4.7	5.4	4.8	4.8	4.2	4.5	6.5	6.9	7.7	5.6	5.5	5.4	11.1	14.4	10.1
Metal manufacturing	132	10.6	9.9	8.0	6.5	3.3	4.5	3.7	4.5	4.7	2.6	-4.8*	2.0	8.0	9.9	7.8
Semifinished products	—	—	7.6	6.5	6.5	4.1	3.4	3.9	4.3	4.4	2.4	-6.3*	3.7	6.7	9.7	8.0
Other metal manufacturing	—	10.6	11.4	9.5	-23.5	2.1	5.8	2.5	5.2	6.2	3.3	3.8	-5.3	12.3	10.4	7.0
Mechanical engineering industries	14	6.9	7.4	8.6	1.2	2.7	4.6	5.5	6.0	6.7	1.8	-0.3	2.1	8.0	9.6	10.1
Capital goods	141	—	—	—	—	—	—	5.1	4.3	6.0	0.4	-1.3	1.9	7.5	9.5	11.7
Consumer durables	142	—	—	—	—	—	—	7.9	9.4	8.5	2.3	1.9	5.0	8.6	10.4	9.0
Agricultural machinery	144	—	—	—	—	—	—	7.6	6.8	7.0	3.0	-0.0	0.7	8.3	9.2	8.1
Other	145	—	—	—	—	—	—	1.5	3.0	5.2	3.0	-0.5	4.9	7.8	11.2	11.5
Cement, concrete products, and lightweight concrete	210 + 220	6.6	8.3	6.5	—	3.6	6.1	8.0	8.2	8.8	7.3	5.7	4.2	9.0	9.5	9.0
Cement	210	—	—	—	—	—	—	8.7	9.5	9.7	7.7	6.1	4.0	8.5	9.0	8.2
Concrete products and lightweight concrete	220	—	—	—	—	—	—	5.2	2.5	4.9	5.7	3.9	5.3	11.1	11.7	12.0
Brickyards	230	4.6	2.9	2.3	7.2*	3.3*	4.4*	1.8*	3.7*	3.5	2.0	-6.4	-3.1	4.5	3.3	5.3
Porcelain and ceramics	24	4.0	5.5	3.9	2.7	-1.2	-0.9	5.9	5.2	7.4	5.0	5.4	-2.3	7.0	6.8	7.4
Glassworks	25	1.8	4.2	4.7	2.2	-1.1	0.8	0.0	-0.2	5.1	5.8	3.9	-0.8	13.4	11.3	7.9
Lumber mills	300	7.5	5.7	7.1	0.1	-2.2	-1.6	2.8*	-2.0*	-1.6	-5.6	-6.1	1.2	7.3	9.5	5.3
Furniture, building joinery, and interior fittings	311-313	4.2	6.0	6.0	1.7	-3.3	-0.5	1.8	-1.6	4.0*	-1.3	-1.4	-0.8	5.8	5.1	5.8
Pulp industry	32	5.4	6.4	7.3	4.4	4.4	5.8	7.4	5.9*	8.0	-2.3*	-0.9*	2.4	6.2	8.3	5.5
Sulphite and sulphate pulp	321 + 322	—	—	—	—	—	—	9.3*	4.2*	6.5	-1.8	-4.4*	1.7	4.9	7.0	3.8
Mechanical pulp	323	—	—	—	—	—	—	-2.8	-4.3	5.1	-7.2	-8.7	1.3	3.0	5.7	4.7
Combined lumber milling and cellulose manufacture	—	—	—	—	—	—	—	7.4	6.5	8.4	-2.2*	-0.4*	2.6	6.7	8.7	6.0
Paper and cardboard	33	5.7	5.8	5.6	1.4	2.0	3.8	4.8	6.2	6.6	2.4	1.9	1.7	4.5	5.4	3.2
Chocolate and candy	411	7.0	8.1	3.8	5.6	6.6	5.8	5.3	6.2	5.9	4.9	3.5	2.9	4.6	3.1	3.6
Oleomargarine	420	1.2	12.6	13.9	4.5	4.8	6.4	9.1	9.1	11.4	9.4	8.5	9.4	7.7	7.4	7.8
Canneries	43	—	—	—	—	—	—	8.1	8.3	8.0	9.3	7.4	7.0	7.6	6.9	7.8
Cotton manufacture	51	3.8	9.1	8.9	5.6	4.4	3.4	6.3	4.4	3.0	4.4	5.0	5.1	6.0	5.5	5.9
Woolen manufacture	52	4.2	3.1	5.1	7.6	1.4	1.7	5.3	4.1	3.5*	5.8	5.1	5.9	9.2	6.2	4.9
Combined cotton and woolen manufacture	—	—	—	—	—	—	—	1.0	-2.8	0.3	1.4	2.6*	4.0	8.4	4.7	5.6
Hosiery manufacture	54	5.3	7.4	9.5	8.2	8.7	7.0	9.9	9.0	7.9	6.9	6.1	6.9	8.6	9.1	8.4
Ready-made clothing and other textile processing	55	10.6	12.5	12.9	5.6	3.4	4.3	5.3	5.6	4.5	5.8	3.7	1.3	7.7	7.9	8.4
Tanneries	610	6.6	8.3	7.8	5.2*	6.4*	2.9	6.3	4.7	4.0	4.0	1.2	2.8	7.1	7.5	5.4
Gloves, leather and fur products	62	13.4	19.2	16.1	2.5	2.9	5.0	7.2	8.3	4.3	8.8	-2.9	6.3	4.4	4.1	3.6
Shoes	630	8.7	8.7	8.1	7.9*	6.8*	4.8*	4.4	4.2	3.5	3.0	-2.6	-0.8	4.1	4.8	4.0
Paints and varnishes	710	—	—	—	—	—	—	6.9	6.6	8.7	6.9	5.6	5.1	7.8	9.0	7.0

FIGURE 12
Major Features of the Industrial Transformation Process, 1913–39

Code

131.	Steel manufacturing
132.	Metal manufacturing
133.	Sheet metal manufacturing
141.	Mechanical engineering, capital goods
142.	Mechanical engineering, consumer durables
144–45.	Other mechanical engineering (145), including agricultural machinery (144)
151.	Electrical engineering, capital goods
152.	Electrical engineering, consumer durables
210.	Cement
220.	Concrete products and lightweight concrete
311.	Furniture
313.	Firms combining furniture, building joinery, and interior fittings
312 & 314.	Building joinery, interior fittings, and prefabricated wooden houses·
321 & 322.	Sulphite and sulphate pulp
323.	Mechanical pulp
331 & 332.	Fine quality paper and other paper industry
351.	Paper packaging industry
352 & 353.	Other paper and cardboard processing
411.	Chocolate and candy products
412.	Fruit preserves
450.	Mineral water and soft drinks
431–33.	Canneries
511–14.	Cotton manufacture
551–56.	Ready-made clothing and other textile processing
541–46.	Hosiery
710.	Paints and varnishes
720.	Oils, soft soap, soap, perfumes, and cosmetics
110.	Steel mills
241.	Porcelain and china ware
242.	Ceramic tiles
243.	Earthenware
251.	Plate glass
252.	Container glass
253.	Household glass
521–24.	Woolen manufacture
621–23.	Gloves, leather, and fur products
420.	Oleomargarine
230.	Brickyards
300.	Lumber mills
610.	Tanneries
630.	Shoe industry

therefore, not be very detailed. Only the most prominent features of the development process will be discussed; hence many simplifications will be made. The discussion should not, therefore, be regarded as self-contained, but rather be considered in the context of the analysis presented in later chapters.[11]

---

[11] Statements made in Chaps. 7 through 9 do in fact in many instances rely on the results of the investigations that are reported and documented in Chaps. 10 through 15. This is true, for example, of the distinction made here between

FIGURE 12 (Continued)
Steel and Nonferrous Metal Manufacturing

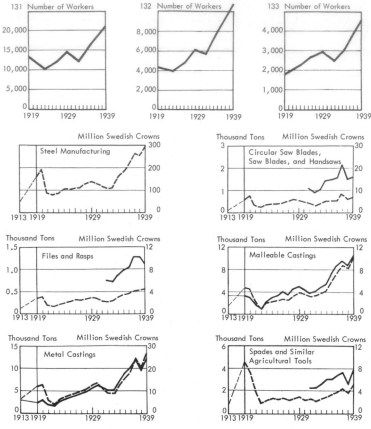

NOTE: Continuous curves represent quantities, dotted curves money values.

The issues formulated here demand, first, a more thorough discussion of the innovation concept than was necessary in Chapter 4.[12] An innovation taking the form of a new production or distribution method[13] may be regarded

---

"active supply-push development" and "demand-pull development"—a distinction which has often required a detailed study of the course of events. The exposition, in other words, follows to a certain extent a different sequence of topics than did the research itself. This has been done for purposes of organization and heuristic advantage.

[12] The distinction between "invention" and "innovation" has already been emphasized in Chap. 4. "Inventions" as such are of no interest in the economic analysis, whereas "innovations" are of central importance—and, in addition, are more easily subject to observation and evaluation.

[13] An innovation may also consist of a new way of organizing production or distribution (such as continuous production or the development of a producer-owned sales organization). Schumpeter refers to "the opening up of a new market" as an innovation. It seems more logical, however, to regard the organizational or other novelties involved in such a process as innovations.

FIGURE 12 (Continued)

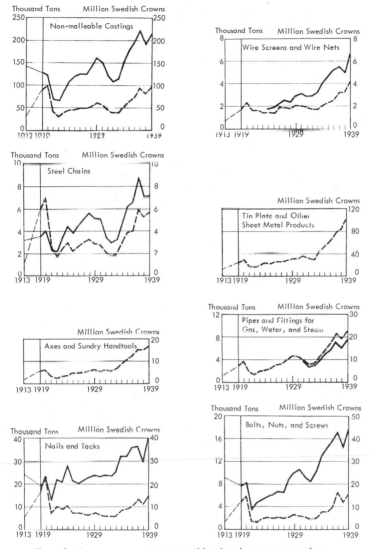

NOTE: Continuous curves represent quantities, dotted curves money values.

as either *primary* or *secondary*.[14] These new processes are often based on some new machine, which in turn is a product innovation in the industry in which it is produced. A primary innovation creates a completely new process, or a product of entirely new character; a secondary innovation alters

---

[14] Schumpeter does not explicitly introduce such a distinction but focuses only on innovations of "the first order" (cf. *Business Cycles*, Vol. I, p. 94). His work does, however, implicitly utilize the distinction in question.

FIGURE 12 (Continued)
Mechanical Engineering, Capital Goods

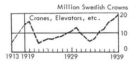

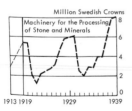

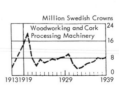

NOTE: Continuous curves represent quantities, dotted curves money values.

FIGURE 12 (Continued)
Mechanical Engineering, Consumer Durables, and Agricultural Machinery, etc.

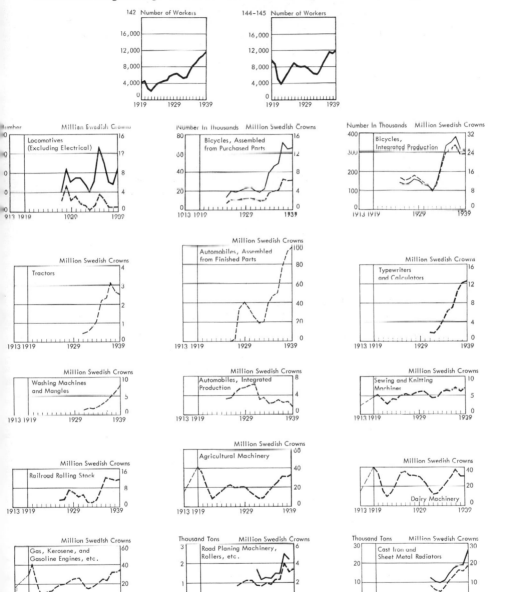

NOTE: Continuous curves represent quantities, dotted curves money values.

FIGURE 12 (Continued)
Electrical Engineering, Consumer Durables

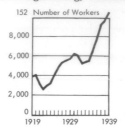

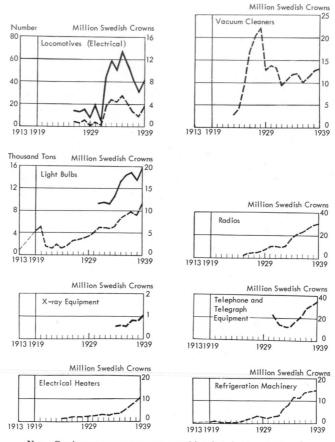

NOTE: Continuous curves represent quantities, dotted curves money values.

an existing process, or product, without changing its basic character. A primary product innovation, as a rule, is based on production equipment constructed for the specific purpose, while a secondary innovation can usually be produced with old equipment. Roller bearings, for example, were a primary innovation, but secondary innovations have improved the production process

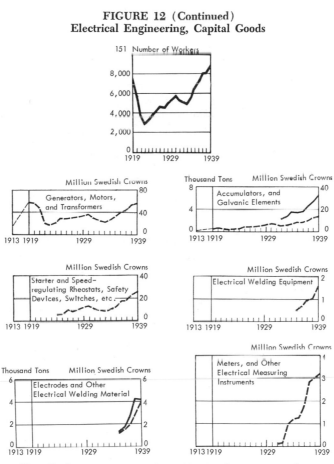

FIGURE 12 (Continued)
Electrical Engineering, Capital Goods

NOTE: Continuous curves represent quantities, dotted curves money values.

and multiplied the types of bearings. The first radio marketed was a primary innovation. It was followed by many secondary ones. Secondary innovations are often defensive measures adopted to combat the threat to an old process or product arising from a new one. Such a threat may occasionally be countered successfully, but as a rule only temporarily. The distinction between primary and secondary innovations is, of course, often difficult to draw.

FIGURE 12 (Continued)
Cement, Concrete Products, and Lightweight Concrete

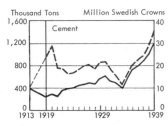

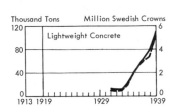

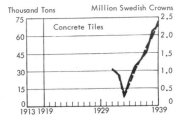

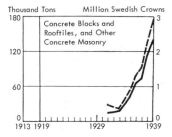

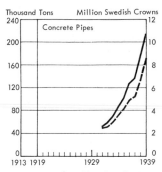

NOTE: Continuous curves represent quantities, dotted curves money values.

FIGURE 12 (Continued)
Woodworking Industries

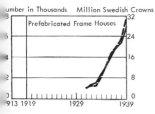 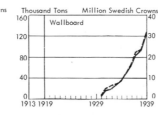 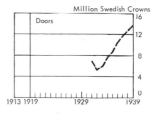

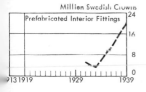  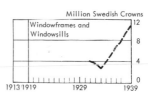

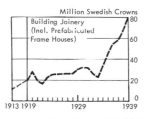 

NOTE: Continuous curves represent quantities, dotted curves represent money values.

FIGURE 12 (Continued)
Pulp Industry and Paper Mills

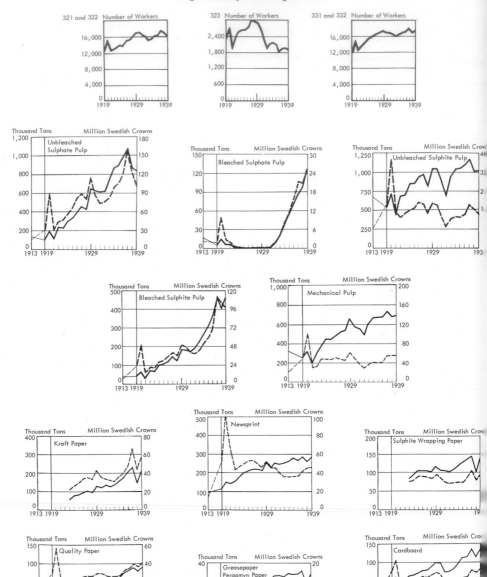

NOTE: Continuous curves represent quantities, dotted curves money values.

Much depends upon what is meant by a "product"[15] or how broadly the concept of "new process" is interpreted. In practice, however, this difficulty becomes a minor matter. Most actual cases are far from doubtful.

The use of the innovation concept leads to a number of problems in statistical measurement in the following causal analysis. While not insurmountable, they are nonetheless difficult to cope with. The importance of product

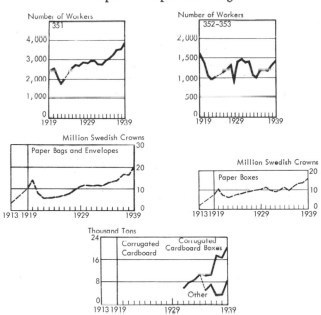

FIGURE 12 (Continued)
Paper and Paper Processing

NOTE: Continuous curves represent quantities, dotted curves money values.

innovations may, theoretically, be estimated by comparing the quantity of the new product to that of older products of the industry in question. In practice, however, it is not always possible to do this because the basic statistical data are not sufficiently detailed.[16] The difficulties are even worse in

---

[15] It seems most appropriate here not to commit oneself to a once and for all fixed definition but instead to retain the option of varying the definition as the context of the analysis demands. Cf. Kristensson, *Studier i svenska textila industriers struktur*, publ. by IUI (Stockholm, 1946), pp. 45 ff.

[16] The official Industry Statistics (IS) does provide a more detailed breakdown for the latter than for the early part of the interwar period. To the extent that this more detailed breakdown only covers a few years, however, it is still impossible to trace the new commodities back over a longer time span.

FIGURE 12 (Continued)
Confectionery Industry

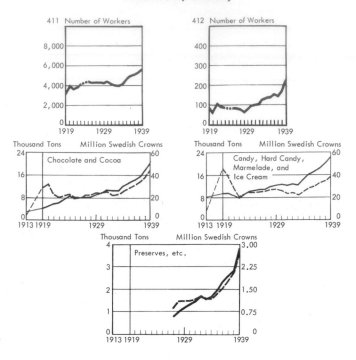

Mineral Water and Soft Drinks

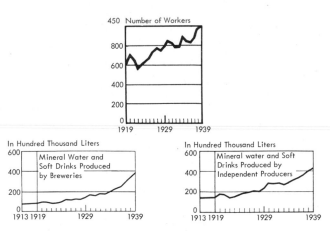

NOTE: Continuous curves represent quantities, dotted curves money values.

FIGURE 12 (Continued)
Canneries

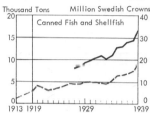

Cotton Manufacture

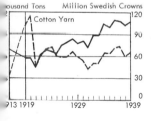

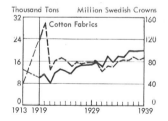

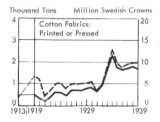

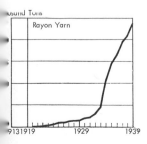

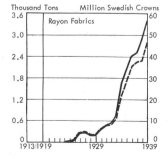

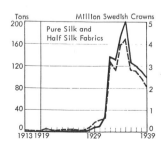

NOTE: Continuous curves represent quantities, dotted curves money values.

FIGURE 12 (Continued)
Ready-Made Clothing

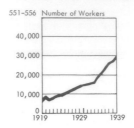

551–556 Number of Workers

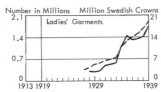

Hosiery

541–546 Number of Workers

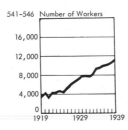

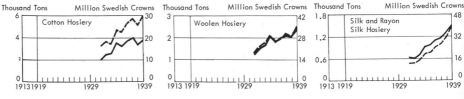

NOTE: Continuous curves represent quantities, dotted curves money values.

FIGURE 12 (Continued)
Paints and Varnishes

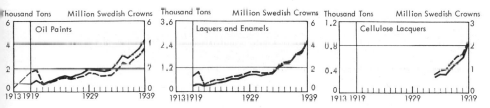

Light Chemicals: Oil, Soft Soap, Soap, Perfumes, and Cosmetics

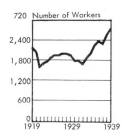

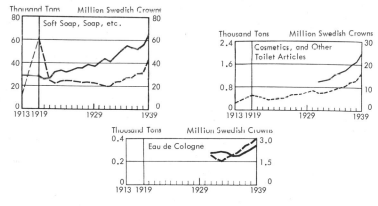

NOTE: Continuous curves represent quantities, dotted curves money values.

the case of process innovations. Their direct importance should be measured, among other things, by their cost-reducing effects. Most often, however, such a measurement proves impossible, although a study of prices sometimes may be made to serve the same purpose. A study of output per man-hour—

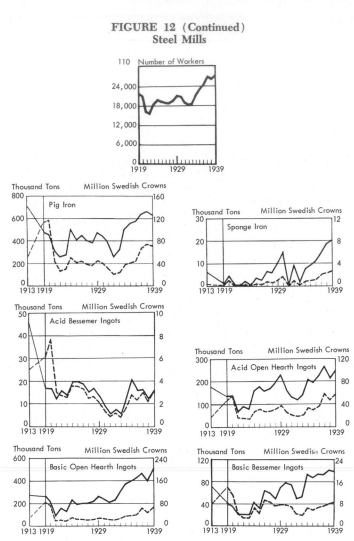

FIGURE 12 (Continued)
Steel Mills

NOTE: Continuous curves represent quantities, dotted curves money values.

productivity—must therefore be used as a preliminary "measure" in order to sort out the more significant developments among the myriad process innovations which the real world exhibits. This will help one to perceive, also, the many cases where a number of small innovations taken together

FIGURE 12 (Continued)
Steel Mills

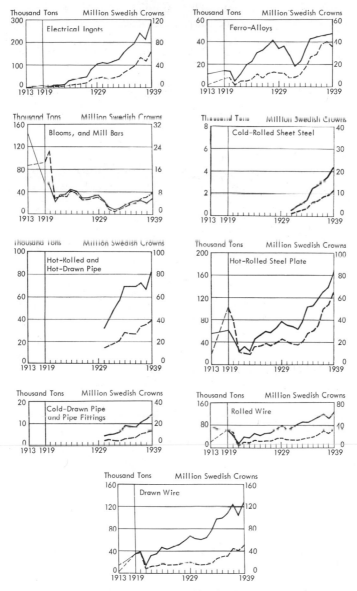

NOTE: Continuous curves represent quantities, dotted curves money values.

FIGURE 12 (Continued)
Porcelain and Ceramics

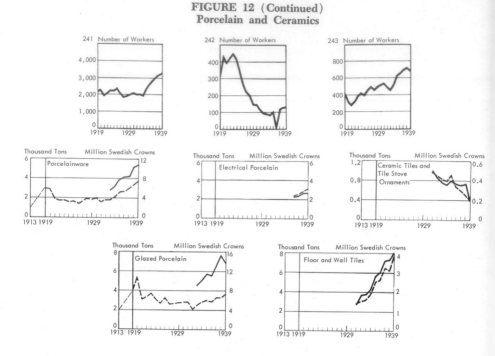

Glassworks

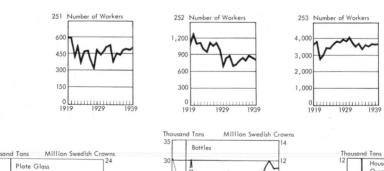

NOTE: Continuous curves represent quantities, dotted curves money values.

FIGURE 12 (Continued)
Woolen Manufacture

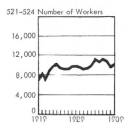

521–524 Number of Workers

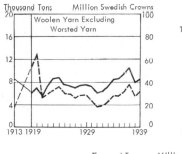

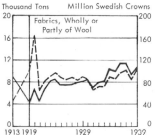

NOTE: Continuous curves represent quantities, dotted curves money values.

will be more important than a single large and more obvious one.[17] A study of raw material or fuel consumption per unit output may also be of great value. In addition, capacity figures for certain machines, or stages of a produc-

---

[17] To the extent that the character of output development makes such computations advisable, the output per man-hour index has been calculated according to the criteria described in I. Svennilson, "Industriarbetets vaxande avkastning i belysning av svenska erfarenheter," in *Studier i ekonomi och historia, tillägnade Eli F. Heckscher* (Uppsala, 1944). On the meaning of the "output per man-hour" concept, cf. also E. Ruist, "Produktionen per arbetstimme som mått på industriföretagets effektivitet," *Affärsekonomi* (1948), No. 6. Output per man-hour alone will not be a good indicator of the significance of process innovations, even apart from those weaknesses that are inherent in the fact that quality changes and shifts in the composition of output cannot, as a rule, be taken adequately into account. Thus if a firm stops buying a semifinished product and starts to produce it itself—or vice versa—this will affect the output per man-hour measure in a way which is analytically completely irrelevant in the present context.

FIGURE 12 (Continued)
Gloves, Leather, and Fur Products

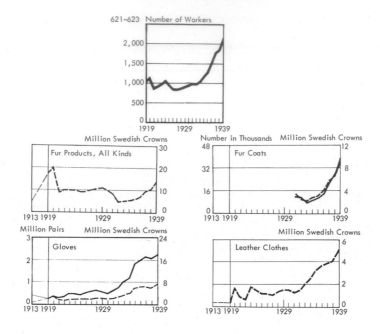

Oleomargarine

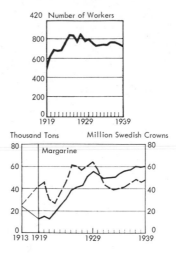

NOTE: Continuous curves represent quantities, dotted curves money values.

FIGURE 12 (Continued)
Brickyards

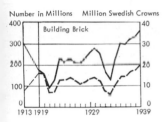

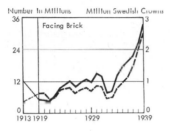

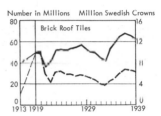

Lumber Mills

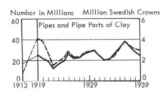

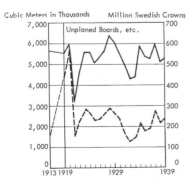

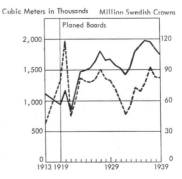

NOTE: Continuous curves represent quantities, dotted curves money values.

FIGURE 12 (Concluded)
Tanneries and Leather Shoes

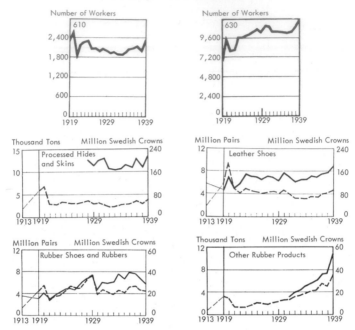

NOTE: Continuous curves represent quantities, dotted curves money values.

tion process, may be analyzed. The relation between installed horsepowers and the number of workers also gives some guidance.[18] One must above

---

[18] "Installed horsepower" refers to total effective horsepower in engines for the direct operation of machinery. The data have been taken from IS. The time series are reported in Appendix 4 of the Swedish edition. The system of utilizing a central power source linked through transmissions, belts, etc., to the individual machines was gradually replaced during the interwar period by a system where motors are linked directly to each machine or group of machines (so-called individual operation). As a consequence, the statistics on installed horsepower do not provide an altogether adequate measure of the "degree of mechanization." Since individual operation reduces transmission losses, total installed horsepower should be less, *ceteris paribus*, than where a central power source is used, even though the degree of mechanization is the same. The actual increase in installed horsepower according to IS is consequently likely to be an underestimate of the increase in mechanization, even though it is not always necessary to have a central power source capable of operating all machines simultaneously while the total horsepower of all the small motors would suffice to do so. The increase in mechanization is further underestimated due to the increasing effectivenes of the power sources and to the occurrence of process innovations reducing energy demands in the operation of machines. Several other circumstances must also be taken into account in estimating installed horsepower per worker. One should above all study the data on installed horsepower and on work force separately while also taking changes in the number of plants into account. Labor-input requirements can be reduced also in other ways than through mechanization, and a strong increase or decrease in the number of plants may make the figures obtained incommensurable.

all depend upon the trade journals and other trade literature in the economic-technical area, although such sources seldom yield quantitative data.[19] Finally, judgments on the significance of various process innovations have been made on the basis of systematic interviews with a number of entrepreneurs (see Appendix 1 of Swedish edition).

The element of arbitrariness which in this way enters the analysis is not serious. The primary function of many of the trade journals has been to follow technical and organizational developments. It seems improbable that any primary innovations of major importance would have escaped mention. That the trade press and literature can be relied upon to mention everything of fundamental importance has, as a rule, become evident in the interviews. The latter have been of great assistance in obtaining some idea of the quantitative importance of the innovations once they were introduced; the trade press is often but little interested in historical recapitulations, so the introduction of an innovation often spells its disappearance from the discussion. A series of minor process innovations, each of too little significance to be registered even in the trade press, may together amount to an important innovation. This constitutes a difficulty which may not always have been adequately overcome. In practice, it has often been possible to register and point out such a conglomerate of connected innovations, namely, when it emerges as a self-contained development within a clearly demarcated time period. When, for example, a series of new dryer constructions appeared in the woodworking industries and in the course of a few years drastically reduced the drying time for wood, this could be registered as a unit. It is unnecessary to distinguish all the different stages.

The picture of innovational activity and its significance that emerges in this way has not been detailed in the following analysis. In general, only the most important innovations receive explicit mention. Less important innovations have been mentioned in exceptional cases, when of some special significance.[20]

The two concepts (*active*) *supply push* and *demand-pull* also require more attention before we proceed. The instrumental character of these concepts should be particularly emphasized. The growth of an industry may be demand-pull induced even though progress in part of that industry is of the supply-push type—if the latter development is at the expense of the rest

---

[19] In the preliminary stages of this investigation, the second volume of the Report of the Rationalization Committee (*Rationaliseringsutredningens betänkande*, II, SOU, 1939, No. 14) proved to be of some help. Unfortunately, however, all the raw data assembled for this investigation were indiscriminately declared secret until 1957. Thus since even the lists of the firms that were in one way or another involved in the study were so declared, it has not even been possible to approach them with a request to study the material—a request which undoubtedly would have been granted in the majority of cases.

Apart from specialized monographs, a number of Swedish trade journals proved to be by far the most important source and have been systematically utilized. References to these journals appear in connection with the later analysis.

[20] For practical reasons, references have generally been confined to surveys in trade journals and to monographs of particular interest. For the rest, the bibliography (of the Swedish edition) provides a general overview of the printed or unprinted sources that have been utilized in addition to the interview material.

of the industry. The progressive development of the furniture industry in the interwar period was basically due to demand-pull—a rising rate of household formation resulted in a rising demand for furniture, while novel types of furniture can hardly have significantly increased furniture sales in general. But the same period also saw the emergence of a new branch of the industry (i.e., the manufacture of upholstered furniture). The output of the latter has grown at the expense of the production of older types of furniture. Were one, then, to limit an inquiry to this segment of the industry, its development would be regarded as of the supply-push type. From the point of view of an individual firm, finally, we may well have supply-push even though development for the larger group of which the firm is a member is of the demand-pull type, and vice versa. Firms may always expand their market at the expense of others in their particular branch.

It should be pointed out that the distinction between the two types of process relates to *progressive* processes. A given development does not necessarily fall into either of these two categories. In the first place, there are the cases where cost-reducing and price-reducing process innovations do not lead to supply-push growth but merely to a retention of the previous market. In the absence of innovations the market would, in other words, have shrunk. In other instances innovations may prevent cost increases on, say, raw materials from leading to sales-reducing price increases.

One problem is the difficulty of measuring supply-push and of determining the active process type. The distinction between the different types of process does not present any insurmountable theoretical obstacles (see the discussion in Chapter 4), and a rigorous analysis along these lines is, in principle, possible. In practice, however, this would require such a detailed dissection of the processes that the scope of the study would have to be completely altered, even assuming the undertaking were possible with the existing, or obtainable, data. A careful investigation of the type of process applicable to the clothing industry, for example, would first require a detailed study to show as far as possible what the course of development would have been with unchanged technology and products, given the development of population, income, occupational distribution, and so forth. A judgment would also have to be made concerning the influence on this hypothetical development of price changes on tailor-made products which might have come about independently of the rise of the ready-made clothing industry. Only then could conclusions be drawn from a comparison with the actual development of output. Such a study would obviously require a chapter in itself. While this would provide an elaborate and detailed picture, the marginal return from the great amount of extra work required hardly warrants the effort; a less thorough analysis has, therefore, been deemed more appropriate. This leaves some dubious cases unclassified, but their number is relatively small. The following is a freely constructed example of the schematic analysis attempted:

If a home-market industry, selling almost exclusively to the construction industry, shows a faster rate of output growth than the construction industry, this would usually indicate a supply-push process. In the converse case, a loss of market to another construction material industry is more often indicated. If, for example, the building joinery industry expands at a faster rate than the construction industry, we have at least circumstantial evidence of a process in which supply-push factors dominate; in the opposite case a demand-pull process is indicated. Evidence of the first kind is never conclusive, however—carpenters' on-site wages may have risen so sharply that the use of prefabricated materials became more profitable than before. The process would then actually be of the demand-pull type.[21]

The rate of household formation is an indication of the strength of the demand-pull acting on the furniture industry, which is protected from import competition. If the output of furniture does not grow considerably faster than household formation, a demand-pull process is normally indicated. The growth of population and real per capita income[22] suggests the extent of demand-pull in the shoe manufacturing industry, although shifts in age distribution and occupation distribution, as well as the income elasticities of demand for different income groups, should also be taken into account.[23] If, however, the production of leather shoes increases more slowly than this indicator, while the output of rubber-soled shoes grows considerably faster, it suggests that the former industry is losing out in competition with the latter. If the decline of the leather shoe industry has been accompanied by substantial price increases due to the rising cost of raw material, the development of the rubber-soled shoe industry may not have been of the supply-push type—nothing may have happened within the industry itself. If, instead, there are price reductions on rubber-soled shoes due to process innovations, this would indicate that the industry was actively expanding its market at the expense of the leather shoe industry.

Comparisons of this type cannot alone lead to firm conclusions—one must always try to trace the driving forces. Such comparisons may be very misleading when applied to a raw material or an intermediate product. If cement production, for instance, increases especially rapidly, this may very well be due to innovations in the manufacturing of concrete products.[24] Finally, a study of the price policies of individual firms may yield a number of suggestions even though these, too, will not be conclusive. The opportunities for

---

[21] The driving force behind an innovation may in certain circumstances be demand-pull. A rise in wages may make feasible the practical realization of a technical advance in the production of fixtures that previously was not profitable (cf. Chap. 5, pp. 74f). If a wage increase of this sort is observed in conjunction with the introduction of an innovation, the analysis will have to aim at pinpointing the driving force.

[22] "Real national income" is, of course, a rather strange concept (cf. Chap. 3, p. 24), but it still has its uses in contexts such as the present one when minor aggregation errors are of no consequence.

[23] Certain commodity groups, such as confectionery or fur products, may be subject to demand-pull due to shifts in the distribution of income, even when aggregate income remains unchanged. In this connection, the parenthetical reflection may also be made that in estimating, say, consumption functions one should always as a matter of course investigate whether the commodities in question did or did not exert supply-push during the period studied.

[24] These innovations could perhaps be said to "expand" the current market actively, but in order to be systematic, we will still use the term "demand-pull" to characterize the process from the standpoint of the current industry. The concrete products industry, on the other hand, deserves the "supply-push" label.

basing conclusions on price statistics are generally very limited, particularly since the various products seldom remain homogeneous over long periods of time. To the extent that a product has stayed comparatively homogeneous, however, demand-pull processes are often—but far from always—characterized by rising prices. Price increases as a rule indicate demand-pull. This is especially the case with intercyclical price increases. Cases of supply-push through process innovation are normally accompanied by absolute price reductions, but in many cases only by relative price reductions. In the process of creating the market for a new product, price is most often held relatively constant at the beginning and then declines gradually. A price increase could endanger expansion opportunities or lure an unnecessary number of competitors into the new area. A price reduction, on the other hand, would seem rather unnecessary as long as the pioneering, price-leading firms are able to sell their capacity output.

There is no reason to dwell further on the technical difficulties of the analysis. The theoretical models have been analyzed in Chapter 4; the following causal analysis and the classification to which it leads will speak for itself. Elements of different process types are almost always present in actual processes, and a penetrating analysis will always reveal reality to be more complicated than initially assumed. An analysis that cannot enter into details, both because of need for comprehensiveness and because of the practical possibilities of obtaining empirical data, must of necessity, therefore, be schematic and simplified. It is, perhaps, especially important to stress that though an industry is classified as of the supply-push type due to the introduction of new products, demand-pull is not necessarily less than in an industry classified as of the demand-pull type. The classification only indicates that the new products have been considered more important than the demand-pull which also was present. In the present context there is only one case of this which is of interest. With reference to the 1930's, the development of the building joinery industry is put in the supply-push category while that of the glass container industry is classified as demand-pull, although demand-pull in itself certainly was stronger in the former case.

C. Summary Analysis

Chapters 7 through 9 are devoted to an industry-by-industry analysis of the transformation process. Progressive, regressive, and stagnating industries are discussed by using the analytical schema outlined above. The various industries are considered in the same order employed previously.

While the importance of the different types of processes varies from branch to branch and industry to industry, the results of the analysis warrant the following generalizations:

It is evident that *new products* played an extremely important role in the material progress achieved. A survey of production at the close of the interwar period shows that there were a great number of commodities that at the outset either were not produced at all, or were at the very beginning of their development without yet having captured even a fraction of the markets they would control two decades later. Stainless steel and lightweight metals, plastics, airplanes, automobiles, electric refrigerators, electric locomotives, concrete products and lightweight concrete, prefabricated fittings and houses, modern cardboard and paper packaging, canned foods (especially fish, fruit, and vegetables), soft drinks, rayon products, ready-made clothing, cellulose enamels and synthetic paints, synthetic nitrogen fertilizers, new explosives, and drugs—all played important roles in the material prosperity of the late 1930's. But these products did not exist at all, or only to a limited extent, 20 years earlier.

Table 4 presents an estimate of the proportion of the total value of sales for various industries in 1939 accounted for by new or quite "young" commodities. The estimate is necessarily somewhat schematic due to the character of the statistical material used. The figures undoubtedly underestimate the importance of the new products; many commodity groups that are not included contained new products which could not be accounted for individually. An additional factor is perhaps even more important. The "young" commodities often showed declining prices through the interwar period in relation to older products—a typical pattern for products in the process of creating or extending their markets. The percentage of total value of sales in 1919 accounted for by the new products exaggerates their quantitative importance in relation to 1939. Finally, the quality and design of older products sometimes developed so rapidly that the distinction between primary and secondary innovations often is difficult to draw. Thus the study of the industrial transformation leads one to emphasize the role of the new and young commodities even when the time period covered is as short as two decades.

In many industries by contrast, the role of *new processes* in the production of largely unchanged products was much less conspicuous. Indeed, most process innovations were inseparably linked with product innovations. It is also striking that new, cheaper processes often appeared as defensive measures for an old product struggling with a new one. It was often this type of struggle rather than competition among different firms producing the same commodity which was the driving force behind the "modernization" movement. The modernization prevented stagnation in output per man-hour and defeated attempts to limit competition through cartels. This conclusion stands even if the criteria for judging a commodity as "new" rather than just "improved" are made very strict. It can be asserted without undue simplification that the struggle between the two components of the development process raged in many industries among products rather than among processes. Financial difficulties developed more in connection with the product struggle than with the process struggle.

The *progressive* development of a number of industries thus depended

TABLE 4

Survey of the Transformation of Production in the Interwar Period
(sales value of production in tenths of 1 percent of the
aggregate sales value of Swedish industrial production°)

	1919	1939
Sponge iron	0.0	0.3
Electro-steel	1.3	9.7
Various alloys	0.1	3.8
Various new rolled (especially cold rolled) and drawn products, etc....	—	8.6
Aluminum and aluminum products	0.3	2.6
Various manufactures (including fittings) not produced by the steel industry	0.3	6.2
Various nonferrous metal castings	2.1	3.4
Central-heating boilers and low pressure steam boilers	—	1.4
Central heating radiators	0.2	2.5
Airplanes and automobiles	1.1	20.9
Motor cycles and bicycles	3.5	5.9
Various new transport equipment, etc	—	1.9
Electrical heaters, etc	0.3	1.4
Radio receivers	—	3.9
Various electrical household appliances	0.2	5.0
Various new electrical equipment	—	5.1
Pumps, fans, air conditioning equipment, etc	0.9	3.9
Typewriters, calculators, etc	—	1.8
Various new instruments and tools (e.g. pneumatic)	—	2.7
Various new types of industrial machinery	—	8.5
Various new agricultural and dairy machinery	—	2.0
Various concrete goods and lightweight concrete	1.8	4.3
Electrical and sanitary porcelain	—	0.5
Various new types of bricks, pottery products, etc	—	2.5
Glasswool and miscellaneous new glassware	—	0.4
Plywood	0.1	1.1
Wallboard	—	4.1
Prefabricated wooden houses	—	4.1
Prefabricated interior fittings and other new joinery products	—	3.9
Various wood products (e.g. impregnated)	0.1	0.6
Bleached sulphite pulp (e.g. viscose cellulose)	4.1	12.9
Bleached sulphate pulp (of an entirely new character)	—	3.3
Various types of paper and paperboard	0.7	7.1
Hard corrugated board	—	1.2
Various new paper and paperboard products	—	2.4
Mineral water and soft drinks	2.0	3.6
Various canned foods, jam, juice, etc	1.1	4.5
Various foods (e.g. milk powder, condensed milk)	0.0	0.6
Cattle feed	1.8	7.0
Various textiles (e.g. machine felt, binder twine)	0.3	1.6
Rayon products	—	13.1
Garments and other ready-made textile products	13.6	29.6
Various fur, rubber and leather products	0.7	8.0
Cellulose enamels, synthetic enamels and varnishes, etc	—	1.6
Miscellaneous new drugs, cosmetic products, etc	—	1.1
Synthetic nitrogen products	—	0.6
Mineral oils, bakelite, vegetable oils, medical preparations, etc	1.2	7.9
Total	37.8	230.2
Total, percentage figures	3.8%	23.0%

* Excluding mining, gold and silverware, armaments, flour mill, dairy and meat packing products.

to a great extent on new or young products. These constituted the primary driving force in the development process and pushed many "old" commodities over to the negative side. The processes were primarily of the active, supply-push type. This was the case during the entire interwar period, both in electric and nonelectric consumer-durables manufacturing, in metal and sheet metal manufacturing, in the concrete and lightweight concrete industry, and in the building joinery industry. Paper processing and cardboard processing also belonged to the group of industries that expanded rapidly in connection with significant product innovations. The situation was similar with the canned food and fruit processing industries, with the soft drink industry during the entire interwar period, and with the fur industry in the thirties. Other examples were hosiery, clothing, and paints and varnishes, where this type of development obtained for the whole interwar period. In the cases enumerated, product innovation was not merely prominent but, indeed, dominating. Without it, the development would have taken an entirely different course. It is particularly remarkable that the new products served mainly to expand domestic markets; they were seldom exported.

Another major class is composed of industries whose main products were already generally known by the end of World War I and where novelties and improvements in production and distribution methods were the driving force and the mainstay of their progressive development. The process innovations served to expand markets either absolutely or by displacing previous imports. A complete absence of new products in these industries would of course have altered the development picture but not fundamentally. New commodities were either few and/or insignificant or else their struggle to replace older commodities took place entirely within the industry, often inside a single firm.

Demand-pull alone could not have lead to a progressive development in these industries—either because it was not significant enough or because it would merely have led to increased imports. Demand-pull factors were not decisive in the emergence of innovations, but in many cases they did facilitate their dissemination. The cement industry and the pulp industry—which simultaneously experienced a strong demand-pull in the domestic market—belonged in this category (as did the paper industry in the 1920's). Other examples are the quality steel producers in the 1930's, and the cotton mills throughout the period. Further candidates for this group are the electric and nonelectric capital goods industries and the glass container and plate glass works in the 1930's, the oleomargarine industry in the 1920's, and the porcelain and ceramics industry of the 1930's.

A third major category includes industries whose development was primarily due to demand-pull. To the extent that major process innovations occurred, their supply-push effects were not great. When they led to price reductions, the main result was simply that purchasing power was set free for other purposes. New products were also insignificant or were introduced as a passive adaptation to a market situation changed by demand-pull factors. They were not the primary driving force in the development process. These industries would have exhibited a progressive development even if no significant innovations had taken place. The previously mentioned industries cannot be so characterized. In contrast to the first two groups of industries, the progressive development of those in the third category did not take place at the expense of older commodities or older methods in other industries or branches. Thus the industries that fall into this group produced either products already well-known at the beginning of the period or new or young products that displaced older commodities primarily within the same industry. The class includes furniture, chocolate and candy, and light chemicals (oils, soap, perfume, and cosmetics) through the whole interwar period, and paper, woolens, household glass, gloves and hides in the 1930's. The commercial iron producers in the 1930's should also be placed in this class.

Among the *stagnating* industries, one distinguishable subcategory would comprise those in which process innovations, in particular, but also secondary product innovations to some extent prevented a regressive development. The brickyards, the lumber mills, the tanneries, and the leather shoe industry belong here for the whole interwar period, as does the entire iron and steel industry, together with the glassworks and the porcelain and ceramics industry, in the 1920's. Demand-pull was without decisive importance in these cases—although the roof-tile brickyards were an exception.

Another overlapping subgroup of the *stagnating* or *regressive* industries worth noting comprises cases where new or young products or processes, in Sweden or abroad, threatened to place a number of product lines in the relevant industries on the negative side of the development process. Such a situation would often be the converse of a progressive supply-push process elsewhere. This was the case, for example, with the brickyards, the tanneries, and the leather shoe industry, as well as with the lumber mills (where, however, the shrinking raw material base of many mills also played an important role). The most important examples were the iron and steel industry and the porcelain and ceramics industries in the 1920's.

Rates of return normally differed significantly between the progressive industries, on the one hand, and stagnating and especially regressive industries, on the other hand—particularly when regression in the latter case was a symptom of the negative development component. When this was not the case, however, rates of return could be at least as high in stagnating as in progressive industries. Profits were, on the average, considerably higher in the 1930's than in the 1920's. Interfirm differences were great, particularly during the 1920's and in industries where innovations were very important. The profits of pioneer firms were generally distinctly above average, despite an apparent tendency for their wages to be higher than in other firms.[25] They were, however, few in number. This explains, in a purely statistical sense, why demand-pull processes normally yielded higher and more evenly distributed profits. The *causal* explanation is simply that while innovations typically provide profits for some firms, they will simultaneously, through competition, result in losses for others. Profits and losses, in other words, frequently were two sides of the same coin. The normally good and evenly distributed returns involved in demand-pull processes have a simple explanation—primarily the economies of high capacity utilization.

A closer study of the transformation process shows, among other things, that the decade of the 1920's was without comparison with respect to advances in production techniques, even though there often was not time for such advances to be generally disseminated and given all their more obvious applications. The 1930's, on the other hand, were definitely a period of dissemination of previously made innovations. The strong demand-pull which characterized the 1930's, partly due to the economic policy pursued, undoubtedly furthered the modernization of the industrial capital stock in various ways through facilitating this dissemination process. But dissemination would obviously still have taken place as a consequence of the pioneer efforts of the previous decade.

It is difficult, in these circumstances, to make a fair comparison of the rates of progress between the two decades. The difficulty exists, even apart from the nonmeasurable advances, with respect, for example, to various services, leisure time, and so forth. A judgment is, incidentally, just as difficult in the area of product innovations, where the situation is similar. Most products that were novel to the interwar period first emerged in the 1920's but only captured the markets during the 1930's when truly novel commodities were relatively few.

A more complete discussion of the relation between developments in the two decades will be given in Chapter 16, following the detailed historical analysis to be provided in Chapters 7 through 15. It will then be possible to follow the development process more closely and to coordinate the transformation analysis with an analysis of its business cycle aspects, along the lines indicated in Chapter 4.

---

[25] Cf. B. Ohlin, "Lönenivåns söndersplittring," *Verkstäderna* (1926), p. 247.

7 Analysis of Progressive Industries

Engineering Industries

The three main branches of the engineering group—(a) *iron, steel, and metal manufacturing*, (b) *mechanical engineering*, and (c) *electrical engineering*—all belonged to the progressive industries during the entire interwar period.[1] In the electrical engineering industry, all indicators point in this direction. It is not so immediately evident in the other two industries. Thus, the work force, for example, increased only moderately, and the official *Industry Statistics* (*IS*) figures on total market value of output, as well as any estimates of output volume based on these figures, tend to be misleading.[2] Time series on the output of individual final products, however, show quite clearly that all three branches were progressive. This is evident also from the fact that the moderate growth of the work force was due largely to labor-saving rationalization efforts.[3]

---

[1] The borderline between the various branches will sometimes be rather arbitrary. Many firms straddle the border between two or more such branches.

[2] Thus one of the most conspicuous features of this industry was the development of its productive structure toward an elaborate subcontracting system. Consequently, the market value of industry output shows too rapid a rise, since semifinished products are excluded if subject to further manufacturing within the same plant but will be included if completion of the product takes place in another firm.

[3] According to the definition adopted by the 1927 economic world congress in Geneva "rationalization" refers to "the use of such technical and organizational methods as will minimize material and labor losses. Rationalization means scientific direction of the work, norms being set for materials as well as products, simplification of work procedures and improvement of transport and marketing methods." Literally, therefore, this means producing the same product in a different way,

The process innovations involved in this rationalization had their origin principally in wartime American industry, and they came to be especially characteristic of the 1920's. In this period, in fact, they played a more prominent and significant role than did new products. With some slight exaggeration it may be stated that the novel element lay mostly in new ways of using already existing machines and equipment. Planning, time-and-motion studies, assembly-line production, and product standardization were very important. However, these innovations were still accompanied by increased mechanization and considerable improvement in the stock of equipment. One important element in this context was the so-called individual operation which implied that each machine was equipped with its own motor.[4] But the factor which undoubtedly was most significant in principle was found in the more organizational type of innovation.[5] It is quite evident that the legislation establishing shorter working hours intensified interest in labor-saving process innovations.[6]

Entirely new products were not of dominating importance in the 1920's. Primary product innovations were rather few. Automobiles and bicycles had been manufactured since the turn of the century. Combustion engines, using kerosene, oil, or gasoline, had come into production in the mid-1890's and had developed especially rapidly after the invention of the two-phase engine in the first years of the new century. Traverse cranes, conveyors, and various other types of internal transport equipment achieved revolutionary significance in the modernization of production, particularly within the heavy manufacturing industry, although they had

---

while changes that lead to a new product are not considered to be "rationalization." Thus the definition cited, in fact, overlaps with that given to the concept of "process innovations." Cf. n. 5 below.

[4] One measure, albeit an imperfect one, of the pace of mechanization is the number of installed horsepower units (Cf. Chap. 6, p. 116n.). Between 1919 and 1939, horsepower per worker increased by from 10 to 50 percent in the various branches of the engineering industry. (Cf. Appendix 4 of Swedish edition.)

[5] It has been argued that "rationalization" as defined above was an entirely new phenomenon in the interwar period [cf. J. Reinholds, "Rationaliseringen och dess uppgift inom folkhushållet," *Affärsekonomi* (1937), No. 3] and that it meant something more than "mechanization" or "creative improvements" of plant and equipment. The latter type of innovation is said to have been predominant up through the early years of the century, while "rationalization" was then not needed, since as yet it "was not more difficult to sell than to produce" (*op. cit.*, p. 104). When following World War I, it did become more difficult to sell than to produce, rationalization supposedly became the order of the day. There is surely a great deal of truth in this, and the Swedish engineering industry provides a good illustration. According to the definition given above, however, it is evident that mechanization is a form of rationalization and a form that was about as common before as after World War I.

It was not rationalization as such, in other words, that was novel but the type of rationalization that mainly concerns *organizational* aspects. In earlier periods it had mostly been a question of mechanization in the literal sense; after World War I organization and planning of production received more attention than before.

[6] Cf. "Statistiska undersökningar angående åttatimmarslagens och bagerilagens verkningar," *Statens Offentliga Utredningar* (SOU), (1925, No. 45).

already been constructed and produced before World War I. The production of roller bearings, the importance of which can hardly be exaggerated, had reached considerable proportions before the war, as had the production of the revolutionary precision measurement tools invented by C. E. Johansson. The use of new alloys in lathes and other machines, which made possible a considerable increase in operating speeds, also dates back to the prewar period. Production of electric generators, motors, transformers, and accumulators, which were to have great significance not only in providing energy for stationary machines but for transportation both inside and outside industrial plants, began in the late 1800's.

Telephones stem from the same period. Even though the vacuum cleaner was no novelty in the 1920's, its widespread dissemination, both domestically and in export markets, was a spectacular interwar phenomenon. Separators and several other products based on the inventions of de Laval were of similar age as were compressor refrigerators. Agricultural machinery as well as machines for the mining industry, the brickyards, road construction, and so forth, of the same basic types that came into general use in the interwar period, had already been produced and had begun to replace many manual implements in the 1870's. There was no Swedish-built tractor until the 1920's, although a self-propelled plow had been produced. Dalén's inventions of various kinds of light apparatus had been made around the turn of the century and led to full-scale production at that time. This was also true of kerosene stoves. Welding equipment, of great importance to industrial development between the wars, was of approximately the same age. A survey of the equipment used in the engineering industries and in the pulp, paper, and other forest-based industries shows that most of the more fundamental innovations were one or more decades old at the beginning of the interwar period. The main principles for lathes and cutters were well known, as was the case with various pneumatic tools, with chucks, reamers, and so forth. Radiators had been manufactured for some time. Safety razors and blades had been produced since 1914.

Important exceptions to the generalization that most items of real significance to the expansion were of earlier origin are found primarily in the electrical engineering industry. Primary innovations that occurred in the 1920's included radios, absorption-principle refrigerators, mangles, washers, and dishwashers, floor polishers, electric ranges, and various types of heaters and ventilation equipment. In the mechanical engineering industry, calculators and several other types of office equipment constituted primary innovations.[7] The Ljungström turbine locomotive should be mentioned also.

---

[7] An exhibition in Stockholm in 1929—the first of its kind in Sweden—gave a representative picture of the innovations in the area of office equipment. Cf. Affärsekonomi (1929), No. 5.

Thus the real novelties came mostly in the area of consumer durables. Exceptions from our general rule were few in the capital goods industries. An exception of great importance based on the breakthrough of pulver metallurgy in the iron and steel industry, was the use of hard metal alloys in tools, which allowed considerably higher operating speeds than before.[8] Only one really new machine tool of importance dates from this period, namely, the centerless grinding machine. Apart from machine tools, the so-called Imo-pump was the most prominent among the few really significant Swedish primary innovations. Various stainless steel articles for both households and industry, and light metal products of many different kinds, were important novelties in the area of iron, steel and metal manufacturing. While light metal products became especially important in the 1930's, the pioneer efforts, leading among other things to great improvements in press foundry techniques, generally dated from the 1920's.

There are many examples of secondary innovations. The new products that were created before and during World War I gave rise to many new product lines with novel properties, usually undergoing radical improvements in the process. The trend in the electrical engineering industry, for example, was to utilize progressively higher voltages and machine effects, and small motors were developed. These could be built into various machine tools, thus replacing the older, larger motors which powered many different machines simultaneously. In the roller bearing industry, spherical bearings were developed; in the automobile industry, the Hesselman auto diesel; in the shipyards, methods for electric welding of entire ships, and so on. The general evolution toward larger machine units, on the one hand, and toward smaller specialized machines for turning out details, on the other, should also be emphasized.[9]

On the negative side of the development process, no important commodities or large commodity groups were markedly regressive, although production of a number of wartime products was discontinued after the end of World War I—among them some originally destined for export to Russia. The continuing construction of cargo sailing vessels should be mentioned, perhaps, as an example. Keels were laid for such ships as late as the early 1920's. But the negative component of the development process showed up everywhere in the disappearance of old production processes. As a rule, however, this took place within the firms in such way as to make the struggle between new and old processes rather unnoticeable to outside observers.

---

[8] Cf. "Några moderna verktygsmaskiner av inhemsk tillverkning" (unsigned), *Teknisk Tidskrift* (1935), No. 45, A 409, and H. Kjerrman, "Verktygsstål och hårdmetall," *Teknisk Tidskrift* (1935), No. 18, A 194.

[9] Cf. esp. C. G. Brodén, "Verkstadsteknik förr och nu. Maskiner och verktyg," *Tekniken och framtiden*, Vol. II (Stockholm, 1945).

Progress in the 1920's was to a large extent based on innovations in productive processes and productive organization. The relative or absolute reductions in prices, and/or improvements in quality, that these innovations made possible created new markets both at home and abroad. This implies, of course, that the development process was of the active supply-push type. The new consumer durables obviously helped to make it so, as did many "young" commodities which, having been unknown to many potential consumers at the beginning of the interwar period, continued to grow in importance. Demand-pull factors were of little consequence. Imports could take place on the required scale in most areas. The engineering industries were not protected from foreign competition to any great extent; instead, they were exposed to very severe competition in many areas.

The great process innovations, the numerous young, if not new, products of growing importance, and the lack of major regressive commodity groups, would lead one to expect rather prosperous conditions for the engineering industries in the 1920's once the initial, acute deflation crisis had been overcome. But good times did not come until toward the end of the decade, and then it was the consumer-durables industries that, typically, benefited the most (see Table 3, Chapter 6 and Appendix 3 in Swedish edition). This weakness during the greater part of the decade was undoubtedly due to the lack of any general demand-pull. The turning point arrived rather suddenly and was connected with the modernization movement and with the decline in German dumping after the stabilization of the German economy. Innovations on the scale of those undertaken in this period naturally took years to complete and could not bear fruit immediately. It is true that they could yield good economic results quite early in certain quarters. But they could not generate improved business conditions in general for the simple reason that they were not disseminated very widely, being concentrated in a rather limited number of firms. Instead, they often made life difficult for other competing, but not innovating, firms. A demand-pull process, with the resulting tendency toward better utilization of capacity, would, on the other hand, have led to a more general improvement in earnings.

The progress of the engineering industries was even more pronounced in the 1930's. The work force increased considerably between 1929 and 1939, and most statistical series for individual commodities pointed strongly upward. In this decade, too, modernization characterized the development process to a very great extent. Primarily it was a time for harvesting the fruits of the innovations that had been introduced in the 1920's and that had only begun to take effect at the end of the decade. These innovations were now disseminated through the greater part of the respective industries. In the early 1920's, the prewar innovations no longer promised much gain. Progress before 1914 proceeded largely on another plane, and in addition, the war brought great changes in all areas so that there were no traditional lines to follow. In the late 1920's and early 1930's, a more or less thorough modernization had in many cases just reached completion, and all the firms which had not yet had time, or for one reason or another had not yet been able, to carry through such modernization had the example of the pioneering firms to follow. Both the incentive and the opportunity to do so were, in addition, strengthened by the strong demand-pull that emerged in the 1930's.[10] Thus the late 1920's mark the dividing line between two periods for more than one reason.

New products were rare in the 1930's. This conclusion appears to be unavoidable despite all the reservations that are appropriate, given our perspective—for such a recent period the novel commodities may be hard to pinpoint.[11] There were, however, a large number of small, but in the aggregate significant, secondary innovations in the form of improvements on older products.[12] In this regard, the 1930's hardly lagged behind the 1920's. In one specific area, moreover, new products emerged more frequently in the 1930's than earlier, namely, among commodities that had previously been imported. It is evident that these import substitutes played a definite role in the progressive development process. They emerged in part as a result of the devaluation of the Swedish *krona* in 1931 and in part independently of this development. Though an unqualified conclusion is difficult to reach, it appears that the devaluation was not of predominant importance. Imports of engineering products increased in absolute figures during the 1930's also.

Negative development effects appeared in the 1930's in approximately the same fashion as in the 1920's. Many "old" processes disappeared. Automobile production, for example, declined steeply, while the output of cars assembled in Sweden increased rapidly. Widely diversified production in the manner of the traditional unspecialized workshop came to play a less prominent role. There were no major regressive commodities or commodity groups, but as was the case earlier, examples were plentiful of old product types being superseded by new and/or progressive ones.

The importance of demand-pull factors in the thirties has already been mentioned in connection with the devaluation of the *krona* in 1931, which weakened foreign competition in Swedish markets. But domestically generated demand-pull was of far greater importance. Population growth and household formation together with the high level of

---

[10] Cf. Chap. 7, p. 132n.

[11] Comparing the volumes of *Teknisk Tidskrift* and *Verkstäderna* from the 1930's with those from the 1920's suggests very strongly that this was the case.

[12] Developments in the production of office machines are illustrative of large segments of the engineering industries. Cf. C. B. Nyströmer, "Kunna affärsföretagen inrikta kontorsmaskinindustriens fortsatta utveckling?" *Affärsekonomi* (1937), No. 19. Also C. G. Brodén, *op. cit.*

construction activity, which was partly due to and partly independent of demographic developments, were very important in this connection (see Figures 1 and 7). This was the origin of many demand impulses which, when they impinged on the engineering industries, led to expansion unconnected with active innovative efforts. In this respect the 1930's stand in clear contrast to the 1920's, even though in many areas this contrast was merely a question of degree.

The profit picture improved considerably as shown in Table 3 and in Appendix 3 (of the Swedish edition). In the context of what has already been said, this is not hard to explain. Both the dissemination of innovations and the demand-pull contributed toward a more general improvement of earnings following the depression in the 1930's than had taken place after the depression in the 1920's. The demand-pull caused higher earnings and improved liquidity and thus made it easier to replace old plants with new and modern ones. This effect, incidentally, did not work only through profits and liquidity. The improved prospects for operating at greater capacity would sometimes also lead to investment in new plants in which new and better techniques could be utilized.[13] In some areas, cartel cooperation and monopoly positions undoubtedly contributed to relatively high earnings, at least over the short run.

The Cement Industry

Cement production in Sweden dates back to the 1870's. The interwar period brought a number of improvements in products although there

---

[13] At this point, however, theoretical clarity requires some important interpretative comments. Whether there is demand-pull or not should be irrelevant to the optimality of a given method of production if the individual firm would be able to conquer the markets of its competitors by lowering its price. The increased demand, which makes the utilization of the larger and more modern capacity possible, should then emerge following a price-reducing innovation. In other words, given this assumption, an autonomous increase in demand—i.e., an increase independent of the innovation—such as actually experienced by large segments of the engineering industry, cannot be regarded as an independent causal factor or precondition for the realization of the innovation in question. When demand-pull nonetheless is sometimes seen to contribute to the introduction and dissemination of an innovation, this is due to inflexibility of customer relationships, the prevalence of monopolistic but above all oligopolistic competition, etc., having within certain limits eliminated price competition. In such market situations it is frequently more difficult for a firm to capture the market of another firm through price cuts than to find outlets in an expanding total market. Since a market situation of this kind was characteristic of the engineering industries in many areas during the interwar period, one may infer that the demand-pull of the 1930's served to accelerate the introduction and dissemination of innovations. But it is then important to emphasize the actual, special circumstances obtaining in this case. A general discussion of the tendency of demand increases to speed up the modernization of plant and equipment can be found, e.g., in I. Svennilson, "Industrialismens växande avkastning i belysning av svenska erfarenheter," *Studier i ekonomi och historia* (Uppsala, 1944). The topic is also discussed with reference to the wood-processing industries in Th. Streyffert, "Den norrländska träförädlingsindustrien," *Norrland, natur, befolkning och näringar*, IUI (Stockholm, 1942), p. 528.

were no entirely novel products. Aluminate cement, silicate cement, and the so-called armor-cement are examples of new types of cement with special properties.[14] Cement also came to be used in many new ways not only because of the new product types but also because of technological advances in the use of concrete. The work force declined in the 1930's despite the strong growth of output. This is explained by the very intensive modernization of the industry. Although basic production principles remained unchanged, machines, ovens, and transport devices developed very rapidly. Installed horsepower per worker increased almost threefold (see Appendix 4 of Swedish edition). Output per man-hour, which in this case can be estimated with reasonable accuracy, also showed a very rapid increase (i.e., from 41 in 1915 to 199 in 1939, with an index based on 1929 = 100). No other industry can match this performance. Cement prices are also significant: They fell, practically without interruption, throughout the interwar period. The price decline from 1926 to 1934 amounted to almost 50 percent.[15]

The rapid development of concrete technology and consequently in the use of concrete for the construction of houses, bridges, and roads led to the development of new uses for concrete.[16] To the extent that this was due to improvements in cement quality, active supply-push expansion took place. The quality improvements do not seem to have been too important; the technological advances in the use of concrete should, rather, be regarded as having created a demand-pull for the cement industry. Research on concrete—where Sweden often pioneered—was sponsored by the cement industry; and the Swedish Cement Association, formed in 1926, was very active in disseminating information on uses for cement. As price reductions induced by process innovations probably led to increased cement consumption, it seems logical to consider the process one of gradual supply-push. Domestic cement consumption, however, did not grow conspicuously faster than construction activity until the late thirties, when a number of new concrete products established a place for themselves in conjunction with new concrete construction methods.[17]

The cement industry exhibited the frequently observed interaction between good profits—achieved even in the depression years—and innovations. Profits were obviously boosted by innovations and stayed at a

---

[14] Cf. T. Bilde, "Cement och betong," *Tekniskt folkbibliotek* (Stockholm, 1940); and *Skandinaviska Bankens kvartalsskrift* (1936), No. 1.

[15] *Skandinaviska Bankens Kvartalsskrift* (1936), No. 1.

[16] Cf. the section on concrete products and lightweight concrete industry.

[17] Exports reached a considerable volume in the late 1920's. Approximately one third of total output was exported. During the 1930's, the volume of exports declined almost without interruption, primarily because of the growth of an indigenous industry in the former customer countries. Some importation also took place during the entire interwar period but on a small scale. Cf. L. Bjerning, *Skånes jord- och stenindustri* (Hälsingborg, 1947), pp. 173–74

high level through both decades. Good returns were the signal for the adoption of capital-demanding innovations, although here the liquid position of the cement industry at the beginning of the period also played a part (due to cautious policies the industry had gone through the 1921–22 crisis relatively unscathed). Better distribution, accomplished through cooperation in the marketing corporation, Cementa, should also be mentioned in this connection.[18]

The Concrete and Lightweight Concrete Industry

The progressive development of this industry was based primarily on new or quite young products that throughout the period were in the process of getting established in the domestic market.

Concrete pipe had been produced since the late 1890's, but the quality left much to be desired. Only in the 1920's did it begin to compete seriously with glazed clay pipe. In general use in the 1930's, the product benefited from lively construction activity and from rising standards for sanitary installations in urban and rural areas, which created strong demand-pull. At the same time, it is evident that concrete pipe considerably facilitated the improvement of sanitary installations during this decade.

"Nopsa"-stone was a Finnish innovation imported during the 1920's. This is a solid brick of concrete of about the same size as an ordinary brick and having the same uses. The product came to be particularly important in rural areas where it was used in the construction of barns, and so forth. "Silurian" stone, although not strictly a concrete product, should also be mentioned. Its introduction led directly to product innovations in the brickyards (i.e., porous, lightweight brick. See pp. 172f).

"Hole-blocks" made of cement were used during World War I as foundation stone and as wall stone, but they did not become very significant because of poor quality. In the interwar period this product was used almost exclusively in foundations, and since great quality improvements had been accomplished, it became a quite important product, particularly in connection with the great success that the new prefabricated frame houses enjoyed in this period. The availability of hole-blocks made it very easy to lay the foundation for such houses.

Production of lightweight concrete from slate ash and lime began in 1924. The invention was Swedish but it was based on ideas originating in the United States. Steam-hardened lightweight concrete was introduced a few years later and proved to be the decisive innovation in the lightweight concrete industry. This product became extremely important in the 1940's, but had seen widespread use as early as the 1930's

---

[18] *Skandinaviska Bankens Kvartalsskrift* (1936), No. 1. Concerning this move toward monopoly and its consequences, cf. "Organiserad samverkan inom svenskt näringsliv," *SOU* (1940, No. 45).

as a wall stone both in one-family dwellings and in large apartment houses. Along with other types of brick substitutes, it became a progressively more serious rival to ordinary brick and natural stone (see the brick industry). The negative effects of these developments were felt in the brick and stone industries. They were of no consequence in the branches discussed here, even though they also had product innovations to cope with—in the 1930's, the nopsa-stone was superseded by lightweight concrete, and the earlier versions of this product were, in their turn, superseded by steam-hardened concrete.

A completely reliable judgment on the profitability of the concrete products and lightweight concrete industry cannot be provided here. Only a few of he firms could be included in our investigation on rates of return, and several of these firms were engaged in other activities as well, such as contracting. But everything indicates that the profit picture was favorable, particularly in the late 1930's.

Woodworking Industries

These industries were among the most progressive of the industries studied. Both work force and output grew in all of the major branches. While the rate of growth appears to have been relatively moderate during the 1920's—at least in the building joinery branch—it was all the more rapid in the following decade. The growth of the furniture industry and particularly of the building joineries is apparently exaggerated, however, by the Industry Statistics figures. Both the value of output series and the various volume estimates based on these data must be regarded with skepticism. The growing importance of subcontracting (in connection, for example, with the strongly expanding production of prefabricated frame houses as well as in the upholstered furniture branch)[19] is a source of error in the data. But it is clear that the record is one of strong expansion, even when allowance is made for this error.

In *building joinery* there were many important new products. Although prefabricated houses were not, strictly speaking, a novelty,[20] the new types which began to be produced in the 1920's must still be regarded as representing primary innovations. In this period the industry began to supply not just summer cabins but all-year housing in this fashion. The success of prefabricated housing depended also in part on the service and advice that producers began to provide to builders. The

---

[19] Semifinished products that undergo further processing within the same plant are counted only once in the market value of industry output, while they are double-counted when this processing takes place in another plant.

[20] The Chinese pavilion in the park of Drottingsholm Castle was a prefabricated frame house—erected in the mid-18th century! For the rest, less successful production experiments had been undertaken beginning in the years around 1900.

adoption of such modern marketing methods may indeed have been the decisive innovation in this branch.

Factory-made fittings and fixtures for kitchens, shops, banks, schools, and so forth were relatively new in the 1920's. They were the driving force in a development toward increasing prefabrication even of many details. This process was hastened by the adoption, in the mid-1930's, of a new system for computing joiners' wages. This system led to higher wages for those relatively few joiners still working on the construction sites, and increasing pressure for shorter construction periods was a contributory cause. Thus the supply-push elements in the development of this industry were gradually complemented by considerable demand-pull.

Factory production of doors and windows originated long before World War I—partly for export. In the twenties, frames and fittings also began to be made in factories. The flush door was an innovation introduced from Germany in the 1930's. It rapidly superseded the old and heavy, paneled door. Another novelty was the picture window. Laminated parquet flooring was a novel product which rapidly began to replace parquet blocks in the 1930's.

The production of plywood antedated World War I and thus was no novelty in the interwar period.[21] There were, however, a number of secondary innovations, especially in gluing techniques, that significantly improved product quality and led to strong expansion of output. Wallboard was completely new to Sweden in the interwar period and generated significant supply-push. The basic invention originated in the United States in 1915, and in the early 1920's there were several American wallboard plants.[22] In Sweden, wallboard production dates from 1929, when it began on American license under the Masonite trademark. Wallboard production was very progressive throughout the 1930's. At the end of the interwar period, Sweden was second to the United States in wallboard capacity. It was characteristic of this completely new industry that the depression which hit the economy in the early years of its development did not affect its growth.

In the nature of things, completely new products can hardly be claimed for the *furniture industry*. Nevertheless, several new trends can be observed, not to mention a general improvement in product quality. In the 1920's, most of the output consisted of complete room furnishings

---

[21] Cf. A. Mebius, "Något om fanerindustrien i Sverige och utlandet," *Kommersiella Meddelanden* (1931), Nos. 3–4.

[22] Production is based on the utilization of lumber mill shavings and/or roundwood which is, popularly speaking, milled, ground, and pressed into boards of various degrees of hardness. Three grades are distinguished: porous, semiporous, and hard boards. For additional information on the production methods, cf. A. Eriksson, "Några uppgifter om wallboardindustrien i Sverige och utlandet," *Kommersiella Meddelanden* (1938), No. 2, p. 65.

of the same style, usually big, heavy, and designed for old-fashioned housing.[23] In the upholsterers' shops of the time, production was organized along craft lines and their most important product was leather furniture. In the early 1930's, the switch to one-piece furniture began.[24] Upholstered easy chairs and sofas were increasingly manufactured in factories buying the unfinished frame from outside suppliers. Easy chairs and sofas with spring seats on the American pattern were also introduced at this time. This new spring-seat furniture became known in Sweden primarily under the Dux brand name. The switch to one-piece upholstered furniture was due in part to the type of apartment housing built in this period. The new small apartments could seldom accommodate the old massive furniture sets and did not provide separate studies, dining rooms, bed-rooms, and so forth. In the 1920's, wholly new types of specially designed office furniture were also introduced. Furniture specifically designed for office use had previously been relatively uncommon. As a rule, ordinary study or lounge furniture was used. With the interest in modern office organization that began to emerge in the 1920's, these were no longer satisfactory.

The important process innovations in the *building joineries* were connected with the organization of series manufacturing, frequently accompanied by product standardization. Mechanization became more extensive, particularly in the export branches. There were no revolutionary new machines. The so-called dovetailing machine, a German innovation with a multitude of uses, should perhaps be mentioned. Initially, standardization concerned mostly the factory-made doors and windows. The beginnings of this movement were hesitant and ill-defined and it is, therefore, difficult to date. The best estimate would be the late 1920's.[25] It spread gradually through the industry without becoming truly general. Only in the 1940's did standardization become the rule among the building joineries.

The thorough-going transformation of production makes a meaningful estimate of output per man-hour impossible. Installed horsepower per worker cannot be estimated separately for the two main branches. For the two together, it rose from 1.7 in 1919 to 2.7 in 1939.

Series production had existed in the *furniture industry* prior to World

[23] But the production of matched sets of furniture did not have a long history behind it. When furniture production was initially industrialized, the decisive role was played by single-piece products and most of all plain wooden chairs. Cf. T. Gårdlund, *Industrialismens samhälle*, (Stockholm, 1942).

[24] Cf. E. Miltopæus, "Något om svensk möbelindustri," *Teknisk Tidskrift* (1930), No. 23½, A 340; G. Johansson, "Efter 1930," *Form* (1938), No. 6 [cf. also *Möbel-världen* (1938) No. 8]; and E. Ljung, "Varför är möblerna dyra?" *Industria* (1946), No. 4.

[25] Serious consideration of the problem began, however, within the "Committee on Standards of Swedish Industries" (Svenska industriens standardiseringskommission) already in the early 1920's. Cf. *Teknisk Tidskrift* (1921), No. 20.

War I, but the practice of long runs had spread very slowly.[26] This development accelerated in the interwar period, however, and was quite advanced by the end of the period. As a consequence, specialization began to characterize the industry although it was not yet dominant. New machines—generally of the same types as those introduced in the building joinery industry—were important but not revolutionary. Their introduction was frequently connected with the switch to series manufacture. Apart from the dovetailing machine, the hydraulic veneer press and some entirely new types of driers were of particular significance to the furniture branch, as were cellulose varnishing and spray painting. All these innovations occurred in the 1920's. Most of them came from the United States, where they had been developed in the automobile and aircraft industries.[27] Finally, one innovation from the late 1930's, namely, the so-called drygluing method, should also be mentioned.[28] Output per man-hour cannot be meaningfully estimated for the furniture industry. The index of horsepower per worker has already been discussed.

Neither industry provided any dramatic examples of the negative effects of the development process. The steadily shrinking market for paneled doors and the corresponding expansion for flush doors was a characteristic phenomenon of this type, but the process was completed only in the 1940's. The old parquet blocks were superseded by laminated floors in the late 1930's. For the rest, the negative development effects were noticeable chiefly outside the building joinery industry proper. The growing importance of prefabricated houses and fixtures caused a decline in joinery work on the construction sites and, indirectly, a decline in the production of those intermediate products which the joineries and lumber mills had previously supplied to the on-site joiners and carpenters. The same thing occurred where factory-made doors and windows were adopted.

In the furniture area, complete furniture sets and leather pieces were replaced to a certain extent by series-manufactured upholstered and single-piece furniture. The ordinary study and lounge furniture, which had been in use in offices, etc., far into the 1920's, gave way to specially designed office furniture. Movable wardrobes and, in particular, linen cabinets were forced out by factory-made, built-in closets. As a material, oak gave way, slowly but surely, to birch and elm, just as inlaid and carved furniture gave way to clean and plain designs. Most of these developments took place during the 1930's, though the pioneering work had been done in the late 1920's and had been publicly demonstrated at the Stockholm exhibition of 1930. In the area of production processes,

---

[26] Cf. S. Ålund, "Möbelindustrins uppkomst och första utveckling i Virserum och Tibro," *Möbelvärlden* (1946), Nos. 4 ff.

[27] Miltopæus, *op. cit.*

[28] Cf. "Torrlimning," (unsigned) *Möbelvärlden* (1938), No. 3.

series manufacture and resulting specialization led to a slow relative decline for the unspecialized producers. Cabinet-making, as a craft, held its position surprisingly well however.

The interwar development of the furniture industry was predominantly of the demand-pull type; in the joineries it was mainly of the supply-push type. The furniture industry was by and large protected from foreign competition so that the great expansion of construction activity, the 50 percent increase in the annual number of marriages, and the higher living standards would have caused a strong expansion even in the absence of innovations. For the new or quite young joineries, on the other hand, new products were decisive in actively expanding markets. The organized home-ownership movement could hardly have become so extensive had it not been for the prefabricated frame houses. Factory-made fixtures created their own market at the expense of on-site joinery. The general renovation of retail store premises in this period was closely connected with the modernization possibilities offered by the new fixtures. There was no product innovation of corresponding importance in furniture—the growth of the upholstered furniture sector did not expand the furniture market as a whole to the same extent. Cabinetmaking, to repeat, did not disappear. Nor did upholstered furniture speed up the modernization of old homes in the way that new store fixtures accelerated the modernization of existing shops. If certain subsidiary branches are considered in isolation, there are, of course, some supply-push cases. Obviously, demand-pull was particularly strong in office furniture. The rapid expansion of national and local government administration contributed heavily to the growth in demand. There was a similar case of strong, and pure, demand-pull in the area of school furniture. The new office furniture did not cause "bureau formation"; neither did factory-made school furniture cause school construction.

The relationship between demand-pull, on the one hand, and the introduction and dissemination of innovations, on the other, which played an important role in the development of the engineering industries, did not play a significant role in the woodworking industries. These industries were composed of many small, similar firms producing the same products; competition was markedly free with little rigidity in customer relations. This meant intensive price competition which, in turn, meant that the direct link between demand-pull and innovative activity was weak. The indirect link by way of profits and liquidity was probably stronger. But this mechanism was not of much importance either—despite the growth of demand, most firms in the industry were in unsatisfactory shape in both these respects.

The innovating firms showed respectable earnings records but this could not make up for the low earnings of the great majority of firms. Although earnings may have improved toward the end of the thirties, dividends typically remained very low. Except in plywood, wallboard, and parquet, there was practically no effective, organized curtailment of competition. The question of why profits were not better under the prevailing conditions of demand-pull is of great interest, but an answer must await the analysis of the following chapters.

The Pulp Industry

Output as well as the number of workers grew in all three main branches of the pulp industry during the 1920's. Output continued to increase through the 1930's, but the work force stagnated. Sales increased,

FIGURE 13
Output and Exports of Pulp, 1919–39

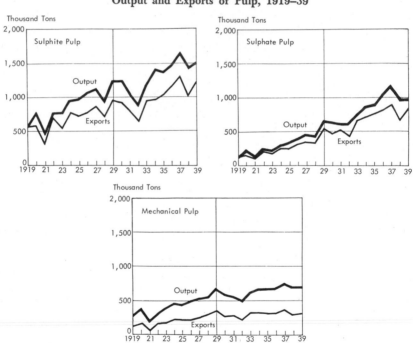

SOURCES: *IS* and *HS.*

both at home and in export markets. The sulphate pulp branch was the most progressive, with sulphite pulp second. Although the mechanical pulp industry expanded greatly in the 1920's, it stagnated in the next decade. The development of output and exports is summarized in Figure 13.

Quantitatively, the old products dominated. One very important primary innovation dating from 1920 should be mentioned, however,— namely sulphite pulp for rayon production. Even though this so-called viscose pulp required little more than a special boiling and bleaching of the sulphite pulp—and perhaps had been produced before—the first delivery explicitly labeled "rayon pulp" seems to have been made in 1920.[29] The output of this new product expanded considerably throughout the interwar period, and a significant secondary innovation followed in the 1930's with the introduction of refined cellulose (i.e., a specially prepared pulp for the production of celluloid, film, plastics, and so forth). There were many other secondary product innovations but none that demanded completely new production equipment. Rather they were based on new ways of boiling and bleaching the pulp. In the early 1930's bleached sulphate pulp, produced with the new methods, was a noteworthy and successful novelty that came to be used in the production of paper and paper products of all types.[30] There were important advances in sulphite production also at this time. A type of pulp, intended specifically for wallboard production, was a purely Swedish novelty (Asplund pulp) from the late 1920's and mid-1930's, and must be considered a primary innovation.

Oddly enough, there were no great novelties in pulp by-products in the interwar period. The impetus which the production of such by-products received during World War I did not lead to further development, except in a few cases. One reason for this was that obstacles were created by legislation sponsored by farm and temperance groups.[31] The exceptions comprised mostly a number of chemical products based on sulphite alcohol. These innovations occurred in the very beginning of the interwar period and to some extent in the mid-1920's. Developments in this area, however, gained real momentum only during World War II.

All three branches of the pulp industry achieved exceptional improvement in production processes throughout the interwar period, although they were not as revolutionary as the introduction of the chemical processes a generation or so earlier. The most important innovations, apart from those already mentioned, which resulted in new products were (a) friction barking, which replaced knife barking and resulted in a raw material saving that was badly needed because of increasing scarcity; (b) fuel-saving improvements which, among other things, made the mills self-supporting with respect to steam heating; (c) drying with fans; (d)

---

[29] Cf. E. Bosæus, *Utveckling av produktion och teknik i svensk massaindustri 1857–1939*, (Uppsala, 1949). Also W. Améen, "Silkesmassa, översikt av silkesmassans utveckling sedan dess första framträdande som råmaterial för konstsilke," *Cellulosa och papper*, (publ. by the Swedish Association of Paper and Pulp Engineers: Stockholm, 1948).

[30] One precondition for the uptilization of these new methods was the availability of corrosion-resistant steel due to innovations in the steel industry. Cf. Chap. 8, p. 160, and R. Söderquist, "Blekt sulfatmassa," *Näringsliv och kultur, en samling uppsatser*, (Stockholm, 1945).

[31] Cf. Bosæus, *op. cit.*

labor-saving transport equipment; and (*e*) automatic production control. Great advantages, finally, were realized in the boiling and bleaching stages of the chemical pulp processes through extensive investment in valuable equipment of acidproof steel, equipment made possible by innovations in the steel industry.[32] A characteristic feature of this innovation process—which affected all stages of production from the barking of the logs to the packaging of the pulp—was that the really important advances, particularly in the 1930's, resulted from systematic scientific research and not just from pragmatic experimentation in the plants. Another remarkable development in this connection is the disappearance in the same period of the industry's earlier tradition of secretiveness.

The new processes are clearly reflected in the output per man-hour index and, also, in the near doubling of units of installed horsepower per worker. With output per man-hour in 1929 set equal to 100, the index shows 60 in 1915, and 172 in 1939. The index is significant because output is not too heterogeneous. The index errs, if anything, on the low side since the process innovations were often combined with at least secondary innovations which tended to improve the quality of output. The shift from unbleached to bleached products should be mentioned in this connection.

Negative development effects were of little consequence in the pulp industry. Improved product qualities did, of course, displace the older product grades, but this was not a very dramatic process. Nor was the negative component very prominent in the area of production processes.

The products that were new to the interwar period—such as viscose and refined cellulose and also the new type of bleached sulphate—to a large extent created their own markets, but they did not dominate the development of the industry as a whole. Instead, the new processes were the predominant feature. They led to a great expansion of exports, both through the improved quality of products that they made possible and by offering greater opportunities for engaging in price competition in a world market characterized by falling prices. At the same time, the industry also benefited from strong demand-pull, at least in the domestic market. This was to a large extent a result of the growing interest in, and need of, paper for packaging purposes, and demand-pull was consequently particularly strong in the sulphate branch. Thus the rapid supply-push expansion of the paper and cardboard industry (see below), caused by the product innovations in those areas, led to strong demand-pull for the pulp industry. The interaction between the two industries went both ways, however—the new bleached sulphate, for example, created new opportunities for the packaging industry. The rapid growth

---

[32] For a more detailed discussion of technological developments, cf. Bosæus, *op. cit.*, and Améen, *op. cit.*

of the newspaper industry, on the other hand, was relatively independent of improvements in the pulp industry and should, therefore, be regarded as a "pure" demand-pull phenomenon. An important factor here was the brand-name system which emerged along with the packaging industry, and which led to increased advertising and consequently to a growing demand for newsprint.[33] These demand-pull conditions were indirectly of great importance to the dissemination of the innovations.[34]

Considering the new products and processes, the demand-pull, and the relative insignificance of negative development effects in the product area, higher average profits might have been expected than were in fact earned.[35] Competition in the interwar years, and particularly in the 1930's, was stronger than before World War I, when profits attributable to innovations dominated the picture in an entirely different manner. It is worth noting that, in contrast to other industries, returns were no higher in the 1930's than in the 1920's. They would, indeed, have been very low had not the process innovations been both important and numerous. At the same time, it should be emphasized that the markets, especially for sulphite and mechanical pulp, were supported by European cooperation in the form of quota or price agreements, especially from the mid-1930's on.[36]

The Paper and Cardboard Industry

In this industry both work force and output grew in the 1920's; in the 1930's, the work force stagnated but output continued to increase at a rapid pace. Markets for all of the more important types of paper expanded throughout the interwar period both at home and abroad—most strongly for the finer grades. The rate of expansion was approximately the same in export markets as in the home market; the domestic market may have expanded somewhat faster in the 1930's (see Figure 14).[37]

Product developments were characterized by many new and varied

[33] Cf. J. Rausing, "Cellulosaexport och varudistribution," *Studier i svenskt näringsliv, tillägnade Jacob Wallenberg,* (Stockholm, 1942).

[34] Compare the previous comments on the analogous phenomenon in the engineering industries. While the comments made about the engineering industries hardly apply at all to the millwork and furniture industry, they do apply by and large as they stand to the pulp industry. Cf. also Streyffert, *op. cit.,* and Svennilson, *op. cit.*

[35] A fairly detailed study covering the 1920's has been made by Th. Streyffert, "Den svenska träförädlingsindustriens räntabilitet och produktionskostnader," *Svenska Skogsvårdsföreningens tidskrift* (1933), No. 3.

[36] Cf. news items on this in the various volumes of *Svensk Pappermassetidning,* and E. Ruist and I. Svennilson, *Den norrländska skogsnäringens konjunkturkänslighet under mellankrigsperioden,* (Stockholm, 1948) pp. 37–46.

[37] Cf. R. Hellberg, "Pappersindustriens roll i det svenska näringslivet," *Svenska Pappersbruksföreningen 1923–1948, Minnesskrift vid 50-årsjubileet* (Stockholm, 1948).

FIGURE 14
Output and Exports of Paper and
Cardboard, 1919–39.

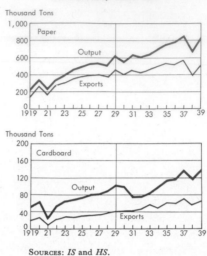

SOURCES: *IS* and *HS*.

qualities of paper but these could generally be produced with equipment
no different in principle from that previously used. Paper was adapted
to steadily more numerous uses, particularly in connection with the development of the graphics industry and the paper and cardboard processing
industries. There were, on the other hand, no great primary product
innovations except the coarse paper sack and asphalt paper. Some of
the secondary innovations from the 1920's, such as greaseproof paper
and kraft wrapping paper, might however be considered as bordering
on primary innovations. The new bleached sulphate became of great
importance to the paper mills.

Attempts at standardization of products, with respect to both sizes
and grades, began in earnest in the early 1920's. While achievements
in this area were less than spectacular, there was still considerable success
in counteracting the increasing proliferation of types and grades of products that customer demands tended to bring about.[38] These efforts prevented the development of an uneconomic fragmentation of production
in the mills.

There were no revolutionary advances but there were a great number
of improvements in the area of production processes.[39] At almost all
stages of the production process, machines were improved. The better
grades of paper that were now demanded required improvements in water

---

[38] Cf. "Svensk pappersstandardisering, Affärsekonomis bordssamtal om pappersstandardisering," *Affärsekonomi* (1942), Nos. 9 and 11.

[39] Cf. E. Schiller, "Pappersindustriens tekniska utveckling," *Svenska Pappersbruksföreningen 1923–1948* (Stockholm, 1948).

purification and better Hollanders (i.e., the machine preceding the actual papermaking machine in the production process). The papermaking machine was equipped with a new apparatus for removing impurities and was redesigned in many details, making possible faster operating speeds and better product grades. Advances in production and quality control were also significant.

The increasing mechanization of the industry was reflected in a near doubling of the units of installed horsepower per worker. The output of the paper industry is more heterogeneous and difficult to compare over time than that of the pulp industry. The margin of error involved in any index of output per man-hour is necessarily considerable. An attempt at estimation, using conventional methods, yields a result of 57 for 1915 and 131 for 1939 (1929 = 100). This sizable increase reflects, but does not exaggerate, the importance of the process innovations which took place in the industry.

No important commodity groups were on the negative side of the development process. The only item worth mentioning in a schematic survey is sulphite wrapping paper, sales of which declined somewhat as a consequence of the especially great advances in the kraft paper area. Since the process innovations were all secondary, there were no particularly dramatic examples in this area either.

The industry experienced strong demand-pull through the better part of the interwar period. At times, however, continued expansion was contingent on the process innovations. This was particularly true in the late 1920's and early 1930's, when price competition in export markets was fierce, and important customer countries increased their tariffs on paper. The development of the newspaper and magazine industry and the rapid expansion of the paper and cardboard processing industry are good indicators of the demand-pull that dominated the rest of the 1930's. This demand-pull, moreover, was the foremost driving force behind the innovations, both in the product and in the process area. The need for more and more paper, and for more and more kinds of paper, necessitated a steady stream of changes and improvements in production processes, product grades, and product types.[40] At the same time, supply-push impulses emanated from the innovations, but these were of relatively limited significance since the struggle between old and new products took place mostly within the individual paper mills. The encroachment of paper products on various textile markets (tablecloths, napkins, handtowels, and so forth) took place mainly in the 1940's. Large cotton or jute sacks had lost ground to kraft paper sacks in the 1930's, just as wooden kegs had been replaced by coarse-grade paper sacks for cement in the 1920's.

---

[40] Cf. Schiller, *ibid.*

In view of the prevalence of cartels in domestic markets—and to some extent also in export markets—it is strange that profits in the paper and cardboard industry were not better. These cartels were certainly not completely effective, but they did succeed rather well, at least in certain areas.[41] During the depression of the early 1930's, however, the industry reported relatively acceptable earnings.

The Paper and Cardboard Processing Industry[42]

New products requiring new specialized equipment were instrumental in the rapid growth of this industry, which in this respect affords a contrast to the paper industry proper. Although soft cardboard was a well-known product at the beginning of the period and found a few new uses, hard cardboard and the so-called solid board were introduced after the end of World War I and became very important in one area after another. Other great advances in the area of paper and cardboard packaging were achieved around 1930. At the initiative of the industry, more and more products came to be marketed in ready-made, specially designed packages. This led to immense gains in the efficiency of distribution. Together with the spreading brand-name movement, it was to be a fundamental influence on the development of many industries as well as on other areas of the economy and society. The rapid proliferation of paper and cardboard articles for advertising purposes and similar uses should also be mentioned. Finally, there were many novel products for modern office use.[43]

In the area of production processes, several new machines were introduced, some of which were prerequisites for the new products. Continuing substitution of machines for manual labor took place even in those lines in which there was no drastic change in the nature of the product—for example, in the manufacture of bags and envelopes. In many mills this was connected with the introduction of assembly-line techniques based on time studies.

A meaningful estimate of output per man-hour cannot be made for this heterogeneous branch, where production was so radically transformed

---

[41] On this topic, cf. L. Sjunnesson, "Svenska Pappersbruksföreningen 1923–1947," *Svenska Pappersbruksföreningen 1923–1948*, and H. Gemmel, "Tredje sektionens betydelse för svensk finpappersmarknad," *En bok om papper, tillägnad C. J. Malmros av AB Klippans Finpappersbruk* (Uppsala, 1944).

[42] All goods for which cardboard or paper constitutes the main raw material have been included in this category. Kraft paper sacks constitute one exception and have been put in the paper industry (cf. above). This product could, of course, also have been considered as belonging to paper processing.

[43] A perusal of the volumes of *Affärsekonomi* from 1928 on will give a good survey of the supply-push innovations that took place in the paper-processing and cardboard-processing industry.

in some areas. Installed horsepower per worker increased from 0.4 in 1919 to 0.9 in 1939, which gives some indication of the role played by the process innovations mentioned.

In the main, the negative effects of these developments had their impact outside the industry itself. One may note that the output of paper bags did not decline despite the partial displacement of bags by specially designed packages. The reason was, of course, that the consumption of bags also depended on the growing total volume of retail trade. The rapid development of the paper-packaging industry led, on the other hand, to stagnation for many parts of the wood-packaging industry. Even here, however, the expansion of the economy as a whole meant that considerable room remained for the old product lines.

The above-mentioned strong supply-push was accompanied by considerable demand-pull during the entire interwar period —particularly so during the 1930's. The growth of the economy meant a growing freight volume and hence a growing demand also for the older packaging products of the paper and cardboard processing industry. The industry was, in part, closely connected with the graphics industry, and the rapid development of the latter was another important factor.

Confectionery Industry

There were no significant new candy and chocolate products, although a few fruit preserves products of some importance—mainly new types of fruit juices, jams, and so forth—were developed. On the other hand considerable development in the mechanization both of production proper and in packaging occurred. The only negative development effect worth mentioning is the displacement of manual production methods. Since output developments were rather heterogeneous, the estimate of output per man-hour is a doubtful indicator, but the increase in the index from 75 in 1915 to 169 in 1939 (1929 = 100) must still be regarded as significant. The growth in number of horsepower installed per worker from 0.9 in 1919 to 2.5 in 1939 reflects the role played by mechanization.

The candy industry developed primarily in response to the demand-pull generated by the country's general economic growth and the commercialization of the rural areas. The growth of output at a rate faster than that of income must be attributed mainly to these factors and doubtless to the considerable income elasticity of demand for these products. The demand-pull was obviously of greater importance than the innovations, although quality improvements resulted in a certain supply-push. The marked decline in imports in the 1930's was to some extent a consequence of supply-push of this sort, but most of it was simply the result of the decision of a foreign exporter to locate his manufacturing operations within Sweden. Only in the fruit preserves branch can one regard the supply-push elements as predominant. Here a market for the industrially manufactured products was created in part by displacing household production. Although this development may not have proceeded very far before World War II, it was nevertheless in full swing.

This industry can hardly be classed with the more profitable ones in the period between the wars. Dividends were small. The general picture of its development would lead one to expect better profits. Competition was free and strong, however, and it was, as a rule, easy to expand output.

Mineral Water and Soft Drinks

As a branch independent[44] of the breweries, this industry was rather insignificant at the beginning of the interwar period.[45] Subsequently, it grew rapidly in terms of volume of output, even though the share of the breweries in the total output of soft drinks increased. Important product innovations, which must be regarded at least as secondary, brought improved types and qualities of products. These were introduced with intensive advertising following the end of World War I, and they contributed greatly to the rapid expansion both within and without the breweries. The growth in the output of soft drinks became especially prominent in the 1940's, when the output of mineral water—which had grown at a comparable rate in the interwar period—stagnated.

While this development was mainly the result of the state of military preparedness and of the tax policies of the time, it was also connected with new products.[46] Product and process innovations combined to keep

---

[44] "Independent" here means separate plants. Many of these, however, belonged to breweries and still more of them came to do so during the interwar period.

[45] The production of soft drinks is based on extracts and concentrates of a variety of types. At the beginning of the interwar period, these were to a large extent imported but have later increasingly come to be produced domestically both independently of and in connection with the bottling of soft drinks. The product innovations in the mineral water and soft drinks industry mentioned below refer to the use of new extracts and concentrates. With few exceptions, these have during the whole period been sold to producers all over the country without the use of tie-in clauses in contracts. At the same time the bottling plants have as a rule bought their liquid carbonate from independent carbonate producers.

[46] Since the excise taxes were imposed per liter of output, the cheaper mineral waters were harder hit than the more expensive soft drinks when these taxes were raised in several stages during the 1940's. But other factors probably also contributed to the drop in sales of carbonated water. One such factor was the reduction of the adult ration of hard liquor from four to three liters a month. Probably even more important was the emergence on the market of the so-called folk-cognac (the popular term, approximately rendered as "bum brandy" is more descriptive). There was less hard liquor available for mixed drinks and the quality of the "bum brandy" was such that it had to be mixed with sweet soft drinks in order to eliminate the taste—to the extent that gin was not used instead, in which case sweet soft drinks were also required.

prices down, and increase the market for soft drinks. This supply-push expansion seemed to take place particularly at the expense of beer, which was becoming steadily more expensive. At the same time, however, strong demand-pull—due to the growth of national income—was also a very important factor.

Following epoch-making pioneering work in the early 1930's, new processing methods were of great significance, particularly with regard to the mechanization of the rinsing, filling, sealing, and labeling stages. This largely paralleled developments in the breweries. Installed horsepower per worker nearly tripled, the increase being especially rapid in the 1930's. The output per man-hour index rose from 100 in 1920 to 162 in 1939 (1929 = 100). Furthermore, distribution became considerably more efficient, mostly through the substitution of trucks for horse-drawn vehicles.

Negative development effects are revealed mainly in the disappearance of older product types and in the decline of manual production methods in favor of mechanized production methods—a very noticeable trend in some areas.

The earnings of the independent soft drink producers were apparently fairly good. In the 1920's, this was partly due to the existence of a cartel which held prices relatively high, while in the 1930's process innovations and demand-pull factors appear to have been more important.

The Canning Industry

Product and process innovations in the canning industry were closely interwoven. The novelties which were of most importance to the industry's interwar development, however, had been introduced before World War I. The production of tinned semipreserves dated from the 1880's— the founding period of the canning industry proper. Fully preserved canned goods had been produced since the 1890's, but their great potential began to be realized only when the so-called autoclave made sterilization in open vats unnecessary.[47] This innovation, which was decisive for the subsequent development of the industry, was introduced in Sweden immediately prior to World War I. Difficulties with tin canning, however, held back developments during the war. The very rapid expansion which the fully preserved fish and vegetable foods—and somewhat later also canned meat—achieved in the interwar period was based, therefore, on quite young products and processes. Considerable quality improvements and a whole range of both fully preserved and semipreserved canned goods constituted secondary innovations of great importance to the con-

---

[47] Semipreserves are not sterilized and consequently cannot be stored for more than six months. The sterilized preserves, on the other hand, may be stored almost indefinitely.

sumption of canned foods in the country. But it could hardly be claimed that the process innovations were either numerous or especially significant in the interwar period. Growth was most rapid in the 1940's. A meaningful comparison of output per man-hour cannot be made because of the rapid expansion of the new, fully preserved goods. The interwar increase in installed horsepower per worker was insignificant.

There were no negative development effects worth mentioning. Manual production methods were displaced slowly since process innovations were rather insignificant.

Although demand-pull was strong, especially in the 1930's, as a consequence of the general increase in the nation's living standard, the fully preserved foods and the new types of products quite obviously had a marked supply-push effect. The fact that factory-canned goods to a considerable extent had replaced home-made preserves in the interwar period supports this contention, even though the most rapid development in this area occurred in the 1940's.

Earnings were very good during most of the period and particularly in the depression years, 1931–33. Only in the mid- and late 1930's did hardening competition squeeze profit margins in the older firms to some extent.

Cotton Manufacturing[48]

There were hardly any new products of great significance in this industry. But there were a number of quality improvements, such as the introduction of sanforized textiles in the 1930's. A shift toward lighter, pressed, and printed cottons also took place, partly in connection with the increasing use of rayon silk[49] and rayon wool.[50] At the same time cotton goods encroached on some of the earlier woolen markets, as exemplified by the use of blue twill in work clothes, a development dating from the 1920's. To some extent the expansion of cotton goods was caused by the very rapid modernization of the industry. While ring-spinning was not an interwar novelty in the cotton textile industry, the modern multiple-loom system was introduced in the 1920's and came into general use in the following decade. The importance of this system as an innovation is reflected in the fact that, according to Industry Statistics, the number of looms could be reduced by 25 percent between 1929 and 1939 despite a strong increase in output. The organization of production according to modern principles was also carried out earlier and faster than in the woolen industry, which did not to the same extent rely on a

---

[48] The structure of the cotton textile industry around 1936–38 (partly in the context of its historical background) is discussed in Kristensson, *Studier i svenska textila industriers struktur*, (Stockholm, 1946).

[49] Synthetic silk yarn was, however, not produced within the cotton textile industry, while this came to be the case with synthetic wool yarn during the 1930's.

[50] Cf. Kristensson, *op. cit.*, pp. 256 and 320 ff.

relatively few staple commodities. This took place in the early 1920's and to a large extent with the help of American experts—an initiative subsequently copied in many other areas. The rise in the index of output per man-hour shows the importance of these modernization efforts. The computation of this index along traditional lines yields a reasonably meaningful result for the cotton textile industry. The index had reached a value of 154 in 1939 compared with 85 in 1915 (1929 = 100).[51] Installed horsepower per worker increased by nearly 25 percent in the interwar period.

Heavier textiles gave way to lighter ones. Rayon-silk yarn, for example, was substituted for cotton yarn in the manufacture of stockings (see the hosiery industry). High quality cotton fabrics declined relative to new lighter, pressed, and printed cotton and woolen goods. Similarly, woven cotton underwear lost ground to the hosiery industry, and cotton sacks to paper sacks. Negative development effects in the area of production processes were undramatic.

Demand-pull was insignificant during the 1920's due, among other things, to foreign competition. It became strong in the 1930's however. The increased protection against foreign competition which resulted from the depreciation of the *krona* played a certain role in this connection, but imports remained substantial. The expansion of the entire economy was the most important demand-pull factor. At the same time, the innovations were fairly important. Relative or absolute price cuts, made possible through modernization, expanded the markets for cotton fabrics and helped stave off foreign competition. But the new products were not in themselves important enough to give the industry's development the marked characteristics of a supply-push process. The new fabrics for work clothes may seem to constitute an exception, but growth in this area was in fact caused mainly by the innovations that took place in the clothing industry.

Earnings in cotton textiles were rather low during the 1920's—it should be noted that taxable income at the end of the decade was substantially below reported earnings—but improved subsequently, particularly in the pioneering firms. No serious attempts at organized curtailment of competition appear to have been made.

Ready-Made Clothing

Throughout the entire interwar period, the clothing industry progressed more rapidly than almost all other industries. Innovations were both great and numerous. A whole range of new machines and new

---

[51] Kristensson, *op. cit.*, pp. 258 ff., has reworked the *IS* data in order to obtain, among other things, figures on output per man-hour. His results show a particularly strong increase in output per man-hour for the weaving mills, which should be attributed in part to the above-mentioned innovations.

types of machines complementing the ordinary sewing machine played a predominant role in the development process from the early 1920's onward. Especially important were a completely new type of buttonhole machine, machines for sewing on buttons, for quilting and for perforating, and also the mechanical pressing machines. Assembly-line "tempo work," with a far more detailed division of labor than before, was introduced after the American pattern. Its adoption was made possible by important changes in rate-setting rules agreed to in the collective bargaining of 1926. Assembly-line techniques were first introduced in men's clothing but were rapidly disseminated and became of revolutionary significance. The period of the late 1920's was one of systematic modernization involving production planning and time and motion studies. The rise in productivity was undoubtedly very rapid, but it cannot be measured on the basis of existing source material. One might refer to a series of striking data on the operating speed of the new machinery, but an ordinary estimate of output per man-hour becomes meaningless in view of the improved product quality and the transformation of industry output. The growth in horsepower installed per worker, from 0.12 in 1919 to 0.21 in 1939 is indicative however.

Assembly-line techniques could be utilized to full advantage only in firms of considerable size. Simultaneously with their introduction, a significant change took place in the area of distribution. Large sums were invested in brand-name national advertising, directing attention to the vast improvements in the quality of ready-made clothing which had occurred since World War I with the use of the new machinery and to the new styling. American styles had largely displaced the earlier ones in which German influence dominated. Some firms combined these promotional efforts with a drastic cut-price policy designed to expand their markets over the long run.[52] Clothes made to measurement—in effect a new product—were another novelty with supply-push potential dating from the early 1920's.

There was also a series of other product innovations in this decade. Improvements in the type and quality of ready-made clothing were such that new products were, in effect, created. Blue twill work clothes and overalls patterned after those of the U. S. Army were introduced immediately after the war and shortly thereafter achieved a quantitative breakthrough concurrent with the introduction of new machinery. Modern sport clothes were another novelty. Significant expansion in the ladies' clothing industry accompanied the change-over to production of reasonably priced daytime dresses instead of the more expensive party dresses. This change occurred in the 1920's, and was subsequently greatly encouraged by the availability of suitable fabrics (i.e., rayon wools and

---

[52] This cut-price policy is reflected with unusual clarity in Figure 12 (the series for men's clothing).

rayon silks in particular). These textiles also gave rise to new kinds of underwear. Finally, in the early 1930's, the production of ladies' suits began on a significant scale.

The positive development component was thus very evident, both with respect to new processes and new products. Negative development effects were most noticeable in the decline of home sewing on contract for industrial firms. To some extent this development was due to the increasing number of new types of machines. In addition, the improved quality of products—partly due to these new machines, partly to the pioneering efforts to promote certain brand-names—played an important role in the decline of home sewing. In the plants, manual methods disappeared gradually with the introduction of new machinery, but this development caused little attention since no unemployment resulted.

Tailoring should also be mentioned in connection with the negative development effects. By and large, however, this branch maintained itself rather well, at least so far as the number of independent tailors was concerned. As far as can be judged, the number did not decline, possibly not even in relation to the population, although the number of tailors' employees certainly declined. The clothing industry recruited a large proportion of its supervisory employees from among the former employees of independent tailors during the whole interwar period, and thus it did not have to undertake the training of supervisors. Although the number of seamstresses moving among the homes of customers appears to have declined both relatively and absolutely, the total number of seamstresses probably did not. The reason why craft-type production of clothes was far from displaced by the rapidly expanding clothing industry was the strong decline in home sewing for domestic needs—or perhaps, rather, the change of its character from sewing of new clothes to repairs and alterations. Another reason was, of course, the strong demand-pull that characterized the whole interwar period, which left room for tailoring.

Demand-pull continued to be strong, particularly during the 1930's when foreign competition declined in several areas. The general rise in income levels, especially in the lower brackets, also played a very important part. Demographic developments—the growth in productive age groups, particularly the increasing number of women in the labor force—were other extremely significant factors. Nor should the commercialization of rural areas and increased rural-urban contacts due to automobiles and buses be overlooked. This development opened a large, partly new, market for ready-made clothing. Several other factors could be mentioned, but taken one by one they were of less significance. One of them which was of great importance for heavier ladies' clothes might be mentioned, however, as an example of demand-pull. The Swedish market for ladies' clothing had been supplied to a rather large extent by imports from Jewish-owned German firms located mainly in Berlin. The genocide of German Jews which began in 1933 spelled the disappearance of these firms. This created a vacuum in the Swedish market which was filled by Swedish producers.

In evaluating the significance of the young products and of the process innovations relative to the demand-pull factors, it appears that the growth of the industry was dominated by the supply-push effects of the product innovations, although demand-pull was at the same time of very considerable importance. When many people came to have a wardrobe containing more than one everyday suit, this was not just because of rising incomes. Consumption of ready-made clothing increased at a much higher rate than real national income. The indirect connection, through profitability and liquidity, between the demand-pull and the innovations, which had been emphasized in connection with several of the previously discussed industries, was undoubtedly of considerable importance to the ready-made clothing industry. The direct connection seems to have been of little significance, however, since market conditions apparently would have permitted the individual firm to expand at almost any rate.[53] The entire industry was characterized by great mobility and by the total absence of organized restraints of trade.

In view of the nature of this development process, the favorable earnings record of the industry is not surprising. Profit margins must be considered quite adequate, at least during the 1930's, and it is worth noting that this was true also for the depression years.

The Hosiery Industry

The rapid development of this industry was to a large extent based on the new rayon-silk goods, in particular rayon-silk stockings, which were new to the interwar period.[54] While cotton hosiery was not new in this period, it came into increasing use in areas previously dominated by woolens. At the same time, knitted goods in general tended to displace, for example, woven underwear made of cotton or linen. Secondary innovations were of considerable importance with regard to both new products and new processes. Product quality was generally improved, and many new product types were added, particularly in sportswear and so-called light hosiery goods.[55] In general, these new products were developed in connection with the introduction of new machinery. Many new machines—some of a general purpose character and others used for quite specialized processes—were introduced in this period; examples are the so-called interlock machine and the machine which made possible full-

[53] Cf. Chap. 7, p. 132n.
[54] Cf. Kristensson, *op. cit.*
[55] Cf. Kristensson, *op. cit.*, p. 328.

fashioned stockings of high quality. The efficiency of a number of other machines was considerably improved, and many other new types were introduced. Frequently these new machines were the necessary prerequisite for the new "light" types of goods just mentioned. Since a meaningful index of output volume cannot be obtained, a quantitative measure of the effects of these process innovations in terms of output per man-hour cannot be made. There was no increase in the amount of horsepower used per worker during the interwar period since the innovations in this industry had very little to do with substitution of machines for human muscle.

The negative aspects of the development process were seen in the loss of markets of certain hosiery goods to the new rayon-silk underwear. Satin dresses as well as certain heavier hosiery goods, mostly woolens, were other examples. Cotton stockings also lost out in the competition with the new rayon-silk stockings. Although the industry at times had problems due to rather heavy import of cheap, foreign hosiery, the interwar period was on the whole characterized by demand-pull. The growth in domestic demand was based on much the same conditions as in the case of the ready-made clothing industry, and the demand-pull was strongly enhanced by the 1931 devaluation of the Swedish *krona*. But the demand-pull coincided with the strong supply-push effects of innovative activity. Looking at the interwar period as a whole, we must put this latter factor in the foreground. This was particularly the case with the rayon-silk hosieries, but the general encroachment of hosiery goods on the previous markets for woven cotton and linen goods should also be considered. With regard to rayon goods, product innovation was combined with successive price cuts due to the fall in raw material prices, which proceeded despite increased tariffs, excise taxes, and exchange depreciation.

While foreign and domestic competition did permit rather healthy rates of return in hosieries of woolen and cotton, it prevented high average earnings. In contrast, producers of rayon goods, and particularly of silk stockings, enjoyed more favorable conditions. Not only was the basic innovation a profitable one, but this branch experienced demand-pull which became particularly strong in the 1930's. This branch of industry, moreover, was already at an early stage characterized by well-developed production techniques and efficient organization, a fact which contributed to the high earnings. No effective, organized curtailment of competition existed.

Light Chemicals

No significant primary product innovations occurred in the production of oils, soft soap, soap, perfumes, or cosmetics. In the paint and varnishes industry, on the other hand, the cellulose enamels and varnishes and the synthetic lacquers were great novelties. Production of the former began in Sweden in the 1920's following the fundamental innovations accomplished primarily by the American explosives industry.[56] Since the war, this industry had had surpluses of gun cotton and had systematically sought new uses for it. At the same time, oil enameling had proved a bottleneck in the rapidly expanding American automobile industry. The synthetic lacquers were introduced in Sweden somewhat later than the cellulose enamels.

Whether or not a great many secondary innovations could be claimed for the toiletries and soap industry depends on whether all the newly introduced brand-name products, which were the objects of exceedingly intensive advertising, should be regarded, in a sense, as new products. To a far lesser degree, this problem also arises with regard to paints and varnishes.

Process innovations were quite significant, even though one cannot point to any revolutionary developments. Output per man-hour cannot be measured meaningfully, but an increase in the installed power per worker of 33 percent in paints and varnishes and of 50 percent in the rest of the light chemical industry is of some significance.

With regard to negative development effects, old products were displaced primarily in one area, i.e., the spirit and oil enamel paints. These were displaced by cellulose and synthetic lacquers, particularly after production of efficient spray guns began in Sweden in the early 1930's. The case was different with oil paints, since these had no good substitutes in exterior painting. Production by pure handicraft methods survived stubbornly, particularly in the soap works and the cosmetics branch, even though such techniques gradually lost significance as brand-name products, with their costly advertising, came to dominate the market.

Strong demand-pull dominated in the development of oils, soft soap, soap, perfumes, and cosmetics, although to some extent the cosmetic products did create their own markets by intensive advertising.[57] This was the case, at least, from the mid-1920's on. Demand for these products, many of which must be characterized as luxury goods, depended primarily upon the growth of national income. The devaluation and the

---

[56] The production of ready-mixed oil paints and oil enamel paints, which existed in the beginning of the interwar period, was a fairly simple operation combining imported pigments with imported linseed oil and in the enamels, with copal. The oil varnishes were at the same time produced quite simply by boiling the imported linseed oil.

[57] One should note that advertising was a supply-push factor only to the extent that it increased total industry sales. This was undoubtedly the case, e.g., with hair tonics and toothpastes. To the extent that it only expanded the market for the particular product being advertised at the expense of another product of the industry, it did not expand the market for the industry as a whole.

new revenue tariffs also played a part. In the paints and varnishes branch, on the other hand, supply-push factors must be regarded as predominant. The new cellulose and synthetic lacquers not only displaced the older spirit and oil enamel paints but created a larger market for paints generally. They made painting an easier task, and customers came increasingly to insist on the attractive surfaces that the new paints made possible.

It is hardly possible to make a summary statement on the overall profitability of these very heterogeneous light chemical industries. Rates of return differed to an unusual extent between the branches and, in addition, fluctuated widely from one time to another. In soaps, cosmetics, and so forth, the simple production technology made for strong competition and narrow profit margins,[58] but good profits could, on the other hand, sometimes be made on certain specialties. Except in the case of the soap works, there does not seem to have been an effective, organized curtailment of competition, if the results of some sizable mergers are disregarded.[59]

---

[58] Cf. Hj. Heimbürger, "Några drag ur tvättmedelsindustriens utveckling och samma industris ställning i vårt land," *Teknisk Tidskrift* (1925), K 25.

[59] Cf. *SOU* (1940, No. 35), p. 74.

8 Analysis of Stagnating and Progressive Industries

The Iron and Steel Works[1]

After World War I, it proved impossible to maintain pig iron production at the prewar level. Foreign importers were less dependent on Swedish charcoal pig iron[2] because of the great advances that had been made abroad in both operation of blast furnaces and oxidation. Other old products were affected in a similar way. Producers of puddled iron were hard hit and, to a lesser extent, so were producers of acid Bessemer steel. These products, on retreat ever since the turn of the century, now lost most of their remaining markets. Not only the output data but the price series give unmistakable evidence of the situation. Attempts were made to mechanize the production of these products, but they were not of decisive significance and could not save the situation. Even the production of crucible steel lost ground because steel of the very highest grades could now generally be produced by more efficient methods. The expansion of the foreign steel industry, with its numerous large-scale units, put many of the Swedish commercial iron firms under severe competitive pressures even in their home market.[3] The producers of commercial iron

---

[1] The output produced by the manufacturing divisions of steel mills has been included here and in the following discussion of the steel industry, although it should really have been put under iron and steel manufacturing.

[2] Great advances have been made abroad particularly in the production of electric steel, and this has meant a decline for crucible steel. Since electric steel was far less dependent on high-grade Swedish pig iron, this development meant a severe setback for the Swedish producers of pig iron for export. Cf. N. Danielson, "Något om den tekniska utvecklingen inom järn- och stålindustrin under världskriget och tiden därefter," *Teknisk Tidskrift* (1923), A 43.

[3] "Commercial iron" is the term used for ordinary steel for construction purposes and the like which does not stem principally from charcoal-produced pig iron

had previously enjoyed significant tariff protection which had made possible the rapid development of this branch from the 1890's up to World War I despite its comparative disadvantages.

Many iron works were expanded during the war in order to replace imports and to support the defense effort. At the end of the war, these firms had to contend with competition from an expanded foreign industry while effective tariff barriers were considerably lower than before. The duties were specific, rather than *ad valorem*, and the purchasing power of the Swedish krona had declined. The picture of stagnation reflected in Figure 12 in the production of basic open-hearth and Bessemer ingots as well as in the output of rolled wire and hot-rolled sheet steel is, therefore, easily understandable.

Furthermore, the wartime expansion of capacity created two quite specific problems in the ensuing peace years. During the war, the engineering industries had expanded, and their expansion had in part been geared to the production of armaments and import substitutes. Two sets of factors, one direct and one indirect, therefore combined to cause the concentration of the iron and steel works on such production. Directly, the industry had to replace imports and to provide for the increased need for iron and steel by the armed forces; indirectly, the exceptional demand for semifinished products by the heavy engineering industry, the steel industry's largest customer, further enlarged the demands put on the industry. The difficulties which the industry had to face after the end of the war boom were correspondingly multiplied. The conversion of the heavy engineering industry to peacetime production usually could not be a simple matter of a return to prewar production patterns. As a rule, these firms had to engage in a costly and time-consuming process of adjustment to the new situation. During this period, there was a persistent structural imbalance between the iron and steel works on the one hand and the heavy engineering industry on the other. The capacity of the former was too large in relation to the latter. This structural imbalance characterized the situation during the major part of the 1920's. The situation was the more serious because of the large investments made during the war which had often been financed by borrowing.[4]

---

of low phosphorus content. "Swedish quality iron" (or high-grade steel), on the other hand, refers to sheet steel or wrought iron products that could not meet customer specifications unless produced almost exclusively from phosphorus-poor, charcoal pig iron. During virtually the entire interwar period, most Swedish steel mills produced quality steel intended for tools, machines, and construction purposes. Only 10 or so, i.e., not much more than one-fourth, concentrated exclusively or almost exclusively on commercial iron. A few had their output about equally divided between the two kinds of steel.

[4] Cf. "Betänkande med förslag angående åtgärder till handelsjärnhanteringens stödjande," *SOU* (1928, No. 6). The problems of the commercial iron mills led to

Developments were more favorable for the producers of high-grade steel, although they also suffered from the same structural imbalance in relation to the heavy engineering industry as the commercial iron producers did. This branch could be characterized as stagnating, but hardly as contracting, during the 1920's. This is evident, for example, from the output data on acid open-hearth ingots. Prices were relatively stable. To a great extent, increased specialization and concentration on particularly high-grade products accounted for the degree to which these firms succeeded in compensating both for the structural imbalance at home and for the frequently weakened competitive position in world markets of their old products which innovations in the foreign steel industry had brought about. In giving ground in areas where new methods abroad made possible a product of comparable quality but lower price than the Swedish product, the industry followed a pattern from the prewar period. In this connection, the conversions and expansions of plants for the production of rolled products are particularly worthy of attention (see, for example, the time series on output of cold-drawn pipe and pipe parts and on cold-rolled thin plate).

Other, equally significant, development trends in steel manufacturing are not as clearly reflected in statistical time series. Beginning in the early 1920's, a whole array of very significant innovations was introduced in the producton of acidproof and stainless steel;[5] the same was true for the production of razor blades, machine-tool steel, suspension steel, and steel wire.[6] Other examples were the ferro-alloys and electrical steel, and, last but not least, the hard metals developed in the field of powder metallurgy. Although these more or less novel products and processes did not turn the stagnation of the twenties into expansion, they did prevent an actual contraction. At the same time, the industry stood ready for strong expansion in the following decade.

The postwar decade was a period of preparation in another exceedingly important respect. As had been the case in so many other industries, the modernization of the firms producing high-grade steel had been made more difficult in the beginning by the lack of risk capital. Many steel works had suffered serious losses during the deflation, and some of them were taken over by creditors, primarily banks. Through the combined

---

repeated but resultless pleas for increased tariff protection, and their situation was painted in the darkest colors. Cf. Gust. Ekman, "Framtidsutsikterna för Sveriges järnhantering," *Affärsvärlden 1901–1926. Första kvartseklets festskrift* (Stockholm, 1926), and in the same volume H. v. Eckermann, "En exposé över svensk järnindustri," and G. Dillner, "Järnhanteringens tullfråga."

[5] The decisive advances in the area of stainless steel occurred when a quality of steel was obtained that made a cutting edge possible and when new methods reduced the costs of production.

[6] Cf. C. G. Brodén, "Verkstadsteknik förr och nu. Maskiner och verktyg," *Tekniken och framtiden*, Vol. II, (Stockholm, 1945), esp. p. 576.

efforts of management and banks, a very extensive and thoroughgoing modernization was gradually and successfully completed. These efforts were particularly intensive in the last years of the 1920's. Modernization meant increasing specialization, particularly in the case of the rolling mills. On the marketing side, worldwide sales organizations were built up. In part, this was motivated by the increasing share of manufactured products in total output, as in the case of the Sandviken company 50 years earlier, but it was also motivated by severe competition from the new products and methods of foreign firms. It was this foreign competition, rather than competition among Swedish steelworks, that stimulated the process innovations.

In summary, large segments of the Swedish iron and steel industry went through a period of transition in the 1920's. On the one hand, the situation was characterized by negative development effects in the form of disappearance or weakening of old markets for many products, while many of the steelworks were at the same time encumbered by large debts. Furthermore, the balance between the ironworks and steelworks and their most important domestic customers was not good. On the other hand, new production processes, new products, and new markets were introduced or created both in the iron and steel industry itself and among its important customers. These factors, however, did not have time to become of decisive importance in this decade.

From the accounts of the situation given by industry spokesmen in the 1920's, one might have expected the advent of the worldwide depression to signal the *coup de grâce* to the severely strained Swedish steel industry. Actually the industry weathered the crisis fairly well. The innovations, which have just been discussed, proved to be essential to its ability to do so. One finds only a few strategic malinvestments, made during the 1920's, which created difficulties during the following depression.

The radical changes in the conditions facing the industry, which characterized the 1930's, are clearly visible in the growth of both employment and output for most individual products. The just noted reorganization, particularly of some of the firms producing high-grade steel, and the new production processes that simultaneously began to emerge provided the foundation for the development of the steel industry during the 1930's. A rough estimate of output per man-hour shows the index (1929 = 100) rising rapidly from a value of 78 in 1915 to 143 in 1939. The growth in installed horsepower per worker is also significant: from 9.5 in 1929 to 10.9 in 1930. The corresponding number for 1919 was 7.4.

Many of the new high-grade steel products did well in export markets and also broke new ground in the domestic market while contributing to the expansion of the heavy engineering industry. The commercial iron branch exhibited a development of particular interest. Producers in this sector began to run their mills considerably closer to capacity limits than before, despite the fact that market prices stayed at a level which had previously been considered too low for profitable operation to be possible. This effort reduced unit costs to such an extent that good results were achieved even during the depression years, and the Swedish works captured a significant portion of the home market from their foreign competitors. The internal modernization of the works played an important role in this connection, while the commercial iron producers did little in the way of specializing among themselves.[7] It was gradually realized that commercial iron production did not necessarily require operation on a gigantic scale.

FIGURE 15
The Steel Market, 1913–39.
(Output, imports, exports, and consumption
of wrought and rolled iron and steel)

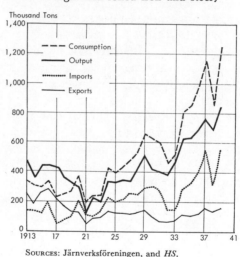

SOURCES: Järnverksföreningen, and *HS*.

The development of the iron and steel industry, however, was also stimulated by the demand-pull which began to set in, both abroad and at home, a few years into the 1930's, and which made this decade such a contrast to the 1920's. The foreign demand-pull directly stimulated the high-grade steel sector and, indirectly, the commercial iron sector since it meant gradually less severe foreign competition for the Swedish home market. As the 1930's wore on, it became more and more closely connected with the international armaments boom. The domestic de-

---

[7] Cf., e.g., "De svenska järnverkens prispolitik," *Affärsvärlden* (1936), No. 49.

mand-pull was part of the general expansion of the Swedish economy. Toward the end of the 1920's, moreover, the structural imbalance between the steel industry and the heavy engineering industry had been redressed due to the reconversion of the latter to peace conditions and, also, to the general expansion of the economy.

Figure 15 presents a summary picture of the development of exports and output in the iron and steel industry since 1913. The contrasts between the two interwar decades are clearly evident. This contrast is also apparent in data on rates of return. Earnings in the Swedish steel industry were low in the 1920's, good in the 1930's. The high figures for taxable income in the late 1930's are particularly worth noting. Dividends remained small however. The striving for financial consolidation was notably strong everywhere. Agreements tending to curtail competition cannot have been of much consequence. In export markets, especially, competition was severe.

The Chinaware and Ceramics Industry

With regard to household porcelain, one must, to a certain extent, take product innovations into account, for there was a new orientation toward artistically designed household articles. These, however, did not demand any new productive equipment, nor did they achieve major quantitative significance. Floor and wall tiles were of relatively greater importance, but although there were several novel items, their production was not based on new equipment either. Electrical and sanitary porcelain products were not new to the interwar period. In the case of electrical porcelain, however, production began only in the last phase of World War I, and a rapid expansion took place in the late 1920's. The safety fuse was a new product in the early 1930's. The production of sanitary porcelain had previously been discontinued but was taken up by other producers in the mid-1930's, from which time output grew at a rapid pace, with the result that imports lost considerably in importance. Thus expansion was very rapid in both cases, and it was based on quality improvements as well as on great improvements in production technology. The tunnel kiln deserves special mention since it proved to be of the greatest importance. The first such kiln was built in 1923 and was followed by several more modern ones 10 years later. The first electric kiln was completed in 1925.[8] Only toward the end of the interwar period, however, did the dissemination of the electric kiln begin to gather speed. There were advances also in the production of household chinaware, but innovations in this area were of more limited significance. For exam-

---

[8] A. S. W. Odelberg, "Elektriska ugnar för porslinsbränning," *Teknisk Tidskrift* (1927), K 61.

ple, electric firing could not be introduced into the manufacture of hard porcelain. Neither did mechanization become general because, among other things, the available types of machinery were of too large a capacity for many firms.[9]

The 1930's saw a renovation of large segments of the chinaware and ceramics industry. This is, to some extent, reflected in the increase in the output per man-hour index to 115 over the base year of 1929, and also in the growth in installed horsepower per worker from 0.98 in 1919 to 1.38 in 1939. With respect to the output per man-hour index, a comparison with 1915 is not very meaningful since the changes in the composition of output during and immediately after the war were too drastic, due, among other things, to the introduction of electrical porcelain.

The only negative development effect worth mentioning on the product side concerned the stove tiles which went the way of the tile stove. The struggle between new and old production processes was undramatic. One may note, however, that the old-fashioned, fuel-consuming kilns, which still existed into the middle 1920's, contributed considerably to the difficult economic situation of the industry.

In the household china branch, the Swedish firms experienced no demand-pull at all during the 1920's, while demand-pull for the rest of the industry was weak despite the high level of construction activity. The greater part of the interwar period was characterized by idle capacity. This was primarily because of the large volume of imports, particularly of household and sanitary porcelain. Importation remained possible and, from many points of view, advantageous despite higher tariffs on household chinaware. Even during the latter part of the 1930's, complaints about foreign competition and occasionally of dumping were heard everywhere. The situation of the domestic industry was eased, however, when foreign exporters responded to the threat of further tariff increases by raising their prices on exports to Sweden.[10] This contributed to some extent to the more favorable development of the industry in the 1930's. But it was not of great consequence since all foreign competition could not be warded off in this manner. The whole industry advanced not only in response to the growth of demand but also as a result of important process innovations which played a decisive role in increasing the industry's ability to meet foreign competition in the 1930's.

Earnings were low in the first half of the 1920's but fairly satisfactory in the second half. It should be pointed out, however, that taxable income, as well as dividends, remained relatively low in the late 1920's. In the 1930's, returns improved considerably as a result of the innovations

[9] Cf. Gösta E. Sandström, "Keramiska industrin i nya fina kläder, *Industria* (1948), No. 12.

[10] Cf. K. E. Gillberg and C. Bohman, *Konsumentkooperationen och det enskilda näringslivet* (Stockholm, 1948), pp. 134 ff.

and, to a degree, of demand-pull. Typically, rates of return were rather well maintained during the depression years.

The Glassworks

No new products of any great importance were introduced in the four main branches of this industry. While an increased concentration on artistic design on the part of the craft glassworks did lead to new products in a sense, this development was not based on new production equipment. Production of ground plate glass for mirrors was begun on a small scale in the early 1930's. The Swedish producers of this product found it exceedingly difficult, however, to meet foreign competition without tariff protection. The large glass beer jugs which replaced the old wooden kegs in the early 1920's were typical of the modest product innovations in this industry.

With respect to production processes, there is at least one very important innovation to be noted, namely, the mechanization of the manufacture of plate glass. This was achieved for the first time in 1927 and led to almost a doubling of output per man-hour in the pioneering firm.[11] From 1923, when machine plate glass was first imported to Sweden on a large scale, to 1935, when the foreign and Swedish machine-made product entirely dominated the market, the price of plate glass declined by more than a third. The glass container works had been mechanized immediately before World War I; new types of machines were introduced throughout the interwar period, making it possible to produce an increasing number of types of bottles, and so forth, by mechanized techniques. This development is reflected in the considerable growth in both installed horsepower and output per man-hour during the 1930's. The output per man-hour index shows a value of 78 for 1915 and of 136 for 1939, 1929 being the base year; installed horsepower per worker increased from 0.60 in 1919 to 0.96 in 1939. Since the craft glassworks, producing household and ornamental glass, had continued their largely unaltered, nonmechanized glassblowing techniques throughout the interwar period, the developments reflected in the above indices were confined to the other branches of the industry.

As for negative development effects, there were no particularly noteworthy developments in products. The glass container producers, it is true, did encounter competition from the paper-packaging industry in some of their markets, and this contributed to the relatively modest growth of this branch in the 1930's. But this development did not represent a loss of old markets but a decreasing share of the generally growing packaging market. With respect to production processes, the most impor-

---

[11] Cf. *Rationaliseringsutredningens betänkande*, Vol. II, *SOU* (1939, No. 14), p. 112.

tant development was the decline of nonmechanized plate glass production.

In the 1920's, the industry benefited very little from demand-pull. This was true not only of the plate glass branch, which had to contend with a large volume of imports, particularly before 1926 when tariffs were raised, but also for the other branches, where imports were of less consequence. In the 1930's, on the other hand, a combination of exogenous factors contributed to a more rapid growth of the industry's markets. Thus, construction activity and the rate of household formation increased, while imports encountered new obstacles after the economic and political changes of 1931 and the tariff increases in subsequent years. Nevertheless, all four glassworks branches suffered from idle capacity. It was the demand-pull of the 1930's and not innovations that ended the stagnation of the household glass branch. The dominant factor in its expansion was domestic consumption, and it did not increase more rapidly than real national income or the rate of household formation. In the other branches, in contrast, process innovations must be regarded as of great importance since, among other things, they enhanced the possibilities of effectively competing with imports. It is indicative of the changed position of these branches that some of their output even was exported during this period.

Earnings were modest in this industry through the greater part of the interwar period. This was particularly the case with the household glassworks, where, in contrast to the other branches, no effective collusive agreements existed. Although such agreements did not in themselves ensure good returns for the plate glass and glass container branches, one still finds a considerable improvement in their returns during the 1930's, an improvement which probably must be ascribed in part to the existence of such agreements. Also, dividends, which had been low for a long time, became relatively satisfactory in this period. There can be no doubt, however, that process innovations were the most important factor. The profits of the pioneering firms were particularly high. These firms did well even during the general depression years of the early 1930's.

The Woolen Industry[12]

There were few, if any, completely new products in this industry. Many product innovations based on rayon fibers must be regarded at least as secondary, however.[13] Rayon wool, originally referred to as cellu-

---

[12] The structure of the woolen textile industry around 1936–38 has been studied in detail by F. Kristensson, *Studier i svenska textila industriers struktur* (Stockholm, 1946), who to some extent also considers its historical background.

[13] The volumes of *Skandinavisk Tidskrift för Textilindustri* (Sk*TT*) from the late twenties give captivating testimony to the growing importance of this new product.

lose wool or staple fiber, was a secondary innovation in relation to rayon silk and was introduced somewhat later, around 1930.[14] The success of the rayon products meant a general shift toward lighter fabrics, and at the same time, it led to increasing product differentiation and more fashion-oriented production programs. The increased use of worsteds also played a major role in this connection. The industry adapted to these changes relatively slowly. As a result, the volume of imports was considerable during the 1920's and late 1930's.

Improvements in production technology and productive organization were of great importance, although they proceeded in general at a slower pace than in the cotton industry, which was less dependent upon changing fashions. The modernization process began in earnest in the late 1920's, partly in connection with a number of mergers, and continued throughout the following decade by means of systematic production planning, time-and-motion studies, and so forth. The most important developments were, however, the conversion to the so-called multiple-loom system, made possible by the increased automation of looms, and advances in dyeing and finishing techniques. As in the cotton industry, the number of looms could be reduced despite the increase in output. The changeover from self-acting mule frames to ring spinners—an innovation that approximately doubled the output per man-hour in spinning[15]—had begun in the production of worsted yarn long before World War I. For carded woolen yarn technical conditions were less favorable, and the changeover to ring spinners had hardly started even at the outset of World War II. Even so, innovations in the spinning mills were more significant than in the weaving mills. With regard to distribution, the industry began in the mid-1930's to free itself from its dependence on the textile wholesalers.[16]

The importance of the great process innovations, which the new products to a large extent made necessary, is clearly evident from the increase in output per man-hour that took place in the 1930's. The total input of man-hours remained approximately constant in this period. It should be noted that the index used understates the actual increase in output per man-hour because of the shift in the composition of output toward lighter fabrics demanding a relatively higher labor input.[17] Conventionally computed, the index shows a value of 93 in 1915 and of 122 in 1939 (1929 is again the base year). Installed horsepower per worker increased insignificantly between 1919 and 1939. This undoubtedly indicates that

---

[14] Cf. *SkTT*.

[15] Cf. Kristensson, *op. cit.*, p. 185.

[16] Cf. G. Rosenberg, "Nyborgs Yllefabriks nya distributionssystem: En omvälvning inom beklädnadsbranschen," *Affärsekonomi* (1936), No. 14.

[17] Kristensson, *op. cit.*, pp. 122 ff., 181, and 184 ff. Kristensson has provided the most accurate calculation of output per man-hour possible. His figures have been calculated utilizing the *IS* raw data.

mechanization of production was less important than organizational innovations.

On the negative side of the transformation process, there were no dramatic developments. Producers of carded woolen yarn, of fabrics made from such yarn, and of heavier worsteds had problems due to the shift, mentioned earlier, toward lighter hosieries and lighter woolen fabrics and the consequent growth in demand for finer yarns and worsted fabrics, a demand that was in part met by imports. The situation in the woolen industry in the 1920's was dominated by the struggle between the coarser product grades and the new products. Better housing as well as other factors caused a rapid growth of markets for the new products, and the woolen industry found it difficult to adjust quickly enough to these developments.[18] Still, the use of rayon staple did not encroach very far on the use of wool. Woolen muslin, which almost completely disappeared, is an exception.

The 1920's were a period of transition for the woolen industry, and its stagnation during this decade must be seen primarily against this background. On the one hand, pressure from foreign competitors had increased due to the effects of World War I inflation on effective tariff rates and as a result of the shift of demand toward lighter products. On the other hand, the industry still had to catch up with contemporary technology and organization in many areas. In part the situation was reminiscent of conditions in the iron and steel industry. The Swedish firms experienced very little demand-pull stimulus during this decade. Plant capacity was far from fully utilized. The growth of domestic demand was to a considerable extent met by imports. In the following decade, in contrast, the industry benefited considerably from demand-pull, and the utilization of capacity increased commensurately. First, foreign exporters faced a more difficult situation, particularly after the undervaluation of the Swedish krona in relation to the British pound in 1933, although foreign competition gradually became stronger and imports revived. Second, the overall development of the economy meant a more rapid rate of growth in the demand for textiles than during the 1920's. This was due particularly to the extraordinarily rapid growth of the ready-made clothing industry. This development, in which innovations in the woolen industry played at best a minor role, made it possible for the woolen cloth manufacturers to standardize output and to work with longer production runs to a greater extent than previously. The growth of the woolen industry in this period is thus a good example of a relatively passive adjustment to a growth in demand caused by exogenous factors.

---

[18] Cf. the contemporary statements of the business situation faced by the woolen textile industry in the twenties, e.g., in *Texilarbetaren* and in *SkTT*.

The considerable improvement in earnings from the low levels characteristic of the 1920's—particularly noticeable in taxable income—to the levels common in the 1930's is hardly surprising in view of the above sketch of the industry's development. The improvement between the late years of the 1920's and the early years of the following decade is particularly worth noting. The superior performance of the pioneer firms is clearly evident. There does not seem to have been any successful attempts at organized curtailment of competition.

Gloves, Leather, and Fur Products

No completely new products of importance were introduced in this industry, but the production of leather clothes and of coarser work gloves increased very rapidly from a very modest beginning to a rather large volume. This was true also of fur products, where there were numerous new types of product, and where, in particular, the production of full-length, ready-made fur coats and fur trimmings for coats increased from an insignificant level as late as in the mid-1920's to become of considerable importance in the 1930's and even more so in the 1940's. In the 1930's, in particular, the industry emphasized furs of more inexpensive pelts and succeeded, in this way, to introduce fur products for everyday use. Up to this time, almost all fur products had been luxury goods. All three main branches of the industry showed an increase in mechanized production at the expense of manual methods, although there were no new revolutionary machines or methods. In the manufacturing of furs no standardization of output or thoroughgoing mechanization was possible since pelts proved too heterogeneous a raw material. In this respect, the conditions were more favorable in the curing of skins and in the manufacture of gloves. The production of gloves, in particular, was simplified in several important respects. Output per man-hour, however, cannot be computed in a meaningful way for this industry. Installed horsepower per worker increased from almost nothing in 1919 to 0.3 in 1939.

The negative development effects are evident in the decline in the output of fur capes, fur collars, muffs, fur caps, half-length fur coats, and so forth, while the production of full-length fur coats and coat trimmings was expanded. The industry's stagnation during the 1920's was essentially a result of the decline in demand for the former group. Declining demand for men's fur coats also played a role. The fur manufacturing industry showed a completely different composition of output at the end of the interwar period from that at the beginning. There were no such changes of corresponding significance in the skin-curing and glove-manufacturing branches.

There is no doubt that the demand-pull generated by rising incomes was of considerable importance to the fur products branch in the 1930's.[19] At the same time, however, there were a number of strong supply-push elements in the picture which, taken together, must be regarded as the predominant influence on the development of this branch. Among these were improvements in quality and styling, price reductions in many cases, and advertising. Most important in this connection were the "young" ready-made, and relatively inexpensive fur coats.

In other branches of the industry, however, it is fairly obvious that demand-pull dominated. New products were not of comparable importance, and the growth of these branches was clearly connected with the advent of the automobile era. In glove manufacturing, the output of high-quality gloves for town wear and similar luxury items paralleled the general rise in incomes, just as the output of heavy-duty work gloves paralleled the industrialization of the economy.

There is little doubt that at least for many fur-goods producers rates of return were rather good. But risks were great in a branch so sensitive to cyclical fluctuations, so exposed to wide fluctuations in raw material prices and with such a relatively heavy concentration on the production of luxury goods. These factors often led to losses. Negative development effects were apparently seldom serious, since changes in the output mix usually could be accomplished with relative ease. There was apparently no effective organized curtailment of competition.

The Margarine Industry

The conversion from animal to vegetable margarine had been completed before World War I. The new type of margarine almost completely displaced the old one, but animal margarine was still produced at the end of the interwar period for certain special purposes. The margarine industry underwent thoroughgoing modernization of production techniques and productive organization involving improvements in machines, transport, and packaging. To some extent this is reflected in the output per man-hour index, which increased from 60 in 1915 to 106 in 1939 (1929 being the base year). Installed horsepower per worker increased from 1919 to 1929 by 60 percent. The modernization of production was paralleled in the late 1920's by considerable modernization of distribution following the cooperative agreement involving a majority of the industry's firms that was concluded at this time.[20]

The innovations led to sizable price reductions, which expanded the

---

[19] One may note that, whereas the raising of revenue tariffs in the early 1920's discouraged the importation of processed fur products, this did not affect the industry greatly since the tariffs applied as well to the furs which were for the most part also imported. The competition from imports was at times very strong.

[20] Cf. Gillberg and Bohman, *op. cit.*, p. 70.

market for margarine. The decline in raw material prices during the 1920's had the same effect. In the 1930's, the excise tax on margarine introduced by the government worked both directly and indirectly (see below) to restrain further price reductions.

The modernization efforts did much to improve earnings, particularly since the cartel succeeded to some extent in preventing the previously very wide price fluctuations. The cartel, however, could not gain a monopoly position, since KF—the Swedish Cooperative Union—was active in the industry during almost all of the interwar period. Developments in the margarine industry are of particular interest, however, in that rates of return remained above the average level for industry as a whole despite the competition. The reason for this, apparently, was that price competition was not particularly strong. It was reasonable for producers to expect that further price reductions, beyond those actually accomplished, would simply lead to a corresponding increase of the excise tax, since the government's farm policy would not permit butter to be completely displaced by margarine.

9 Analysis of Stagnating Industries

The Brickworks

Pressured by supply-push innovations in other construction material industries, the brickworks were forced into both product and process innovations. Still, the picture is that of a stagnating industry.[1] In the late 1920's, one began to mix sawdust into the brick clay in order to obtain high-porosity brick and lightweight brick.[2] For both these new products smaller sizes were adopted since their insulation capacity was superior to that of older types. Refractory brick was not a novelty in the interwar period, but the importance of this product increased along with the great improvements in type and quality which yielded many kinds of special brick for a variety of industrial purposes. But, typically, these did not demand major changes in plant and equipment.

The changeover from seasonal to year-round operation, and the changes in equipment and so forth which this entailed, was the most important method innovation. The first successful attempts in this direction were made in the late 1920's. Apart from this, advances were few and did not become widely disseminated until near the end of the 1930's. Low

---

[1] Compare the concrete products industry. The decline in the relative importance of bricks was not initially due to low prices on, or a qualitative superiority of, the new construction materials, but instead to the fact that labor costs per square meter of walls were lower. Rising wages for masons thus hurt the brickyards while the competing industries benefited. Cf., *Tegel* (1931), p. 76. On the other hand, the wage rates for concrete work set by the building unions have (to a fairly large extent) adjusted in such a way that the advantages of using concrete have become less pronounced than they otherwise would have been.

[2] Modern steel frame construction has led to a reduced demand for brick of maximum strength, and this also contributed to the growing importance of the new brick types. Cf. *Tegel* (1931), p. 11.

rates of return and inadequate liquidity were among the factors retarding progress. It was frequently very difficult to incorporate the often bulky and expensive new machines and other equipment into the small brick-works of the old type.[3] Progress with the mechanization of the industry is to some extent reflected in the increase by some 50 percent in installed horsepower per worker, though this figure does not reveal the wide variation among individual firms. The output per man-hour index stood at 84 in 1915 and at 107 in 1939 (1929 being the base year).

Product innovations without doubt explain the fact that the industry managed to maintain its position relatively well in the 1930's. Demand-pull was hardly a major factor, despite the growing volume of construction, since the use of other, new materials increased rapidly. In brick roof tiles, however, demand-pull played a certain role because tightened fire insurance stipulations made necessary a general conversion of old thatched roofs.

Returns were very low in the 1920's, except in firms pioneering in the introduction of new processes or in the new porous and lightweight products.[4] Earnings would certainly have been as bad in the following decade, had it not been for the more general dissemination of the innovations. In the late 1920's, serious attempts were again made at cartel cooperation. In many areas this contributed to the improved situation. It is worth noting that in the late 1930's taxable incomes exceeded reported earnings instead of the other way around as had been the case previously. The higher earnings were above all used for the modernization of plants and for financial consolidation. Characteristically, dividends remained small throughout the period.

The Lumber Mill Industry

Employment in this industry remained fairly high in the 1920's, but a considerable reduction took place in the next decade. Of the two main product groups, unplaned products declined while planed products expanded. The development of this industry was further characterized by a considerable decline in the prices of lumber-mill products.

In the lumber-mill industry proper, no product innovations of great significance appeared. Lumber-mill firms, on the other hand, frequently took up the further processing of their products (e.g., the manufacture of prefabricated frame houses, wallboard, coreboard, laminated floor tile, etc.). Developments in the area of production processes during the 1920's

---

[3] Cf. *Tegel* (1930), p. 67, and *ibid.* (1931), pp. 62 and 90.

[4] It is interesting to note that prices on large-size building brick, which had been kept constant for a long time through cartel agreement, fell by approximately 25 percent during 1927. C. A. Strömberg, "Statistisk överblick av tegelindustrien och dess produkter," *Byggmästaren* (1935), No. 3.

were hardly significant either—in any case not until the end of the decade when modernization, especially of the lumberyard work, began. One explanation for this was the lack of capital in a branch where the future seemed beset with uncertainties. In the 1930's, on the other hand, many lumber mills underwent rapid modernization affecting all stages of the production process. Methods of barking were considerably improved, the saws were automated, and saw speeds increased quite dramatically. Improved sawing equipment contributed to this development also. Sorting plants were also vastly improved. Gantry cranes and other transport equipment for handling the lumber in the mills and in the yards were among the most important novelties. Their introduction increased turnover in the yards and made the drying and storing of lumber an acute problem. Technical-structural balance thus required kiln-drying, and kilns were introduced in most mills. Finally, great advances in fuel economy should be mentioned.

These innovations are reflected in the output per man-hour index. With 1929 as the base year, the value of the index for 1939 was 115, while the figure for 1915 was 73.[5] The reduction in the work force in part reflects the same development. Installed horsepower per worker increased by somewhat less than 20 percent in the 1920's but by more than 50 percent in the 1930's. This sizeable increase in the rate of growth of this index is no doubt indicative also. Finally, it should be noted that the so-called circular saws underwent great improvements in several respects. Sawing techniques were improved as well the power sources— diesels or electrical motors—which were often made mobile by using trucks.[6]

Substitutes for lumber products became important in many areas, while at the same time competition in export markets became more severe and the obstacles to international trade grew. The decline of unplaned products was especially severe. Of these, crossties and pit props were the most important—one suffered from the great decline in railroad construction, the other from the difficulties of the British coal mines as well as from the conversion in the mines to concrete props. The production of barrel staves and boxboards, which was important to many lumber mills, also fell off rapidly as a consequence of the growing use of paper and cardboard packaging materials.[7] Small-board sawing of this kind de-

---

[5] The figure 115 may seem low. The explanation is that the innovations were to an unusual extent unevenly disseminated. The difference between the pioneering firms and the great majority was very great and considerably greater than within the pulp industry. Cf. P. E. Werner, "Träbearbetningsmaskiner," *Teknisk Tidskrift* (1936), No. 17, Å 187.

[6] Cf. S. Grundström, "Cirkelsågningen i Norrbottens Iän," *Svensk Geografisk Årsbok* (1949), pp. 267 ff.

[7] Cf. J. A. Sundin, "Utvecklingen inom sågverksindustrien," *Affärsekonomi* (1937), No. 19.

clined generally. With regard to production processes, one notes the diminishing role of manual work in the operation of the lumberyards, while the new methods otherwise displaced older ones in a less noticeable manner.

These innovations were above all designed to make feasible the gradual achievement of reasonably profitable operation of the lumber mills. These efforts took place in a market where output prices were falling almost without interruption while at the same time wage rates and raw material prices rose and a scarcity of lumber made itself felt, particularly in the northern provinces. If Swedish lumber fared relatively well in the world market, it was due to these innovations. Had production techniques in the 1930's remained the same as in the 1920's, the export markets would certainly have been lost. A similar observation can be made of domestic markets: without the innovations, other construction materials would have encroached on the markets to a far greater extent than was actually the case. The absence of demand-pull characterized the entire development of the industry. The lumber mill industry as a whole suffered from excess capacity at the end of the interwar period, as it had at the beginning.

Earnings were exceedingly low in the 1920's.[8] Many firms were able to continue as going concerns only because they combined lumber milling with some other activity, usually pulp production. Where the operation of a lumber mill was based on forests owned by the same firm, this also proved to be a source of financial strength. In the 1930's, the situation improved considerably and, as was the case with many other industries, taxable income typically exceeded reported earnings—a reversal of the relationship characteristic of the 1920's. As has already been suggested, this is explained by those process innovations which, though partially utilized in the 1920's, were generally carried out in the 1930's.

The industry's improved financial situation is explained, however, not only by the process innovations but also by the complementary product lines just mentioned and, from 1936 onward, to some extent by cartel cooperation on an international basis.[9] A number of other explanatory factors can also be adduced. A discussion of these other factors will, however, have to await our study of the transformation process from the standpoint of the development of industry structure. Despite the great improvement in earnings in the late 1930's, dividends were maintained at a low level. Profits were generally plowed back and facilitated the modernization.

---

[8] Cf. Th. Streyffert, "Den svenska träförädlingsindustriens räntabilitet och produktionskostnader," *Svenska Skogsvårdsföreningens Tidskrift* (1933).

[9] Sundin, *op. cit.* Cf. also E. Ruist and I. Svennilson, *Den svenska skogsnäringens konjunkturkänslighet under mellankrigsperioden* (Stockholm, 1948), pp. 32–33.

The Tanneries and the Leather Shoe Manufacturing Industry

This is one of the few industries where doubts may be entertained concerning the right classification. In the shoe manufacturing branch, employment increased rather considerably in the 1920's while output was clearly stagnating. At the same time, however, the trend in the composition of output was toward lighter weight shoes of a higher quality. In the 1930's, output increased more than the work force, but neither variable increased by much, particularly if one takes into account the fact that the figures for 1939 were influenced by the outbreak of war. With regard to the tanneries, output figures show almost exactly the same pattern as in shoe manufacturing, while the work force hardly increased at all. Nor do the statistics for individual products give a clear basis for classification. The two branches have been tentatively grouped here among the stagnating industries on the basis of two considerations. First, the industry's development borders on stagnation, according to our criteria, when its interwar record is compared with the development during the decades preceding 1914. Second, the industry had already during World War I reached a capacity by and large sufficient for its output in the late 1930's. This was at any rate true for the shoe manufacturing branch.[10]

There were no primary product innovations to record in either branch. The improvement in product quality, however, was marked in both cases, and a fair number of new product types were developed, partly as a result of the introduction of new production processes.[11] In the shoe manufacturing branch, cemented shoes and Veldtschoen are particularly worth mentioning.[12] Apart from this, technical advances were most significant in the tanneries without, however, being particularly dramatic even there. Installed horsepower per worker increased considerably during the 1920's but not in the 1930's. By and large the shoe manufacturing industry had the same machine equipment at the end of the interwar period as it had had at the beginning. Upper stitching and punching, however, became somewhat more mechanized. Technological progress was otherwise relatively limited, a fact reflected in the rather small increase in the horsepower-per-worker index. On the other hand, improvements in the organization of production were of considerable significance and took the form, for example, of increased reliance on serial operation and as-

---

[10] Cf. R. Elinder, *Studier i den svenska skoindustriens struktur*, IUI (Stockholm, 1948), p. 14. This work contains a detailed analysis of the leather shoe industry in the late thirties. Articles and news items in the 1919–39 volumes of *Sveriges Läder- och Skoindustri* give a clear picture of the stagnation of the tanneries and leather shoe industry through the entire interwar period.

[11] Elinder, *op. cit.*, pp. 30 ff.

[12] Cf. "Vad en agoman minns," *Svensk skotidning* (1949), No. 23.

sembly-line production and of systematic production planning. Time-and-motion studies were not utilized, however, until the late 1940's.

Neither industry showed much of an increase in output per man-hour. The index for the tanneries stood at 106 in 1939 compared with 71 in 1915 (1929 = 100); the corresponding figures for the shoe manufacturing industry were 100 and 93. But these figures say little more than that the quality of products improved—partly in connection with the trend toward lighter products in both branches and, in shoe manufacturing, toward a more fashion-oriented production. With regard to the latter branch, it is especially important to note the major role played in this development by the rubber footwear industry, which captured a good deal of the market for inexpensive, everyday shoes.[13]

Negative development effects were of considerable importance. The rubber footwear industry expanded in many areas at the expense of the leather shoe manufacturing industry, and thus at the expense of the tanneries also.[14] The trend in fashions from boots to oxfords meant a declining demand for leather suitable for uppers. The most dramatic development took place in the tanneries where the quick-tanning method made the equipment of many tanneries outdated—a process that had begun as far back as the 1870's.[15] In shoe manufacturing, the struggle between new and old methods was not spectacular. Hand-crafted shoes had practically disappeared by the turn of the century. Among the processes that had difficulty surviving in competition (e.g., with the cemented method and the stitch-down method), the turnshoe method and the so-called machine-sewn method should be mentioned.

Product innovation in the two branches did not lead to any significant increase in the consumption of leather and leather shoes. The industry was on the defensive. Without the comparatively modest innovations, both branches would have contracted to the advantage both of imports and domestic rubber footwear production. If one were to classify the tanneries and leather shoe producers during the 1930's as belonging to the slowly expanding industries, the role of the process innovations and secondary product innovations would have to be emphasized.

Rates of return were fairly satisfactory among the larger, modern tanneries but were very low in many small firms.[16] In leather shoe manufacturing, earnings were low during the whole interwar period in almost all categories of firms, and the number of firms that reported losses was large.[17] Dividends were very small. While the large number of family

---

[13] Cf. Elinder, *op. cit.*, pp. 111 ff. and 169.

[14] The cited volumes of *Sveriges Läder- och Skoindustri* provide clear evidence of the hard struggle against the rubber-soled shoes.

[15] Cf. Chap. 5, p. 85.

[16] Cf. *Sveriges Läder- och Skoindustri* (1929), p. 5, and *ibid.* (1937), No. 3, p. 9.

[17] Cf. Elinder, *op. cit.*, pp. 138 ff. Also *Sveriges Läder- och Skoindustri* (1935), p. 3.

firms partially accounts for this observation, it is undoubtedly still indicative of low returns in this industry. There were no successful moves toward organized curtailment of competition. One such attempt was made in the latter half of the 1930's when shoe producers and tannery owners together tried to achieve control of new entry into shoe manufacturing. The results of this effort were of no practical consequence however.[18]

---

[18] Cf. Elinder, *op. cit.*, p. 190.

Part III

Formation, Development, and Disappearance of Industrial Firms in the Interwar period

10 General Survey of Rates of Formation and Disappearance of Firms

A. Issues, Concepts, and the Empirical Data

In Chapters 6 to 9 an outline of the industrial transformation process in the interwar period has been presented together with an analysis of some of its aspects. Following the plan presented in Chapter 4, the main objective of this chapter and the next one will be to study this process from yet another perspective, namely, that of the formation, the development, and the disappearance of firms.[1] From this standpoint, what can be said about the development histories of progressive, stagnating, and regressive industries? Did progressive industries generally show high rates of formation of new firms and relatively low rates of exit, and did stagnating or regressive industries have relatively low formation rates and high disappearance rates? Did industries which showed different types of development, according to the classification in Chapters 6 to 9, differ also with respect to the formation, development, and disappearance of firms? Other related questions pertain to cyclical fluctuations in the formation and disappearance of firms and to the entry size and subsequent development of new firms in comparison with previously existing firms.

A study of these problems leads to yet other questions dealing with the characteristics of different types of firms. To what extent, and in what ways, do new firms in principle differ from old ones? To what extent did the new firms introduce innovations, and to what extent were the innovations introduced by new firms? The underlying issue is not

---

[1] It follows as a corollary to the criteria used in Chaps. 6 through 9 in handling the *IS* raw data that many firms will not fit completely into any one of the given industry categories. Whenever such ambiguities have been significant in a way relevant to the analysis, this has always been made explicit.

only the extent to which material progress has been based on new products, but also the extent to which it has been based on new firms during the relatively short time period considered here.

The data published in the official *Industry Statistics* (*IS*) are of little help in answering these questions. Nor is it possible to obtain sufficient information by further processing the raw data. The published data are inadequate for two reasons: first, because *IS* reports only the net change in the number of firms year by year, but not the total number of new firms or of discontinued firms; second, no inferences can be made on the basis of this source about the role which changes in the number of firms have played in the development of industry output over time. In addition, firms appear or disappear from these records as they make, or fail to make, an arbitrary "statistical threshold"—as a rule put at a market value of annual output of 15,000 *kronor*.[2] Only in exceptional cases does the unpublished raw material give any guidance for judging the year in which a particular firm has been formed or discontinued.[3]

Nevertheless, primary data gathered for *IS* must form the initial foundation for the present investigation. No other previously collected material is available. Questions relating to the quality of the *IS* data are discussed in Appendix 1 of the Swedish edition and may therefore be bypassed here with the general comment that the data are sufficiently representative for the main purposes of the present work, although certain gaps in the coverage, as well as other weaknesses, must be taken into consideration.

The *IS primary material* has been utilized to obtain data on the number of workers and salaried personnel and on the market value of output for the period 1915–42. The specific industries involved are listed in Appendix 1 [in Swedish edition], in which some of the problems met in processing the data are also discussed. This appendix also reproduces the *questionnaire* that was sent to those firms which appeared in *IS* for the first time in 1919 or later, and which, in addition, belong to the industries involved in *project B* of the present work. Firms in industries involved in our *project A* but not included in *project B* did not receive the questionnaire. For the most part, it has been possible to obtain information on "birth years" and "death years" from other sources (Appendix 1 of Swedish edition). Data were obtained for a number of years prior to 1919 and subsequent to 1939, since those firms which were in existence only during the first few, or last few, years of the interwar period would otherwise have been overlooked in many instances. Firms which disap-

---

[2] Cf. Appendix 1 of the Swedish edition.

[3] When Kommerskollegium learns of the existence of a firm for the first time, e.g., through it being included in *Handelsregistret*, the firm is requested in writing to provide information on the year in which operation was begun, on whether it has taken over some already existing plant, etc. Unfortunately, the returns to these inquiries have not been retained for more than four or five years.

peared at the beginning of the period would thus have been overlooked if the market value of their output or the size of their work force had prior to 1919 declined below the "statistical threshold" set by the Board of Commerce. Similarly, firms established prior to 1939 would have been missed if they had not reached the threshold by that year. Despite this, and apart from the question of how complete the *IS* material is, it is likely that the number of firms in existence during these years has been somewhat underestimated. Experience gained from the study of the material for the interwar period as a whole has shown that the length of the period between the time at which a firm was established and the time at which it appears in the official statistics often exceeds one or two years. In some cases, the period is considerably longer. Although the potential error involved is not very serious, some caution should be exercised—particularly in comparing the rate of formation of new firms in the last years of the interwar period with that of earlier years.[4]

It was clear at the outset of this investigation that to gather all of the material according to the principles indicated would be a very laborious undertaking. This raised the question of whether the work could be reduced by using representative samples. Actually, this possibility could be utilized for only a few industries; the main reason for this was that there were not enough firms and the industries were not sufficiently homogeneous. Two considerations were important in this connection. First, the data covered a great number of branches with too few firms in each separate branch to make sampling a reliable approach to a more detailed analysis of the character of the firms. Stratified sampling methods (i.e., sampling based on a prior grouping of the data into sufficiently homogeneous branches) were, of course, of no help here because stratification according to branches could not be achieved in many cases without a detailed study of the entire material—exactly what sampling was supposed to save us from. Second, the desirability of analyzing geographical aspects of the material provided another obstacle because even with considerably larger and more homogeneous branches, the geographical distribution of the firms would have meant too much fragmentation of the basic data. Thus, sampling was used only for obtaining dates of establishment of firms in certain less thoroughly studied branches (the shoe industry, the mineral water and soft drink industry, and the concrete products and lightweight concrete industry). A more simple questionnaire was used in these cases also. These industries are not included in projects A and B [see Appendix 1, Swedish edition].

Processing of those questionnaires which were returned made it possible to determine fairly well the years in which firms were established and discontinued in accordance with certain predetermined principles

---

[4] Cf. Chap. 11, p. 221 f.

(see below).[5] The questionnaires have generally provided the basic material for the analysis. They have, however, been complemented with other information. The Swedish *Commercial Directory* was a most important source. It and several other directories and reference works have been gone through year by year.[6] Information obtained in this way has been compared with that from *IS* primary data and from the returned questionnaires. Additional primary data were gathered through study trips to numerous manufacturing towns, through interviews, and through extensive correspondence.[7] The information gathered by these means, together with other printed sources, has provided the third set of empirical data on which the analysis has been based. Experience has shown that it would not have been sufficient to rely on only one of the mentioned sources or procedures since this would have introduced errors that would have been both intolerably large and impossible to detect. Thus it became evident, for example, that the views of individual entrepreneurs of past conditions in the branch outside their own firms were frequently erroneous. The ability to forget, as well as the tendency to generalize from one's own experiences, is as striking as it is natural. In this connection, therefore, one can only rely on a combination of the testimonies of several persons and established facts. By combining information from different sources in this way, it has also been possible to correct many errors in the statistics, even though it has not always been possible to ferret out all such errors or to obtain and thoroughly corroborate all desired information. Since the reliability of the utilized materials differs considerably from case to case, the reliability of our conclusions is best considered in direct connection with the analysis and the discussion of the results of the investigation.

The gathering and processing of this empirical primary material demanded solutions to a whole array of definitional problems. These questions must be discussed in detail since the definitions adopted are of decisive importance to the statistical picture which emerges from the processing of the data.[8]

The term *enterprise* may refer to (1) a technical entity, such as a work location, or a plant, or it may refer to (2) that financial unit for which it is sought, schematically speaking, to maximize net revenue.[9] An *enterprise*

[5] For the proportion of questionnaires returned, cf. the account given in Appendix 1 of the Swedish edition. This appendix also provides a critical methodological account of the construction of the questionnaires.

[6] An account of these sources and the problems met in utilizing the data is given in Appendix 1 of the Swedish edition.

[7] Cf. Appendix 1 of the Swedish edition.

[8] Readers who have no need to judge the methodological and statistical problems and are interested only in an outline of the main results may—although hardly to advantage—skip this discussion and go directly to section *B*, 190.

[9] Readers who dislike this characterization of "the enterprise" may very well

may also be (3) a legal entity—a firm. A firm may be either an economically and organizationally independent unit or only a legal person with no independent existence in the "financial" sense. An enterprise in the financial sense may thus comprise several firms as well as several plants. This is not necessary, however—it may simply be coexistent with the legal entity and have a single plant. If the "technical" criterion is chosen, the enterprise could never comprise several firms. On the basis of such a definition of "enterprise," however, several enterprises could belong to the same firm as well as to a single enterprise in the financial sense.[10]

The study of the formation, development, and disappearance of enterprises or firms may be based on any one of these three alternative definitions. The third alternative (i.e., enterprise defined as the legal entity) appears to be the least suitable point of departure, although the legal concept of a firm sometimes is a necessary complementary concept. In the present context, the legal definition of "firm" has little analytical relevance apart from those aspects of the problem which can be handled equally well by the use of one or the other of the first two alternatives. Where a firm is also an independent financial entity, the second alternative is equally suitable; where the firm is a subsidiary, the most relevant alternative is the second one when dealing with financial aspects of the problem, and the first one when dealing with the firm as a work location or plant. Alternative 3 may therefore be ignored in the analysis of the formation of firms. But the investigation not only can, but should, be planned with both alternatives 1 and 2 in mind so that the development process may be studied from two different points of view. Each of these viewpoints is significant in itself. In the present work, however, the first definition will be the dominant one.[11] *Except where*

---

interchange it with some other definition with less emphasis on profit maximization. The main consideration is to have a definition referring to an organization in which decisions are to a certain extent made under central direction. The maximization of net revenue need not be the only objective of the management group. Cf. S. Carlson, *Företagsledning och företagsledare* (Stockholm, 1945). Carlson defines the financial, economic-organizational unit of an "enterprise" as "that sphere of action in the economic system within which regulation by the price system is replaced by the control by centrally organized management." (*Op. cit.*, p. 13).

[10] A concrete Swedish case may clarify the implication of the alternatives mentioned in the text. ASEA (Allmänna Svenska Elektriska Aktiebolaget), for example, may be considered as consisting of a large number of "enterprises," in the sense of "plants," some of which are "firms" (Luth & Roséns Elektriska AB, etc.), some not (the plants in Västerås, Ludvika, Stockholm, etc.). Alternatively, one might refer to an "enterprise" with several firms and plants and thus use "enterprise" restrictively as connoting the entire multidivision company.

[11] When the "technical" criterion is the one used, a certain unfortunate incongruence results in relation to everyday usage. Strictly speaking, we should use, e.g., "plant formation" instead of "firm formation." But since everyday usage is anything but decisive on this terminological point, it seems better to avoid such clumsy constructions and to stick with "firm formation." It is still possible to make a special note of those cases in which an already existing firm builds a new plant and to distinguish these cases from those in which a firm is formed at the same time as a new plant by either private individuals or an existing firm. The "technical" criterion is the one used both in *Industry Statistics* (*IS*) and in the 1931 census of firms. In these sources, this criterion is, in fact, the only one considered in contrast to the case here.

a different usage is expressly indicated, the terms "firm" and "enterprise" will refer to a "plant." In certain special cases, however, several plants belonging to the same firm will be treated as one, namely, when they are all situated in the same geographical location.[12] Since in reality most plants are also found to be independent financial entities, this definition leads, in the great majority of cases, to the same results as alternative 2. If special attention is to be given to firms with several plants or to firms which control a group of companies, the financial definition should be used. It will be used here in dealing with enterprises of the type just mentioned, *but only insofar as the analysis of the financial aspects of the problem makes it essential to do so.* This limitation has been imposed here not only because of the necessity of largely disregarding a number of problems, an adequate treatment of which would require far too much space for our present purposes, but also because other investigators are studying Swedish manufacturing from this financial viewpoint.[13]

The distinction between "industrial activities" and "crafts" poses a special problem. It has already been argued, in an earlier connection, that no advantage is gained by basing the distinction on the same general criteria in all cases (see p. 61 fn. 1). Somewhat different distinctions have been found suitable for the analysis of different branches. The definitions which have been chosen, and on which the statistical processing and analysis are based, are reported in Appendix 1 (Swedish edition). Here we need only point out, therefore, that the criteria considered by and large fall into three different categories. As a rule, the concept of "craft" has been related to one or the other of the following: (*a*) repair and service activity, (*b*) organization of production and the distribution of output, or (*c*) the purely technical character of production. In the mechanical engineering branches, for example, firms have been classified under the heading "craft" when all but exclusively engaged in repair activity and when manufacturing has been limited to spare parts needed for this purpose or, at the very most, to production for the purpose of maintaining employment in periods of slack demand for the firm's services. In the clothing branch, as another example, firms have been classified in this way when producing individual pieces to order or short series for direct sale to the final consumer. Finally, the purely technical character of production in combination with sale through the firm's own retail outlet has been the criterion chosen in dealing with firms in the confectionery industry and in the various branches of the chemical industry.

---

[12] While logically unsatisfactory, this exception has been made principally because the statistical raw material is less than dependable in the reporting of each plant when the same firm owns several in the same geographical location. To some extent, however, there is also an analytical reason for so doing since the difference is often minimal between, on the one hand, several plants in the same location and, on the other, several divisions within the same plant. In addition, there is frequently more overlap in management when plants are located in the same town than when they are geographically separated.

[13] Thus studies of this type are being undertaken in the Department of Economics at the University of Uppsala under the direction of G. Lindgren and by H. Hagnell at Svenska Metallindustriarbetarförbundet (Swedish Union of Metal Industry Workers). The latter study is exclusively concerned with the iron, steel, and metal manufacturing industries.

The definition of a firm that has been chosen here makes it necessary to consider the question of in which cases one should refer to a firm as new, i.e., *to the formation of a firm* as opposed to the reconstruction of an earlier firm. On the one hand, it would be inappropriate to exclude from the study of the formation of firms all cases where a plant is taken over from an already existing firm. On the other hand, it would also be inappropriate always to consider, for example, the construction of a new plant to replace an old one as constituting the formation of a new firm.

To begin with, there are certain clear cases of the formation of new firms—i.e., when one or more individuals, or an already existing firm or company group, start a new plant to supplement an old one (but in a different geographical locality) and in premises newly constructed for the purpose or in rented premises not directly taken over from an existing firm. But as soon as the premises, and perhaps also work force and technical management, are taken over, the question arises as to whether the enterprise should be referred to as a "new" firm or not. The best solution seems to be to regard *the bankruptcy of the earlier firm as a necessary condition for referring to a firm as new* in cases of this sort.[14] This would indicate that a major part of the original capital has been consumed, and it seems natural to tie the concept of "new" firm to the injection of new risk capital. Bankruptcy of the earlier firm is, however, not a sufficient condition. One must also require either that the enterprise comes under *new management*[15] or that *product lines belonging to a different major industry branch* become the firm's primary business.[16] When neither of these latter conditions is fulfilled,

---

[14] Unfortunately, the line cannot be drawn at a deed of agreement with creditors even though this, in fact, often amounts to bankruptcy. As a rule, it proves nearly impossible in practice to obtain accurate information on such agreements.

[15] When it is a question of unincorporated enterprises, it will be considered as coming under new management when registered in the name of a new owner. In the case of corporations, a new board of directors will be considered as constituting new management. If the board is not entirely new, changes in the chairmanship and managing director's post may be regarded as decisive. Thus the term "management" is used here not only to denote the top executives but the owners or their agents. To look at the titular owner and the board, respectively, is a makeshift expedient in this context. Such a schematic procedure may obviously be a source of errors of various kinds. It is especially risky whenever there is reason to suspect a "front" of some kind for the real controlling interests. By and large, however, this potential source of error probably lacks any practical significance.

Another problem arises when a bank, for example, is forced to take over the operation of a firm and to hire a new manager. Should one consider new management, and consequently a new firm, as occurring on this date or only at the later date when the bank has sold the firm and the new owner takes over management? The first alternative does not seem acceptable since it is seldom a matter of a new initiative when forced takeover occurs. But if the latter date is considered as the one at which new management takes over and the new firm is formed, the result is an interregnum between the bankruptcy and the formation of the new firm which appears particularly peculiar if the operations were never interrupted. But this still seems the only acceptable alternative. Cf., however, below regarding those cases in which bankruptcy and new management are not to be considered as constituting the formation of a new firm.

[16] Concerning the concept of "major industry branch" ("huvudbransch"), cf. Appendix 1 of the Swedish edition.

the case should be considered to be one of *financial reconstruction*. In many cases, it also seems more appropriate to refer to financial reconstruction rather than to the formation of a new firm, even when new management is brought in after a bankruptcy—namely, when production is kept up without interruption and with the same output mix, when distribution patterns and customer relationships are not disrupted, and when the name of the firm is kept more or less unchanged.

In certain cases it will, however, be advantageous to make exceptions to this main rule which expresses our most inclusive definition of firm formation. If it is desired to focus exclusively on continuity of operation, one would avoid referring to formation of firms even in cases of bankruptcy, new management, and interruptions in the sense indicated. This would then involve a more narrow definition. It will be possible to judge the extent to which the statistical picture would be changed by application of this narrow definition in place of the more inclusive one since the following tables give information on how the "new" firms have originated in those cases of continued operation after bankruptcy, change of management, and other changes of the kind discussed, where, by application of our main rule, the formation of a new firm has been considered to have taken place. It must be emphasized at the outset, however, that for certain industries it has been particularly difficult to obtain information on all bankruptcies, change of management, and so forth. In these industries there have certainly been many cases of formation or disappearance of firms which have not been recorded in the present work. But it is relatively easy to judge for which industries the data are particularly incomplete, and this has been taken into account in the following analysis.

One special case arises when a firm without going through bankruptcy adds a new product to its line which ends up completely dominating its business.[17] When the new product belongs to an "industry branch" in which the firm has not previously been engaged, this is generally considered to be formation of a new firm.[18]

The determination of the *date for the formation of a new firm* raises certain problems even where it is not a question of gradual development, for example, from handicraft or trade. It is doubtful, for example, whether the better criterion would be to consider, on the one hand, the date on which new construction is started or the date on which the firm moves into rented or purchased premises or, on the other hand, the date on which production is started. The first alternative (i.e., the date on which the firm's capital first becomes engaged) seems to provide the most attractive solution. In practice, this criterion would frequently become difficult to apply if it is desired to fix the date more precisely than to a certain *year*. This, however, will not be necessary, so the criterion is quite usable.

---

[17] Note that this special case is relevant only when the new product line is being produced in the same plant as the old (or in a new plant in the same geographical location). If it is being undertaken in a new location, this would not constitute a special case but be considered an ordinary firm formation according to the chosen definition of a "firm."

[18] For the concept of "industry branch," cf. Appendix 1 of the Swedish edition.

The determination of the year in which a firm is started presents a more important problem when one is faced with an industrial firm that has developed out of a retail or wholesale enterprise, or out of a handicraft operation according to some definition of the term. The conceptual problem here is that of drawing the important line between trade and industry and, above all, between handicraft and industry. The difficulties of drawing a clear distinction between commerce and industry arise mostly because the former is often combined with so-called "putting-out" activity and household manufacture. In cases of this sort, the distinction between craft and industry also creates difficulties. Since the definitions of both commerce and craft vary according to the branch studied (see above and Appendix 1 in Swedish edition), *it becomes necessary to apply different criteria to different branches in determining the date when a firm, previously engaged in trade or in craft production, becomes an industrial enterprise.* In this connection, it should be remembered that the criteria which are used here for drawing distinctions between commerce and industry and between industry and craft do not correspond to the criteria on which the official statistics are based. Indeed, *Industrial Statistics (IS)* does not strive for any conceptual distinction. Its criterion is based on the market value of output and the size of the work force. While this is somewhat mechanical, it also has the advantage of eliminating dubious borderline cases.[19]

With regard to the disappearance of firms, three possibilities should be distinguished. The first *(A)* occurs when a plant is *closed down*—not closed down only temporarily, however. Firms are classified as "discontinued" under *(A)* only in those cases where operations and the manufacturing of the product in question have not been resumed before the end of 1942. This time limit is, of course, quite arbitrary—a plant that is closed, for example, in 1933 and reopened in 1941 is not classified as discontinued, while one that is closed down in 1938 and is not in operation at the end of 1942 would be so classified. There does not seem to be any feasible alternative to this procedure however. The disadvantages of the method adopted do not seem serious since, in practice, those cases where a plant remains closed over several years almost always turn out to constitute the discontinuation of the firm according to *(B)* or *(C)*.

Secondly, a firm is, as a rule, to be considered "discontinued" *(B) if the firm owning the plant goes bankrupt, the plant comes under different management, and continuity of operation is interrupted also in other respects (see above)* as well as when, following bankruptcy, new products lines belonging to another major branch of industry are started and these become predominant. If, however, after bankruptcy, operations are continued as before, this would be considered a case of "financial reconstruction."

The third type of discontinuation *(C)* concerns firms that *change over from one branch of industry to another.* This corresponds to the special case of "firm formation" discussed above.

It is, as a rule, less difficult to determine a "death year" than a "birth

---

[19] Cf. Appendix 1 of the Swedish edition.

year." When a bankruptcy is involved, the year selected is that in which bankruptcy proceedings are instituted rather than the year in which they are concluded. Exceptions are made where the operation of a firm is discontinued while bankruptcy proceedings are started only one or more years later. In cases of this sort, the year in which operations are discontinued is considered the death year. If, on the other hand, the firm is closed only after the bankruptcy is concluded, the year in which proceedings were instituted will still be considered the death year.

When a firm is liquidated without going bankrupt, the relevant date is the year in which liquidation was decided upon rather than the year in which liquidation was completed. In this case, however, the date on which actual operations were discontinued takes precedence over the date on which it was decided to liquidate the firm.

B. The Statistical Picture

In Table 5, the available information on changes in the population of firms in different industries and branches during the interwar period has been summarized in the following manner:[20] Column 1 gives the number of firms started between 1919 and 1931 as a proportion of the number of firms still in existence at the end of 1939. Column 4 records the number of firms established before 1919 but discontinued in the interwar period as a proportion of the total number of firms at the beginning of 1919. Columns 2, 3, and 5 show what is termed here *the entry share, the entry quotient,* and *the exit share.* These three ratios are designed to give a picture of the relative importance of the new firms, the old and surviving firms, and the firms that disappeared during the period in relation to total *work force* in the different industries.[21] For the pulp and paper mills, however, it has been necessary to base these computations on output capacity rather than on employment. While it has been possible to get data on capacity, a satisfactory breakdown of the total labor force figures in terms of numbers employed in the production of the various

---

[20] In accordance with our main criterion (cf. p. 187 f.), the widest definition of "new firm" has been used here. Appendix 10 (Swedish edition) shows, however, that a more restrictive definition would leave the picture unchanged in all essentials—the number of new firms in the "reconstruction with new management" category is small. It should also be noted that some uncertainties pertain particularly to the grouping of firms into those started in the twenties and those started in the thirties and also, to some extent, to the classification into "new" and "old." The number of "uncertain" cases, as reported in Appendix 5 of the Swedish edition, is relatively slight, however. A comparison of columns A and B of Appendix 5 will indicate the maximum possible error.

[21] The discussion on p. 187 f. of the alternative definitions of "new firm" applies here as well. The cases of "uncertain" dating of "birth years" and "death years" become still less significant, however, when these quotients and shares are computed, since most of the "uncertain" cases pertain to very small firms. The margin of error is wider, in other words, with regard to the *number* of firms in the various categories than with regard to the shares and quotients.

TABLE 5
Survey of the Formation and Disappearance of Firms in the Interwar Period

Code	Groups and branches of industries	Number of enterprises started 1919–1939 and in operation in 1940 as percent of total number Dec. 31, 1939	α_{23}	β_{23}	Number of enterprises discontinued 1919–1939 and started before 1919 as percent of total number Jan. 1, 1919	γ_{23}
110	Iron and steel mills	0	0	0	53	15
13	Iron, steel and metal manufacturing	50	19	0.62	23	10
131	Iron and steel manufacturing	44	13	0.47	25	10
132	Nonferrous metal manufacturing	57	32	1.05	18	9
133	Sheet metal manufacturing	50	18	0.38	23	9
14	Mechanical engineering industry	42	14	0.48	33	16
141	Capital goods	40	7	0.27	34	15
142	Consumer durables	61	39	1.05	42	32
144	Agricultural machinery	23	6	0.62	15	16
145	Other	26	9	0.26	29	12
15	Electrical engineering industry	74	23	0.66	44	16
151	Capital goods	66	10	0.26	41	17
152	Consumer durables	84	35	1.00	50	16
153	Other	50	14	—	33	4
210	Cement	30	12	0.55	22	26
220	Concrete products and lightweight concrete	(77)	(54)	(2.16)	·	(23)
230	Brickyards	9	6	0.50	15	10
24	Porcelain and ceramics	26	5	0.09	52	36
241	Porcelain	25	4	0.07	14	33
242	Ceramic tiles	0	0	0	73	71
243	Earthenware	35	10	0.23	38	21
25	Glassworks	20	19	—	33	21
251	Plate glass	100	60		100	100
252	Container glass	0	0	0	50	37
253	Household glass	13	12	—	8	4
254	Other	60	70	4.77	0	0
31	Building joinery, millwork, and furniture (wallboard excluded)	61	49	2.48	27	33
311	Furniture	58	41	2.47	26	30
312	Building joinery, interior fittings	67	56	2.30	20	26
313	Firms combining furniture, building joinery, and interior fittings	56	43	1.54	25	46
314	Prefabricated frame houses	100	100	—	100	100
312 &314	Building joinery, interior fittings, and prefabricated frame houses	68	60	2.74	20	27
316	Models and mock-ups	63	61	12.36	20	30
317	Wallboard	100	100	—	0	0
318	Other woodworking	56	45	1.70	37	47
319	Plywood	80	90	24.59	0	0
32	Pulp industry	13	19	0.43	23	8
321	Sulphite pulp	3	2	0.04	4	3
322	Sulphate pulp	31	44	1.23	8	4
323	Mechanical pulp	12	18	0.39	41	24
33	Paper and cardboard industry	18	16	0.40	18	7
331	Quality paper	0	0	0	10	5
332	Other paper and cardboard industry	21	18	0.44	19	7
35	Paper and cardboard processing	58	32	2.70	30	26
351	Paper packaging industry	59	35	1.91	30	27

TABLE 5   (*Continued*)

Code	Groups and branches of industries	Number of enterprises started 1919–1939 and in operation in 1940 as per-cent of total number Dec. 31, 1939	α_{23}	β_{23}	Number of enterprises discontinued 1919–1939 and started before 1919 as percent of total number Jan. 1, 1919	γ_{23}
352	Office supplies	47	14	—	17	19
353	Other	68	53	5.30	44	58
41	Confectionery industry	58	17	0.49	41	15
411	Chocolate and candy products	57	17	0.47	41	14
412	Fruit preserves	63	39	0.89	44	51
420	Oleomargarine industry	58	47	—	32	3
43	Canning	59	46	1.42	26	22
431	Canned fish	61	56	2.49	20	12
432	Canned fruit and vegetables	33	12	0.19	20	24
433	Other canned goods	67	22	0.38	57	44
450	Mineral water and soft drinks	(44)	(26)	(0.74)	(17)	(36)
51	Cotton manufacture	36	3	0.10	27	7
511	Cotton spinning	18	4	0.19	10	0
512	Cotton weaving	46	12	0.49	41	31
513	Firms combining cotton spinning and weaving	0	0	0	14	1
514	Other cotton manufacture	55	25	0.56	30	5
52	Woolen manufacture	15	2	0.05	29	14
521	Wool spinning	6	1	0.02	16	14
522	Wool weaving	40	3	0.05	37	10
523	Firms combining wool spinning and weaving	8	1	0.04	31	14
524	Other wool manufacture	33	42	1.61	50	21
54	Hosiery manufacture	72	38	1.09	28	14
541	Cotton hosiery	62	22	0.48	13	19
542	Woolen hosiery	71	62	4.56	35	37
544	Rayon silk hosiery	97	95	29.62	0	0
545	Stockings	90	71	2.91	60	42
546	Other	46	8	0.16	24	4
55	Clothing and textile manufacturing	77	50	1.59	40	26
551	Men's clothes	78	45	1.03	35	31
552	Ladies' garments	76	44	1.81	53	32
553	Work clothes	95	72	2.60	25	32
554	Children's clothing	93	100	—	0	0
555	Firms combining men's, ladies' and children's ready-made clothing	77	48	2.22	47	17
556	Other	65	57	3.69	30	13
610	Tanneries	12	3	0.12	72	32
62	Gloves, leather, and fur products	68	44	2.13	27	30
621	Gloves	61	29	0.49	33	62
622	Fur products	66	33	3.89	26	25
623	Other leather products	81	85	5.74	14	100
630	Shoe industry	(71)	(31)	(1.26)	.	(26)
710	Paints and varnishes	55	17	0.29	35	25
720	Oils, soft soap, soap, perfumes, and cosmetics	55	25	1.01	44	37

Note: A 0 in the β column indicates that no entry took place while an underscore indicates that there were either no continuing firms or that the work force in continuing firms declined so that the β coefficient could not be computed. A perio indidcates that the data did not permit the percentage to be computed. A relatively large margin of error attaches to the figures put in parentheses; these figures do indicate, however, that entry without a doubt was lively and quantitatively significant (cf. Appendix 1 [in Swedish edition]).

types of pulp and paper cannot be obtained. The table covers all industries analyzed in Chapters 6 through 9, except the lumber mills, for which it has been impossible to provide a completely satisfactory statistical analysis. For certain industries—bricks, concrete products and lightweight concrete, soft drinks, and shoes—the available data underlying the tabulated figures have been less detailed than for other industries.[22] To indicate this, the figures for these industries have generally been put in brackets. Figure 18 (see pp. 212–20) complements Table 5. The graphs show total employment in individual industries over the interwar period and, to the extent that such data has been available on a year-to-year basis, the shares of new firms, continuing firms, and discontinued firms in total industry employment.[23]

Entry shares (α) have been computed both for the 1920's (including 1919), (α_2), and for the 1930's, (α_3), separately, and also for the entire interwar period, (α_{23}). As a rule, entry shares have been defined in terms of employment figures.[24] Thus, α_2 represents the ratio of the number of workers employed in firms started between 1919 and 1929 to total industry employment in 1929, while α_3 is the ratio of workers employed in firms started in 1930–39 to total industry employment in 1939. In each case the ratio thus obtained has been multiplied by 100. An entry share for the entire interwar period (α_{23}) of 30 means, therefore, that 30 percent of a total industry employment at the end of the interwar period (1939) is to be attributed to firms newly established sometime between 1919 and 1939.

The *entry quotient*, (β), has been computed only for the entire interwar period, β_{23}. This figure refers to the share of new firms in the *growth* of industry employment during the period rather than in total employment. The entry quotient is thus defined as total 1939 employment in firms started between 1919 and 1939 divided by the increase in employment in continuing firms over the same period. If the number of workers added to the total labor force of the industry by new firms is equal to that added by old firms, the entry quotient is 1. If the number added by new firms is twice as large, the quotient will be 2, and so forth.

The *exit share*, finally, has been computed for the interwar period

---

[22] Cf. Appendix 1 of the Swedish edition.

[23] Appendixes 6 and 9 of the Swedish edition report on the material in more detail and give the data on work forces on which the calculation of these quotients and shares is based. In Appendix 7, the firms are grouped according to "län" (approx. "county") and according to location in large towns (population greater than 10,000 as of 1929) or smaller towns and rural areas (population less than 10,000 as of 1929). The most important grouping of the firms has been done according to "major branches" within the several "industries" (cf. Appendix 1). A more detailed differentiation of the industries than the one used in Chaps. 6 through 9 has been undertaken in certain instances in order to make a more detailed investigation possible.

[24] In the pulp and paper industry, number of tons.

as a whole, γ_{23}, and is defined as the ratio of the 1919 employment in firms which later disappeared to total industry employment in 1919, multiplied by 100.

Let A represent the number of workers at the end of the relevant period in firms started during the period; C_b, the initial employment in continuing firms; C_e, employment in continuing firms at the close of the relevant period. Then we have:

$$\text{The } entry \text{ } share: \alpha = \frac{A}{A + C_e} \times 100,$$

and

$$\text{The } entry \text{ } quotient: \beta = \frac{A}{C_e - C_b} \times 100.$$

Let B be the number of workers employed at the beginning of the relevant period in firms that later disappeared during the period. Then we have:

$$\text{The } exit \text{ } share: \gamma = \frac{B}{B + C_b} \times 100.$$

The data on the entry size of firms and on their *development types* are given in Appendix 8 of the Swedish edition, and are summerized for all industries together in Table 6. The structure of the different industries at the end of the interwar period is outlined in Appendices 12 and 13 of the Swedish edition, where information on the "terminal size" of firms (in 1939) has been combined with data on "entry size" and "development type."

The classification of new firms in terms of *entry size* has been based on the average number of workers for the first two years. Owners or managers have been included in this figure to the extent that they have directly participated in production. A certain number of exceptions have been made from this main rule, however. Thus the firms have been grouped in the next larger entry size class in cases where it has been evident that they really started on a larger scale than indicated by the employment figures. Employment figures for the immediately following years, or other data (e.g., on initial equity capital or productive capacity) may, for example, indicate that the employment figure for the first two years must be regarded as exceptionally low for one reason or another. These exceptions from the main rule have, however, been so few that they are of little significance. The "old" firms have also been classified according to entry size (i.e., size at the beginning of the interwar period) in order to make a comparison with entering firms possible.

The following entry size classes have been chosen: *Entry Size Class I:* less than 8 workers; *Size Class II:* 8–19 workers, *Size Class III:* 20–99 workers; *Size Class IV:* 100–499 workers; *Size Class V:* 500 workers and more. The increasing class interval must of course be kept in mind. It has been possible, however, to study the distribution within the different classes directly, as

TABLE 6
Initial Size of Enterprise and Development Types
(all industries according to project A)

Initial Size* (Number of Workers)	Continuing Firms						New Firms 1919–39 and in Operation 1940						Firms Discontinued 1919–39											
													Formed before 1919						Formed 1919–39					
	Type of Development†						Type of Development†						Type of Development†						Type of Development†					
	1	2	3	4	5	Total	1	2	3	4	5	Total	1	2	3	4	5	Total	1	2	3	4	5	Total
1–7	822	187	20	11	3	1043	1566	489	62	7	104	2228	413	11	1	34	41	500	315	25	—	5	28	373
8–19	284	139	42	92	1	558	264	183	48	20	69	589	187	18	4	95	69	373	85	18	2	15	20	140
20–99	288	196	97	118	4	703	65	52	75	8	25	225	155	31	1	108	41	335	22	7	2	13	14	58
100–499	81	103	116	31	2	333	8	10	9	—	5	32	12	3	2	32	4	53	1	—	—	2	—	3
500–	11	12	23	3	—	49	—	2	—	—	1	3	1	—	—	2	—	3	—	—	—	—	—	—
Unknown but under 100	31	21	2	4	35	93	52	25	6	10	58	151	20	4	—	18	23	65	46	10	1	14	50	121
Unknown	—	1	—	—	1	2	2	2	—	—	1	3	—	—	—	—	—	—	1	—	—	—	—	1
Total	1517	659	300	259	46	2781	1957	765	200	45	263	3231	788	67	8	289	178	1330	470	60	5	49	112	696

* For continuing enterprises and for enterprises formed prior to 1919 and discontinued 1919–39, initial size refers to size as of 1919.
† 1 = stationary, 2 = moderately progressive, 3 = strongly progressive, 4 = regressive, 5 = unknown.

well as the typical character of firms in each initial size class, in order to evaluate the chosen classification scheme. The class boundaries have been drawn only after a study of the distribution so that the boundaries in question have not been drawn through peaks of the frequency curve.

The old, continuing firms have also been included for purposes of comparison in grouping the firms according to development types. Four such categories have been distinguished: (*A*) stationary firms, (*B*) moderately progressive firms, (*C*) strongly progressive firms, and (*D*) regressive firms. The grouping of firms in terms of these four types has been based, in the first instance, on the development of work force figures (including owners and managers). The following outline gives details on the criteria. The definition of the "stationary" type has not been included since it is residually defined once the other development types have been set forth. Note also that entry size class III has here been divided into IIIA and IIIB, with the line between the two drawn at 50 workers. This has been done in order to provide a more reasonable classification of development types.

Firms in entry size class I (1–7 workers)

Moderately progressive.... More than doubling of size, but at least to 11 workers, while to less than 10 times initial size. Exception: in case of growth to 10 times initial size, but to less than 50, the firm is still classified as "moderately progressive."

Strongly progressive...... Growth to 10 times or more of initial size, but at least to 50 workers.

Regressive............. Decline by at least 67 percent, but only cases with an initial size exceeding 5.

Firms in entry size class II (8–19 workers)

Moderately progressive.... Growth by more than 80 percent but less than 300 percent. Exception: in cases of growth by 300 percent or more but to a terminal size of less than 70, the firm is still classified as "moderately progressive."

Strongly progressive...... Quadrupling of size or more, but at least to 70 workers.

Regressive............. Decline by at least 50 percent.

Firms in entry size class IIIA (20–49 workers)

Moderately progressive.... Growth by more than 67 percent, but at least to 35, while less than 200 percent. Exception: in cases of growth by 200 percent or more, but to less than 90, the firm is still classified as "moderately progressive."

Strongly progressive...... Tripling of size or more, but at least to 90.

Regressive............. Decline by at least 40 percent.

Firms in entry size class IIIB (50–99 workers)

Moderately progressive.... Growth by more than 50 percent, but at least to 85, while less than 200 percent. Exception: in cases of growth by 200 percent or more, but to less than 200, the firm is still classified as "moderately progressive."

Strongly progressive...... Tripling of size or more, but at least to 200.

Regressive............. Decline by at least 33 percent.

Firms in entry size class IV: (100–499 workers)

Moderately progressive.... Growth by more than 33 percent, but at least to 150, while to less than twice the size. Exception: in cases of growth by 100 percent or more, but to less than 300, the firm is still classified as "moderately progressive."

Strongly progressive...... Doubling of size or more, but at least to 300.

The main idea has been to take into account both the relative and the absolute increase or decrease in employment in as reasonable a way as possible. To concentrate exclusively on either one would lead to unreasonable results since, for example, an increase from 3 to 6 workers and an increase from 100 to 200 workers ought not to be regarded as equally progressive. Nor would it be reasonable to classify a firm growing from 100 to 120 and a firm growing from 10 to 30 as equally progressive.

The above criteria are based exclusively on work force figures. Classification according to development type has been altogether avoided in cases where the observations have been too few, as well as in those cases where the type of development has been difficult to evaluate for other reasons—the work force may, for example, have fluctuated to such an extent from year to year that the primary data are suspect. The number of such cases can be seen in Table 6 [and in Appendix 8 in the Swedish edition]. It should also be emphasized that numerous exceptions have been made from the principal criteria set forth above in cases where the work force figures have been obviously misleading. When the growth in the market value of output has been very rapid and it has been possible to attribute it clearly to growth in the volume of output, the firm in question has been classified among the moderately or, in certain cases, the strongly progressive firms, even though it would have belonged to the stationary or moderately progressive firms, respectively, according to the work force criterion. The objective in these cases has, of course, been to avoid an unreasonable classification of those firms which through labor-saving mechanization have achieved a very significant increase in output per man-hour.

It is quite obvious that it has not been possible to avoid a few rather strange results in the classification of individual borderline cases, and it cannot be denied that some exceptions have had to be made simply on an *ad hoc* basis. But the borderline cases are few, and it is hardly possible to avoid arbitrary decisions altogether. To apply the main criteria without exceptions would have led to unfortunate results, and this would have been true even if they were complemented by rigid rules for the computation of output per man-hour based on output-value data, price index series, and so forth. To rely on mechanical procedures of this sort would be to waste the knowledge of individual firms which has been gained through the study of the records underlying *Industry Statistics* with their extensive and diverse information, and through the interview material. It should also be emphasized that the exceptions have been few. This is due primarily to the fact that large increases in the value of output per man-hour in the great majority of cases have been combined with an increase in the number employed of such a magnitude as to indicate the appropriate development type on this latter ground alone.

C. The Formation, Development, and Disappearance of Firms in Relation to the Transformation of Production and Profitability: Preliminary Analysis

A comparison, satisfactory in all essential respects, of the extent of new enterprise formation during the two decades of the interwar period, on the one hand, and the decades immediately preceding World War I, on the other, is unfortunately impossible since fully comparable data for the earlier period cannot be obtained. One question, however, can be answered, namely, whether the number of initially large and/or later rapidly growing firms was higher before or after World War I. According to Table 6, in 1939 there were 6,012 firms in industries represented in our project A [see data in Swedish edition, Appendix 1]. Of this number, approximately 3,231 (i.e., 54 percent) were new in the interwar period. But only 300, at the most, of these 3,231 (i.e., somewhat less than 10 percent) had started with 50 or more workers or had grown out of the "small business" category, here defined to include firms with 1 to 49 employees. The extent of enterprise formation in industries not included in project *A* (i.e., the concrete products and lightweight concrete industry, the brickyards, the soft drink industry, and the leather shoe industry) can only be estimated with a relatively large margin of error. But if these industries are included, the picture still remains unchanged—only about 320 of approximately 3,800 firms new to the interwar period (i.e., not quite 10 percent) were started with more than 50 workers or grew out of the small business category. Thus the interwar period was characterized by a large number of new, stationary, small firms and a few new large and/or strongly progressive firms.

This picture is in stark contrast to that for the period before World War I. Of the 935 firms reported in Chapter 5 as having been started between 1889 and 1909—a period of the same length as the interwar period—no less than 385 either began with 50 or more workers or else grew out of the small business class prior to 1914. Many had been established on a very small scale and had grown very rapidly. Considering the fact that data for this period are far from complete, we can conclude that the number of new firms which by the end of the respective periods had grown out of the small industry class, was much smaller, even in absolute terms, during the interwar period. There is no doubt whatsoever that the *proportion* of such firms was much smaller still, a conclusion that would appear even more self-evident if the lumber mills could have been included. Granted that the 385 firms should not be compared with the 935 in the same manner as the 320 have been compared with the 3,800, since it is the relatively large firms that are comparatively less well-represented in the 935 figure. But from a comparison with the *Industry Statistics* for 1914 it is evident that the number of stationary small firms at the outset of World War I was only a small fraction of what it was 25 years later. Not even the total number of firms in the industries here included was as large in 1914 as the number of firms in the same industries which were established during the interwar period and remained stationary. Since out of the unknown number of firms established between 1889 and 1909 at least 385 had achieved a relatively large size, the proportion of stationary small firms must have been relatively small. This is particularly true if one disregards those small and, in the technical sense, purely handicraft firms of outmoded type which still survived in this period (e.g., among the tanneries).

During World War I, Sweden may therefore be said to have passed an important milestone is its industrial development. The stationary small firms took over the predominant—or at least, the eye-catching—role previously played by the expanding firms. Most industries showed a far more dynamic structure in 1914 than in the interwar period, in the sense that a relatively much greater number of firms were in the process of growing into larger size classes. In addition, the different industries showed a relatively much larger number of firms of the same general type in the earlier period, with firms belonging to different size classes more frequently competing actively with one another. At the end of the interwar period, in contrast, one finds within a whole range of industries that the many new small firms that had emerged complemented the larger and generally older ones rather than competed with them. This important development emerges quite clearly if one disregards firms that had been established or expanded as subsidiaries. Subsidiaries became more common after 1919 than they were before 1914. That the interwar period represented a new development stage becomes still clearer when one notes that the smaller initial size of new firms and their lessened capacity for expansion, which is characteristic of this period, did not depend only on the rapid growth of a number of newly prominent consumption-good industries. The same structural change is visible within "older" branches where the rate of formation of new firms continued high. The strongly expanding firms of the interwar period are found mainly in the ready-made clothing and hosiery industries, while most industries which previously had included many expanding firms had relatively few such firms during the interwar period.

It is clear, however, that these generalizations do not tell us much, even if they do serve to emphasize one important aspect of the changing nature of firm formation. A more detailed analysis of the formation and development of new firms is required.

The first step in such an analysis should be to investigate whether the development types of the new firms were connected with the types of expansion process characterizing the respective industries. Table 7 shows, industry by industry, the number of new firms as a proportion of the total number of firms in 1939, as well as the entry shares for the entire interwar period, with the data grouped according to the type of development process characterizing the respective industries.[25]

---

[25] Certain industries have been labeled as borderline cases in order to emphasize their position between the different process types when this position has been particularly obvious.

An expanding industry development was not always based on a high rate of firm formation. Many highly progressive industries showed very little, and quantitatively insignificant, entry, while in others the formation of new firms was of relatively little quantitative significance though rates of entry were relatively high. In the latter cases new firms were, in other words, started on a small scale and remained, as a rule, small. The cotton goods industry and the paper mills were the most characteristic examples of the first category, while the capital goods industries were equally typical of the latter category. On the other hand, one also finds stagnating or regressive industries where the formation of firms was lively and quantitatively significant. The leather shoe industry is an example. But most stagnating or regressive industries showed little and relatively insignificant entry. Firm mortality, on the other hand, was often (but far from always) important in these industries. Among the progressive industries there were several with high firm mortality.

Thus while expansion of an industry did not always mean lively and quantitatively significant firm formation, the data make it quite evident that this was the rule in cases of supply-push industry development based on new or "young" products. Frequently, but not always, this was also true of demand-pull expansion processes. That a positive correlation between industry expansion and firm formation cannot be generally established turns out, on closer study, to be due to the fact that whenever supply-push processes were based not on new or young products but primarily on new or young methods, they usually did not give rise to lively and quantitatively significant firm formation.

Part I of Table 7 lists industries in which product innovations and young products were important. The formation of new firms in these industries depended, in a manner to be more thoroughly analyzed in Chapter 12, to a substantial extent on this fact. With few exceptions, more than half of the firms in these industries in 1939 were firms that had been established during the interwar period. The entry share usually exceeded 30, and sometimes exceeded 50 by a substantial margin.[26] In addition, the new firms as a rule accounted for a greater share of the growth in total industry employment than did the expansion of old firms. The entry quotient, in other words, was usually larger than unity. Expansion in concrete products and lightweight concrete, building joinery, paper packaging, ready-made clothing, hosiery, canned goods, fruit processing, and fur products, etc., was thus combined with high rates of

---

[26] In some cases, however, the innovations took place only in the 1930's or toward the end of the 1920's so that the many new firms did not have time to grow sufficiently to give rise to a very large entry share. Typically, however, the entrants of the 1930's still brought a larger number of workers into the respective branches in these cases than did the entrants of the 1920's (cf., e.g., sheet metal manufacturing), something which was otherwise seldom the case.

TABLE 7
Survey of Process Types and Formation of Enterprises*

Process Type	Industries Classified as Progressive:					
	During Entire Interwar Period			*During either 20's or 30's*		
	Industry	*Percent*	α_{23}	*Industry*	*Percent*	α_{23}
I. Supply-Push based on New or "Young" Products	Nonferrous metal manufacturing	57	32	Fur products	66	33
	Sheet metal manufacturing	50	18			
	Mechanical engineering, consumer durables	61	39			
	Electrical engineering, consumer durables	84	35			
	Concrete products and lightweight concrete	(77)	(54)			
	Building joinery, interior fittings, and prefabricated frame houses	68	60			
	Paper and cardboard processing	58	32			
	Fruit preserves	63	39			
	Canning	59	46			
	Mineral water and soft drinks	(44)	(26)			
	Hosiery	72	38			
	Ready-made clothing and other textile processing	77	50			
	Paints and varnishes	55	17			
II. Supply-Push based on New or "Young" Processes	Cement	30	12	Porcelain and ceramics	26	5
	Cotton manufacture	36	3	Oleomargarine	58	47
II/III. (Borderline cases)	Steel manufacturing	44	13	Steel mills	0	0
	Mechanical engineering producer goods	40	7	Plate glass	100	60
	Electrical engineering producer goods	66	10	Container glass	0	0
	Pulp industry	13	19			
	Paper and cardboard	18	16			
III. Demand-Pull	Furniture	58	41	Household glass	13	12
	Chocolate and candy	57	17	Wool manufacture	15	2
	Oils, soft soap, soap, perfumes, and cosmetics	55	25	Gloves	61	29
				Other leather products	81	85

* Figures in the "percent" column show the proportion of enterprises formed since 1919 of those still in existence at end of 1939. α_{23} is the entry-share for the entire interwar period measured in number of workers, except for pulp and paper mills where capacity had to be used. Parentheses around figures indicate that the margin of error may be considerable.

entry in these industries. Their entry shares as of 1939 were also quite high despite the small scale on which most of the new firms began, and depite the strong growth of old firms in most of the branches in question. These industries usually had a particularly large number of both new and old firms that were progressive.

Entry into the soft drink industry, however, was quantitatively somewhat less significant, since the many new firms generally remained small. The relatively low entry share in sheet metal manufacturing is explained by the fact that the product innovations in this industry occurred in the early 1930's, while in the other cases the relevant new products belong to the 1920's. In none of these instances was a high entry share or entry quotient attributable to just one firm, or a few new firms. The paints and varnishes industry is the only clear exception to the rule that new supply-push products gave rise to many new and relatively important firms. Although the number of new firms was fairly large in this industry, most of them grew very little, if at all. The entry share, therefore, was relatively small.

Developments in the consumer durables industries offer good examples of the combination of many primary product innovations with lively and quantitatively significant entry. Numerous primary product innovations were the driving forces behind the expansion of both branches (electrical and mechanical) of the consumer durables industry, and each branch exhibited high rates of entry and high entry shares and entry quotients. Two other typical examples may be found in nonferrous metal manufacturing and sheet metal manufacturing. The expansion of these industries was based, to a significant extent, on the new light metal products and stainless steel products, respectively.

As has been indicated previously, rates of return were not always satisfactory in those industries that expanded on the basis of product innovations or young products, and which, therefore, also showed high rates of entry as a rule. If the entire industry is chosen as the unit of observation, one cannot establish any marked positive correlation between rates of return and rates of entry. A closer study shows, however, that those firms that pioneered the innovations in question usually also had the highest earnings, but that the high earnings of these firms were often offset by the lower earnings of others.

Part III of Table 7 lists industries for which the development process was characterized above all by demand-pull. Some of these industries exhibited relatively high rates of entry and comparatively high entry shares and entry quotients together with rapid expansion of older firms. The furniture industry, the chocolate and candy industry, the gloves and fur products industries, and the light chemical industry belong to this category. Here more than half of the firms existing in 1939 were new to the interwar period. Except for furniture and "other fur and leather products," entry shares were generally below 30 and the entry quotients were relatively low. These measures of the significance of new firms consequently yielded generally lower values than for industries characterized by many new or young products. It is interesting to note, furthermore, that compared with the latter industries, the variance of firm growth rates was much higher. A very small proportion of the new firms accounted for the major part of the entry share.

In many other cases where demand-pull gave the impetus to an expansionary development process, firm formation was neither lively nor quantitatively significant. The strong demand-pull experienced, for example, by commercial iron producers, by capital goods producers, and in the 1930's by paper mills gave rise to no new firms at all in the first-mentioned branch, while the latter two had little entry and entry shares and entry quotients that were very low.[27] Nor did the woolen industry and/or the household glassworks show lively or significant firm formation. In all the enumerated cases, one generally finds strong expansion on the part of the older firms however (Cf. Appendix 8 in Swedish edition).

Rates of return were generally satisfactory and, in addition, usually more evenly distributed in industries experiencing demand-pull than in other industries. In some cases, rates of return and rates of entry show a clear, positive correlation. But the above discussion makes it evident that this was far from always the case. The furniture industry, among others, exemplifies the exceptions to this rule. This industry experienced strong demand-pull, and the rate of entry, the entry share, and the entry quotient were high, but earnings were bad.

Part II of Table 7 lists industries in which development was primarily based on innovations in production or distribution methods and/or in which the mostly secondary product innovations usually could be accomplished with productive equipment that was already generally well-known. With few exceptions, associated with special circumstances, these industries showed low rates of entry, small entry shares, and small entry quotients. Most firms in 1939 were, as a rule, old; entry shares were, with a couple of exceptions, less than 20; and entry quotients were significantly below 1. The old firms, however, grew more or less rapidly during the entire interwar period. The cement industry, the cotton goods industry, and the glass container producers are examples of industries belonging to this third major category. Since earnings were, for the most part, good in industries belonging to this category, and particularly so for firms that pioneered in carrying through the innovations, one cannot in this case establish any definite relationship between rates of returns and rates of entry.

---

[27] The new paper mills were, for that matter, with few exceptions subsidiary companies or, more correctly, subsidiary plants.

In the category of stagnating or regressive industries, numerous and/or important new firms are observed only in exceptional cases. The most notable exception is that of the leather shoe industry. New firms in this industry were established on a small scale and remained small, but they were so numerous that the entry share became quite large nevertheless. Profits were, of course, seldom satisfactory in the stagnating or regressive industries so that, with the exception just mentioned, this category shows a combination of low rates of entry and low rates of return.

The discussion so far does not tell us anything about the types of firms in which the pioneering enterprises are to be found. One should not conclude, for example, that the new firms were particularly responsible for the development of their respective industries in the sense of being foremost in introducing innovations. Actually, this was seldom the case. Few new firms began as pioneers. Highly progressive firms—whether old or new—were, on the other hand, almost without exception successful because of their, at least secondary, innovations. Stagnation or retrogression was the rule for firms in which such initative was lacking, and firms belonging to industries that as a whole were characterized by strong demand-pull and rapid growth were no exceptions in this regard. Nothing could be more erroneous than the generalization that new and young firms more than others were the ones that infused new life into Swedish industry during the interwar period and thus prevented stagnation and decline.

It is on the contrary quite clear that the characteristic activity that was always the deciding factor in the introduction of innovations of any kind was not especially prevalent in new firms. In the interwar period, for several different reasons, there was a distinct tendency for this characteristic to be found in older firms to a greater extent than previously. This was the case not only absolutely speaking—which would be somewhat self-evident with respect to the more long-established industries—but also relatively speaking. Wherever this reinvigorating human factor was missing—and it became rarer with the age of the entrepreneur—decline sooner or later followed. New, fresh initiatives—which as a rule meant young, though not very young men—gave new impetus to old firms just about as frequently in this period as they gave rise to successful new enterprises.[28] The generalization mentioned above is therefore invalid. The combination, "many new products—many new firms," which we have found to be the rule, must be explained instead by focusing on the nature of the expansion process that the industries in question went through.

---

[28] The average age of managers was lower in "young" than in "older" firms, but the age of founders was not particularly low and usually above 30 (Cf. Appendix 15 of the Swedish edition).

New or young products generally had the greatest potential in creating a growth of demand. The pioneering firms, which were the first to market the new goods, were actually often incapable—for purely technical or organizational reasons—of entirely satisfying the demand to which their innovations gave rise with their own productive capacity or through their own distribution channels. The "market vacuum" created in this manner proved more than anything else an inducement to the entry of new firms that were attracted by the ease with with which a share of the new market could be captured. Entrepreneurship of a particularly high order was not always necessary in order for a new firm to grow under these conditions. It should be noted that, on the other hand, the very speed with which new firms sprang up often meant that the already existing firms never became conscious of the existence of such a market vacuum. In many instances, of course, the new entrants did not just exploit the "vacuum" but also encroached on that part of the market which the older firms should have been easily able to cover.

In *demand-pull processes,* the already existing firms were normally in a more favorable position to meet the growth in demand. Growing demand would ordinarily follow older, well-established distribution channels, based on existing, habitual customer-supplier relationships in the product area in question. In this respect, potential entrants were at a disadvantage, in addition to frequently being at a technological handicap relative to existing firms. Well-managed, older firms, as well as those new firms that were successful in establishing themselves on the market, were able to expand rapidly, while others fell behind. Such rapid expansion generally required the firm to be in the vanguard in adopting innovations. This explains why the expansion of industry output was more unevenly distributed between firms in demand-pull than in supply-push processes. In the latter case, it was usually easier for almost any firm to expand. One should also note that the demand-pull process was especially conducive to the establishment of new firms of a type different from the existing ones, particularly subcontractors.

In spite of the supply-push effects frequently associated with *process innovations,* the industries in which such innovations were important only rarely showed a rate of demand growth exceeding that which existing firms were able to meet without technical or other difficulties. Since the products were already familiar, established distribution channels proved an important advantage to existing firms here also. In addition, the older firms usually had the better chances of being in the forefront with innovations of this type simply because of their greater experience and their superior position with regard to the mobilization of risk capital.

Chapter 12 and later chapters will be devoted to the analysis of these process types as well as to a general investigation of the nature of the formation and development of firms in the different industries.

Preliminary studies of *firm mortality* data for the different industries, and of the same data together with the data on earnings, do not yield as clear a picture as in the case of the formation of firms. In this connection, more detailed definition of the questions, and a correspondingly more detailed differentiation of the empirical material, is particularly necessary. One fact stands out, however—overall firm mortality rates were quite high. Table 6, which summarizes the project *A* data, shows that of 4,100 firms in existence at the end of 1918, no less than 1,330—one third of the original population—had disappeared prior to 1940. If the most restrictive definition of "firm death" is applied, the number of discontinued firms would be reduced somewhat, but on the other hand, there were a great many financial reconstruction cases bordering on discontinuation of the firm. A rough calculation shows that in all probability considerably more than 50 percent of the firms in existence at the end of World War I either disappeared or else went bankrupt but were reconstructed, prior to 1940. Approximately one fifth of the 1919 labor force was employed in firms that disappeared during the interwar period—a figure which indicates that this fate generally befell smaller firms, although not the very smallest. If workers in firms that required financial reconstruction were included, the figure would surely come close to 50 percent.

There is, unfortunately, no possibility of providing reliable figures for those industries that were not covered by the project *A* investigation. For reasons indicated in our previous discussion of the available data, estimates of the number and mortality of firms in these industries are subject to a relatively substantial margin of error. But there is no doubt that the general picture of high firm mortality would remain unchanged.

There was also frequently considerable mortality among the firms established after 1918, even in the rapidly growing industries. This immediately raises the question of whether these almost universally high mortality rates were due to strategic malinvestments playing a prominent role even in the expanding industries—i.e., whether the reason was that so many fatal mistakes were made in starting new firms and in expanding the older ones. The analysis of the following chapters will show that the answer to this question is in the negative. The explanation is quite different—roughly stated, negative development effects overshadowed the role of strategic malinvestments in almost all industries, including most of the expanding ones. The disappearance of firms was, above all, due to the new products and processes introduced by a frequently small number of progressive firms, domestic or foreign. These innovations rendered other firms noncompetitive, even though they had not committed mistakes that would in themselves have been fatal. In general, disappearing firms were simply unable to survive in the evolutionary struggle.

That mistakes and malinvestments were the cause of many financial reconstructions and of great losses to individuals, particularly during the 1920's, is another matter. The emerging picture is clear. In order to explain it, however, one must investigate questions analogous to those raised in the discussion of the formation of new firms: To what extent was the discontinuation or financial reconstruction of firms preceded by a period of progressive or regressive development for the firms in question? To what extent did this development depend upon stagnating or declining products? To what extent was it due to process innovations introduced by old or new competitors? Table 6 shows that firms that were either stationary or regressive accounted for the overwhelming proportion of all discontinuations. Considering only those firms for which it has been possible to determine the development type, only 140 of the 1,736 firms which disappeared (i.e., 8 percent) had grown appreciably in the latter part of their life spans. One of the objectives of the next chapter will be to shed additional light on this matter, while later chapters will further investigate the question of the nature of firm mortality. First, however, the cyclical variations in the formation, development, and disappearance of firms should be studied.

11 Cyclical Aspects

A. The Questions

This chapter considers the following questions: (1) What were the year-to-year variations in the number of new firms started? (2) What were the cyclical variations in the initial scale on which new firms were established and the effects of new starts on aggregate employment? (3) What were the year-to-year variations in the total number of firms discontinued, the firm-size distributions of this total, and the effects of firm mortality on employment? (4) What were the ages of firms that disappeared? With regard to the last question, data on the year of establishment are as a rule lacking for the period prior to 1919. As far as possible, older firms have been grouped into those established before 1914 and those established between 1914 and 1919. The fourth question must therefore be reformulated: How many of the firms which disappeared, say, during the depression of the early 1930's were started during the boom of the 1920's and how many dated from an earlier period?

Our previous discussion of the rules applied in the determination of the dates for the formation and disappearance of firms need not be repeated here. It should be recalled, however, that the margin of error is occasionally fairly substantial. But the reliability of the results can be judged by consulting the appendices in which the doubtful cases have been especially indicated. For our present purposes, the reliability of these data will be quite sufficient.

B. The Data

The answer to our first question is contained in Figure 16 and in Appendix 5 [in Swedish edition].[1] As in Figure 18, the time series are

---

[1] The figures refer to special study *A* (cf. Chap. 10, p. 182).

based on the most inclusive definition of "new" firm, but where a more restrictive definition yields a substantially different result, this has been explicitly noted. Figure 18 and Appendixes 9 and 11 contain the answer to our second question. For easy cross reference, some additional series with the same index base are also plotted in Figure 18.[2] The third question

TABLE 8
Mortality of Firms of Different Size Classes

Industry	Code	*Number of discontinued firms established before 1919 as percent of all firms in 1919 grouped according to size of work force*						Total
		1–7	8–19	20–99	100–499	500–	1–99*	
Iron and steel mills..............	11	100	100	67	24	—	—	53
Iron, steel, and metal manufacturing.............	13	19	34	19	5	—	88	23
Mechanical engineering.........	14	34	41	32	16	13	—	33
Electrical engineering..........	15	57	76	21	43	—	—	44
Woodworking industries (wallboard excluded)............	31	18	36	40	22	—	30	27
Pulp..........................	32	83	53	25	4	—	—	23
Paper and cardboard...........	33	50	29	22	—	—	—	18
Paper and cardboard processing..	35	20	32	28	38	—	80	30
Confectionery.................	41	45	42	33	—	—	100	41
Canning......................	43	36	13	18	—	—	100	26
Cotton and woolen manufacturing.......	⎰ 51 ⎱ 52	36	42	25	9	—	100	28
Hosiery.......................	54	29	50	16	22	—	67	28
Clothing and textile manufacturing.............	55	34	58	41	22	—	37	40
Tanneries.....................	610	82	38	50	13	—	—	72
Gloves, leather, and fur products.	62	33	30	29	50	—	—	27
Paints and varnishes...........	710	39	36	—	—	—	—	35
Oils, soft soap, soap, perfumes, and cosmetics..............	720	48	44	31	50	—	100	44

* Includes firms of which it is known only that they had a work force between 1 and 99. A more exact figure has not been obtainable.

is answered in Figures 17 and 18, Table 8, and in Appendixes 5, 9, and 11 all of which are based on the most inclusive definition of "discontinuation of a firm." The answer to the fourth question, as reformulated, is summarized in the data provided on page 225. The inclusive definition is used here as well. The data in Figures 16, 17, and 18 have been recorded both for industry groups and for the more important branches. Appendixes 5 and 9 include time series also for some branches not represented in

---

[2] Firms that were started but also disappeared during the interwar period have not been included in the figures but are only reported in Appendix 9 (Swedish edition). Usually, their role has not been significant enough to be very noticeable in the figures.

FIGURE 16
The Formation of Firms, 1919–39

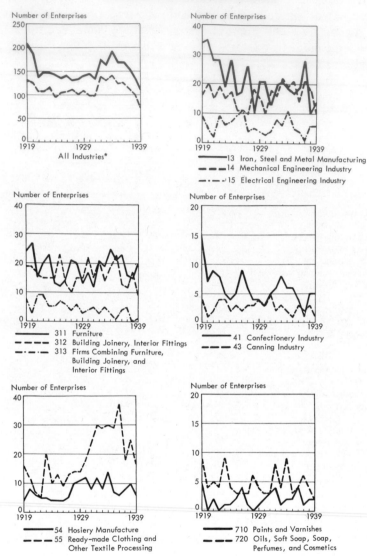

Number of Enterprises

All Industries*

13 Iron, Steel and Metal Manufacturing
14 Mechanical Engineering Industry
15 Electrical Engineering Industry

311 Furniture
312 Building Joinery, Interior Fittings
313 Firms Combining Furniture,
     Building Joinery, and
     Interior Fittings

41 Confectionery Industry
43 Canning Industry

54 Hosiery Manufacture
55 Ready-made Clothing and
   Other Textile Processing

710 Paints and Varnishes
720 Oils, Soft Soap, Soap,
    Perfumes, and Cosmetics

* Continuous curve represents all enterprises except those about which it is known only that they were formed in the interwar period. Dotted curve represents those enterprises for which the exact start-year has been determined.

FIGURE 17
Discontinuation of Firms, 1919–39

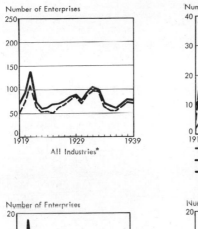

All Industries*

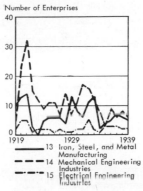

——— 13 Iron, Steel, and Metal
Manufacturing
– – – 14 Mechanical Engineering
Industries
–·–·– 15 Electrical Engineering
Industries

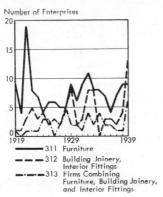

——— 311 Furniture
– – – 312 Building Joinery,
Interior Fittings
–·–·– 313 Firms Combining
Furniture, Building Joinery,
and Interior Fittings

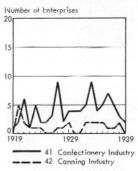

——— 41 Confectionery Industry
– – – 42 Canning Industry

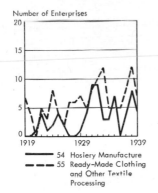

——— 54 Hosiery Manufacture
– – – 55 Ready-Made Clothing
and Other Textile
Processing

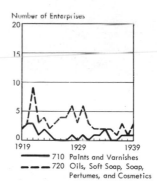

——— 710 Paints and Varnishes
– – – 720 Oils, Soft Soap, Soap,
Perfumes, and Cosmetics

* Continuous curve represents all enterprises except those about which it is
known only that they were discontinued in the interwar period. Dotted curve
represents those enterprises for which the exact year of discontinuation has been
determined.

FIGURE 18
Number of Workers in Firms of Different Categories, 1919–39

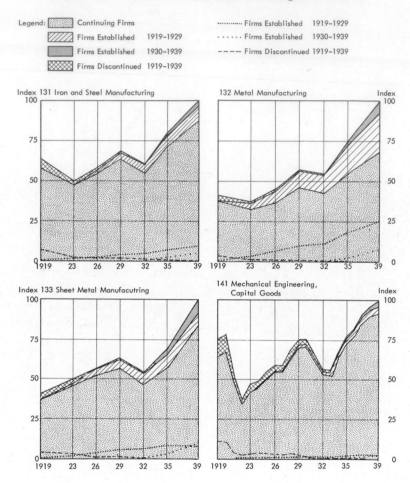

FIGURE 18 (Continued)

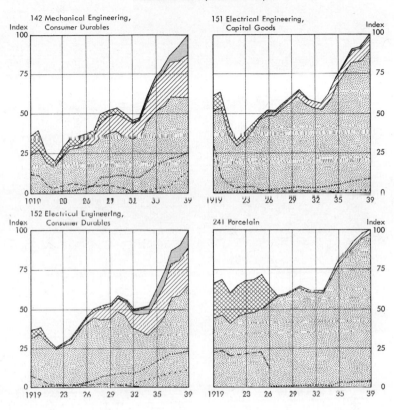

FIGURE 18 (Continued)

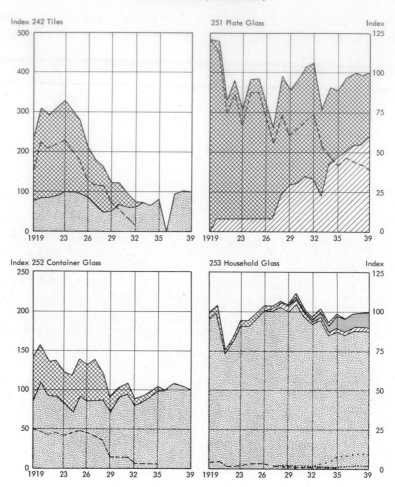

FIGURE 18 (Continued)

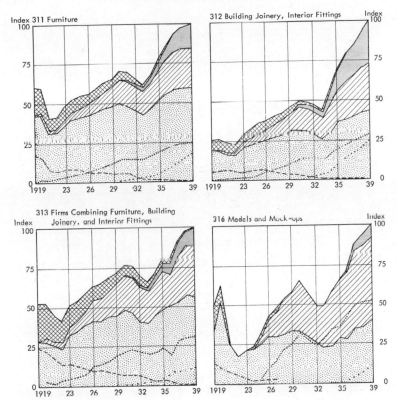

FIGURE 18 (Continued)

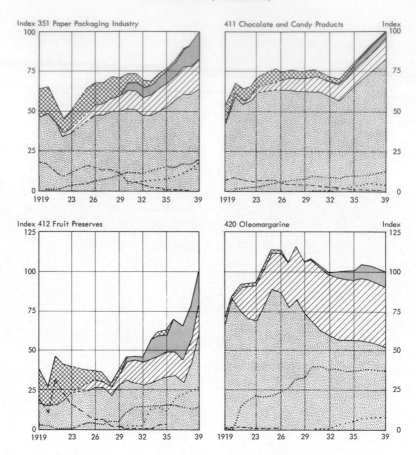

FIGURE 18 (Continued)

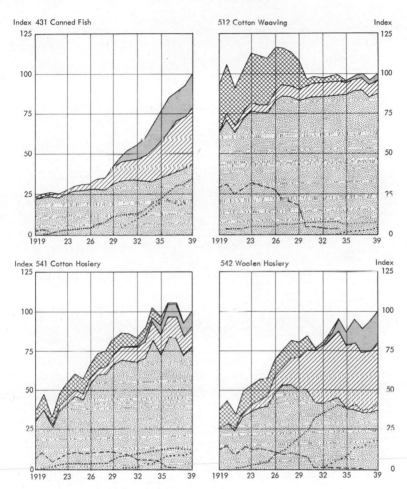

FIGURE 18 (Continued)

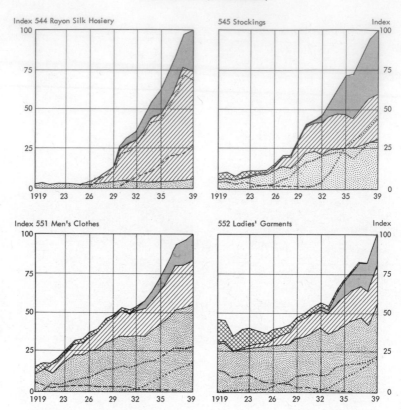

FIGURE 18 (Continued)

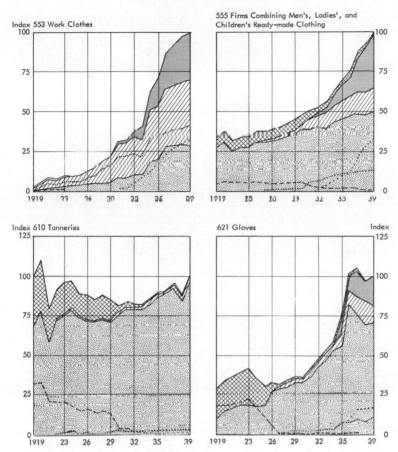

FIGURE 18 (Concluded)

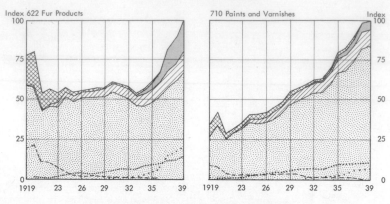

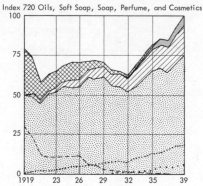

the diagrams. In addition, Appendix 5 records the number of cases in which birth years and death years have been definitely established.[3]

A comparison between the "totals" and "definitely established" in Figures 16 and 17 will show, to begin with, that discrepancies are as a rule relatively insignificant. In most instances, the analysis may be based on those series that include the "uncertain" cases. The three years 1919, 1920, and 1930, are the only ones for which the number of "uncertain" cases significantly affects the picture of *firm formation*. In these instances the number was unusually large. A not insignificant proportion of the firms registered as started in 1919–20 but noted as "uncertain" may well have been started during World War I or even earlier. But the very high rate of firm formation in 1919 and 1920 remains a fact, as does the decline in 1930 *or* 1931. Nor is the picture decisively altered if those cases are sorted out in which discontinuation was immediately followed by the formation of a new firm.[4]

The time series on new starts provide additional information of interest. Except for the years immediately after World War I, when entry rates were high for two years and then declined, the data show little relation to the fluctuations in aggregate activity. The decline after 1920 was mild in view of the strength of the depression. The data for the early 1930's are remarkable: Not only was the depression only faintly reflected in the insignificant reduction in entry rates for 1930 and 1931, but the rates at which new firms were established rose most dramatically between 1931 and 1932—i.e., in the worst year.[5] The level reached in 1932 was high and was maintained up through 1937. This year is followed by a considerable decline. The magnitude of this decline is open to some doubt; it may not be entirely misleading but it probably exaggerates the decline over the remaining years of the period.

One source of bias in the basic data has already been emphasized previously, namely, the underestimation of new starts in the late 1930's due to the fact that, as a rule, only those firms which had had time by 1942 to surmount the "threshold" of the official *Industry Statistics* (*IS*) were observable. Another bias arises because of firms that disappeared in 1940. In all probability the number of such firms was uncommonly large due to the extraordinary conditions of that year, particularly the general mobilization. Thus many small businesses started in the late 1930's, which under normal circumstances would have passed the statistical threshold in the 1940–42 period, were never

---

[3] Appendices referred to throughout this paragraph may be found in the Swedish edition.

[4] Firms listed under type of origin "5" in Appendix 10 (Swedish edition) were not sufficiently important in 1921–22 or 1931–33 for their elimination (i.e., by using the more restrictive definition of "new firm") significantly to affect the series on firm-formation 1919–39.

[5] In this connection it should be noted that A. Oxenfeldt, *New Firms and Free Enterprise* (Washington 1943), infers a relatively low cyclical sensitivity of U.S. firm formation. Oxenfeldt's data, however, do not permit very strong conclusions.

FIGURE 19
Number of Plants, 1919–39, According to the Present
Study (E.D.) and According to the Official *Industry
Statistics* (*IS*) for all Industries Included in Figure 16.
Formation and Discontinuation of Firms as Measured
in the Present Study.

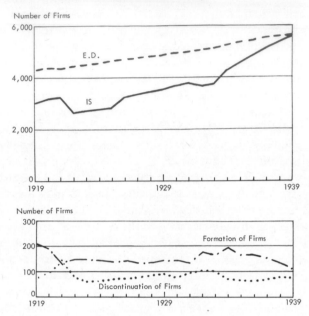

recorded. Unfortunately, it is impossible to obtain a fully reliable estimate
of the significance of these sources of error. Samples from *IS* data on firms
passing the threshold in 1946, however, have been made. A significant number
of firms that were started in 1937–39 and not recorded prior to 1946 turned
up in these samples. But so did some that were started even earlier. Again,
it is quite clear that the decline really was less significant than it appears
from the tables and diagrams presented here, but that a decline in all probability did take place. The inflation of 1939–42 meant that the time interval
before a new firm passed the statistical threshold was significantly shortened.

A comparison with the annual figures on the total number of firms
reported in *Industry Statistics* is of some interest. Figure 19 shows the
number of firms in the industries included in Figure 16 according to
IS and according to the data compiled for the present study.[6] Our series
on rates of entry and exit have also been included. The increase in the

---

[6] One problem here has been that plumbing contractors and repair shops were
included in the *IS* figures for engineering firms up to 1927 and 1935, respectively,
without also being reported separately. The only available solution for this problem
has been to extrapolate the trend from 1927–33 and 1935–39, respectively, backward
to 1919 and then to subtract the number of plumbing contractors and repair shops

number of firms reported in *IS* for the years 1919 and 1920 obviously does not give a good indication of the rate at which new firms were established. The main reason is that the inflation during the year 1920 pulled in a number of firms that would have remained unreported had the purchasing power of money been unchanged. According to *IS*, the total number of firms declined again in 1922. This agrees with the data on new starts and disappearances in that year (with regard to the latter, see below). This decline may be explained in part by the decline in output and by the deflation which caused many firms to sink below the statistical threshold.[7] But the small number of firms rising *above* the threshold in this particular year is probably a more important factor. Expanding firms, which would have been recorded at a stable price level or, particularly, if the inflation had continued, remained below the statistical threshold due to the deflation.

With regard to the early 1930's, one finds that *IS* gives a particularly unreliable picture of the fluctuations in rates of entry and exit. It is especially noteworthy that *IS* records a decrease in the number of firms between 1931 and 1932, while rates of entry actually increased considerably. The factors that distort the *IS* picture here are probably by and large the same as in 1922, although the increase in the number of disappearances was less significant than in that year. Finally, it should be pointed out that the rapid growth in the number of firms recorded by *IS* for the 1933–39 period does not correspond at all well to the actual rate of entry, which did not increase substantially. To a significant extent, the *IS* figures must instead be explained in part by the numerous, previously excluded firms that were included from 1934 onward as a consequence of the 1931 census of firms, and in part by the inflation and generally high levels of activity that gradually brought an increasing number of firms over the threshold. To some extent, one should probably also take into account a gradual improvement in the comprehensiveness of *IS*, even apart from the 1931 census. The main conclusion to be drawn from this is that *IS* gives an exaggerated impression of rates of entry in the 1930's relative to those prevailing in the preceding decade. This conclusion stands also if consideration is given to errors in the data, which probably have imparted more of an upward bias to the figures for the 1920's than for the 1930's.

It is clear, too, that the more rapid growth in the number of firms

---

thus estimated. (The figures for 1933 and 1934 were not utilized in computing the trend since 1934 represents the first year in which the firms that were "newly discovered" in the 1931 census of firms were included.) Although this procedure involves a very rough approximation, it still gives a less misleading result than if no correction were made at all.

[7] This factor should not be assigned too much weight, however, since firms are as a rule not removed from *IS* until they have remained below the statistical threshold for several years.

in the later decade resulted partly from a decline in *mortality rates*. Figure 17 shows that the higher rates in the 1920's are to be explained primarily, though not exclusively, by the greater impact of the depression following World War I compared to that of the depression of the 1930's. The rise in the number of disappearances during the latter crisis is indeed notably small. The great depression of the 1930's, remarkably enough, did not increase the ratio of disappearances to existing firms. Both in absolute numbers and percentagewise, disappearances in the second half of the 1930's were below the levels recorded for the last half of the earlier decade. It is interesting, also, that·the troughs of these series are found in 1923–24 and 1934–35. In each case, the upswing was then definitely underway, but the peak of the cycle had not yet been reached.

The main part of our analysis of the data summarized here follows in later chapters. In the present connection, a few additional observations, relevant to the questions raised above, should be made. Closer scrutiny of the size of new entrants reveals no definite tendency for new firms to be established on smaller initial scale in depression years than in boom years (Cf., Appendix 11 of Swedish edition). A weighting of the number of starts by entry size does not change the general picture. In most industries, however, firms started in the 1930's generally entered on a bigger scale than those in the 1920's. Mortality was not always highest among the smallest firms. Table 8 shows the incidence of disappearance for different size classes of firms in existence at the end of World War I. Table 6 and Appendix 11 [of the Swedish edition] give the same information for firms formed during the interwar period. Excessive mortality among firms in the 1919 size class of 8–19 workers is apparent in several industries, as well as among firms started on a relatively large scale. This suggests that being "very small" did not mean being extremely vulnerable. This conclusion will seem even more warranted if the data on tanneries and steel mills are excluded, and there were a number of quite special circumstances which combined to eliminate the smallest firms in these two particular industries. But the relatively low mortality in the smallest size class of many industries was also due to the fact that young firms, which simply had not had the time to expand significantly, were less vulnerable than older firms.

The summary below shows that only one third of the firms that succumbed to the depression in the 1930's had been started during the 1920's. As for those firms that disappeared in 1920–22, a notably large number dated to the period before 1914. Table 6 and Appendix 8 show that the great majority of the firms that disappeared had been stationary or regressive during the immediately preceding boom. This observation, which there will be several occasions to recall later, also suggests that young, and consequently often small, firms by no means always were the most vulnerable.

Some reservations, however, must be made. The data indicate that only a small proportion of the firms that were discontinued in these periods had been started during the preceding boom. The question is whether this result is reliable. Could it not have been that many small firms were started in the boom periods but never grew to the threshold size before they disappeared and, therefore, were not included either in *IS* or this study? To this question one may answer, first, that even if this were the case, these firms would not be very important in the overall picture. They would, for example, not affect employment significantly. Second, it seems improbable that the result is unreliable, since new firms in the lowest registered size class are not found to be predominant among total disappearances. In most industries, in fact, mortality rates were higher the higher the size class. Thus it is improbable, albeit not impossible, that a particularly large number of firms spent their entire life span below the statistical threshold of *IS*.

Firms Discontinued 1920–22

Total number	305
started prior to 1914	144
started 1914–19	33
started prior to 1920, but not known whether before 1914 or not	120

Firms Discontinued 1931–33

Total number	300
started prior to 1914	130
started 1914–19	7
started prior to 1920, but not known whether before 1914 or not	26
started 1920–29	
(Max. estimate)	128
(Min. estimate)	57

Two other reservations are probably more important. First, bankruptcies, with consequent changes of ownership, are probably more easily missed when they occur in the smallest class of firms. In such cases, then, exits and entries are not recorded. Second, one must infer that in this size class the prelude to changes in ownership was often an economic failure such that, for the purposes of this study, it ought to be equated with bankruptcy, even though legally no bankruptcy took place. To the extent that such cases were frequent, the mortality rate for the smallest firms would be underestimated here. A closer study, penetrating beneath the statistically quantifiable data, yields the strong impression that the actual situation in this regard varied drastically from industry to industry. At present, therefore, it is best to postpone further discussion of this problem to later chapters. At this point, we will only note that the observations made above do not warrant the conclusion that the smallest and/or youngest firms really possessed economic strength superior to that of the larger firms. The ability to survive, according to the criteria used here, is not to be equated with strength.

In preparation for the analysis of later chapters, we should emphasize, finally, some of the results that emerge from a closer study of individual industries. At present, we will, however, focus attention only on some individual instances that diverge notably from the general picture. The more detailed discussion belongs in the later context of our analysis of the nature of the formation, development, and discontinuation of firms.

It is important to point out, first, that no industry exhibits a marked cyclical sensitivity of entry rates, and that the high level in 1919-20, the remarkable rise between 1931 and 1932, and the decline in the late 1930's emerges almost everywhere. The rise in entry rates in 1931-32 was by no means limited to industries that stood to gain the most from the increased tariff protection which was part of the general revamping of government economic policies in 1931.

Firm formation was more lively during the years 1932-37 than in the 1923-30 period. While the difference is not very marked, it is of considerable interest to note that the rise in the total entry rate was almost entirely due to developments in the ready-made clothing and hosiery industries. In these two, entry rates almost doubled, while the level remained much the same in the great engineeing industries, among the joineries, and in the food and chemical industries. In the textile branches mentioned, the depression of the thirties is not reflected in any decline of new entry. Instead, entry increased. These conclusions are not significantly affected if one applies the more restrictive definition of "new firm," which eliminates the case in which a "new" start is tied to an immediately preceding disappearance. If the industries are grouped as far as possible into capital goods and consumption goods industries, no marked cyclical sensitivity of entry rates in the former class emerges.

It has already been mentioned that the high mortality figures for the first postwar decade derive not only from the fact that the depression of the early 1920's had a more serious effect than that of the early 1930's, but also from the high disappearance figures for the rest of the 1920's. A closer study reveals that this conclusion pertains particularly to the engineering industries, to the steel mills, and to the tanneries. With regard to these industries, the conclusion also holds true for the totals, and not only in relation to the number of firms at the beginning of the respective decade. Quite the opposite situation is found in the ready-made clothing industry. Since this branch had a considerably larger firm population in 1930 than in 1920, there is nothing remarkable in the industry's divergence from the more general pattern.

The capital goods industries generally showed decidedly higher mortality rates. In the engineering industries, the crisis of the 1930's had a severe impact on capital goods producers but did not affect the mortality of producers of consumer durables. It is worth noting that the various textile branches came through the early 1920's relatively unscathed but showed a clear rise in mortality rates toward the end of the decade. The cotton and woolen branches showed no mortality increase in the crisis of the early 1930's, but rather a decline. These results remain unchanged if the narrow definition of "discontinuation" is used.

12 Analysis of Industries with High Rates of Entry

Chapters 6 through 9 have provided a broad outline of the transformation of Swedish industry in the interwar period and have also, to a certain extent, analyzed the different types of developmental processes. Chapters 10 and 11 have presented quantitative evidence on the formation, development, and discontinuation of firms—first for the interwar period in its entirety, then for the two decades separately, and finally on a year-by-year basis. We have seen that formation of new firms was lively—in most industries the number of new starts exceeded the number of firms in existence at the end of 1918. Most of the firms in existence by 1939 had been formed during the interwar period. In many branches, however, rates of entry were declining. Compared with the period before World War I, new entry relatively seldom led to the establishment of big and/or strongly progressive firms. Most large and/or strongly progressive new enterprises were subsidiaries. The major portion of the 1939 work force was found in firms which dated to the period before 1919. Entry rates showed little sensitivity to fluctuations in aggregate activity. There was a notable rise in 1932 and apparently a certain decline during the last two years of the 1930's.

Among industries that developed mainly on a supply-push pattern, it was found that those with many new or young products as a rule showed lively and quantitatively significant entry, while those in which new production methods were of predominant importance showed few new firms but often exhibited rapid growth of existing firms. Rapid demand-growth, not associated with new products or new processes, led to lively and, usually, quantitatively significant entry, but not to the same extent as in industries where new products were important. In these demand-pull cases, moreover, it was usually only a few firms which accounted for most of the industry's growth, while in supply-push industries, the new firms as a rule were more generally successful in expanding.

Realized rates of return showed no simple relation to rates of entry— high average earnings in an industry were not always associated with a substantial number of new firms, nor low returns with a small number of entrants. Disappearances were found overwhelmingly among old, stationary, or regressive firms, and they were not closely correlated with the business cycle. Mortality rates were considerably higher in the 1920's than in the 1930's. In both decades, they were found to be lowest in the early part of the cyclical upswing.

So far, a whole array of questions have been left open. The answers to these questions require a detailed analysis of the *nature* of the formation, development, and discontinuation of firms, not just of the quantitative extent of these phenomena. Chapters 12 through 15 are devoted to these questions, as well as to a number of other problems relevant to the present study which will emerge in the course of the discussion. The industries are dealt with largely in the same order as in Chapter 6. Since it has been judged desirable to make each industry section self-contained so that it can be read separately, a good deal of repetition has been unavoidable. Since the analysis must survey a large field, it has, on the other hand, been necessary to discuss certain causal relationships, which are relevant in several separate instances, only in connection with that industry for which the relationship has been most important. Repetition has in this way been kept within limits. To avoid making the discussion more tedious than necessary for readers who go through all of the sections, a certain variation in the plan of discussion has been attempted. For the same reason, explicit references to earlier chapters have not always been made. Formulations have been purposely varied to a somewhat greater extent than strict requirements of consistency would recommend. The disadvantages of this procedure are not serious, however, since the discussion in Chapter 16, in which results are surveyed, deals in general terms rather than with each industry separately.

The Engineering Industries

The majority of the new firms in these industries were started on a small scale and remained small (see Appendix 8 of Swedish edition). They very frequently complemented the existing big enterprises. The "underbrush" of small firms competing with the products of medium-sized or big firms was insignificant. Industry structure was fairly stable also in the sense that, at the end of the interwar period, there was no special category of firms that was doomed to disappear, whereas somewhat obsolete types of firms had been present at the beginning of the period. Appendix 8 shows that about 38 percent of the new capital goods producing firms were started with less than eight workers and remained stationary. In the other branches, the corresponding figure was 38 percent for consumer durables producers, 56 percent in iron and steel manufacturing, 66 percent in (nonferrous) metal manufacturing, and 44 percent in sheet metal manufacturing. Appendix 12 [in Swedish edition] reveals another characteristic picture. A fairly small proportion of the medium-sized and big firms that were in existence at the end of the period and that had been started after the end of World War I were started on a very small scale. It is worth noting, also, that almost all of the big firms in existence in 1939 could look back on the interwar period as a period of rapid expansion (see Appendix 13 of Swedish edition). The data on the

FIGURE 20
Concentration of Engineering Industries in 1919 and 1939

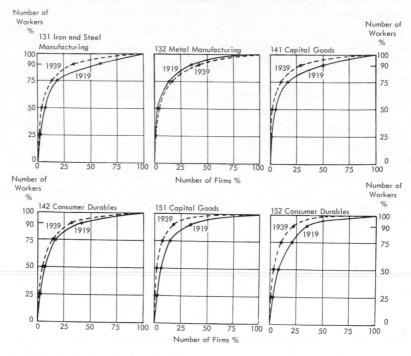

firm distribution of the labor force show a considerable degree of industry concentration. On this measure, industry concentration also increased through the interwar period, despite a considerable increase in the number of small firms relative to that of medium-sized and large enterprises (see Figure 20).

The situation typical of the interwar period was no doubt characteristic of the 1940's also. The number of small firms continued to grow. To a substantial extent, this was due to the strong inflationary pressures, to price control which generally favored new producers, to the curtailment of imports, and so forth. But in part this development was a continuation of interwar developments. The structure of the engineering industries at the end of the 1940's must be judged less stable than earlier since many of the new firms, which owe their existence to the factors just mentioned, surely will disappear. To some extent this weeding-out process began in 1949. But despite this element of instability, there is little doubt that the somewhat novel type of industry structure which emerged in the interwar period and became more marked by the late forties will be lasting. A closer study of the nature of the formation, development, and disappearance of firms in the 1919–39 period will clarify the reasons for this prognosis.

Four Categories of New Enterprises. In the various engineering industries, four major types of new firms may be distinguished, although "pure" specimens of these types are seldom found.

The first category concerns a small group of firms that were *established directly in connection with the expansion of other firms in other industry branches.* Here one would include firms that began producing for a particular industry, or even for a single firm, usually in the same town or at least in the same region. A number of machine shops, producing tools and other implements for the quarries and canneries in the province of Bohuslän or for the glassworks in Småland, are examples belonging to this group. The industries placing the orders for these products were quite dependent on the new firms and generally absorbed their entire output.

The second category consists of *subcontractors to firms in the same or in a closely related branch.* The output of these firms consisted of *semifinished products,* i.e., either products finished in another firm or finished parts of another product. We may also include here the production of *tools.* While tools are definitely final products, they were, after all, to a substantial extent produced also by the firms for their own needs. In a sense, therefore, they may be regarded as semifinished goods. This definition of "subcontracting" is not altogether satisfactory since its strict application would mean, for example, that AB Svenska Kullargerfabriken (S.K.F.) would be included in this category. While in this instance the result would be unreasonable, the definition still yields a useful general rule. As an example of a semifinished product class of the first type, one may mention the greater part of the output of machine castings. A whole range of metal castings belongs here. As examples of the second type, we have parts for bicycles and automobiles. In the interwar period, such semifinished products, or finished parts for final products, as well as many types of tools, came increasingly to be produced by independent firms instead of by the firms marketing the final product in the more definite sense of the term.

In clear contrast to the situation before World War I, firms belonging to this second category were quite prominent in the overall picture of enterprise formation in the engineering industries between the wars.[1] Since in numerous cases the proper classification of firms remains in doubt, the total number of firms in this subcontracting category can only be estimated in a very approximate fashion. But at least 200 of the new firms in all the engineering industries (i.e., somewhat more than 20 percent) are to be regarded as definitely in the subcontractor category. Among the close to 1,000 continuing firms, the number belonging to this category was at most 40 or 45 (i.e., 4 or 4.5 percent of the total). The difference is so marked that it cannot possibly fall within the margin of error. It should also be noted that a considerable proportion of the smallest firms, not reported in *Industry Statistics* (*IS*), certainly must have belonged in the subcontractor category. It appears that firms of this type were even predominant in the establishment of new firms during the 1940's. New small firms have emerged in great numbers, particularly after the end of World War II, a development which is to be attributed primarily to the general inflationary pressure, to the import difficulties, and to the continuing tendency, dating back to the prewar period, toward expansion of the subcontracting system.

The third and the fourth groups of new firms both comprise firms that began producing final products but should be distinguished from the first category above. Firms in the third category entered into the production of goods that were already manufactured domestically or imported from abroad.[2] New entry in this more narrow and conventional sense of the term leads to what may be called "parallel competition." The fourth category comprises firms established to produce new final products.

In the engineering industries, one finds *only a few new firms producing final products that were already being produced domestically at the end of World War I and were at that time so well-known that their markets could expand only through demand-pull or through price reductions and/or improvements in quality and type.*[3] It was unusual, in other words,

---

[1] Whenever subcontracting has accounted for the preponderant part of a firm's output, the firm has been classified in this category.

[2] "Parallel competition" may differ from "price competition" to the extent that a more or less prominent element of product differentiation by quality enters in. Most quality differences do not constitute a distinction between two different products. Parallel competition appeared also among the firms in the subcontracting category but was less prominent there since the relationships between suppliers and customers generally were firmer.

[3] Price reductions and/or quality improvements may, of course, enlarge the market for the product in question, but they need not do so if competitors lose ground.

for new enterprises of some considerable importance to win a share of a market growing primarily on the basis of demand-pull or process innovations. Cases of this type most often involved new firms, induced to entry by the formation of monopolies or cartels, which then remained in the shadow of a cartel. In some other, and sometimes similar, cases, the new firms saw their chance to enter by choosing to produce items that were not among the standardized products of the large enterprises. Many new firms producing wire nails and screws can be mentioned as examples. Numerous new firms producing electrical fixtures belong here, but in this branch there was strong "parallel competition" as well.

Not many new firms went into *parallel competition with earlier imported products*. There were few areas in which the tariff changes made during this period had any decisive significance. The most important such change was the reduction of the import duty on automobile parts in conjunction with a certain upward adjustment of the duty on assembled automobiles (see below). For the rest it was mostly a question of restoring protection that had been eroded by internal inflation. Of the product lines that were new to the domestic scene, only a few were taken up by new firms from their start. Although few firms were established for the principal purpose of producing previously imported goods, it was nonetheless common that the new firms gradually complemented their programs with such products. These were not infrequently well-suited for small enterprises, since they often enjoyed only a relatively limited market in Sweden.

Many new firms engaged in *parallel competition by following on the heels of a new or established firm that was in the process of creating a market for a certain product*. This often did not require a comparative advantage over, or even equal efficiency with, the older firms. This type of process was found also among the subcontracting firms but was less frequent due to firmer relationships between suppliers and customers. Together with the proliferation of subcontracting firms, the new firms emerging in this way account for the greater part of new entry in the engineering industries during the interwar period. New and young products played a far greater role in the industries producing consumer durables and in nonferrous metal and sheet metal manufacturing than they did in the capital goods producing industries. It is typical that the former dominated the formation of new firms in the engineering industries, particularly during the 1930's. This seems to have been the case, also, in the 1940's, but the emphasis during this later decade was probably partly on subcontracting firms and partly on import-replacing firms.

The fourth and last category, *new enterprises pioneering in product innovations*, comprised a relatively modest number of firms. In the capital goods producing industries, whether in electrical or mechanical engineering, the number was particularly small. But then, the number of new or young products was also relatively small in these branches. This observation seems to apply to the 1940's as well as to the interwar period.

Of these four categories, the first may be disregarded in a closer analysis of the formation and development of firms as being of little significance and as posing few problems of analytical interest. The remaining three, particularly the second, are the more interesting ones.

Subcontracting Firms. The continuing firms did not generally develop toward a noticeably greater degree of specialization.[4] Although there were some instances in which increasing concentration on certain product lines left room for new firms to take up the discarded ones, such cases were of little quantitative significance. But the production of the main product lines frequently became increasingly more complicated technically, and this made it desirable to arrange for the production of a growing number of semifinished goods, various small components, and finished parts for the final product outside the firm. The improved machine tools marketed in this period, the new light metal materials, the new stamped foundry products, and so forth, all meant that there were many things suitable for production by small shops. Similarly, it was advantageous to have the continuing firm's own tools produced by other firms to a larger extent than previously.[5] In this connection, one should mention that wooden foundry models came to be produced by independent woodworking shops to a far greater extent than earlier (cf. the section on the woodworking industry).

To continue the internal production of semifinished products, tools, and models to the same extent as in earlier periods, when production processes were far less complicated, would have meant excessive diversification. This would have been particularly true before the products of these more complicated processes found a sufficiently large established market, permitting long production runs. To the extent that a development of the latter type took place, there was often a tendency to reintegrate the production of semifinished goods into the firm itself. This helps to explain the fact that subcontracting firms seldom remained purely subcontractors over the longer run. One finds that by the end of the interwar period, such firms were very frequently engaged also in the production of some finished product of a simple kind. But for the engineering industries as a whole, the first-mentioned tendency dominated throughout the interwar period. This meant that there was considerable scope for small businesses that would contract to deliver semifinished

---

[4] "Specialization" here means that an individual firm devotes itself in the main to one or two products. "Concentration" is a complementary concept but concerns the industry as a whole and refers to the extent to which the production of a product is concentrated to one or a few firms without regard to the degree of specialization of these firms.

[5] Originally, the engineering mills made all their tools for themselves. The tendency of letting other firms make them started very early, however.

products and/or finished parts and tools. Many of these firms were at the same time engaged in service-related activities of one kind or another and often resembled the burgeoning category of automotive repair shops.

The following cases of formation of new firms are typical:

In 1929 a foundry foreman from a large steel mill started a metal foundry in rented facilities. The location of the firm—a medium-sized town—was selected because it was his wife's birthplace. The owner had moderate savings and borrowed approximately the same amount from relatives with life insurance as collateral. The only cosigners he could find were his father and brother. From the start, the firm concentrated exclusively on semifinished products of the then novel light metals. There was a definite demand for such items on the part of large engineering firms, and he had few difficulties in marketing most of the output outside the town. These customers of the firm "had found it cheaper to purchase semifabricates and to restrict themselves to the mechanical processing of them."

In 1924, a Stockholm foreman started a firm solely for the production of "precision-manufactured parts and instrument components." He found regular customers "among larger firms which had to turn to specialized shops for components that were not manufactured in quantity."

One firm was started in Malmö for the production and cutting of cogwheels and chainwheels, "when I found out that these products could be made both cheaper and better with automatic cutters and that for certain industries and firms, which do not require large quantities but do require many different types of wheels, it did not pay to invest in these machines."

The large number of such subcontractors and producers of special tools is part of the explanation for the combination of a high rate of entry and a quite low entry share ($\alpha_{23} = 8$) found in capital goods manufacturing. It also helps to explain why the entry shares for the consumer durables branches, metal, and sheet metal manufacturing industries were not still larger ($\alpha_{23} = 37, 32$ and 18), despite a high number of entrants relative to continuing firms, and despite a couple of very large new firms in the first of the three—most significantly, AB Volvo and General Motors Nordiska AB. Firms of the subcontracting type usually had few of the prerequisites for, and/or little incentive toward, expanding in the manner of other types of firms, particularly since many of them produced for a local or regional market.[6]

The important role of subcontracting firms is also reflected in the data on market orientation, summarized in Appendix 16 [in Swedish edition]. It is quite evident that the new firms started in the interwar period were oriented toward export markets only to a relatively insignificant extent.[7] The firms founded in the 1930's, in particular, were overwhelm-

---

[6] A second factor contributing to the increasing importance of the small, stationary firms will be discussed below.

[7] This indicates a significant change in the situation relative to the period prior to World War I. Before 1914, the export markets had been generally regarded

ingly oriented toward domestic markets. This statistical evidence is perhaps not so remarkable in and of itself, since recently started firms seldom are successful in export markets immediately, even when their longer run market orientation lies in this direction. One should also recall the basis on which the classification into export firms and domestic firms has been made.[8] Strictly speaking, the data prove only that the new firms seldom went directly into exports or had their own foreign customers, and so forth. But a study of the products usually produced by these firms does give a firm foundation for the conclusion that the orientation toward foreign markets had become completely subsidiary, particularly among the new firms established in the 1930's. The semifabricates, the parts for finished products, the tools, etc., were export goods only in exceptional cases.

The great significance of this largely novel type of firm during the interwar period was due also to factors other than those already emphasized (i.e., the growing role of subcontracting arrangements, the introduction of new machines, new materials and new product types suitable for small businesses, and the difficulties encountered in export markets). Two sets of preconditions should be particularly emphasized in this connection. One of these has often been stressed in the literature, namely, the favorable conditions created for small businesses of an industrial nature in the new era of electric power and of the automobile.[9]

The second set of preconditions, however, has been more or less ignored, *viz.*, *the expanding base for the recruitment of new entrepreneurs.* Since this factor is of interest from a number of different viewpoints, it is desirable to study it in some detail without, however, in any way pushing the first-mentioned factor into the background.

Appendix 14 [in Swedish edition] summarizes the data on the recruitment of founders of firms in the engineering industries. The age of founders at the start of the new firms is also of some interest. Appendix 15 shows it to have been relatively high. New firms were seldom started by very young men.[10]

---

as less risky than the home market. Cf. E. Linder, "Den svenska mekaniska verkstadsindustriens utveckling intill krigsutbrottet," *Tull- och Traktatkommitténs betänkande, SOU* (1923, No. 31).

[8] To the extent that information directly from the firms has proved impossible to obtain, *Svensk Exportkalender* has been used. Those firms that never appeared in this reference work have been classified as producing for the home market. The Swedish export directory, however, does not list all firms with some production for export, not even when the firms themselves sell directly to foreign customers. Apart from this, moreover, there is a source of error in that many firms may be exporting indirectly, i.e., through some other firm or through wholesalers or machine manufacturers.

[9] Cf. Eli F. Heckscher, "Efterkrigstidens ekonomiska och sociala förskjutningar," *Ekonomisk-historiska studier* (Stockholm, 1936).

[10] For the concept of "enterprise founder" and the material underlying the statistical calculations, cf. Appendix 1 of the Swedish edition, p. 14. Concerning the

The great importance of workers, supervisors, and foremen is evident. Two thirds of the known founders belonged to this blue-collar category.[11] Engineers also played a relatively significant role in the interwar period, particularly in the electrical engineering industry. While merchants and landowners had played a very prominent role prior to World War I, these groups receded completely into the background after the war. Table 9 indicates the number of cases for which data on the background of the founder was available, and in which a firm, founded during the period and still in existence in 1940, had been started by a worker—alone or with others. The percentage of responses has surely been lower among "blue-collar firms" than among other firms; so the table probably underestimates the actual share of such firms. It should be added that workers and foremen formed partnerships with salesmen, office workers, and persons of similar background less frequently in the engineering industries than in some other industries.

There can be no doubt that this strong shift in recruitment from merchants toward industrial workers took place during the entire period after 1900 and that it became especially pronounced in the interwar period. It is true that study of the recruitment of enterprise founders before World War I reveals a significant number of workers also in this period.[12] The number of such cases increased in the interwar period but this is not the only significant change that occurred between the two periods. It is also true that the older "blue-collar firms" characteristically differed from those founded in the latter period in that they typically developed out of a craft shop of the old type, such as a smithy, a simple repair ship, and so forth. In the interwar period, on the other hand, most of the newly formed small businesses were of a type quite distinct from the old crafts right from the start, and this was true also among the firms started by workers.

The recruitment of new entrepreneurs in the engineering industries was basically limited to persons already employed in these industries. Thus the general expansion of the engineering industries led to a cumulative broadening of the recruitment base. A steadily growing number of workers acquired industrial experience, while at the same time the

age of founders, Oxenfeldt, *New Firms and Free Enterprise, op. cit.,* Chapter VI reports some data which indicate a relatively high average age also for founders in the United States.

[11] It should be recalled here that repair shops, smithies, etc., have not been included.

[12] It has not been possible to study recruitment in this period at all as thoroughly as for the interwar period. A rather large number of questionnaires were, however, answered by firms established a long time prior to World War I. (All firms that had not been included in *IS* until after 1918 received questionnaires but a fair number of them turned out to be older.) In addition, information on recruitment has also been obtained through the various *Festschrifts,* brochures, etc., which the older firms, in particular, have had the time to publish on various occasions.

general educational level and the level of technical knowledge rose. The growing demand emanating from the established firms for relatively simple semifabricates, components, and tools meant that the demands on the size of initial capital, on sales organization, on established credit, and so forth, were lowered. In the light of these developments, the lively formation of new blue-collar enterprises is not so surprising.

The recruitment base explains to some extent the high propensity to start subcontracting firms. Apart from this, it also helps to explain the remarkable fact that the great majority of the new enterprises remained stationary or grew only to a rather insignificant extent (see Appendix 8 of Swedish edition). It seems that a very large proportion of the new firms, particularly those started by workers, were formed without any intention of substantial expansion. The main motive was simply to obtain a comfortable income for the entrepreneur. In this respect, these firms were no different from the old craft shops or, for that matter, from ordinary wage-earning employment. But in certain instances, there was a psychological difference in relation to the latter alternative—the desire to become independent often played a role in the decision to start a business. This desire was often a more important motive than the desire to earn more money than needed for a decent standard of living. In still other cases, the will to become independent was quite subsidiary, while the simple, overriding necessity to find a source of income for the entrepreneur and his family was decisive. Many firms were started on this *"livelihood principle."* This explains the finding reported in Chapter

TABLE 9
Survey of Engineering Firms Founded by Workers, Foremen, etc.

Industry	Number started 1919–39 and in operation 1940	Number for which previous occupation of founder is known	Firms founded by workers, foremen, etc.	
			Number	Percent
Iron, steel and metal manufacturing...	485	326	236	72
Mechanical engineering............	320	222	134	60
Electrical engineering..............	101	79	29	37
Total......................	906	627	399	64

11, namely, the absence of any cyclical decline in the rate of formation of new firms in the years 1931–33.[13] Prior to World War I, in contrast, when the number of worker-owned firms was considerably lower, the

---

[13] Cf. Oxenfeldt, *op. cit.,* Chapter X. Oxenfeldt points out that, in the United States also, unemployment has given rise to formation of new firms.

rate of firm formation was highly correlated with fluctuations in aggregate activity.

New Final Goods Producers Engaging in Parallel Competition. While there were thus several different reasons why the situation was promising for subcontracting firms, the conditions were generally unfavorable for new firms that entered into direct competition with established firms in the markets for final goods. Markets, especially for capital goods, either did not expand at all or their growth was characterized by demand-pull or by process innovations. This generally meant that large and capital-demanding risks had to be accepted in any attempt to dislodge an older firm from its market. Nor was it an easy task to prevent established firms from appropriating an expanding market.[14] There were some exceptions—in cases where the new firm, at least temporarily, could find customers in a local market in which the large firms made little sales effort, and where a personal relationship between producer and customer existed. Other exceptions are found in those instances where the products were too expensive to transport over long distances. New population agglomerations would then demand new producers. Finally, one should mention those cases in which the attempt of older firms to relinquish old wholesale connections created a favorable opportunity for new firms (see below).

In other instances, parallel competition generally required that the new enterprise be technically and organizationally considerably more efficient than its established competitors. Older firms often had firmly established customer connections, and oligopolistic markets existed in many areas. As long as the older firms did not bungle their customer relations, customers usually were not apt to desert to other suppliers until faced with large and long-established differentials in price, quality, product type, or service. It should be noted that pure price competition was relatively unusual. When lower prices were offered, they were undoubtedly often connected with lower quality. Usually product differentiation and service competition predominated, since the chances of dislodging established firms from their markets through price cutting were often quite slim, particularly since many of the new enterprises started with machinery and equipment that had been discarded by existing firms.

In those engineering branches that developed more on the basis of secondary, rather than primary, innovations, the new firms were generally

---

[14] Old firms just as well as potential entrants would much rather hunt for new products. *Verkstäderna* (1931), p. 217, cites the advice of a well-known American industrialist which the Swedish business world surely was generally prone to follow: "You should rather adopt the production of a technical novelty than compete with others over the market for already established products. But the new product should then be superior to whatever already exists to serve the same purpose. Under these conditions you do not have to fight with the knife at your throat but will have enough breathing room to get the new product established." One might add, however, that frequently a cutthroat struggle of this sort need not occur when the parallel competition takes place in an expanding market (cf. below).

handicapped.[15] The older firms usually had larger financial resources. In addition, it was not uncommon for older firms to operate with a fixed plant which had been written down to a very low figure (e.g., because of large capital losses suffered by earlier owners) so that these firms had a smaller equity to earn a return on than a newly established enterprise.[16] Even when a new firm was the first to carry out a good idea, and thus initially get an advantage, the established firms usually were able to channel larger resources of different kinds—money, sales organization, and so forth—into its exploitation, and in this manner to overtake and vanquish the new firm. This prospect often scared off prospective entrants. Thus the individual with such an idea would rather seek the support of an older and/or larger firm. The usual result would be either that a subsidiary was formed or that the innovation was realized within the established firm. The policy of the banks, which were often contacted by individuals with ideas and the desire to start a new enterprise, was of considerable importance in this connection. In the interwar period, the banks almost always tried to tie prospective innovators to an already existing firm whenever they found the idea worth exploiting. Before World War I, in contrast, the policy had generally been to help the individual start his own firm.

Finally, it should be noted that there was a large number of cases in which a new firm that expanded on its own was bought up or assimilated in some other way by some larger firm or group of companies. Table 10 shows quite clearly that an uncommonly large proportion of the progressive firms were no longer independent by the end of the interwar period. Very frequently this was explained by the advantages to be gained from exploiting the already established sales organization of an older firm. In many instances, it was not very tempting to build an expensive sales organization just for a single new firm or, perhaps, just for a single product, when older firms could offer the services of an already established distributive network. Prior to World War I, on the other hand, there was frequently no choice because the number of established sales organizations was small.

Parallel competition thus required new entrepreneurs to accept great risks and demanded sizable amounts of risk capital. This undoubtedly circumscribed the recruitment base for enterprise founders. It is clear, to begin with, that managers, engineers, and high-level executives were reluctant to accept these risks and generally preferred to remain in sal-

---

[15] It should be emphasized that this in no way required that all the old firms had an advantage over the entrants. This, in fact, was very seldom the case. But it was often sufficient that one older firm had such an advantage.

[16] Since the significance of this factor for the competitive position of entrants played a more important role in certain other industries, it will be discussed in more detail later on.

TABLE 10

Engineering Firms Grouped according to Development Type and Status* in 1939 or When Discontinued

Type†	Continuing Firms				Firms Started 1919–39 and in Operation 1940				Firms Discontinued 1919–39							
									Started before 1919				Started 1919–39			
	Inde-pen-dent	Sub-sidi-ary	Un-known	Total	Inde-pen-dent	Sub-sidi-ary	Un-known	Total	Inde-pen-dent	Sub-sidi-ary	Un-known	Total	Inde-pen-dent	Sub-sidi-ary	Un-known	Total
1.........	441	42	89	572	486	16	58	560	135	15	75	225	66	7	30	103
2.........	149	31	33	213	178	18	33	229	7	5	5	17	10	2	2	14
3.........	55	28	4	87	40	20	15	75	1	1	—	2	—	—	—	—
4.........	64	13	17	94	5	1	—	6	64	10	27	101	7	2	4	13
5.........	1	1	—	2	20	8	8	36	17	9	18	44	7	3	4	14
Total	710	115	143	968	729	63	114	906	224	40	125	389	90	14	40	144

* Firms in which another manufacturing enterprise had a more than 50 percent interest or which were owned together with others by a financial holding company have been classified as "subsidiaries." "Independent" status does not exclude a linkage to other firms through an individual. Many such cases, of course, may in reality be comparable to subsidiary status.

† 1 = stationary, 2 = fairly progressive, 3 = strongly progressive, 4 = regressive, 5 = unknown.

aried positions.[17] While these groups generally had better opportunities than the blue-collar groups to raise the necessary beginning capital, they also had relatively less to gain and more to lose as independent entrepreneurs. An engineer, for example, who failed as an entrepreneur would find it more difficult to find new employment than would a former worker or foreman for whom a bankruptcy, for example, would be less serious.

Raising capital was generally the decisive problem. In the engineering industries, the formation of a new firm generally required a sizable financial investment as soon as it was not simply a question of producing as a subcontractor or for a small market, marginal to the mass-produced, standardized lines of the big firms. In comparison with earlier periods when machines were few and simple, the ability to compete hinged increasingly on the acquisition of expensive equipment. This became particularly true in the 1930's. Despite the undoubtedly growing number of new subcontractors, this period shows a tendency toward a larger initial scale of entrants (see Appendix 11 of Swedish edition)—a fact which to some extent reflects the role of the increasing outlays for equipment that was required. The difficult conditions in foreign markets also put heavier demands on the financial resources of new enterprises because a good sales organization was more necessary than ever. This required that the new firm invest considerable amounts if it did not choose to associate itself with an existing firm having an established distribution network. Opportunities for raising sufficient starting capital from private individuals were much smaller in the interwar period than earlier. There were several reasons for this, and their relative importance is difficult to gauge. Since a separate chapter will be devoted to these financing problems, the discussion of this issue may be postponed.

Next, we should consider those new enterprises which engaged in parallel competition with older firms in markets which expanded due to the supply-push of a new or "young" product. Effective cartel arrangements were seldom found in markets of this kind. As previously noted, new entry of this type was particularly common in the consumer durables branches and in metal and sheet metal manufacturing.[18] Most of the

---

[17] One entrepreneur, with a background as a worker with only primary school education, expressed this very well: "Had I not been so inexperienced and ignorant, I would never have started my business." He did start, however, and developed through hard work a successful enterprise based on a product innovation of his own design. The initial capital was Sw. cr. 1,200 and the beginning was made in a basement. The firm was sold to an old and large company during the 1940's. This company, in turn, entered into an agreement with the sole Swedish competitor whereby the latter firm ceased its operations. The firm was thereupon modernized and underwent a still more rapid development than previously.

[18] Cartel agreements were naturally unlikely to be established in those cases where a product was gaining ground rapidly. On the one hand there was little reason to form a cartel when the market was large enough for everybody; on

new or young products mentioned in Chapter 7 are good examples of the product types that gave rise to many new firms. It may be noted that KF (the Cooperative Union) and the large new "dimestore" chains were big customers of these new firms.[19] In addition to this, there were numerous products of a more specialized nature, each with a relatively small, and frequently locally or regionally circumscribed, market. These products were often of a type which, though consumed in all areas of the country, were so simple to manufacture that any little firm could enter and find customers, for example, among hardware stores in the vicinity where the proprietors would be old acquaintances of the entrepreneur's. Sundry household articles are good examples. In other instances it was a question of products for which long transports were uneconomical and/or personal contact with the ultimate customer was of great importance. This was often the case, for example, in the construction materials branch.

If we confine ourselves to parallel competition firms which either started on a relatively large scale (i.e., with 50 or more workers) or started on a small scale but reached the indicated size before the mid-1940's, the number of such firms in the engineering industries is not so large that these firms cannot advantageously be enumerated in order to give a more concrete idea of the more outstanding features of the evolutionary process.[20] Characteristically, there are few new producers of machinery, while radiators, fittings, and sundry consumer durables predominate among the products of these new enterprises. The producers of interior fittings are of special interest in this connection. The large number of progressive new firms is to be explained, *inter alia*, by the decision of the big, established firms to attempt to circumvent the wholesalers and sell directly to construction contractors. This caused the wholesalers to offer the new producers favorable marketing outlets. The corresponding phenomenon is found also in some other areas, particularly when the products were relatively simple, as with interior fittings.

Only a few of the following 86 firms can be counted as "big companies," if by "big" one means firms with several hundred employees. Such firms have been marked with a dagger following the year of establishment. An asterisk indicates that the company began on a small scale.

---

the other, it was more difficult to do so, since it was no easy task to cover the entire market.

[19] Cf. the *Annual Report* of the board of the Cooperative Union (KF) for 1933, p. 71.

[20] Among the firms enumerated, some were also responsible for innovations of some importance. But, in general, they do not belong in the same class as the firms listed later as pioneering innovators. The development of the firms in the latter category was almost entirely based on their innovating contributions. In a few cases, the name of a firm will recur also in our later enumeration of product-innovating firms, namely, when product innovations played a large, though not predominant, role in its growth.

A "D" indicates a firm formed as a subsidiary—a common case. Together with firms that were taken over by another and, most often, older company at a later date, the subsidiaries account for almost one third of the total number. That so many of the progressive firms were absorbed by other, usually old and big, companies is particularly worth noting. In the majority of these cases, rapid expansion dates from the time of the takeover. The products mainly responsible for the firm's development have been indicated where the name of the company does not make it superfluous. The firms are generally listed under their present name, but previous names have also been indicated to the extent that these have been carried for a long enough period for the firm to become widely known under them.[21]

Iron, Steel, and Nonferrous Metal Manufacturing

AB Bendor, Stockholm, 1928. Nuts and bolts, etc.

AB Sandins Metallfabrik, Sundbyberg, 1934. Metal fittings.

Svenska Skandex AB, Stockholm, 1932. File cabinets.

Tekaverken AB, Stockholm, 1919* (later Alingsås). Curtain rods, etc.

AB J. R. Andersson & Co., Stockholm, 1927. Merged into A. Johnson & Co. Stainless steel products.

AB Stålfjädrar, Stockholm, 1934.* Steel springs.

AB Nordiska Metallduksväveriet, Uppsala, 1924. Screen netting.

Holms Industri AB, Motala, 1927. Horseshoes, agricultural tools, etc.

Prestoverken i Motala, AB (previously Holmsbruks Gjuteri AB), Motala, 1924. Central heating equipment.

AB P. M. Liljeqvist, Anderstorp, 1935.* Steel couches, staircase and balcony railings, etc.

Ljungby Armatur & Metallfabr. AB, Ljungby, 1928* Merged into AB C. T. C., Göteborg. Water heaters.

AB Svenska Strebelverken (previously AB Fundo), Västervik, 1924. Taken over first by Strebelverk, Mannheim, Germany, later by K. F. (Swedish Cooperative Union). Central heating equipment.

AB Färe Armaturfabrik, Sibbhult, 1922.† Interior fittings.

AB Bergmans Chuckfabrik, Tyringe, 1922.

AB Ystads Metallindustri, Ystad, 1920. Metal ornaments.

AB Matadorverken, Halmstad, 1927–29.* Razor blades, etc.

Rakbladsfabriken Sollex, Halmstad, 1933* (later Jönköping). Razor blades.

AB Göteborgs Bleckvarufabrik, Göteborg, 1924.† Merged into AB Plåtmanufaktur. Sheet metal products.

AB Fixfabriken, Göteborg, 1925. Metal fittings, etc.

---

[21] The dates here denote the year in which the firm was started, according to the criteria of this study. They will not always, therefore, conform with the dates specified by the firms themselves as their year of establishment, e.g., for inclusion in *Industrikalendern*. Thus it has been common for a firm to have its products produced by other enterprises before entering industrial production on its own. In such a case, the criteria of this study will indicate the date at which the firm enters manufacturing on its own as the "year of formation."

AB Lysekils Emballagefabrik, Lysekil, 1937. Merged into AB Plåtmanufaktur. Tin containers, etc.

J. A. Wirén Gjuteri & Mek. Verkstad, Sävedalen, 1919. Pumps, etc.

AB Vårgårda Armaturfabrik, Vårgårda, 1920. Interior fittings.

Industri IWO AB, Mariestad, 1938. Lighting fixtures.

Necks Verkstäder, Kommanditbolag, Nossebro, 1919. Sheet metal and wrought iron work, etc.

AB Svenska Stållinor, Kristinehamn, 1928. Merged into Hellefors Bruks AB. Steel cable.

Lindesbergs Gjuteri & Mek. Verkstads AB, Lindesberg, 1920.

AB Köpings Armaturfabrik, Köping, 1920.

Erik Sörberg, Armaturfabrik, Kungsör, 1936

Mora Armaturfabrik AB, Mora, 1927.

Gävle Galvaniseringsfabrik AB, Gävle, 1929.*

Mechanical Engineering

AB G. E. Finquists Verkstäder, Ålvsjö, 1919.* Cogwheel gears, etc.

General Motors Nordiska AB, Stockholm, 1928,† D. Automobiles.

AB Augustendals Industrier (AB Svenska Bilfabriken), Stockholm, 1928,† D. Automobiles.

Verkstads AB Tibo (previously AB Elg & Thorén), Stockholm, 1936.* Machine frames, containers.

Ingenjörsfirman Ventilator, S. Romedahl, Stockholm, 1931.

F. Ecks fabriker AB, Nacka, 1925. Radiators. Absorbed by radiator cartel.

AB Johan Sörling, Märsta, 1924.* Truck hoists.

AB Nyköpings Automobilfabrik, Nyköping, 1937,† D.

M. Berlin & Co. AB, Värnamo, 1934. Bicycles.

AB Bruzaholms Bruk, Bruzaholm, 1931. Radiators.

Nya Mek. Taberg AB, Smålands Taberg, 1920.* Textile machinery, mangles, etc.

Maskin- & Gjuteri AB, Kalmar, 1924. Transport equipment.

Osbyverken H. Lönqvist, Osby, 1927. Woodworking machinery.

AB Vattenvärmare-Kompaniet, Osby, 1935.* Water heaters.

AB K. J. Levin, Malmö, 1925. Refrigeration machinery and vending machines.

AB Plåtindustri, Limhamn, 1935. Steel plate and sheet metal work.

AB Järnmontering, Limhamn, 1938, D. Steel structures for buildings.

AB Nyhems Mek. Verkstad, Halmstad, 1919.* Shovels and luggage carriers.

Origoverken, Bröd. Johanson, Smålandsstenar, 1935* (later Halmstad). Jacks, locks, shackles, beds, etc.

AB Svetsmekano, Göteborg, 1937, D. Welding.

Korp & Söners Verkstäder, Vänersborg, 1935. Sundry machine tools and other machinery.

AB Värmeverken, Lerum, 1932.* Merged into AB C. T. C. Central heating equipment.

Fjellmans Mek. verkstads AB, Mariestad (1914), 1925.* Woodworking machinery.

AB Tidaholmsverken, Tidaholm, 1935.† D. Gun carriages.

AB Lidköpings Värmelednings industri, Lidköping, 1921* (later Järpås). Radiators.

AB Thermiaverken, Arvika, 1923. Heating equipment.

AB Örebro Radiatorfabrik, Örebro, 1937.

AB Hägglund & Söner, Örnsköldsvik (1899), 1920's.*† Car bodies, electrical motors, etc.

AB Maskinfabriken i Örnsköldsvik, Örnsköldsvik (1918), 1920's.*† Saws.

Fabriks AB Forslund & Co, Skellefteå, 1936. Truck hoists.

Electrical Engineering

AB Asea Svetsmaskiner, Stockholm, 1938, D. Welding equipment.

Dux Radio AB, Stockholm, 1926.

Elektr. AB Helios, Stockholm, 1919. Merged into Asea. Electrical heaters.

AB Gylling & Co, Stockholm, 1931. Radios.

Lumalampan AB (previously AB Hammarbylampan), Stockholm, 1931.† K. F. Light bulbs.

Skand. Radio AB, Stockholm, 1935.

Standard Radiofabrik, Stockholm, 1938. D.

AB Stern & Stern, Stockholm, 1925. Radios.

Svenska Radio AB, Stockholm, 1919.† Merged into Telefon AB L. M. Ericsson.

Tjernelds Radiofabrik, Stockholm, 1923.

A. Wessel & Co, Stockholm, 1939, D. Switches.

Svenska Torrelement AB, Stockholm, 1927. Dry cell batteries.

Aga-Baltic AB, Sundbyberg, 1924 (later Lidingö). Merged into AB Gasaccumulator. Radios.

AB L. Johanssons Radiofabrik, Sundbyberg, 1923.

Pertrixverken, Acc. Fabriks AB Tudor, Sundyberg, 1932, D.

Elektr. AB Skandia, Eskilstuna, 1924 (later Arboga). Merged with Elektramek. Industri AB, Hälsingborg (L. M. Ericsson).

Charles Westerberg & Co, Nyköping, 1922.* Electrical equipment for elevators, automatic switches, etc.

Svenska AB Le Carbone, Linköping, 1926* (later Sundbyberg). Dry cell batteries.

AB Svenska Transformatorfabriken, Linköping, 1919.

Luxor Radio AB, Motala, 1927.

Norrköpings Elektrotekn. Fabriker AB (NEFA), Norrköping, 1930,† D.

G. C. Faxe AB, Malmö, 1923. Dry cell batteries.

Bjurhagens Fabrikers AB, Malmö, 1924. Merged into Asea. Electrical cables.

Bröd. Anderssons Velociped- & Radiofabr. AB, Göteborg (1912), 1932.

El. AB Morén, Partille (1907), 1925. Merged into Asea. Electrical motors.

AB Arbogamaskiner, Arboga, 1932.* Electrical machine tools.

The cases in which many new firms eagerly entered into the production of a new or young "supply-push" product have several interesting aspects and, therefore, deserve detailed analysis. Since they were more prominent in industries other than engineering, such an analysis will be postponed for the present. It should be noted, however, that the pioneering firms sometimes were not able, did not try, or did not have the time to expand at a rate fast enough to enable them to cover the market created by a new product. One important reason for this was lack of equity capital and the fear of excessive indebtedness.[22] In some instances the reason was simply insufficient entrepreneurial skill or else purely technical obstacles to a rapid expansion of capacity. In certain cases, firmly established sole distributorships also played a part. When a new product became known but was marketed, say, only through certain machine dealers, other firms of this type would often encounter a demand for the product in question and would then search out other firms or individuals willing to enter into the production of the new product.

It might be expected that patent protection would often prevent new firms from flowing into a new market in the wake of a pioneering firm. But the new products were frequently such that effective patent protection proved impossible. The novelty might lie, for example, in the raw materials utilized rather than in the design of the product. In other cases it was often possible to imitate the design without coming into conflict with the patent laws. One should note in this connection that pioneering firms often avoided early advertising for fear that other firms would throw themselves into the production of the new product. It was a general rule in the advertising field that a new product should be on the market in considerable quantity before a promotional campaign was started. The pioneering firm, therefore, would first try to establish a market for a new product among its regular customers—particularly among wholesalers and retailers. This would also gain added time for the creation of needed production capacity, which made it easier to keep ahead of prospective competitors.[23] Even in such cases, however, competitors were frequently induced to enter, since pioneering firms sometimes put a rather high price on a product in order to exploit an early lead (e.g., in production techniques). A high price was sometimes motivated, also, by the desire to recoup development costs, etc. Imitators, who did not need to cover such costs, were then induced to enter the market with a lower price.

On the other hand, there were cases where the pioneering firm introduced a product at a price below the unit cost for the quantity that could be sold initially. The idea was that a higher price would make a significant sales volume impossible. At the lower price, it was expected that the product would gradually gain a large market so that unit costs would fall below the price established. But low-price policies of this type put heavy demands on liquid resources and could, therefore, seldom be pursued by a new enterprise. Since such a policy was open primarily to older firms, it was generally the most effective method for preventing the inflow of a large number of new producers. One method frequently

---

[22] Cf. Chap. 14.
[23] Cf. the quote from *Verkstäderna*, (1931), p. 217, above p. 239 n.

used, but primarily open to older, diversified enterprises, was to budget costs in such a way, for example, that a new product would be charged with costs lower than those actually incurred, while older, established products carried more than their share of the total costs.

Firms Pioneering with Product Innovations. There is no doubt that the points just made give one of the reasons why *the number of new firms with product innovations was relatively insignificant in the interwar period.* It was not easy for a new firm to raise sufficient capital to follow the low-price policy that was often required in order to gain a large market for a new product. Other reasons have been suggested previously in connection with our discussion of the willingness to accept risks among different categories of potential enterprise founders. These risks must always be taken into account even though, in general, starting a new firm on the basis of a product innovation was a less risky venture than starting a firm to engage in parallel competition with established firms in an "old" market. During the first few years of its existence, a new firm striving to introduce a new product almost always ran into considerable difficulties in the form of consumer conservatism and/or intensified competition from older firms which felt threatened by the new product. Considerable strength was then required in order to survive.

If the discussion is limited to new firms in the same size class as the previous list, the number of examples worth mentioning is small enough to be enumerated here also. It is characteristic that many of these firms grew to large size, often with the help of the sales organization and the financial strength of another firm that was already in the "big business" category. The majority of these successful enterprises relinquished little of their market to other firms, either because a very rapid expansion proved feasible or because the new product was quite "exclusive." Thus the previous discussion of supply-push processes on a scale exceeding the resources of pioneering firms applies primarily to firms other than those ennumerated below.

AB Cryptoteknik, Stockholm, 1924.*

Hugin Kassaregister AB, Stockholm, 1930. K. F. Cash registers.

AB Imoindustri, Stockholm, 1931. Pumps.

AB Linham, Stockholm, 1927. Grease cups.

Ulvsunda Verkstäder AB (previously AB Nomy), Stockholm, 1928. Merged into AB Volvo. Slide bearings.

AB Max Sievert Lödlampsfabrik, Sundyberg, 1922. Light bulbs.

Hesselman Motor Corp. AB, Nacka, 1929. Pumps for engines.

AB W. Dan Bergman, Södertälje, 1919.*† Merged into AB Bofors. Aluminum products.

Domkraft AB Nike (previously H. Landin), Eskilstuna, 1925.* Merged into K. F. Jacks.

Svenska Aeroplan AB (SAAB), Linköping, 1937.† D. Airplanes.

AB Facit, Åtvidaberg, 1922 (1918).† Calculators.

AB Ljungmans Verkstäder, Malmö, 1924.† Measurement equipment for liquids, etc.

AB Volvo, Göteborg, 1926.† D. Automobiles.[24]

Svenska Flygmotor AB, Trollhättan, 1930.† D. Airplane engines.

AB Ecco-verken (previously E. Järnåker), Skara, 1931.* Merged into AB Atlas-Diesel. Aircompressors (for spray painting).

AB Kanthal, Hallstahammar, 1931.† D. Merged into Bultfabriks AB. Materials for electrical resistors.

Georg Schönander, Stockholm, 1930. X-ray tubes, etc.

AB Artic, Motala, 1923.† Merged into AB Elektrolux. Absorption principle refrigerators.

AB Hägglund & Söner, Örnskoldsvik (1899), 1920's.*† Welded car bodies.

Charles Westerberg & Co., Nyköping, 1922.* Automatic switches, etc.

While a list including the smaller firms in this category would not be particularly long, such firms were individually of little significance, and hence their enumeration would not serve much purpose.

Cyclical Variations in Entry Rates. Figure 16 and Appendix 5 of the Swedish edition show that the somewhat declining trend of entry rates in the engineering industries would have been still more pronounced had not the consumer durable branches attracted an increasing number of new enterprises during the boom of the 1930's. In the late 1930's, the annual number of new consumer durable producers exceeded that of new capital goods producers—a reversal of the situation that prevailed in the twenties. This was undoubtedly due in part to the greater incidence of young products in this sector, and in part to the construction boom that characterized the 1930's.

Apart from this, the observation that must be stressed in considering cyclical variations in entry rates is the reduction in enterprise formation in the initial year of the two depressions, 1921 and 1930, and in the recession year of 1938. Still, in each instance, the reduction was remarkably small. The years of real depression, i.e., 1922 and 1932 (the late 1930's recession, of course, never developed into a depression with large-scale unemployment) show increases in the number of new firms. This picture, which is repeated in many other industries, can, as has been suggested already, be explained as follows. The initial phases of the downturn were dominated by a general shortening of planning horizons and a pessimistic or hesitant business attitude. In the later phases, with unemployment growing to larger proportions, firm formation on the

---

[24] Although several firms had previously manufactured automobiles in Sweden, they had not been organized for mass production and had hardly used any subcontractors. Volvo was almost entirely built on a system of subcontractors and organized its production according to modern principles. The older firms had been loss-makers while Volvo, after a few years in the red, gradually became a profitable enterprise. It may be mentioned in passing that the initiative to Volvo's establishment was not taken by the management of the parent company (S.K.F.) but by private individuals who received the strong support of S.K.F.

"livelihood principle" began. The substantial number of new firms in both 1922 and 1932 is principally to be explained in this way. In both these years, another factor seems to have been significant also, namely, the ease with which inexpensive machinery could be acquired—either from older and/or discontinued firms in the form of discarded equipment, or directly from producers willing to supply at prices below those of the boom years. The devaluation of 1932, on the other hand, did not significantly affect the situation that year. This can readily be ascertained from a study of the firms that are relevant here.

In the cyclical upswings, the formation of new firms was not stimulated to the same extent by the search for a source of family income. The main impetus in such periods derived from the business situation in general and, more particularly, from the increased propensity of larger enterprises to arrange for the production of semifabricates and of non-standardized items on the outside. The peaks of 1919–20 and the trough of 1939 in entry rates are not hard to explain. While it is true that the period immediately after World War I was not in general a good one for the engineering industries, it is clear that the considerable improvement in the supply of raw materials encouraged the establishment of new firms in many areas. It is also evident that the electrification of the countryside, which rather suddenly picked up momentum on a broad front at the end of the war, led to the establishment of many new electrical engineering firms while, at the same time, it created more favorable conditions for new rural enterprises generally.

Finally, planning horizons were relatively long, and long-term expectations were rather buoyant in anticipation of improved business conditions following the peace, even if these were slow in coming. This situation had more of an effect on the formation of new firms than on business conditions for the engineering industries in general. Short-term expectations explain the 1939 picture, particularly following the outbreak of World War II. At that time, the formation of new firms was more affected than was the general business situation for the engineering industries.

The Degree of Product Specialization.   The preceding discussion has suggested that new firms were, as a rule, more specialized than the older ones. Table 11, which is based on a rough index of specialization, shows this clearly.[25] One group, in particular, shows a rather low degree of specialization, namely, those firms that had been founded prior to 1919 but disappeared during the interwar period. Table 12, which is based

---

[25] The firms included in the primary data of this study was assigned numbers ranging from 1 to 10 on the basis of information on their output mix and their size as of either the year of establishment or 1919. The "10" category represents pronounced specialization, and the columns labeled "specialized" in Table 11 includes firms from this category only. The remainder (including those which for various reasons could not be classified) were considered as "diversified."

TABLE 11
Specialization of Engineering Firms
(as of 1919 or year of establishment if later)

| | Firms Started before 1919 | | | | Firms Started 1919–39 | | | |
| | Continuing | | Discontinued 1919–39 | | In Operation 1940 | | Discontinued 1919–39 | |
Size of Work Force in 1919 or in Year of Establishment	Number	Percent Specialized	Number	Percent Specialized	Number	Percent Specialized	Number	Percent Specialized
1–7	365	46	126	33	612	58	63	49
8–19	216	45	129	40	133	65	36	58
20–99	236	35	88	36	37	70	4	—
100–499	91	34	12	25	3	—	2	—
500–	20	25	2	—	—	—	—	—
Total	928	41	357	36	785	60	105	53

TABLE 12
Specialization of Engineering Firms in 1939

| | Continuing Firms | | Firms Started 1919–39 and in Operation 1940 | | Total | |
Value of Output, 1939 (in thousands of Swedish crowns)	Number	Percent Specialized	Number	Percent Specialized	Number	Percent Specialized
0–50	35	34	54	48	89	43
51–100	26	46	30	60	56	54
101–200	31	65	32	53	63	59
201–500	56	50	24	58	80	53
501–1000	32	41	8	75	40	48
1001–5000	48	42	4	100	52	46
5001–	21	48	4	100	25	56
Total	249	44	156	57	405	49

on a numerical analysis of the raw data underlying *Industry Statistics* and which has thus been compiled quite independently of Table 11, yields a similar picture, but its statistical reliability is no more than barely satisfactory.[26] It is not just a coincidence that the older firms often had

[26] Here a firm has been classified as "specialized" when one "product" alone accounted for more than 75 percent of the market value of its output. ("Product" was here defined in accordance with the 1939 product classification scheme of *IS*.) This procedure has the advantage of being less arbitrary than that used to obtain Table 11. But the classification of Table 12 is then also more schematic, and it does not take the size of the firm into account. Everything indicates, moreover, that it was typical for many engineering firms during this period to drop a whole range of minor products, a development that the calculations made here would often fail to reflect.

names such as "Middletown Foundry and Steel Manufacturing Corporation," while the newer enterprises frequently had more specific names,
sometimes linked with a trademark.

The very fact that they were new, rather than any particular propensity to specialize, explains in part the higher degree of specialization
of the new firms. With the exceptions noted below, the general rule
in the engineering industries has always been for new firms to start
with one or a few products and only gradually expand into other product
lines without entirely relinquishing the older ones. A development of
this type must be seen in the context of the firm's market situation.
During bad years, especially, many firms were forced to search for new
product lines in order to maintain utilization of the plant. New customers
won in this way were no more readily relinquished than old ones, once
business conditions improved again. The desire of many customers to
place orders with the same enterprise for a number of different products
also acted in the direction of increased diversification. A study of the
output structure of firms at different dates during the interwar period
indicates the strength of these competitive pressures toward diversification. One finds remarkably few enterprises in which the same product
remained predominant over the entire period. This observation emerges
from a year-by-year study of the main *IS* forms and would undoubtedly
show up still more clearly if a more detailed breakdown by product
groups had been available.[27]

But these competitive pressures do not altogether explain why, in the
engineering industry, the older firms were generally more diversified
and the new firms more specialized. Part of the explanation lies in the
fact that the new subcontracting firms generally showed less of a tendency than the majority of final goods producers to diversify when exposed
to competitive pressures. Thus it is the special character of these subcontracting enterprises, rather than the fact that they were "new," which
accounts for the higher degree of specialization among the new firms.
It is evident that the increased importance of these firms gave the engineering industries a more specialized branch structure by the end of
the interwar period than they had at the beginning.[28]

---

[27] This does not contradict the previously mentioned fact that parallel competition
was not in general regarded as an attractive prospect. Thus such competition was
not unusual in product areas with expanding markets, and furthermore, the earlier
comment referred specifically to new firms. Several of the circumstances that deterred new firms from entering into parallel competition did not at all apply
to older firms. Competition of this type, in fact, was a common phenomenon
among the older enterprises. New firms, in other words, were seldom formed
in order to enter into parallel competition but were later frequently forced into
it gradually. Competition in the areas of quality, product type, and service was,
however, much more common than price competition, even among older firms.

[28] The very oldest firms had initially been diversified mechanical shops producing
to individual order, and many of them had retained this character. Many of the

This more specialized branch structure at the end of the interwar period depended not only on the nature of the new firms, but also on that of disappearing firms. Before going into this matter, we will touch on the role of collusive practices.

Collusive Practices in Restraint of Competition. There are no indications of any significant attempts to control entry through control of the supply of production equipment needed by entering firms. On the contrary, the sale by older firms of used machinery often encouraged the establishment of new firms. Nor were there apparently any effective agreements with raw material suppliers in order to exclude firms from the sources of supply. Instead, the supplying firms encouraged new enterprises by their sales policies, particularly during bad years. On the other hand, there were cases in which newly established firms were induced to discontinue or to sell out. In this connection, furthermore, the entrepreneur in question was at times required to agree not to start again in the same branch—a commitment which was also made in some cases where an older firm was bought and/or induced to discontinue. But the most common attempt to keep entry in check—apart from ordinary competition, naturally—seems to have been through cooperation with wholesalers. Wholesalers were often granted sole distribution rights in exchange for their promise not to handle the business of new firms.[29]

It is far from certain, however, that the absence of any type of control on entry would have significantly affected rates of entry in any of the main engineering industry branches. The electrical capital goods industry is a possible exception. This does not exclude the possibility that such attempts to control entry were effective in certain minor branches. But, apparently, entry could often be kept in check only for relatively brief periods. There were often ample opportunities to rely on "outsiders" among wholesalers and retailers. This was particularly the case, of course, when certain wholesalers had been purposely left out of a cartel agreement. An official investigation in 1940 (SOU, 1940, No. 35, p. 205) noted that within the Swedish economy it is "almost the rule that some firms operate and are permitted to operate outside the cartels." Our research has not uncovered any evidence contradicting this conclusion. Even in the

---

"middle aged" firms were, however, also diversified from the beginning to an extent that was unusual among the firms entering the industry between the wars. One may therefore refer, schematically, to three epochs in the formation of new enterprises. The first, lasting from the 1840's into the 1880's, gave rise above all to extremely diversified firms producing to order (cf. Chap. 5). The second, from the 1880's or 1890's up through World War I, gave rise both to diversified mechanical firms of much the same type as the oldest firms and to specialized firms based on specific inventions (telephones, ball bearings, vacuum cleaners, etc.). In addition to producers of small and relatively simple finished products (most often consumer durables), the third epoch, the interwar period, gave rise to conspicuously many specialized subcontractors and producers of specialized tools.

[29] Cf. *Kartellregistret* (1947), p. 12.

electrical capital goods industry it should be noted that general conditions were not very favorable for lively and significant entry. The innovations in this industry were generally of a secondary nature, and survival in competition with the big, older enterprises would in any case have required considerable financial strength in most instances. The firm of Charles Westerberg & Co. is one example of successful entry and represents, at the same time, one of the best examples of a blue-collar enterprise which managed to expand rapidly while retaining its independent position. AB Hägglund & Söner may also be mentioned in this connection.

With regard to collusive agreements of other kinds than those designed to control entry, the conclusion seems warranted that, in certain branches of the engineering industries, these occasioned the establishment of a number of firms which otherwise would not have been started. But it is difficult to separate these cases from those in which the immediate cause lay, for example, in the standardization of output and specialization of production brought about by a cartel. This question has already been discussed above.[30]

Collusive agreements were in all probability more important to the development than to the founding of firms. New firms frequently found it difficult to grow and to catch up with older enterprises, both in cases where attempts to control entry had failed and where such attempts had not been the subject of explicit agreements. To expand while relying exclusively on customers who were not tied to a cartel by contract was certainly more difficult, as a rule, than to gain an initial foothold in the market. It is significant that many, if not most, new firms that were started outside a cartel entered it after some time, either voluntarily or under some duress.[31] In numerous instances, however, growth opportunities were limited simply because the new firm concentrated on nonstandardized products that did not compete directly with the mass-produced products of the larger enterprises. These two circumstances help to explain the evolution of small firms, typical particularly among capital goods producers. But it is evident from the above discussion of other aspects of the formation and development of firms in these industries, that this alone is not the whole explanation.

---

[30] Cf. p. 233.

[31] But there are also many interesting examples of a struggle between a cartel on the one hand and one or more firms on the other. It was not uncommon for these firms to participate in the cartel for more or less lengthy intervals. The motive for opposing the cartel according to the outside firms has been that the prices that it wished to maintain were too high or else the cartel was too restrictive in some other aspects of its efforts to curtail competition. There are, in fact, few examples of cartels operating for long, continuous periods with a minimum of friction and without struggles with outsiders. AB Cykelfabriken Monark, located in Varberg, is a dramatic example of a firm (in this case an older one) struggling against a cartelized industry. This firm, which was founded by a worker, developed at an extraordinary pace between the wars and outgrew the majority of its competitors.

One should add, finally, that cartel agreements in numerous instances increased the opportunities for firms to expand even when they did not eliminate competition from new entry. Cartel cooperation did eliminate the chronic "dumping" competition of firms which calculated only with variable costs, and which time and again failed, only to be revived with injections of new capital. The finances of the remaining firms were thus improved. Chronic dumping of this sort became a much less common condition during the 1930's than it had been in the previous decade. This was due in part to more extensive cartel agreements, but also to demand-pull conditions becoming more prevalent. There are a number of different aspects to this dumping problem which we will have occasion to return to in connection with the analysis of other industries.

The relationship between organized collusive practices and the disappearance of firms will be discussed below.

Firm Mortality and Its Cyclical Variation. Figures relating to firm disappearances in the largest engineering branches are given in Appendices 5 and 6 [in the Swedish edition] and in Table 5. Figure 17 should also be consulted.

Although mortality rates in several industries were considerably above those in the engineering industries, the latter must still be regarded as significant. In the three largest branches, about 30 percent of the firms in existence at the end of World War I had disappeared before 1940. Table 8, page 209, and Appendices 6 and 8 show that this was not a question of just small businesses. It is evident, however, that this discontinuation of firms was less important as a factor creating unemployment or, more generally, as a factor releasing labor than were developments within other firms [see Figure 18 and Appendix 19].

Closer study of the data shows that the majority of the firms that later disappeared were stationary or regressive. This is true both of old and of new firms (see p. 224 above and Appendix 8). The first category to be distinguished would comprise firms whose disappearance was connected with the age, illness, or death of the owner or manager. Even though in many cases of this sort the firm was continued by other individuals, often a son, there were quite a few instances of such disappearances. These, however, account for only a relatively small fraction of all discontinuations.

A second category of discontinued firms is characterized by strategic malinvestments. There were relatively few such cases, however, even though the first peacetime crisis, in 1921–22, broke the backs of many of the firms that had been started during the immediately preceding upswing.[32] Obviously, all industries exhibit a certain firm mortality simply

---

[32] A remarkable number of firms failed because of their concentration on exports to the Soviet Union, which proved a bad idea. A still larger number of the "Russian firms" had to undergo financial reconstruction. Another important category of strategic malinvestments were those made in ball-bearing firms. As a rule, the

because incompetent management will always be present to a certain "normal" extent. In the engineering industries, where the incidence of disappearances among newly established firms was not particularly high, a relatively large proportion of total disappearances is to be attributed either to such a lack of entrepreneurial skill or to the factors just discussed in connection with our first category. If we add the rather numerous disappearances connected with efforts at buying up new firms, only a relatively few cases of discontinuation among the new firms remain to be accounted for. The relatively insignificant role of strategic malinvestments seems to indicate that large risks were seldom willingly accepted at the start of a new firm. The formation of a new firm, demanding considerable capital resources, was seldom undertaken if the probability of successful survival was not very high. And a project of this type was not undertaken unless considerable financial backing was assured so that the often troublesome early years before experience was gained and the operation stabilized could be surmounted.[33]

This picture is quite different from that of the earlier stages of the industrialization of Sweden, in particular with regard to the engineering industries. There can be no doubt that in the interwar period the greater risks were taken by the older firms, which had other established product lines to fall back on and which did not need to accept initial costs of the magnitude required at the start of a completely new enterprise. The data still show, however, that not even among the older firms did malinvestments play a particularly important role as a cause of discontinuation—except in the first postwar depression. Indeed, insufficient investments were undoubtedly a more frequent cause of the economic retrogression and mortality of firms observed during the remaining years of the interwar period, including the years 1931–33. It should be noted, however, that individual entrepreneurs frequently were hard hit by large losses, wholly or partly attributable to expansion in periods of high prices, even though these losses did not cause "discontinuation" according to the present definition or more complete financial reconstruction. But in these cases it was not really a question of investments that were unjustified in the longer run. Nor were cases of this type common after the mid-1920's.

The third and last category of disappearances is comprised of firms which, due to their product mix or organization, were slowly but surely forced back, and finally out, by their competitors. In this category, naturally, one finds mostly "old" firms. But in the engineering industries—in contrast to many other industries—it was only seldom a question of firms

---

formation of these companies involved large sums of capital, but most of them had never time to go into production. S.K.F. was too far ahead, and the new enterprises were for the most part ill-conceived anyway.

[33] Cf. p. 240.

getting into difficulties because their products were supplanted by new products. Only a few firms, in other words, failed because their products became obsolete. As a rule, it was fairly easy to replace old products with others while retaining the original equipment with few or no changes a fact that left its impact on the competitive struggle in many areas. Certain, relatively simple, products were forever being taken up by firms striving for at least temporary compensation for shrinking markets for some old products, and the established producers were strongly affected by these adjustments.

On the other hand, the number of cases in which discontinuations were directly due to process innovations by other firms is striking. The most widely diversified engineering firms were especially hard hit by this type of change. In part, one finds this reflected in the considerably higher mortality rate among machine producers compared with the iron, steel, and metal manufacturing branches (see Table 5, p. 191, and Appendix 6). Highly diversified firms were more common among the former than the latter. The relatively high mortality of rather large machine-producing firms reflects the low survival probability of this "jack-of-all-trades" type of enterprise. It was, above all, the medium-sized firms that were insufficiently specialized. The development history of these firms is characteristic and similar from case to case. Disappearances among them were usually definitive, in the sense that operations were not continued aside from the fact that other enterprises sometimes took over the premises.

The finances of these firms were undermined by their low degree of specialization and their inability to judge the profitability of different products on the basis of rational cost estimates. Obsolete equipment and inadequate plant space were often contributing factors. The 1920's were a particularly difficult period for firms of this type because highly significant process innovations were introduced by many other firms and foreign competition hardened in this period. In addition, the first postwar crisis had undermined the finances of many of these firms. Banks and other creditors would often argue as follows: "You must show that the firm can be profitable. We will then not be reluctant to provide additional money for it." Management, on the other hand, could retort: "Our insufficient liquidity prevents the modernization which is necessary if the firm is to be operated profitably. Give us the money, therefore, and we will manage." When creditors and/or financial intermediaries would not, or did not, dare accept the demands of management, this attitude was often based on the fear of throwing good money after bad. One might not have much faith in a certain management yet find it difficult to employ other, and perhaps more capable, management for the firm.

An additional factor, in many instances, was that the old facilities were ill-suited to modernization of the firm's production processes and product mix. A gradual modernization was therefore out of the question, while at the same time the construction of an entirely new plant demanded too much capital. The geographical distribution of this type of firm disappearances should also be noted. Typically, these firms were located in urban areas and had a long history of supplying the region with engineering products of all kinds. Their more simple products for the regional market were later often supplied by small businesses, while other, strongly progressive large enterprises moved into their market for products less suited for small firms.

The disappearing firms had yet another characteristic. They were primarily producers of such final goods as engines, machines and tools, transport equipment, and so forth. The number of semifinished goods producers that disappeared was insignificant in comparison. Firms of this latter type were, of course, rather few in number at the beginning of the interwar period. But this is not the whole explanation. Evidently, many firms with complicated products found it difficult to survive in big business competition, even when their finances were not undermined by excessive diversification or by faulty cost projections. They certainly encountered serious difficulties in raising the new capital required for modernization of plant and equipment and for the expansion of capacity that this frequently required (e.g., when assembly-line techniques were introduced). In the engineering industries, as in so many other industries, it was generally the larger firms which had the largest retained earnings, had been the least affected by the postwar crisis of 1920–22, and/or had secured financial support from banks or others at an early stage, that were also able to take the vanguard in obtaining skilled managers and the other resources required for the modernization. Their success in these respects, directly or indirectly, became the misfortune of their less favorably endowed competitors.

One interesting phenomenon already encountered in the engineering industries should be noted in this connection, even though we will not discuss it in detail here since it was more significant and was revealed more clearly in other industries. As long as the "doomed" firms managed to survive (often, perhaps, to a great extent by calculating with inadequate depreciation allowances, by not making sufficient reinvestments, etc.) this indubitably caused a form of dumping competition in many cases, particularly for certain products.[34] It has been said that these engi-

---

[34] The pricing policies of these firms, which were more or less on the skids, also differed from the pricing policies of those firms that were newly established and/or followed a progressive investment policy. Cf. p. 239. The former in contrast to the latter competed primarily through low prices. Frequently the quality of their products came to suffer, voluntarily or involuntarily, from this policy since the declining firms often lacked sufficient working capital as well as qualified employees.

neering firms "succumbed about every 20 years, since they never managed to set aside sufficient depreciation allowances." These firms depressed prices so far that even firms with far lower costs—but higher depreciation allowances—than the dumping firms suffered. The history of the Swedish engineering industries in the 1920's clearly shows the effects of this characteristic dynamic process. At this time, the firms in question generally had a history of several reconstructions.[35] One should note here, however, that the cartels of the 1930's in certain cases probably led to lower firm mortality in that some weak firms found it easier to survive than previously.

Both these circumstances certainly contributed to a lessening of competitive pressures and to the brighter profit picture for the engineering industry in general, which became characteristic of the later 1930's. A dumping process is, of course, always present to some extent, since new products and processes are always struggling with old ones that prove more or less tenacious because of sunk costs and for other reasons. But one may still regard the early 1930's as the end of an era. These years represented the end of a period during which a particularly large number of old firms waned and vanished under the onslaught of great, *temporally concentrated*, process innovations carried through by a relatively limited number of other enterprises.

Cyclical variations in disappearances show clearly in the engineering industries, although they are pronounced only in connection with the first postwar depression. In this crisis, the engineerng industries, like the steel industry, had to cope with particularly serious problems and suffered from a considerable number of strategic malinvestments.

As with many other industries, data on firm disappearances show lows at the *beginning* of upswings in "general" activity, i.e., in 1923–24 and in 1934–35 (Figure 17, p. 211, and Appendix 5). The previous depression years, on the one hand, had killed off so many of the weakest firms that those remaining were generally not entirely hopeless. On the other hand, the return of a more optimistic—albeit cautiously optimistic—atmosphere, characterized *inter alia* by a general lengthening of planning horizons, certainly played a role also. Both entrepreneurs and credit institutions convinced themselves in many instances that since the worst years had been survived, there was no need to throw in the towel just at the point when better times were apparently around the corner. That the continued upswing later brought higher firm mortality must presumably be explained as a consequence of expectations being disappointed and of unanticipated increases in various costs.

---

[35] Concerning the problems of the engineering industries before World War I, cf. Linder, *op. cit.*

Concrete Products and Lightweight Concrete

The concrete products industry in existence at the end of World War I was engaged primarily in the production of concrete pipe and a range of special concrete products, such as concrete roof tiles. The very significant quality improvements in concrete pipes that took place created the preconditions for the high rate of entry into the industry in the 1920's. These improvements meant that concrete pipe began to encroach seriously on the market for the older, glazed brick pipe and also gained new markets based on novel uses. "Nopsastone" was a new product that played an important role in this respect. These factors continued to contribute toward a high rate of entry in the industry, even during the 1930's. But other concrete products were by then more important, at least in the latter half of the decade. The rapidly growing demand for foundation stone for prefabricated single-family frame houses led to particularly intensive entry and contributed greatly to the very high entry share of approximately 54 percent for the 1919–39 period.[36] But the hundreds of new firms were, with few exceptions, stationary.

First, it was very easy to start a small concrete products plant. At least up until the late 1940's, by which time certain firms had become considerably more mechanized than previously and competition, consequently, had hardened, production could advantageously be managed on a small scale and with very simple and inexpensive equipment. No large fixed plant was required, and production could be stopped and restarted almost at any time without incurring sizable costs. Production could also be carried on as a sideline to farming, a possibility which was very frequently exploited. Everything seems to indicate that in the interwar period most plants were started by persons engaged in farming or related occupations. In this respect, the industry resembles the brick industry and may be regarded as its latter-day heir. The seasonal nature of farming, the availability of sandpits and sometimes of other facilities in the form of old barns played a major role in this connection. Many plants were also started by construction contracting firms.

Second, production of these concrete products could not very well be concentrated in a few large firms. Transport costs were simply too high for bulky and/or heavy products, particularly as long as high quality standards had not yet become generally required.[37] A single firm could not very well supply a large region with concrete products. Thus, the

---

[36] Cf. Chap. 10, p. 191.

[37] During the 1940's the quality regulations of Kommunaltekniska Föreningen made it more difficult for the smaller firms with their handicraft methods to compete while at the same time the opportunities of the larger firms to sell in a wider market improved since the better quality products were better able to stand long-distance transport.

concrete products industry affords a particularly good example of the way in which novel products may create a market so rapidly that opportunity as well as a positive need for new firms emerges. The firms in existence at any given time were unable to cover the entire market because long-distance transportation of their products was uneconomical. Somewhat paradoxically, on the other hand, it appears that in certain areas the high rate of entry put a brake on the supply-push created by these new products. Many firms would use production methods so primitive that the quality became low—with the result that the new products fell into bad repute.

In contrast to concrete products of this type, lightweight concrete products gave rise to relatively few new firms. The production of lightweight concrete involved entirely different requirements with regard to machine equipment, and therefore capital, than did conventional concrete production. The first porous concrete factory was started in 1922 in Borensberg by a lime products firm dating back to World War I. A few years later, Skövde Mek. Stenhuggeri & Kalkbruks AB entered the market with a porous concrete based on schistous ashes and lime. This firm, later operating under the name of Skövde Gasbetong AB, was started before the turn of the century and began to acquire a big business character toward the end of World War I. Steam-hardened lightweight concrete was introduced in 1929 by Yxhults Stenhuggeri AB, which also dates back to the 19th century. This firm purchased the Borensberg factory in the 1930's, from which time this plant also produced the steam-hardened product. The Skövde firm also converted to the same method at about this time. Together with the firms connected with Skånska Cement AB, all of which were started during the 1930's and produced the special type of porous concrete named "Siporex," the firms just mentioned dominated the market. This market was not of a local nature. The new products could be sold throughout the country. All the porous concrete firms were strongly progressive.

The very high rate of entry into most areas of conventional concrete production did not create serious parallel competition. The number of firms in the various local and regional markets did not grow so rapidly that they did not still complement, rather than compete with, each other, despite the absence of significant cartel organization.[38] But in the 1940's, the industry, as already indicated, entered a new era. The firm-structure of the branch gradually became relatively unstable during this decade. New firms continued to enter at such a pace that parallel competition often became very sharp in most areas. One entrepreneur in the county of Kronoberg states: "At the start (1922), there were only two other factories in the county; now (1946) we have about twenty. Most of them

---

[38] Cf. *SOU* (1940, No. 35), p. 52.

have started in the last few years and after the last war." Another entrepreneur in the county of Kalmar says: "No less than eight new firms have been added in the last few years, and this may endanger the survival of our factory." In neither case had the firms had to cope with serious competition during the 1930's.

It follows from what has already been said that there was no cause for substantial firm mortality. Despite the ease with which production could be discontinued, especially since so many producers could fall back on farming, relatively few firms disappeared. There were no firm disappearances to speak of due to negative development effects. Hardly any products of significance were adversely affected in the development process, and parallel competition in the area of production processes did not become strong until well into the 1940's. Nor does one note firm disappearances due to strategic malinvestments. The great majority of discontinuations that took place were occasioned by random factors or by the illness, age, or death of the owner.

The Woodworking Industries

Firm formation among the *building joineries*[39] affords an excellent illustration of the way in which new products, introduced by a few pioneers, created and expanded a market at such a rapid pace that a great deal of room for new producers, and hence also for a large number of new enterprises, resulted. Figure 16, Table 5, and Appendix 6 [of the Swedish edition] clearly show how large numbers of new enterprises were attracted by the market for prefabricated interior fittings, which became a big item in the interwar period. New types of doors and windows played less of a role, but were still significant. Prefabricated frame houses should also be mentioned. The score of firms which were producing such houses by 1939 were all new in the sense that they had not previously been engaged in this activity nor in other types of joinery. Several of them were older enterprises, however, which started the fabrication of houses in a new plant but had previously operated, for example, a lumber mill. The pioneering contributions in the late twenties were due to a few firms only. This was the case in the wallboard branch also. The first firm here was AB Nordmalings Ångsåg, which in the late 1920's introduced "Masonite," produced with an American license. A whole group of other wood-processing firms followed suit with new plants, other product types, and other brand names. The Asplund process for the production of wallboard pulp was an innovation of decisive importance in this branch and came to be adopted by the majority of

---

[39] Concerning the value of α_{23} for varying branch definitions, cf. Appendix 6 of the Swedish edition.

producers.[40] Initial capital requirements were high, but the development of already existing wood-processing firms in this direction was natural, chiefly because of their assured sources of raw material. The production of plywood similarly expanded mainly within older firms. The addition of one new big firm started by an individual—an engineer who had previously held a top management position in a large wood-processing company—should be noted, however. This was AB Furuplywood, established in Kristinehamn in 1926.

Most of the older firms in the building joinery branch proper had initially been engaged in all types of building joinery, as well as in other forms of woodworking, and in repairs connected with the construction contracting, which in an earlier period frequently was combined with the operation of a woodworking factory. Such diversification had primarily been due to the demand of customers for different kinds of joinery work and also to the local or regional market. At the end of World War I, most of the firms still had this diverse character. A small number of firms concentrating on exports, and specializing from an early stage mostly on doors, represented most of the exceptions. Among the older firms, one particular combination was common, i.e., a combination of building joinery and furniture making. This was a natural combination of activities, particularly in more remote areas of the country with bad and/or long communication routes.[41] Characteristically, these firms, as well as those new firms which were very diversified, remained stationary somewhat more frequently than did more specialized enterprises (Tables 13*a*, and 13*b*).[42]

Some of the new firms *specialized* to a greater extent than the old ones. It should be emphasized, however, that specialization often involved great difficulties, since architects, contractors, and other customers generally put up strong resistance to the standardization of product which usually was a precondition for specialization. This was one reason why a high degree of specialization was still rare at the close of the interwar period and even in the late forties. The "specialists" which emerged despite all this most often started on a larger scale than the older, highly diversified firms had done, and they generally grew faster than the latter. This was especially the case with those established during the 1930's. Orientation toward prefabricated interior fittings, laminated doors, and so forth, created the conditions for and demanded, if production were to be rationally managed, a higher degree of specialization and standardization of product as well as production on a larger scale. As regards the interior fittings, a number of new H.S.B. enterprises established during

---

[40] Cf. Chap. 7, section on the pulp industry.

[41] Firms combining these activities were thus particularly common in Norrland (cf. Appendix 7).

[42] Table 13 is based on calculations of the same type as those underlying Table 12.

TABLE 13*a*
Building Joineries Grouped according to Type of
Development and Degree of Specialization

	Continuing Firms			Firms Started 1919–39 and in Operation in 1940		
	Number of Diversified Firms	Specialized Firms		Number of Diversified Firms	Specialized Firms	
		Number	As Percent of Total		Number	As Percent of Total
Total number of firms in 1939.........	243	38	14	384	62	14
Developmental type:						
progressive.............	45	7	13	81	21	21
regressive..............	29	3	9	4	—	—
stationary and unknown..	169	28	14	299	41	12

TABLE 13*b*
Building Joineries Grouped according to Value of
Output and Degree of Specialization

	Continuing Firms			Firms Started 1919–39 and in Operation in 1940		
	Number of Diversified Firms	Specialized Firms		Number of Diversified Firms	Specialized Firms	
		Number	As Percent of Total		Number	As Percent of Total
Total number of firms in 1939.........	243	38	14	384	62	14
Firms with value of output:						
>100,000 crowns.......	83	14	14	69	17	20
<100,000 crowns.......	160	24	13	315	45	13

the twenties were in significant respects the pioneering firms. The H.S.B. apartment cooperatives assured them of a large, nationwide market.[43] Other enterprises were first among the innovators with respect to laminated doors and prefabricated frame houses. But it is worth noting that these pioneers were old firms which thus sought to become more specialized, acquire modern machinery, create a more up-to-date organization, etc. New firms were not particularly prominent in carrying out either product innovations or process innovations.

The older firms were generally forced to adjust to increasing competi-

---

[43] H. S. B. stands for "Hyresgästernas sparkasse- och byggnadsföreningars riksförbund," a national association of a large number of apartment cooperatives.

tion from the more modern and more specialized enterprises with nation-wide markets, either by also attempting to specialize or else by relinquishing part of their local or regional market to the geographically distant firms. In the latter case, the old firms would concentrate on joinery work to individual order of a kind that could not be the object of mass production by the newer type of enterprise. House repairs would be an example. The different ways in which the building joinery industry developed in the larger urban areas and in the smaller towns and countryside reflect, in part, this change in industry structure. Most of the new and initially large firms were established in small towns or in the countryside (Appendix 7). Other factors, however, also contributed to this development, i.e., rapidly increasing wage rates and land values and new building codes in the cities, as well as electrification of the countryside and the general improvement in communications. Among the old firms the expansionary ones were generally also found in smaller towns (Appendix 8).

One should also note that during the interwar period there were relatively fewer new firms combining building joinery and furniture making than new firms specializing in either one or the other. It is especially typical that the former type of firm was rare in the 1930's. The exceptions to this were characteristically found in Norrland, where difficult communications made this combination of activities more appropriate than in other parts of the country. The addition of new firms marketing their products over the entire country and the related shift of industry structure are clearly reflected in Figure 3, Chapter 15. The beginning of the concentration of building joineries in the province of Småland dates to the interwar period, while in furniture manufacturing the same phenomenon goes farther back in time. By the end of the interwar period the building joinery industry still was more dispersed over the whole country than was the furniture industry (see Figures 2 and 3, Chapter 15).

In addition to the fairly specialized firms with relatively modern equipment discussed so far, the interwar period also gave rise to a large number of new firms of a rather different type. First, there were a number of usually stationary *subcontracting* firms, i.e., enterprises which manufactured fittings, doors, or windows for the firms that had entered into the production of prefabricated frame houses.[44] The number of these firms is difficult to estimate because only seldom did they confine themselves entirely to subcontracting. There were probably at least 50. The producers of prefabricated houses tended, however, to relinquish subcontracting arrangements as they grew larger. The smaller firms to which

---

[44] Another branch of the millwork industry also gave rise to many subcontractors. Many millwork shops were started, particularly during the twenties, as a direct consequence of developments in the engineering industries. These shops supplied mock-ups to the foundries which the latter no longer regarded as advantageous to make for themselves.

they had given rise then had to search for other outlets. Thus, this process illustrates how a new product may cause the formation of new firms not only directly but also indirectly.

Second, many of the new firms *were of the same type as the old*, i.e., very diversified, and operating with fairly outdated equipment—a type of entrant which was rare in the engineering industries, for example. These new building joineries of the "old" type were most often stationary or moderately progressive, and accounted for about 400 or 450 of the 597 total new firms. They often had a local or regional market. The formation of such a firm was often occasioned by the market vacuum left by the disappearance of an old firm or by a rise in the local demand for all kinds of building joinery in connection with especially lively construction activity. But it was frequently induced by unemployment or the threat of unemployment. Firms were thus frequently started on the "livelihood principle," i.e., without the objective of rapid expansion or large-scale marketing. This type of firm, engaging in parallel competition, was of remarkably great importance. This deserves explanation. The explanation is found to a large extent in the recruitment of founders.

The history of the building joineries before World War I shows that most of the firms were started and operated either by contractors or in conjunction with a lumber mill and/or a lumber yard. The production of millwork was to a large extent conducted by contractors in the construction off-season, and the millwork—at that time mostly doors and windows—would be stored to meet the needs of the warm seasons. It was also fairly natural for owners of lumber mills and yards to operate a building joinery as a sideline because the builders who bought their lumber would frequently at the same time demand the related millwork products. While one still finds examples of this origin among new building joineries in the interwar period, it is notable that most founders were by then workers, foremen, or persons with similar backgounds (Appendix 14). Table 14 shows that such individuals were involved from the start in 185 of the 226 new firms that were in existence in 1940 and for which it has been possible to determine the founders. It was only with regard to the firms producing prefabricated houses, laminated doors, and those specializing most heavily in interior fittings, that workers played a relatively small role. In these areas, most new factories were started by old firms, belonging primarily to the lumber mill industry.[45] Unfortunately, it is not possible to compile a table for the period before World War I corresponding to Appendix 14. But a study of the raw data shows that the recruitment of new entrepreneurs among contractors, and so forth, became relatively less frequent in the 1930's than it had been in the 1920's.

---

[45] The production and sale of prefabricated frame houses demanded more capital than other types of millwork. Furthermore, many lumber mills began producing prefabricated houses since the lumber mill business in general was not very profitable.

TABLE 14
Survey of Joineries Established by Workers, Foremen, etc.

Major Branches	Number of Firms Established in 1919–39 and in Operation in 1940	Number of Firms for Which Previous Occupation of Founder Is Known	Firms Founded by Workers, Foremen, Etc.	
			Number	Percent
Furniture......................	459	226	194	86
Building joinery, interior fittings.....................	382	164	129	79
Firms combining furniture, building joinery, and interior fittings..............	104	62	56	90
Total........................	945	452	379	84

This undoubtedly represents the continuation of a trend going back to the prewar decades.

As in the engineering industries, this change in recruitment can to some extent be seen as reflecting the change in generations. A gradually more democratic society meant a broader basis for the recruitment of enterprise founders. One should also note that the growing importance of prefabricated interior fittings meant that the occupations of carpenters and joiners were on the retreat on the construction sites. This factor should not be exaggerated, however, because the rapid expansion of construction activity in the country as a whole counteracted the strong tendency toward a reduction of demand for such workers which the development of the joinery industry created. But it is clear that construction carpenters and joiners faced declining employment opportunities in many areas. It is impossible to determine quantitatively the extent to which this led them to start their own firms, but one finds a significant number of examples of this. The long periods of low employment in the building joinery industry itself were of far greater importance. The need to earn a livelihood was a strong inducement. That the branch suffered from few new orders would, therefore, not deter people from starting new firms in competition with old firms, even when the latter were operating at less than full capacity. For that matter, it was precisely during such bad years that it was particularly easy to acquire the simple, and in most cases inexpensive, mechanical equipment required for a small new joinery firm.

Nothing indicates that there were any organized attempts to control entry in any way. The firms producing wood-processing machinery were quite willing to grant advantageous payment conditions. Many lumber mills and yard owners similarly encouraged new firms, especially in periods of declining sales. They attempted, in other words, to transfer their sales difficulties to the next link of the production chain. Both construction carpenters and workers in the joinery industry, as well as many others, possessed the requisite technical knowledge. Less capital was needed to start a diversified and not too modern firm in the woodworking industry than, for example, in the engineering industries or for starting a fairly specialized and rather well-equipped factory for interior fittings. While in the engineering industries, the broadening of the recruitment base gave rise primarily to subcontractors and firms specializing in some simple final product with a limited market, here the same development gave rise to a large extent to somewhat old-fashioned building joineries engaging in parallel competition with existing firms.

Many of the new firms started in this manner were unprofitable. In many instances, the business gave a surfeit of work for earnings that were extremely low on an hourly basis and only sufficed for a decent livelihood because of the usually long work week. From a general economic standpoint, this type of mostly stationary firms represents a remarkable phenomenon. They were particularly common in the joinery industry, where they to a large extent "neutralized" the tendency toward increasing specialization in the industry created by the more specialized, new enterprises.

Many of the new firms were started by young men. The average age of founders was lower in the joinery industry than in any other industry (see Appendix 15). In the beginning, these men had a great capacity for work and frequently took little account of the costs, which in later years would come in the form of reduced ability to work, age, illness, and so forth. Nor were sufficient depreciation allowances always made. Frequently, rational depreciation calculations were simply not made at all. The fact that the plants of bankrupt firms could often be bought cheaply was significant in this connection; large expenditures would only come when the need for reinvestment arose. Furthermore, certain administrative costs would in many cases become necessary only through growth of the firm. The formation of a new firm of the "old" type to engage in parallel competition with the final products of existing firms may have appeared more attractive, therefore, than it ought to. Only when such a firm had passed its early youth did a combination of several factors reveal the operation as unremunerative. But a firm could be operated for a considerable period even when unremunerative from the start. In many cases operations continued until the initial equity was consumed.

The parallel competition in which firms of this type engaged contributed strongly toward narrowing profit margins even for the more specialized and more modern firms. Since this type of entry continued throughout the entire interwar period, it had an effect similar to "chronic dumping." While the effects were in part the same as in cases where older firms engaged in dumping during a period of transition (see the section on the engineering industries above), the two situations should be clearly distinguished. This type of entry was particularly troublesome in years of depression, both because sales expanded only for certain new products, if at all, and because the "supply" of new entrepreneurs was especially high in such years. A study of firm disappearances throws further light on this phenomenon.

The very high mortality[46] of both old and new firms must be considered in relation to the characteristics of the overall development process described above. Actually, it was even higher than it appears from the figures presented in this study. There were numerous instances in which an accord with creditors was asked and reached and new management took over while at the same time the continuity of production and of customer relationships, and so forth, was broken (see Chapter 10, p. 189). Many of these are undoubtedly missing in the statistics here utilized. The significance of these "hidden" firm disappearances became apparent in the course of the author's study trips to the various building joinery towns. To begin with, there were, as usual, a number of cases of mismanagement. But the competition in this industry also killed off many firms which could not be called mismanaged. The incidence of discontinuations was particularly high among the very diversified firms, which were hard pressed by more specialized enterprises, both new and old. Thus the mortality, for example, of the firms combining building joinery with furniture production was particularly high [as shown in the Swedish edition in Appendix 6].

But many firms were, for reasons already indicated, obstinately long-lived and often contributed to the "chronic dumping" situation. Machinery as well as buildings could often be operated for prolonged periods with less than full maintenance. It was frequently not necessary to burden cost calculations with sizable depreciation allowances. The process innovations, as we stressed in Chapter 7, were not revolutionary but fairly continuous; so equipment obsolescence set in rather slowly. The human factor must be emphasized in this connection. It represented a strong element of inertia—for example, because the firms were so often managed on the "livelihood principle" by workers with little long-term indebtedness. In the building joinery industry, unincorporated businesses with single owners were the rule, and company subsidiaries were very rare. In all areas, therefore, one finds numerous examples of firms continuing operations for the simple reason that the owner-manager survived. Throughout the entire interwar period, many basically obsolete businesses remained, and then disappeared only with the death of the owner-manager.[47]

---

[46] Concerning the value of α_{23} for varying branch definitions, cf. Appendix 6 of the Swedish edition.

[47] In many cases, naturally, the firm was instead sold to a more "modern" entrepreneur. In other instances one or more sons took over and often reorganized the firm.

The *furniture industry* shows a development in many respects similar to that of the building joineries ($\alpha_{23} = 41$). Furniture production, however, had by and large already become industrialized by 1919, although cabinetmaking as a craft survived everywhere and particularly in the cities. The building joinery industry, in contrast, was just entering a period of very extensive industrialization at this time.[48] The maps in Chapter 15 clearly show the differences between the two main branches of the woodworking industry. The industry's interwar development is portrayed in Table 5, p. 191, and in Figure 16, p. 210. It is charactistic, furthermore, that at the end of World War I, 75 percent of the industry's labor force was employed in 27 percent of the firms, while at the end of the interwar period a greater proportion of the firms (i.e., about 32 percent) was needed to account for this percentage of the labor force. There is hardly any other industry in which small businesses played such an important role, and only a few industries resembled the furniture industry in having a less concentrated structure in 1939 than in 1919.

Some new firms were attracted by office furniture, but these were remarkably few. The pioneers in this area were old firms, and they dominated most of the market. They were able to expand production very rapidly, partly because of subcontracting arrangements and production in long, standardized series, and partly because one important firm, AB Åtvidabergs Industrier, was to offer other office equipment at the same time, such as typewriters and calculators.

The shift in the composition of output toward one-piece furniture, described in Chapter 7, was associated with a very high rate of firm formation. The new upholstered furniture, which to a certain extent created its own market at the expense of other furniture types, attracted a large number of new firms during the interwar period and still more in the 1940's. These firms were industrialized upholsterers, but they seldom developed out of the old upholstery shops. The special section of the Swedish Furniture Manufacturers' Association formed by the manufacturers of upholstered furniture had 75 members by 1947. Three fourths of these firms had been established either before the war or in the 1940's, while only one fourth belonged to the old, continuing firms that had not been founded specifically to produce upholstered furniture. Most of these firms were progressive, while for the furniture industry as a whole the opposite was true (see below).

The concentration of the new firms discussed so far, and especially of the progressive ones, to the countryside and smaller towns is very noticeable. Certain parishes with old furnituremaking traditions experienced particularly high rates of formation. Kyrkefalla parish, with the

---

[48] Concerning the definition of "handicraft," cf. p. 186 and Appendix 1 of the Swedish edition.

town of Tibro as its center, in the county of Skaraborg, and Virserum in the county of Kalmar should be mentioned here (see Figure 2, Chapter 15).[49] Remarkably few new firms appeared in the larger towns. Firm mortality was far higher in the cities than in other areas (see below in connection with disappearances). Appendix 7 [in the Swedish edition] shows that in 1919, 22 percent of all the firms were located in the larger towns. In 1939, the percentage was only 11, and these firms were considerably smaller on the average than those in smaller towns and in the countryside.

This undoubtedly reflects the fact that the industrial production of one-piece furniture, and so forth, for nationwide marketing forced aside the older type of furnituremaking bordering on handicraft (i.e., the manufacture of entire sets of furniture frequently for a local market and sometimes to direct individual order). This development is reflected also in the initial sizes of new firms, which increased particularly toward the end of the 1930's (see Appendix 11). The new machines, which were gradually introduced, also worked in this direction, to the extent that firms did not specialize on some simple product type such as unfinished furniture. In the latter case, it was possible to get by with simple equipment and only a few employees.[50]

It is evident that the old, often small, furniture factories, bordering on handicraft and located in the cities, seldom developed into industrial establishments. Few new firms of this "old" type were started. Only a few of the new firms appearing during the interwar period can be classified as having developed from craft shops (Appendix 10). This is hardly surprising. Not even in its very beginning did the furniture industry develop out of the old craft of cabinetmaking (see Chapter 5). The old cabinetmakers who were primarily located in the cities often regarded the industrial furniture with contempt. In addition, their facilities in the cities seldom offered opportunities for expansion. Higher wage rates, higher real estate values, and more restrictive building ordinances were other factors that undoubtedly contributed significantly to the strangulation of the industry in the cities.[51]

Finally, one should also mention the rapid development of furniture retailing. Specialized furniture shops were very rare up until the end

---

[49] Cf. S. Ålund, "Möbelindustrins uppkomst och första utreckling i Virserum och Tibro," *Möbelvärlden* (1946), and H. Stalberg, *Smalands skogs- och träförädlings-industrier*, (Lund, 1947).

[50] Cf. also below concerning the new subcontracting firms of this type. The presence of these subcontractors in the sample tends to conceal the trend toward entry on a larger scale to which the factors mentioned otherwise contributed. Had it been possible to sort these subcontractors out, this trend would, in other words, have emerged much more clearly than it does in Appendix 11.

[51] With regard to wage rates, cf. "Möbler," *Betänkande avgivet av 1946 års möbelutredning, SOU* (1947, No. 52) p. 114.

of the 19th century; hence it was quite natural to find furniture production located where consumption demand was concentrated. In this early period there was only one characteristic and significant exception to this, namely, the mass production of standardized, wooden chairs. The rapid development of furniture retailing removed a major reason for the old location pattern. It also reduced the incentive for continuing with a high degree of diversification. Furniture-producing firms were in general somewhat more specialized at the end of the interwar period than they had been at its beginning.

There is little reason to single out a particular firm as the pioneer in the area of one-piece and upholstered furniture. These new developments appeared simultaneously in several firms, both old and new, in the latter half of the 1920's. It is therefore difficult to pinpoint pioneers, in particular since the innovations were generally of a secondary nature. There is reason, instead, to study in more detail the predominant pattern of parallel competition which prevailed in part as a consequence of the entry discussed above. What is most remarkable in this connection is the fact that the high rate of entry so intensified the parallel competition that the situation resembled one of competition in a stagnating market. This was true of supply-push and particularly of demand-pull processes. Demand-growth was never so rapid that the firms in existence at the time found themselves unable or unwilling to meet it. In most cases, it did not require any expansion of capacity. On this point, therefore, the development of the industry differed to some extent from that of the interior fittings sector of the building joinery industry, and it differed still more from several sectors of the engineering industry and from various other industries to be discussed later.

The furniture industry also shows an increase in the number of *subcontracting* firms. This is especially true during the 1930's, when many new firms entered the production of unfinished chairs, sofas, and so forth, to be sold to the producers of upholstered furniture, or of types sold to others, such as polishing shops or wholesalers. In northeastern Småland—the old center of the production of wooden chairs—a particularly large number of such firms appeared.[52] They could be started on a small scale and with simple equipment and still often be operated fairly efficiently. Their weakness was the dependence on the customer firm. Some new subcontracting firms chose, therefore, to change over gradually to selling to furniture merchants but then had to give up the simple production of unfinished items. In this way, they came to increase the parallel competition among "ordinary" furniture producers discussed above.

At the same time as the one-piece furniture, the upholstered furniture,

---

[52] Many of these have not been included in *IS* and are, consequently, missing in the present study also.

and the unfinished furniture on subcontracts gave rise to many new firms, the "old" furniture sets also continued to induce entry to some extent. But businesses with such relatively diversified output declined in importance in relation to other firms.

Several different factors contributed to the very high rate of entry. All of them resemble the factors that created such lively parallel competition through new entry into the building joinery industry. One precondition was the ease with which a new furniture firm could be started. Initial costs could be kept low, especially during the 1920's and the first half of the 1930's. There was almost always a ready supply of used machinery, and differences between the old machines and the new types which were introduced were seldom very great since the process innovations were generally of a secondary nature. Recruitment of enterprise founders posed no problems at all. There were always many individuals for whom the idea of starting a furniture factory was tempting and who also had the opportunity. It was an old saying in the industry that if a plant burned down and the employees were unharmed, one or more new firms would instantly arise. Appendix 14 [in the Swedish edition] shows how strongly former workers and foremen predominated among founders. Table 14 shows that of the 226 new firms still in existence by 1940 and for which the founders are known, 194 had been started by workers or individuals with similar backgrounds, or at least had one or more such persons among the founders. On the other hand, one seldom finds the older master craftsmen (i.e., the cabinetmakers) among them. Since the furniture industry as well as the building joinery industry belonged to the so-called low-wage industries, entrepreneurship often seemed to offer the prospect of higher earnings than could be had in employment. Since unemployment and/or inadequate employment opportunities characterized the situation during almost the entire interwar period, many workers, foremen, or other supervisory personnel were induced to start their own firms in order to ensure a livelihood. This is clearly reflected in the data on new entry, particularly during the depression years in the early 1920's and 1930's shown in Figure 16, p. 210 [and Appendix 5 of the Swedish edition]. That the market situation did not deter entry despite almost continuous excess capacity in the industry is demonstrated not only by the large number of new firms in all the categories considered above, but also by a closer study of the character of entry.[53]

---

[53] Here "excess capacity" does not mean simply that full utilization of the industry's total capacity would lead to ruinous prices, although such a situation was common enough. That situation, after all, is fairly "normal" whenever modern and obsolete firms compete. In the present context "excess capacity" refers to a situation in which the total capacity even of the fairly "modern" firms alone is too large in the sense indicated.

It is evident that the furniture dealers switched suppliers relatively frequently. Everything indicates that relationships between producers and distributors, finishing shops, and so forth, were more fluid than, for example, in the engineering industries. Old and new furniture manufacturers would often be played against each other. The market structure generally corresponded more closely to the concept of "pure competition" than in most other industries even though there were significant elements of monopolistic competition, i.e., competition in terms of product types rather than in terms of prices. A new firm could, moreover, almost always find some way of selling the output planned for its initial period of operation. It did not have to be more efficient than existing firms, or even equally efficient. In this respect the situation differed from that usually found in the engineering industries where the market structure was somewhat different. In the furniture industry, entry only required the entrepreneur to shave prices a little below his closest competitor. If this sometimes was done at the expense of quality, the consequences were not always as immediate and as serious as, for example, in the engineering industries where producer-customer relations were easier to survey. Prices in this branch were thus depressed, but each new entrepreneur would always hope to achieve a corresponding cost reduction or be able to raise his prices once he had become well-established. It should also be pointed out that new or financially reconstructed firms frequently got started under favorable conditions simply because the plant of older firms could be purchased very cheaply in connection with a bankruptcy. The initial capital would, of course, in some cases tide the firm over for some time. The attempts to cut costs were, moreover, often successful, although usually only by calculating with too low a wage for the entrepreneur himself and too low depreciation allowances.

Conditions in the furniture industry thus resemble those previously described in connection with the building joinery industry. Characteristically, the stationary firms were exceptionally numerous. [See Appendix 8]. But, as with the building joineries, they showed great ability to survive and engaged in considerable chronic dumping. Many of the furniture factories were undoubtedly unprofitable and underwent frequent changes of ownership. It was not unusual for workers in a firm on the brink of bankruptcy to provide additional capital and take over the management when threatened with the alternative of unemployment. This is one of the reasons why an exceptionally large number of the new furniture firms—i.e., more than one-third—had more than one founder. The situation in the building joinery industry, incidentally, was the same. Only too frequently good money was thrown after bad, and the situation would often be further complicated by the conflicts that thus emerged within the management of these firms.

These conditions in the furniture industry clearly demonstrate that

unusually strong demand-pull and rapid output-growth in an entire industry need not necessarily be associated with rapidly increasing productivity[54] either directly (see p. 132) or as a result of a general improvement in earnings.[55] The generally unsatisfactory earnings that
characterized both of the woodworking industries, and which are
for the most part explained by the factors discussed above, undoubtedly reduced the frequency, and retarded the dissemination, of
process innovations. Low earnings had an unfavorable effect on liquidity,
and financial difficulties were almost continuously the predominant con
cern of most of the firms. Low returns also deterred individuals who
would have been able to provide equity capital in the amounts required
for efficient operation. This was particularly the case with the furniture
industry. This may seem somewhat peculiar, since an industry with such
evident weaknesses in plant and equipment would generally seem an
attractive target for entrepreneurs possessing the ample financial resources
needed to operate a firm efficiently. Part of the explanation has been
suggested already, however. The dumping engaged in by a large number
of firms that underwent frequent changes of ownership meant dimmer
profit prospects for the more efficient firms, especially when the latter
did not work with novel supply-push products. It is still true, however,
that there were some, frequently rather small, furniture firms which
were relatively profitable precisely because they were among the first
with a new product. Firms manufacturing upholstered furniture and relying on subcontractors, for example, were as a rule more profitable than
other firms in the industry. But evidently the furniture industry was
not particularly well-suited to production on a scale sufficiently large to
attract big capitalists and/or markedly progressive entrepreneurs. To
some extent, the office furniture branch was an exception.

Firm mortality was high, particularly among old firms ($\gamma_{23} = 30$).
It was not affected by organized curtailment of competition in either
direction. Except for the already mentioned fact that mortality rates

---

[54] Although is is hardly possible to calculate a meaningful output per man-hour
index, it still seems evident that the furniture industry can not have experienced
a very rapid increase in labor productivity.

[55] In this connection, one issue should be mentioned. It has been argued (cf.
"Möbler," *op. cit.*, p. 113) that the infrequent use of list prices in the furniture
industry served to slow the pace of modernization. The furniture dealers were apt
to use large markups on the less expensive of the high quality items and this served
to reduce the demand that these items otherwise should have met from the purchasing public. The incentive for manufacturers to produce this furniture was in this
way considerably reduced. This is a doubtful argument, however. The manufacturers
almost always had connections with a large number of furniture dealers, and the
opportunities for the individual producer to increase his sales, if he could offer
inexpensive, high-quality furniture, must have been good. The dealers must presumably have been eager to buy such inexpensive, good items that could carry a
large markup. The conclusion must be that the method of pricing hardly can
have thwarted the desire to produce less expensive and better furniture.

were higher in cities and relatively large towns than in small towns and countryside, there is little of interest to note about disappearances. The explanation for this has in effect already been given in the course of the previous analysis. Thus it is evident that many producers of sets of furniture disappeared in competition with the producers of one-piece and upholstered furniture. Here the similarity with the situation in the building joinery branch is striking in that a considerable number of failures among the continuing older firms were hidden behind outwardly insignificant changes.

It has been made clear already that even the new firms showed a relatively high mortality. Apart from the "normal" incidence of cases of mismanagement, strategic malinvestment was a frequent cause. But it is significant that it seldom was a question of firms that entered on a grandiose scale failing. In the main, the strategic malinvestments occurred in the course of entry of the type that was normal in this industry in the way analyzed above. Nor was it a case of firms formed during a boom being particularly likely to fail in the following recession. The malinvestments were generally not of a short-run nature which the firms could, so to speak, "grow into" in the long run.

In conclusion, it should be noted that the structure of the woodworking industries by the end of the interwar period gave an outward appearance of stability. There was no underbrush of small firms in the process of growing out of the small-business class. Although a fair number of very small firms were on their way into the size class of 15–25 workers, the number of strongly progressive firms was small. Not only were the small firms relatively more numerous in 1939 than in 1919, they also played a more important role.

Basically, however, the industry structure was far from stable. Small and large firms did not complement each other to any significant extent by meeting different needs and supplying different markets. Instead, firms of different sizes competed to a large extent directly with each other. There was, moreover, a high rate of turnover of firms in all size classes, particularly among the smallest, both through disappearances and through financial reconstructions. The class of small firms, in particular, was stable only in a statistical sense. Thus the picture one gets of a large number of small, stationary firms in no way indicates an equilibrium of the industry structure. Toward the end of the 1940's, in particular, the structure was probably very unstable, at least for the building joinery branch. The innovational pioneers had by then gained a strong position, and the difference between their efficiency and that of the large mass of smaller firms had increased as a result, among other things, of substantial advances in the standardization of products that favored a certain degree of specialization and mass production. Many small businesses of the traditional type were able to continue operations up to this time, albeit not very profitably, chiefly because of the almost uninterrupted rise in construction activity. But by the late 1940's, they probably represented a type of organization even more outdated than in the interwar period.

Paper and Cardboard Processing Industry

In the *paper packaging industry* ($\alpha_{23} = 35$), the supply-push created by the hard (corrugated) paperboard boxes stimulated some entry.[56] But the establishment of a new firm in this branch required considerable capital, and the firms which arose were therefore not so numerous but instead fairly large and strongly progressive. The pioneer was AB Sveriges Litografiska Tryckeriei (S.L.T.), which bought its machinery from the United States. Four other firms followed in 1924, 1925, and 1929.[57] Two of these—AB Pappemballage in Norrköping and Varnamo Wellpappfabrik—were, however, bought by S.L.T. after a few years; one of them was discontinued, and the other moved to Göteborg. Apart from these new firms, two older producers of soft cardboard entered the hard cardboard field. The innovation profits of the pioneers shrank, which led to the formation of a cartel in 1928. Several large, new firms were formed during the 1930's, and price wars disturbed the cooperation, but in the end all firms joined the cartel.

For reasons already given, no small firms sprang up in the shadow of the cartel.

There were no disappearances, other than those resulting from intentional concentration of production. Apart from those mentioned, the S.L.T. subsidiary, Stockholms Kartong och Litografiska AB, closed down its paperboard division, and another S.L.T. subsidiary, Göteborgs Wellpappfabrik AB, was discontinued, whereupon the S.L.T. Thorsvik plant was expanded. Although S.L.T. pioneered in hard corrugated board, it was a new firm, AB Kraftbox, which introduced the so-called solid board. This firm, however, had developed out of Forsså Bruks AB and was, therefore, not a new enterprise in the financial sense. It began operations in 1925 but, in contrast to the general expectation at the time, never became a serious threat to the corrugated cardboard producers.

The rapid spread of the brand-name system was connected with the

---

[56] The producers of wooden boxes and crates put up hard resistance in the beginning, particularly by reducing their prices. At the same time customers proved conservative. The breakthrough for the corrugated cardboard box came in the mid-1920's when such big consumers as the state tobacco monopoly and Banankompaniet became users.

[57] S.L.T. was a holding company formed in 1913. It took over the shares of no less than 13 different enterprises scattered over the whole country. Most of these were old firms. With time, several additional firms were added to the group.

emergence of a wide range of special cardboard and paper packaging products. This led to considerable entry into the packaging industry, and these firms, in turn, contributed to the dissemination of the system. AB Åkerlund & Rausing, established in the early 1930's, was the pioneer in this area. After a few years of great difficulties, this firm came to dominate the development of the industry.[58] It was hardly possible for other new firms to compete on an equal basis with this firm, which operated on efficient, mass-production principles. But some older firms entered the field, and many new ones took up the production of the usually somewhat more simple cartons and boxes, particularly for brand-name products that were not marketed on a large scale in standardized containers. The large number of new producers was in part a typical case of demand-pull because an increasing consumption of cardboard boxes was an automatic consequence of the overall expansion of the economy. But the formation of many of these new firms can still be explained with reference to the supply-push of the new containers for brand-name products. In either case, the producers of the more simple boxes usually relied on a local or regional market. Cardboard products with a low value per unit weight could in many instances not be economically transported over considerable distances. The geographical shift of the cardboard and paperpackaging industry toward the smaller towns and the countryside (Appendix 7) is partly due to this. It is especially interesting that most of the new firms sprang up in locations where previously no paperpackaging industry existed (see also Chapter 15).

A third branch of the packaging industry is composed of the producers of paper bags and envelopes. This branch managed to maintain its position only because the relative decline in the use of bags in favor of special packages was offset by the rapid expansion of retail turnover in general. There was little entry during the interwar period. It was characteristic for this branch that production became more and more concentrated to large firms, often in connection with paper mills. Cartel agreements tended to prevent the entry of new firms since it became difficult for outsiders to obtain paper at reasonable prices. It was frequently difficult, also, to market the product through the large wholesalers.[59] The cartel, in combination with the technical superiority of the larger enterprises, made life difficult for a large number of older, small businesses producing bags and envelopes along handicraft lines. These small firms were almost completely eliminated from the production of standard types of bags.

---

[58] Cf. R. Rausing, "Ett företags uppkomst," *Företagande, ekonomi och teknik, tillägnad Marcus Wallenberg Jr.* (Stockholm, 1949). AB Åkerlund & Rausing belonged to the rather small group of Swedish manufacturing firms started between the wars that were strongly progressive and made very significant innovations from the very beginning.

[59] Cf. *SOU* (1940, No. 35), pp. 124 ff.

To the extent that they were not discontinued, they often had to concentrate more on the local market than previously, and/or on more special types of bags and envelopes, for which, due to the lack of standardization of product, the large and medium-sized, mechanized firms did not find it profitable to adjust their equipment. The economy's growing demand for many kinds of such specialized articles was undoubtedly the main reason why developments in this branch did not lead to massive elimination of small businesses, as in the otherwise often similar tannery industry. The entry which actually took place in this branch must be viewed in this same context.

The production of sundry *advertising material* was another area characterized by supply-push and lively entry in the same manner as in the first-mentioned branches of the packaging industry. No entirely new large firm arose here, however—only a large number of small enterprises, which did not attain very considerable size during the 1930's, nor did they show promise of future growth.

The *office supplies branch* expanded rapidly due to a mixture of supply-push and demand-pull factors, but entry into the branch was neither lively nor quantitatively significant ($\alpha_{23} = 14$). This may appear strange, since the relevant products would be well suited for small businesses. But it was evidently difficult to enter into parallel competition with the large enterprises, all belonging to S.L.T., which already dominated the branch at the beginning of the interwar period. The main reason seems to have been that this group of companies could offer customers a very wide range of products, i.e., practically everything in office supplies. This was of great importance, since in this branch it is largely a question of a very great number of different items, each of which is generally required only in modest quantities by each of innumerable and widely dispersed customers. The difficulties faced by small firms trying to compete under these conditions could perhaps have been surmounted through reliance on wholesalers, but wholesalers also found it difficult to expand either their market or their share of the total market in competition with the S.L.T. group, which largely acted as its own wholesaler. Another factor which limited the ability of small firms to enter into parallel competition was the fact that, contrary to the situation in so many other branches, the large firms did not leave room for smaller businesses by passing up special orders of different kinds. These firms had a tradition of accepting such individual orders, and their relationships with their customers, e.g., among the large manufacturing firms, were rather close. On the other hand, there does not seem to have been any concerted effort on the part of older producers and independent wholesalers to discourage new entry.

Concentration efforts played a large role in firm disappearances in the paper-processing and cardboard-processing industry ($\gamma_{23} = 26$). About six rather large firms were absorbed by the S.L.T. group, thus accounting for almost two-thirds of the exit share for 1919. Apart from this, firm mortality was not particularly high. The above-mentioned cartel among paper bag producers may possibly have helped a few firms to survive.[60] On the other hand, there were many disappearances of box or bag producers in towns where competition was increased due to the process innovations of other firms. Partly as a corollary to the insignificant entry in other places, one finds very few disappearances outside the traditional locations of the paper-processing and cardboard-processing industry.

While in the early part of the interwar period the industry structure could be regarded as strongly dynamic, mainly due to the prominent role of the new products, it had become more stable toward the end of the period. Few firms were then in the process of expanding from small to large size, and relatively few outmoded firms remained whose disappearance was to be predicted. By and large, the big and small enterprises complemented each other.

The Oleomargarine Industry

The most important event with regard to firm formation was the addition, in 1920, of the Swedish Cooperative Union's (KF) new factory in Norrköping. The rapid expansion of this factory dominates the picture and accounts for the major part of the high entry share at the end of the interwar period ($\alpha_{23} = 47$). This high figure, however, is also due to the intensive modernization efforts in most of the firms, which meant a relatively modest growth of the labor force in the industry as a whole. The second big event was the 1926 formation by the majority of the other firms of Margarinfabrikernas Försäljnings AB, usually referred to as the "Margarine Company." The objective of this merger, which resulted in a common sales organization, was primarily to achieve economies in distribution. While most of the firms previously had had their own sales organizations and inventories in many communities, the merger led to a single sales organization with a single storage facility in each major community. Margarine prices were stabilized and also standardized to some extent. As already noted in Chapter 8, prices were gradually reduced, however, due in part to reduced production and distribution costs, as a consequence of modernization, and to lower raw materials prices. Certain opportunities for outside producers remained however. It is characteristic that several new firms entered the industry after the formation of the Margarine Company [Appendix 5]. These entrants did not let their policies be affected by the considerations which to some extent guided the large enterprises.[61] This enabled them to survive beside the big

---

[60] Cf. *SOU* (1940, No. 35), p. 126.
[61] Cf. Chap. 8, p. 171.

firms, and even to expand somewhat. Since, however, KF controlled a very considerable fraction of the distributive apparatus, and the Margarine Company much of the rest, their chances of achieving substantial size and of expanding beyond the local or regional market were never very good.

It is clear, therefore, why the development of the oleomargarine industry diverged from what could otherwise be expected of an industry in which process innovations played such an important role. Almost all of the new firms involved, incidentally, were absorbed by the Margarine Company during World War II, and production was in several cases discontinued. The government actively encouraged this development. The concentration of production, already rather considerable in 1939, thus progressed still further during the 1940's. From a "financial" standpoint, the industry was already very highly concentrated by 1939.

A few small firms disappeared during the interwar period, but firm mortality was insignificant on the whole ($\gamma_{23} = 3$). In this respect, the industry was typical of industries that developed free from any pressure due to the negative effects of the transformation process.

The Confectionery Industry

The development of the *chocolate and candy industry* was mainly of the demand-pull variety. The most prominent datum about the industry is that the extremely high number of new firms (Table 5, p. 192) gave such a low entry share ($\alpha_{23} = 17$).[62] The only other industry that was comparable in this regard was the capital goods-producing electrical engineering industry.

Two firms, both established immediately after World War I, accounted for a very considerable proportion of the 1939 entry share, *viz.*, somewhat in excess of one-third. The two were Svenska Suchard AB, which started under another name in 1919 and began producing on the basis of Swiss recipes in 1933, and Chokladfabriken Standard, which started on a very small scale in Stockholm in 1920. The great majority of the other 75 entrants started on a very small scale and, with very few ex-

---

[62] In judging the structure of this industry, one must recall the distinction drawn between industry and crafts. Firms which did not make substantial use of machinery in production and which sold their output through their own retail outlet have been classified under "crafts." A considerable proportion of the firms listed in *IS* have been sorted out by the application of this definition. This has been the case, for example, with most of the confectioneries. In many cases, particularly among the firms that later disappeared, it has, however, not been possible to determine the nature of the enterprise. In such uncertain cases, we have followed the rule to include rather than to exclude the firm in question. Several firms must, consequently, have been included in this way that ought to have been eliminated. While the data of this study thus comprise fewer "craft shops" than *IS*, it is not plausible that we have been entirely successful in limiting the material to "industry."

ceptions, remained small (Appendix 8). By 1939, none of them had reached 50 or more employees, and only a handful had 20. By and large the same applies also to the older firms—the few that were relatively large by 1919 expanded strongly, while the great majority of the small ones remained stationary and grew only insignificantly. One should note, however, that AB Chokladfabriken Marabou, which was one of the most successful older firms, had been established as a subsidiary of a Norwegian company as recently as during the last phase of World War I. Another firm, Stens Choklad- och Konfektfabrik AB had also been started by a worker at this same time and subsequently grew rapidly. At the beginning of the interwar period, 18 percent of the firms accounted for three fourths of the industry's labor force. By 1939, just 13 percent of the firms accounted for the same share of the labor force, despite the lively entry.

The lively, but quantitatively rather insignificant, entry is put in still clearer perspective when one notes that a very large number of the entrants disappeared before 1940. Apart from the 77 firms established between 1919 and 1939 which still existed by 1939–40, there had been 61 other entrants that never amounted to much and had succumbed in short order. The mortality rate for the firms in operation in 1919 was also very high. No less than 39 of 96 such firms had disappeared by 1940. That the exit share still was no larger than 14 is explained by the large share of the industry represented by the continuing firms as early as in 1919.

In summary, then, the chocolate and candy industry was characterized, on the one hand, by an exceedingly high turnover of firms and, on the other, by a relatively small number of large, continuing firms which during the whole period accounted for the main part of the branch's total output, and which really constituted a group apart as far as production equipment, sales organization, etc., were concerned. The demand-pull primarily benefited the larger, older firms with well-established names. Since they had already reached a size class that required an administrative apparatus and, to some extent, outside financing, they were not reluctant to expand. New firms with no significant novelties to offer could not elbow their way up among the old ones; and, among the young firms, Marabou was the only one able to grow into the circle of the very largest firms and to successfully compete with them by relying on a high degree of specialization and forceful promotion of its brand name.

Apart from Svenska Suchard AB, which engaged in pure parallel competition with the older, big firms (although after 1933, it partly replaced foreign competition of this type), most of the new firms in the chocolate and candy branch proper typically worked with simple product grades, often without brand-names. Chokladfabriken Standard, mentioned above, belonged to this category, for example. The growth of this firm was based primarily on sales to the dimestore chains. Firms in this category usually held their prices below those of the large or medium-sized enterprises which dominated the industry. Outside the chocolate and candy branch proper, there also arose a considerable number of producers of toffee, cough drops, and sundry confectionery, but with one or two exceptions, these did not grow significantly either. During the interwar period, finally, there was a fair number of new producers of sugar-glazes and fruit-glazes, bordering on the fruit preserves industry. As a rule, these remained stationary, also.

It is not particularly hard to explain this large number of entrants, of which a great many only served a local or regional market. The general precondition was the small investment required to start a new firm. Confectionery, and candy in particular, could be produced with very simple and inexpensive equipment. Also, as long as quality requirements were not very high, not much specialized technical knowledge was required. Consequently, there was a broad basis for the recruitment of entrepreneurs. Producer-customer relationships were also fluid. The market structure was characterized by innumerable, small retailers and thus did not offer any obstacles to a new producer trying to enter. The problem was to survive and, still more, to grow. The industry experienced considerable demand-pull, particularly after the devaluation of 1931, which reduced foreign competition. Since the major producers generally were reluctant to supply anonymous products of too cheap a quality, the new small businesses were given ample opportunities which they carefully exploited. As a typical reflection of the demand-pull conditions, many bakeries and coffeehouses, faced with growing demand, stopped making their own cake decorations, chocolate pastes, and so forth, and began instead to rely on specialized producers. In this respect, the formation of firms reflected the industrialization of the branch.

If it was easy to start small firms for the production of sundry confectionery products, it was also easy to discontinue them. In contrast to the larger, industrial chocolate firms, there were no large fixed plants on which a return had to be earned. Both for this, and for other reasons, these firms seldom had substantial long-term debts. The otherwise common propensity of creditors to forever continue to pump new blood into a sick enterprise—in the hope that it would in the end not only become competitive but also, perhaps, be able to recoup past losses—was, therefore, not operative here. Nor did these firms generally have a large administrative apparatus to dismantle. It was really only a matter of calling a halt to production.

The chocolate and candy industry, moreover, was decidedly an urban industry, even though there was some shift in the formation of new firms toward smaller towns and rural communities [cf. Appendix 7, Swedish edition]. This meant that its structure was more fluid. Apart from factors already mentioned, the larger urban communities generally offered more opportunities for the entrepreneur to transfer to another, closely related, activity than did the small towns or rural communities. Furthermore, the larger urban firms in this, as well as in other industries, were less frequently started and owned by workers or persons with similar backgrounds, i.e., the category that usually showed the greatest endurance even when the economic outcome proved unfavorable. Finally, there were no substantial strategic malinvestments in connection with the establishment of new firms during the interwar period. This is indicated by the fact that, despite the high mortality of new firms, the incidence was remarkably low among firms that had been started on a substantial scale. Neither among new nor among old firms did disappearances concern previously progressive firms.

The many small businesses exerted considerable competitive pressure on the big firms, but this factor must not be overemphasized. As has been indicated already, the market was primarily characterized by the competition between the trademarked products of the large and medium-sized firms within the chocolate industry proper. To a certain extent the small firms generally complemented, rather than competed with, the large and medium-sized ones. Despite the demand-pull, rates of return were not particularly good in the industry; this was due as much to the sharp competition among the dominating large and medium-sized firms and among the smallest firms as to competition between the larger and the smaller firms. In this respect, therefore, the situation differed in some degree from that in several other industries (such as the woodworking industries) where the competition was largely a struggle between the different size classes of firms, albeit small and large firms even there complemented each other to some extent. By the end of the interwar period, the structure of the chocolate and candy industry appears to have been relatively stable.

The *fruit processing industry* may be regarded as on the borderline between the confectionery industry and the canning industry. At the end of the interwar period, this branch stood at the very beginning of its era of rapid, supply-push expansion. Only during the latter half of the 1930's had there been considerable entry into this branch. This had been a period during which many new products were introduced in connection with great advances in preserving techniques and in fruit processing techniques generally. Although the new firms did not have time to develop very far before the outbreak of World War II, the entry share was still sizable ($\alpha_{23} = 39$). It should be noted, however, that the industry's continued rapid development during and after the war depended heavily on two old firms—namely AB Findus in Bjuv, a firm which had been completely modernized and developed by AB Marabou, and the KF plant in Åstorp. It was evidently difficult to enter into competition with these two, financially strong, firms. Despite significant product innovations, the branch experienced only moderate entry during the 1940's.

The Canning Industry

The fully preserved foods—canned fish, vegetables, and meat—were "young" products which, primarily through secondary product innovations and vigorous advertising, created a supply-push development. This became the immediate cause for the establishment of several new firms, so that even by the end of the interwar period the structure of the industry remained relatively dynamic. Strömstads Canning Co. AB was an important pioneer in the area of fully preserved fish products. This firm started in 1930 on a large scale (approximately 70 employees) as a subsidiary of a Norwegian company. Its development, based primarily on sardine and herring products new to Sweden, was very rapid, and the firm accounts for a significant proportion of the industry's entry share as of 1939 ($\alpha_{23} = 46$). The main producer of fully preserved meat, AB Konservfabriken Sirius, was formed in 1929 but did not begin to develop rapidly until 1939.

After the mid-1920's, the market was generally regarded as offering particularly favorable opportunities for new firms, since the high profits earned by the leading group of companies, AB Sveriges Förenade Konservfabriker, were well-known. Nor was it difficult to start a new firm. Initial investments could be kept low since the equipment was inexpensive and the technology did not require operating on a large scale. The distributive structure of the branch was characterized by numerous retail customers and fluid supplier-customer relations, and it did not, therefore, create significant obstacles. A very large proportion of the new firms that were thus established were typically more or less progressive.[63] Many of these new canneries were established by firms previously engaged in the very common combination of fish trade and salting (see Appendix 10). There was, however, one dominant firm in this area—AB Bröderna Ameln, an old fish wholesaler firm which started its cannery in 1928. In 1939, Strömstads Canning and this firm together accounted for 38 percent of all workers in the new firms established during the interwar period. Since a considerable number of the new firms were strongly progressive, while at the same time many old firms grew rapidly, the industry structure underwent a shift toward greater concentration,

---

[63] That this type of origin was so common among the new firms strongly contributed to making the geographical distribution of the canning industry in 1939 much the same as it had been in 1919. Thus the majority of the older firms had also in their time developed out of the combination of fishing-commerce-handicraft that was a distinctive characteristic of this industry.

despite the many small, new firms that were added. Thus in 1939, 24 percent of the firms accounted for 75 percent of the industry labor force, while the corresponding number in 1919 had been 38 percent.

One group of entrants represents a special case in that its members hardly expanded at all. This group comprised almost a score of firms which sprang up primarily on the island of Klädesholmen and were almost without exception directly connected with fishing, fish merchandising, or fish salting. The canneries here were generally small and rather primitive. Although they generally ought to have been profitable, these entrepreneurs as a rule did not want to expand. One reason for this reluctance lay in the administrative apparatus that expansion would require.

Beginning in the mid-1930's, the lively and quantitatively significant entry began to have noticeable effects in the form of hardening competition. Large and small firms alike underbid each other and profits declined. The interwar development of the canning industry represents a relatively good illustration of the classical pure competition model—one of the rather few such illustrations in Sweden during this period. One can, however, hardly regard the industry as having developed any genuine and persistent excess capacity during the 1930's. Profit margins were not compressed to the point where firm mortality became very high. It was, instead, fairly low, despite the absence of large, fixed plants deterring exit and despite the frequently present option of falling back on fishing and/or the fish trade, which was another element tending to reduce the persistence with which entrepreneurs were inclined to pursue canning. Strategic malinvestment with discontinuation in its train was an almost wholly unknown phenomenon. The canning industry generally exhibited rather low mortality for both older and new firms ($\gamma_{23} = 22$ for all canning and 12 for fish canneries). The disappearances that occurred were in several important instances the consequence of concentration efforts initiated, in particular, by the group of companies that enjoyed a dominant role in the industry already by the end of World War I. If these cases are excluded, the remaining disappearances were of remarkably little significance.

In 1950, following World War II, a more difficult period seemed in prospect, however. Many of the firms that were strongly progressive in the interwar period expanded considerably, while, at the same time, both output capacity and the ability to compete increased greatly in many areas due to the introduction of a series of process innovations which surpassed in significance those that occurred before the war. The industry structure gradually became more unstable.

It may be noted, finally, that the new directions in which the food-processing industry began to move in the 1940's, in response to the great innovations in the dehydration and deep-freezing of many types of food, did not stimulate much entry, since the new techniques were rather sophisticated and required substantial investments. Svenska AB Vato, established in 1940, pioneered in the innovation of dehydrated foods.

Mineral Water and Soft Drinks

The mineral water and soft drinks industry also experienced lively and, quantitatively, relatively significant entry ($\alpha_{23} = 26$).[64] Products which were at least partly new created a market at such a rapid pace that local opportunities for many new firms arose throughout the country. At the same time, demand-pull was very important. Transportation of soft drinks over long distances was not economical. In fact, the very possibility of undertaking such transport hardly existed until well into the 1930's, when almost all producers had converted to distribution by truck. Most of the new firms, of which undoubtedly only relatively few were registered by *IS*, were started in smaller communities and supplied, as did the older ones, a local market. The initial investment was as a rule small, especially during the 1920's when little in the way of machine equipment was required. Nor did the recruitment of entrepreneurs meet with any obstacles. Isolated attempts to control new entry through agreements with raw material suppliers were surely without significant effects.[65] Since no special technical knowledge was required, anyone could establish a soft drink plant. Many firms were operated with the help of family members and without wage labor. The character of these new firms is reflected in the fact that practically all of them remained stationary.

Firm mortality was high ($\gamma_{23} = 36$),[66] but this was almost totally due (in more than five sixths of the cases) to discontinuation prompted by concentration efforts. Small firms were bought out and closed up primarily by the breweries and by their subsidiaries in the mineral water and soft drink branch.[67] The fact that, aside from this, firm mortality was so very insignificant must certainly be attributed to the lack of any pressure due to negative effects of the transformation process. As in the concrete products industry, however, the situation began to change in the late 1930's and especially in the 1940's. The existence of many

---

[64] If output figures rather than number of workers had been used to calculate α, a lower value would certainly have resulted. Output per man-hour must have been relatively low in the small and often fairly primitive firms.

[65] Cf. *SOU* (1940, No. 35), p. 65.

[66] For the reason just mentioned, γ would have been less than 36, if measured in terms of output.

[67] Since these firms were usually quite primitive, it was strictly speaking their market rather than their plant and equipment that was purchased. The buyer rarely had any use for the equipment. The efforts of the breweries to acquire soft drink plants are to be explained by their financial strength and by the fact that their own development for various reasons was regressive. Furthermore, the advantages from a distributive standpoint were quite obvious and their full strength came to be felt with the increasing use of trucks.

smaller firms became threatened by the important process innovations which the larger and older firms and the breweries introduced in the course of their increasing mechanization. Apotekarnes Mineralvattens AB in Stockholm was the innovating pioneer in this regard. A new, very modern factory was constructed in the early 1930's, following the 1928 purchase of the firm by AB Stockholms Bryggerier. The smaller firms were also threatened by the higher sanitation requirements that the manufacturers' association sought to put into effect, particularly in the larger urban communities. For much the same reasons that applied in so many other industries, it was often the medium-sized enterprises that suffered the most from competition with the innovators. On the one hand, these firms frequently were unable to modernize and join the ranks of the large firms; on the other hand, they also lacked the advantage of the inexpensive and simple mode of operation of the small family firms.

The Clothing and Hosiery Industries

The *ready-made clothing industry* (including "sundry textile manufacturing") and the *hosiery industry* belong to the group of a few industries in which a single category of new firms completely dominated entry ($\alpha_{23} = 50$, and 38, respectively). *In all of the branches, the great majority of the new firms entered into parallel competition in product areas that were continuously expanding.* In the clothing industry, the "garment contractors" may be regarded to some extent, perhaps, as a different category. Innovation pioneers were only in exceptional cases found among the new firms. The most important innovations were introduced by old firms.

The explanation for this dominance of a single category of firms is not difficult to find. New, or young, products were continuously growing in importance in all areas. Consequently, the firms already in existence at a given time were almost never able, or willing, to expand production sufficiently to satisfy current demand, whether with regard to quantity or to assortment. This was the situation particularly characteristic of the 1930's, when foreign producers had little opportunity to compete, either quantitatively or qualitatively, while the industry at the same time enjoyed a period of strong demand-pull. This gave rise to very lively entry into all branches of the clothing, textile processing, and hosiery industries. Characteristically, most older firms went through very rapid expansion at the same time. [Cf. Appendix 8 of the Swedish edition.]

The industry's structure was still strongly dynamic by the end of the interwar period. There was a considerable underbrush of young firms on their way to becoming large. In relation to the number of stationary firms, the number of progressive ones was very large both among new and old enterprises—typically an indication that new and old firms are of similar character and pursue roughly the same policies. Despite an extremely high rate of entry, therefore, the structure of both industries showed higher concentration by the end of the interwar period than at the beginning. The number of regressive firms was notably small. Those that did exist were primarily located in the cities and represented a special type of firm (see below).

The *garment contractors* represented a form of industrial organization new to the interwar period. They would receive textiles and other materials either from manufacturers or from wholesalers or retailers and would also leave the marketing of the product to them. Before World War I, they had had their predecessors in the cottage industry. Some cottage industry still existed in the interwar period, but it was on its way out everywhere. Garment contracting arose both in the men's clothing and the work-clothes branches.[68] In the former, it was a question of odd garments of simple types, little affected by fashion. The firms producing work clothes provided a modern repetition of the story of the early textile industry. Their emergence was above all due to a technical factor, namely, the twin-needle or triple-needle machines. These first appeared in Sweden during the twenties, but did not become generally known until the turn of the decade. As usual, it was necessary to have the example of a few pioneers to copy. The capacity of these machines and their procurement cost were so great that they could not be used in the home in the same way as the ordinary sewing machine. The dimensions of all other stages in the production process had to be tailored to the capacity of the machines. This required a production operation "under one roof" and led to the development of firms of this type. A concentration of entry to the otherwise unfavorable years of the early 1930's was especially characteristic of the work-clothes branch. This was due precisely to the fact that these machines had by then become generally known and had had their advantages demonstrated by the pioneers of the branch. The rayon-silk textiles contributed to a similar industrialization process in ladies' garments. These fabrics, which were a novelty in the 1920's, were more difficult for the home seamstresses to work with than cotton or woolen fabrics.[69]

In ready-made clothing particularly, the geographical distribution of the firms underwent a strong shift toward rural communities and smaller towns (Appendix 7, Swedish edition). This shift was especially pronounced in men's clothes and in work clothes. The production of ladies' garments was still concentrated in the larger urbanized areas by

---

[68] The number of garment contractors, especially in the production of work clothes, was undoubtedly significantly larger than the figures used for this study would indicate. Many of these firms were too small to be included in *IS*.

[69] Cf. G. Grenander-Nyberg, "Sömnadsindustrien. En översikt av dess uppkomst och utveckling i Sverige," *Daedalus* (Tekniska Museets Årsbok, 1946).

the end of the interwar period, but the same shift can be observed in this branch, also. At the end of World War I, hardly any firms producing ladies' garments existed in the rural communities and small towns, while by the end of the interwar period such a location was not at all uncommon. Nor did firms combining men's, ladies', and children's clothing exist outside the larger urban communities until well into the interwar period. Finally, the production of work clothes, which constituted an entirely new branch, developed primarily in rural and small urban communities. This branch was particularly well represented in the Sjuhärads district. The same locational shift can be observed in the hosiery industry, also. Here, however, rayon hosiery and stockings constitute exceptions.

The strong concentration of new entry in rural and smaller urban communities, which will be studied in more detail in Chapter 15, must be viewed in the light of the nature of the older type of enterprise. A large proportion of the clothing and hosiery manufacturers in existence by the end of World War I combined manufacturing with wholesaling or retailing. Wholesaling was most common in men's clothing, retailing in ladies' garments and hosiery. The new type of enterprise which arose during the interwar period, initially through transformation of older firms, was based on process innovations—such as serial and moving-line production—and it was generally of such a markedly industrial character that the combination of manufacturing and distribution appeared less functional (see below in connection with disappearances). This removed the previously natural tendency for new firms to gravitate toward consumption areas.[70] Obviously the rapid development of transportation also played a big role in this connection, as did the electrification of rural areas. Both these developments improved conditions for firms located in rural communities and small towns. Another important factor was the differentials between wages, real estate values, etc., in and outside the larger urban areas. That rayon-silk hosiery and silk stocking production became more concentrated in the cities was due, among other things, to the somewhat more advanced technology required and to the fact that the expensive raw materials involved in these branches made geographical wage differentials relatively less important. The requirements concerning technical knowledge and financial strength meant that the recruitment of entrepreneurs was limited to categories found primarily in the cities; these people also preferred to locate new enterprises in the cities.[71]

The recruitment of enterprise founders is of interest in other respects,

---

[70] It is significant that the shift toward rural areas and small towns was most pronounced during the 1930's, i.e., the period in which the innovations of the 1920's became widely disseminated.

[71] Cf. also Chap. 15.

also. It is remarkable, to begin with, how very rarely clothing manufacturing firms developed out of the old tailor trade. Appendix 10 [in Swedish edition] shows "developed from handicraft" to be an insignificant category. Instead, there was an evident shift toward workers and foremen (Appendix 14 and Table 15) in most branches of the two industries under consideration. This trend is particularly evident in men's clothing, where the number of new manufacturing shops evolving from retail or wholesale businesses, or otherwise started by merchants, became much smaller in the 1930's than in the 1920's, while the number of firms started by workers, foremen, and so forth, increased considerably.[72] One should recall at this point that almost all clothing firms dating back before World War I had been started by merchants. We have already encountered this trend in the recruitment of founders in the analysis of many other industries. It was particularly pronounced in the clothing industry, however, even though it did not become evident as early as in the 1920's to the same extent as in many other industries. But then the decisive broadening of the recruitment base also occurred later than in the engineering industries, for example, since the great expansion of old firms only took place in the 1920's.

TABLE 15
Survey of Clothing and Textile Manufacturing,
Firms Established by Workers, Foremen, etc.

Major Branches	Number of Firms Established in 1919–39 and in Operation in 1940	Number of Firms for which Previous Occupation of Founder Is Known	Firms Founded by Workers, Foremen, etc.	
			Number	Percent
Men's clothes....................	113	84	35	42
Ladies' garments.................	65	54	10	19
Work clothes....................	54	41	13	32
Children's clothing...............	14	10	—	—
Firms combining men's, ladies' and children's ready-made clothing.....................	57	31	4	13
Other.........................	72	45	12	27
Total.....................	375	265	74	28

It was noted above that very frequently the existing firms were either unable or unwilling to expand sufficiently to meet the growing demand for both ready-made clothing and hosiery and, in particular, rayon hosiery. One reason has already been touched upon in connection with

---

[72] Cf. above concerning the nature of these firms.

the older type of urban firms. The firms combining manufacturing with retailing frequently did not possess premises suitable for expansion. The alternative of building a factory in a separate location often did not appeal to an owner whose primary interest was in the retail establishment. Insufficient expansion opportunities due to lack of suitable premises also constituted an obstacle in several cases where the firm was not confined by its combination of retailing and manufacturing to crowded quarters in the cities. Owners undoubtedly hesitated to undertake a rapid program of expansion even when sales prospects were favorable and physical space did not present a problem. Many an entrepreneur simply did not want his firm to grow to the point where he would have too complex an organization to administer. In this connection one should recall that even a firm of moderate size usually earned a sizeable return.[73] Where the will to expand was present, liquidity problems and/or difficulties in raising sufficient long-term capital often presented obstacles. One gets the impression, however, that it was more often a question of being reluctant to go too deeply into debt than one of insufficient opportunities to borrow. In general, borrowing money was not difficult for firms belonging to branches that were among the most profitable in the country, and in which the number of bankruptcies was less than in most industries (cf. below in connection with disappearances).

Finally, another important factor connected with the marketing structure of the industry should be mentioned. As a rule, older producers were obviously associated mostly with older wholesalers and retailers.[74] The expansion of the market was so strong and rapid everywhere that these older distributors usually were able to handle the entire output of the older producers. The latter, therefore, did not have to search for new customers among new wholesalers and retailers, either very often or very energetically. But the urbanization and increasing commercialization of rural areas led to the establishment of many new retail outlets. These retailers tried, perhaps, to order also from older producers, but often found it easier, under the circumstances, to contact people who were in a position to start, or had recently started, a new firm.

One special factor should be noted here. The brand-name products, which were also new products in several respects, especially in the men's

---

[73] Since the great majority of firms were individually owned or family owned, the desire to expand was frequently curtailed simply because development into "big business" was impossible within the framework of such a firm. It would have required a broadening of the firm's financial base without any attendant guarantee of higher income for the entrepreneur.

[74] Cf. F. Kristensson, *Studier i svenska textila industriers struktur* (Stockholm, 1946), p. 370. Among Kristensson's findings is that of a strong positive correlation between sales per customer and size of firm. His interpretation, namely that "older" firms preferred to sell to "older" customers who were also the dealers with the greatest opportunities to expand, is surely correct.

clothing branch, were introduced with considerable advertising. AB Gunnar Collijn was perhaps foremost in this regard. In this connection, a fairly limited number of the older retailers were sometimes given exclusive marketing rights. When the brand-name products became generally known, the public would also start to ask for them in retail establishments that did not have such marketing rights. Consequently, these retailers became interested in obtaining similar products from other producers. The process illustrates clearly the way in which novel products could create a market at such a rapid pace that new firms found it easy to enter.

In sharp contrast to the woodworking industries, for example, the opportunities for new firms created in this way were not fully. exploited, despite the lively entry. This was particularly true in the ready-made clothing industry. One sign of this is the rate of entry which kept increasing, at least up through the last few years of the 1930's (Figure 16, p. 210). The high profits which indubitably characterized the branch throughout the period, despite the rapid expansion of both old and new firms, are also indicative. Why the existing firms did not expand faster and to such an extent as to bring about a general reduction of average rates of return is a question which has already been answered. Why still more new firms were not started so that the same effect would be achieved is perhaps a more difficult question. It may be inferred, however, that the base for the recruitment of enterprise founders probably was not sufficiently broad to allow a higher rate of formation of new firms, especially not in the ready-made clothing branch. In contrast to the furniture industry, for example, the ready-made clothing industry was small at the beginning of the interwar period, when the strong supply-push due to significant product and process innovations— and somewhat later the strong demand-pull—began. Appendix 14 [in the Swedish edition] shows that the recruitment of entrepreneurs was practically limited to persons with previous employment in the manufacturing or marketing of ready-made clothing. Evidently neither master tailors nor "outsiders" found it easy or attractive to enter the branch. By the end of World War I, the number of persons in the industry with technical or commercial experience was limited. Due to the technical status of the branch at that time, its personnel consisted almost entirely of managers and unskilled workers. Only as the industry grew and technical and organizational development progressed did the recruitment base broaden. Thus it appears that just about as many new firms were established in the clothing industry during the interwar period as was possible, given the existing recruitment base. Perhaps it should be pointed out here that there were hardly any new firms being started on "the livelihood principle" since there was never any considerable unemployment, or risk of unemployment, in the industry. Thus the large "supply" of entrepreneurs which such factors created in other industries was nonexistent.

Recruitment in the hosiery industry showed somewhat similar patterns, at least in the rayon and stocking branches. The situation in woolen and cotton hosiery was rather different since these branches had already developed far by the end of World War I and were technically less demanding. Neither the supply-push nor the demand-pull factors were as strong in these latter branches as in the others, particularly because foreign competition was at times intensive. This factor did not only reduce profits directly but also, in a rather paradoxical manner, indirectly—i.e., by causing increased entry in periods of unemployment or threatening unemployment. This is, in principle, the same mechanism which we found at work in a more pronounced fashion in the furniture industry.

The important process innovations that occurred during the 1920's, particularly in the men's clothing branch, led to a noteworthy change in the initial size of the typical entrant. In this respect, the introduction of assembly-line techniques was most important. Appendix 11 shows clearly that the new firms that appeared during the 1930's generally began operations on a markedly larger scale than did the new firms established in the 1920's. Undoubtedly this was due not only to the many new machines which had come into use and had become necessary for any competitive enterprise, but also to the fact that moving-line production could only be organized advantageously on a scale larger than the one previously most common in the men's clothing branch. It is not just coincidence that the same increase in the size of entrants cannot be observed in the ladies' garments industry. There were few serious attempts at applying assembly-line techniques to the production of the lighter garments that dominated the ladies' clothing branch.[75] Nor is it coincidence that the new hosiery firms were not started on a larger scale in the 1930's than in the 1920's. In this branch, the technical and organizational advantages of greater initial size were not very pronounced.[76]

---

[75] In addition, however, ladies' garments were more dependent on fashions. In order to have good earnings a firm had to keep well abreast of changing fashions, and successes or failures in this respect were much more important than "optimality" on the production side. *Theoretically*, to be sure, there is nothing to imply that the "hunt" for the latest fashions should make it less important to attain "optimality" of size of firm. But, in the real world, we are of course dealing with people whose talents are often suited only for the marketing or for the production management side of the firm's operations.

[76] Certain tendencies toward larger initial firm size are, however, still observable also in light ladies' garments and hosiery, where increased mechanization came to be required in order to compete successfully. Over the span of a couple of decades, the number of machines employed had increased substantially in this area also. That credit was easier to obtain in the 1930's than had been the case in the 1920's may also have played a certain role.

The cyclical fluctuations in the rate of entry (Figure 16, p. 210) are, as has been indicated, of considerable interest, particularly with regard to the ready-made clothing industry. The number of entrants increased drastically in the very midst of the general depression of the early 1930's, only to decline during the last few years of the decade.[77]

There was several reasons behind the increase in the number of new firms in the early 1930's. Although it is impossible to judge their relative importance in a reliable quantitative manner, certainly the most fundamental cause lay in the fact that the great decisive innovations made in products and processes during the 1920's had led to a virtual revolution of the clothing industry. By the late 1920's, the industry was ready for a rapid advance on a broad front due to the large and growing market which these innovations had opened up. Not even a serious depression in the economy as a whole could put serious obstacles in the way. Nor is it a coincidence that the figures on the formation of new firms show no reflection of the depression at all, while the output series for all the different branches show some retardation. The situation in ready-made clothing was such that it had to induce optimistic long-run expectations. These expectations influenced the rate of entry, while current output, on the other hand, could not but be affected by the depression, at least to some extent.

A number of other factors also played a role, however, in determining entry and in making the development of output in the various branches resistant to cyclical influences and the contractionary tendencies temporary. It has already been indicated that in the work clothes branch a purely technological factor caused a high rate of entry in the early 1930's. In this connection, it should be noted that sewing machines and other equipment for the clothing industry, as well as knitting frames, could be bought very inexpensively during the depression years; this contributed to making the formation of new firms more attractive. The marketing policies of the textile mills also had the same effect. There were considerable sales of both cotton and woolen fabrics at low prices, which attracted many people to the production of ready-made clothing where prices held up better than in textiles. A couple of textile and spinning mills also started their own clothing factories and hosiery divisions.[78]

---

[77] Although study of a sample indicates that the decline of the "birth rate" curve for the late 1930's shown in Figure 16 is exaggerated, the decline as such must be regarded as firmly established.

[78] It is remarkable that such integration forward was not more common. Part of the explanation appears to be that the hard times undergone by the weaving and spinning mills were rather rapidly becoming a thing of the past in the early 1930's. It is perhaps more strange that not even the cotton textile industry chose to integrate with hosiery and garments already in the 1920's. The reluctance to compete with customers was probably the decisive consideration. Efforts to integrate spinning with weaving (or the other way around) had already for some time played a large role.

The tendency for prices of final products to decline by less than the prices of materials used is characteristic of the behavior of relative prices in almost every recession. In addition, there was an increased tendency on part of the public to substitute ready-made clothing, which had improved greatly in quality precisely at this time, for the more expensive tailor-made clothes—a tendency which in turn must be viewed in the light of the general reduction in income.[79]

With regard to the hosiery industry, the same innovation process as in the clothing industry was undoubtedly the decisive factor underlying the high rate of entry, especially during the depression of the early 1930's. The best example is the stocking industry, where in the late 1920's one new firm, AB Malmö Strumpfabrik, accounted for important innovations, particularly in the area of sales organization and marketing techniques (brand-name products). At the same time, the devaluation played an important role. It stimulated a good deal of entry also in the other branches of the hosiery industry by easing foreign competition, particularly from Belgian and Czechoslovakian imports.

The fall-off of entry, particularly in the clothing industry, toward the end of the 1930's is not easy to explain. One's first guess, to be sure, is that the extremely intensive entry, together with the rapid expansion of the majority of both new and old firms, finally saturated the market to some extent. Actually, however, this does not seem to be a particularly realistic explanation. It is in any case not a sufficient one. One finds no notable increase in complaints of keen competition in the branches, nor is there anything to suggest that rates of return were generally declining.

With regard to firm disappearances in the interwar period, one remarkable fact should be noted—namely, that despite mortality rates that were high ($\gamma_{23} = 26$ and 14, respectively) considering the strongly progressive development of the ready-made clothing and hosiery industries, strategic malinvestments did not play a significant role.[80] The ready-made clothing industry, in particular, was relatively risk-free as long as the firm was not mismanaged. Those cases of strategic malinvestment that can be ascertained were almost without exception due to outright mismanagement and/or to a complete lack of experience in the industry on part of the entrepreneur at the start of the firm.

There do not appear to have been any planned discontinuations for purposes of concentration. The relatively high mortality of old firms

---

[79] A corresponding shift of demand toward less expensive product types can be observed in the shoe industry. Cf. Swedish Cooperative Union (KF), *Annual Report* (1932), p. 61.

[80] The high exit share, measured in number of workers (cf. Table 5, p. 192 and Appendix 6 of Swedish edition), is undoubtedly higher than it would be if calculated in terms of output. The firms that disappeared in all probability had low output per man-hour (cf. below).

gives, instead, an unusually good example of how innovations made it impossible for old factor combinations to survive. Thus it was in large part the "classic" firm-type which disappeared during the 1920's and in the depression of the 1930's. When new and old firms went in for mass production with assembly-line and other modern methods, those firms that combined wholesale and/or retail merchandizing with production were faced with two alternatives—either they had to discontinue their role in distribution and concentrate wholly on modern, industrial production, or else they had to relinquish manufacturing and concentrate exclusively on trade.[81] Many firms chose the latter alternative (i.e., to discontinue manufacturing), and this, then, meant a high mortality rate among the older firms. This type of firm mortality had a number of distinguishing features. Old firms—frequently very old ones—were more important in the total picture of disappearances than were the new (even though the latter were several times as numerous as the firms in existence in 1919); almost half of the old firms which later disappeared showed regressive development and half of them were stationary—for that matter, the great majority of the stationary ones were so small that a regressive development often was impossible (see the definitions of "regressive" and "stationary" in Chapter 10); only a small minority of the old firms that disappeared were progressive.

With regard to the industry's development during the 1940's, finally, one notes that the rate of entry was very high, particularly in ready-made clothing. It appears, however, that the industry structure was somewhat less dynamic by the end of the decade than previously. In comparison with the interwar period a considerably larger number of firms had stopped growing, at least for the time being. Also many of the new firms—which included a large proportion of garment contractors—were less progressive than the majority of the firms established in the interwar period had been in their time. To the extent that it was not a question just of older firms establishing branch plants in areas with a good supply of female labor, the formation of these new firms must in many industries be considered in the light of the inflationary overheating of the economy—in much the same way as in the engineering industries. Since it can hardly be assumed that these firms represent a lasting phenomenon, their entry in all probability made the industry structure less stable than previously.

Gloves, Leather and Fur Products

If the small number of firms engaged only in curing pelts are disregarded, the *fur products industry* can be divided into two categories. One would include the larger manufacturers who, as a rule, had more

---

[81] Cf. above p. 292.

than 20 workers and sold to a very large number of retailers throughout the country. The other consists of retail stores with their own, usually modest, production of new fur products for local markets. Unfortunately, it is not possible to determine the distribution of total output between these two types of producers. Thus only part of those belonging to the latter category are reported in *IS*, and in addition, all of them were to a great extent employed in renovating furs or in altering furs which they had previously produced or bought from a producer in the first category. It is evident, however, that these retailers accounted for a significant proportion of the industry's output throughout the interwar period.[82]

In both of these categories, the rate of entry was high in the thirties ($\alpha_{23} = 33$), and it became exceptionally high in the years of economic isolation during World War II. The new firms were often progressive. This stands in remarkably sharp contrast to the stationary development which, as a rule, characterized the older firms in the fur products industry ($\beta_{23} = 3.89$; cf. also Appendix 8 in Swedish edition).[83] Those new firms which produced for a nationwide market were progressive almost without exception. Evidently the new types of fur products created a supply-push while at the same time demand-pull was strong. Process innovations, on the other hand, were of little importance. As in the ready-made clothing industry (though in a less pronounced manner), this process offered favorable opportunities for new entrants. Almost the entire increase in the work force of this branch was due to new firms (cf. Appendix 9). In this respect, the situation differed from that found in most other branches that exhibited a similar type of development process. The explanation for this is mainly that the composition of output changed from smaller fur products (such as muffs, fur caps, etc.) toward fur coats, the production of which required less labor. In the older firms, the increased output of fur coats was accomplished primarily by transferring labor from the production of smaller items. The new firms, in

---

[82] Since production in the manufacturing firms took place on much the same lines as in the workshops of the retailers—in neither type of firm had there been any general mechanization (cf. Chap. 8, p. 169)—it hardly seems appropriate to eliminate the retailers as constituting "handicraft." If this is done, however, one will find that the firms that on the basis of their marketing arrangements could be considered as "industrial," had not in general developed out of the retailer-craftshop type. This applies to the prewar as well as to the interwar period. Nor have the fur wholesalers engaged in manufacturing for a national market to any considerable extent. This finding is undeniably surprising.

[83] The gross addition of new firms between 1919 and 1939 was 70 firms (the figure does not include shops curing skins). Of this number, approximately 50 belong in the retailer category. The actual gross addition must surely have been much larger than 70, and almost all of those that were not included in *IS* were undoubtedly of this type.

contrast, began with production of fur coats right from the start. Hence they added a considerably greater number of workers to the branch than did the older firms. Had it been possible to compute the entry share and entry quotient in terms of the output of fur coats, instead of in terms of numbers of workers in all fur products, there is not the slightest doubt that the entry share would have been less than 33.

Firm mortality was insignificant in terms of the number of firms that disappeared, but the discontinued firms were rather large ($\gamma_{23} = 25$). Most of the disappearances occurred during the 1920's (Appendix 5). Losses incurred on inventories of pelts and fur products in connection with the great decline of prices in the first postwar depression were undoubtedly an important cause. To that extent firm mortality was thus associated with strategic malinvestments in inventories. In addition, however, the smaller fur products and men's fur coats went out of fashion, and this created difficulties for firms that did not convert to ladies' fur coats rapidly enough. Thus, these difficulties, which were concentrated to the 1920's, were due to the negative effects of the transformation process. There were hardly any strategic malinvestments in fixed capital.

At the beginning of the interwar period, there were relatively few producers of *gloves*. The domestic consumption of gloves was in large part met through imports. The firms were small—in 1919 none of them had as many as 20 workers. Despite continued large imports, the domestic industry experienced strong demand-pull through the interwar period, and especially during the 1930's. Many of the old firms expanded, while at the same time a rather considerable number of new firms emerged ($\alpha_{23} = 29$). Entry occurred in various parts of the country but was to a remarkable extent concentrated to the Malung district with its old cottage-industry traditions in leather processing. Since many of the entrants remained small, the number of new firms was surely larger than indicated by *IS*, and thus larger than the figures given in the present work. The simplified production methods introduced by some of the new firms were important in stimulating further entry. The new methods made it easier for other new firms to operate, and they also forced the older firms, which were rather tradition-bound and frequently concentrated on particularly high-quality products, to simplify their methods to some extent. The 1927 discontinuation of a major firm (see below), which was not primarily motivated by the market situation, was another development which to some extent must have influenced the formation of new firms. Only a few firms were started in the larger urban areas, and since just as many disappeared, the number of such urban firms in existence by 1939 did not exceed that of 1919.

Firms producing gloves had their most common origin in leather-product commerce. As a rule, the new firms produced for a nationwide market from the start. In both these respects, the branch differed from the fur products branch.

Curiously enough, no new firms were established in such old glove-making centers as Lund and Malmö. Thus one phenomenon, otherwise common, is missing here—i.e., older firms giving rise to new ones started by their employees in the same community. During and after World War II, however, a large number of firms were established by workers—and also in these cities—although the financing of these blue-collar firms was often provided by commercial firms.

The mortality figure ($\gamma_{23} = 62$) largely reflects the closing down of Malmö Handsk- och Glacéläderfabrik in 1927, from which time this firm concentrated exclusively on the operation of its tannery in Kävlinge. Liquidity problems were the main reason behind the decision. Another factor, of less importance, was the opinion that a tannery could not be operated to advantage in combination with the making of gloves as long as it was not feasible to use the entire output within the firm itself.[84] To "compete with one's own customers" was widely regarded as a bad practice. Apart from this case, many old glovemakers closed down. Their handicraft methods made it difficult to survive in competition with the more mechanized manufacturing firms.

Neither in the fur industry nor in the glove industry did a few new firms account for a major part of the entry share. This, however, was the case in the *sundry leather products industry* ($\alpha_{23} = 85$), which cannot be included in either of these two industries. At the begining of the interwar period, this category comprised only a small number of firms, all of insignificant size. Among the many subsequent entrants, which showed a remarkable concentration around Malung, a single enterprise was predominant. This firm, Jonssons Fabriker AB (Jofa), was established in 1926 and produced a very wide assortment of different "leisure time" products—sport equipment, leather clothes, gloves, sport shoes, fur coats, and so forth. The firm grew at an exceptional pace, particularly in the 1930's, and reached a million-kronor turnover as early as in the mid-1930's. The primary reason for this rapid growth was the firm's early entry into the market for sporting goods, as well as its mechanical work-shop for the production of such things as bicycle saddles, lounge chairs, and camping equipment. In 1939, this firm accounted for almost 40 percent of the work force in the *IS* category of "sundry fur and leather products industry." Although several of the other firms also showed

---

[84] Still several glovemakers had started their own tannery with part of the output intended for sale. As a rule, however, the sale of leather would be phased out as it became possible to expand the manufacturing of gloves. In the case of the Malmö firm, also, its glove production was older than the tannery operated in Kävlinge.

a progressive development, none of them had comparable success. The founders of the latter firms were not as a rule the type of entrepreneur who makes growth a primary objective, even though many of them may well have had the ability to bring it about.

Although the branch produced a mixed assortment of goods, relatively new products dominated—automotive accessories and goods related to sports and recreational activities in general. The branch, therefore, showed no sign of negative development effects. There were no products or processes on their way out, and the strong demand-pull meant that the risks of strategic malinvestments were relatively small. Only a few of the new firms disappeared.

The Leather Shoe Industry

Although the leather shoe industry by and large stagnated during the interwar period, it had a high rate of entry, especially during the 1920's ($\alpha_{23} = 31$).[85] Only about one fourth of the new firms showed noticeable growth, while the rest remained stationary or regressed. The latter actually accounted for a considerably larger proportion, since many of them never were registered in *IS*.

The majority of the new firms, however, started on a small scale and remained rather small. Most of them were turn-shoe makers operating basically with handicraft techniques. During World War I, these firms represented by and large a new type, and their appearance was due mainly to the wartime difficulties in importing turn-shoes from Germany.[86] Their output was almost entirely marketed through wholesalers and consisted also after the war of simple types of shoes, particularly children's shoes. The equipment of these small businesses was inexpensive, and the equity needed to start a new firm could be kept to a modest sum, particularly since credit was usually obtainable from the wholesalers who both supplied the raw materials and marketed the final product. On the other hand, the so-called rental system, which otherwise characterized the shoe industry, was of little importance in the formation of this class of firms, since machines were seldom rented to the very small firms. They mostly operated with simple, German-made equipment. Almost all of these turn-shoe shops were typically started by shoe industry workers. As in the prewar period, one finds few cobbler craftsmen among the founders of new firms.

Of the new firms which were not turn-shoe shops but produced a wider assortment of shoes, using more rented machine equipment, many

---

[85] For reasons emphasized in Chap. 10, the margin of error attaching to the estimate of the entry share is rather large here. But there can be no doubt that, as indicated by the value of α, new firms played a very important role.

[86] Cf. B. Forssell, *Handskomakeriet i Närike. Kulturhistoriska anteckningar* (Örebro, 1920).

were started on a somewhat larger scale, although seldom with more than 10 employees.[87] These firms were also as a rule started by workers. In most cases they remained stationary. The interwar period, however, did bring a noticeable shift in the type of entry and in the recruitment of founders. The very large number of new firms that appeared between 1890 and 1914 typically differed from those established after World War I—they were usually started on a somewhat larger scale or, in any case, tended to grow more rapidly than the postwar entrants. Also, they were in most instances founded by wholesalers or other merchants rather than by workers and foremen.[88] The wholesalers, however, continued to play a significant role after World War I in the formation of new firms outside the turn-shoe category by often inducing workers and foremen to start such enterprises. A rather large number of new wholesaler firms were started during the 1920's, and these firms undoubtedly concentrated their sales efforts on retailers in the relatively new and rapidly growing urban communities. These wholesalers were particularly willing to establish relationships with new producers (cf. the clothing industry). Furthermore, the entry of several other new firms was occasioned by the attempts of some older firms, particularly those which had achieved a rather substantial size, to bypass the wholesalers in marketing their products. The wholesalers would then be anxious to make contact with newly started firms. In some instances this chain of causation was reversed. Thus certain wholesale firms started or purchased manufacturing establishments and became factory wholesalers. This caused other manufacturers to begin selling directly to retailers since they did not feel they could count on the factory wholesaler to show the same interest as previously in marketing their products.

The depression years of the early 1930's showed no reduction in the high rate of entry. This was mainly due to high unemployment among shoe industry workers. Subsequently, entry apparently declined somewhat. At least this seems to have been true if the turn-shoe firms are ignored. The low rate of return in the industry could hardly but affect entry in the long run. On the other hand, attempts at organized curtailment of competition with the objective of controlling entry, were far from effective.[89] These attempts took the form of agreements between

---

[87] Concerning the machine-rental policies of the American United Shoe Machinery Corporation, cf. Elinder, *Studier i den svenska skoindustriens struktur* (Stockholm, 1948), p. 200 ff.

[88] Concerning the early history of the shoe industry, cf., e.g., T. Åqvist, "Skoindustriens utveckling i Örebro stad och län," *Nerikes Allehanda*, special anniversary issue (March 4, 1943).

[89] Cf. Elinder, *op. cit.*, p. 190. It may be added that the rate of entry probably was not lower in the late 1930's than it had been in the late 1920's. As Elinder emphasizes, however, his time series is based on the years in which the firms came to be included in *IS*, so its cyclical variations should not be taken too seriously.

shoe manufacturing firms and tanneries, but at least for smaller producers, it was always possible to find raw material suppliers among retailers or wholesalers who were not party to these agreements. During and after World War II, the principles guiding the government regulation of raw materials distribution caused a reduction in entry. Thus, new quotas were granted only in exceptional cases.

The majority of both continuing firms and new firms remained stationary in the sense that the number of their employees did not grow significantly. As a rule, they operated at less than full capacity. But a couple of firms showed strongly progressive development due, among other things, to purchase of other firms. The two most important ones were the Oscaria-group and the KF-owned Svenska Skoindustri AB, both located in Örebro. In both cases, as well as in a few others, the firms followed a policy of vertical integration from tanneries, on the one hand, to wholesaling and retail outlets on the other.

Firm mortality in the interwar period was substantial ($\gamma_{23} = 26$). The figure reflects above all a large *number* of disappearances. A major factor here was the competition from rubber shoe manufacturing. It was also characteristic of the industry, however, that several firms were able to survive only because of their particularly good liquidity and large net worth (cf. Appendix 3 in Swedish edition). Their strong financial condition was due to the industry's high profits during World War I and to the reserves accumulated during the war. Because of low inventories, among other things, the firms managed to conserve these financial reserves rather well through the first postwar deflation. Had this not been true, more firms would in all probability have disappeared during the 1920's.

The incidence of disappearance among the smallest firms was low. The many turn-shoe shops that appeared during World War I were as a rule able to continue in operation, even though they were far from profitable in most cases (see below). Their ability to survive was remarkable in view of the evident superiority of the new cement and Veldtshoen processes over the old turn-shoe process used by the small firms. The explanation is simply that it was not very difficult to convert to the new processes.

Strategic malinvestments were the cause of discontinuation in only a few instances. One case is of special interest here, namely, that of a new, modern factory which was established in Jönköping in the early 1930's. Following its failure, it was taken over and closed down by a group of older firms. The failures of firms and the closing of plants in the shoe industry during the interwar period are of particular interest in that they frequently involved combinations of older firms which sought to prevent the plant and equipment of the bankrupt firm from being sold cheaply to new owners. The resulting low fixed costs would enable the new owners to continue operating in the manner characterized as "dumping" in our previous discussion of the woodworking industries. This remarkable policy of the older, independent shoe producers does not seem to have been seriously attempted in any other industry. In general, the policy was unsuccessful. For example, it proved difficult to prevent the machinery of the failed firm from being used in one way or another to start a new enterprise. It was undoubtedly a rather common and chronic phenomenon in the shoe industry, too, that firms recovered only variable costs. Under these circumstances, competition between different size-classes of firms· became intensive. This led to repeated financial reconstructions which, if more information had been available, in many instances should have been recorded in the present work as failures followed by a new start.[90] Substantial amounts of capital were in this way invested in the shoe industry in the interwar period— and then lost. The causes and consequences of a situation of this kind have already been discussed in detail, particularly in connection with the joineries, and may therefore be passed over without further comment. The leather-shoe industry, in much the same way as the woodworking industries, was too large in relation to its market.[91]

Paints and Varnishes

This industry stands out as one of the few exceptions to the general rule that a new, supply-push product leads to lively and quantitatively significant entry. It is thus of particular interest for the study of the formation and evolution of firms ($\alpha_{23} = 17$; $\beta_{23} = 0.29$). It is particularly remarkable that while many small firms certainly appeared—55 percent of the firms in the industry by 1939 were new—all of them remained stationary, despite the fact that they produced the new cellulose enamels and synthetic paints from the start. This was true also of those new firms that began with oil paints and oil enamel paints but later added the new products to their lines. In this group, there was one single exception—Färg-och Fernissfabriks AB Arvid Lindgren & Co., located in Märsta in the province of Uppland. This firm pioneered with the synthetic enamels. Of the older firms, on the other hand, the majority adopted the new products and showed progressive development. Thus in 1939 only 21 percent of the firms accounted for 75 percent of the industry work force, while in 1919 the figure had been 28 percent. Two of the older firms, Ferniss AB and AB Wilhelm Becker, pioneered with the cellulose enamels in Sweden.

The production of these new paints did not per se require particularly large plants and expensive equipment, even though the technical advantages of operating on a large scale gradually became more and more

---

[90] Cf. Chap. 10, p. 190.
[91] Cf. p. 273 n.

apparent. There were consequently few if any obstacles of this kind
to lively and quantitatively significant entry. But the rapid technical
progress, due among other things to continuously improving raw materials, meant that the existing firms had a certain advantage over potential
entrants. The larger firms were in a better position to maintain their
own laboratories, where the novelties could be tested and developed for
industrial production, and through which one could keep abreast of new
developments abroad. But most important to the dominance of the older
firms in this branch, which expanded rapidly on the basis of new, supply-
push products, were the well-established and extensive distribution networks, often including wholly owned wholesale and retail outlets, with
which these older firms stood ready when the new products were introduced in Sweden. They found it easy to promote the sale of the new
products through the old distribution channels of the oil enamel paints.
New firms, on the other hand, faced the laborious and risky task of
building their own sales organizations in competition with the established
ones of older firms. This task was even more difficult because most wholesalers either had their own manufacturing plants or had arrangements
with the older producers. Thus the situation within the paints and varnishes industry provides a good illustration of how "organic" produc-
tion/distribution relationships may give the formation and evolution of
firms in an industry a character that diverges from what otherwise would
be expected. Under these circumstances, it is not so difficult to explain
why even though new firms emerged they were almost without exception
unable to elbow their way up and capture any considerable part of the
growing market. It is significant that the single progressive firm accounted
for a considerable proportion of the entry share. It is no coincidence
that the other light chemicals industries show a larger entry share than
this industry even though their development was not of the supply-push
type to the same extent. The industry producing oils, soft soap, soap,
perfumes, and cosmetics also developed in rather close connection with
commerce. But it was not characterized by the same organic ties with
wholesalers as in the paints and varnishes branch (cf. below).

The industry's old ties with commerce largely explain its big city
character at the end of World War I. Also many of the new firms
were started by merchants (or at least sales executives, and so forth)
or emerged in direct conjunction with a commercial firm. Another factor
behind the big city locational pattern should also be noted—namely,
that the industry operated with expensive raw materials and relatively
little labor. The high and rising urban wages, therefore, did not offer
the same incentive for firms to locate outside the major urban areas as
in other, relatively more labor-intensive industries.

Little need be said about firm mortality. The rather high exit share
in 1939 ($\gamma_{23} = 25$) was mainly due to mergers. The one that caused

the most attention was the merger of AB Wilhelm Becker and Ferniss AB during the 1920's, which brought a very hard struggle between these two competitors to an end. Apart from the mergers, some firms which had manufactured substitute products during World War I failed in the early 1920's. The number of disappearances after the mid-1920's was remarkably small. There were hardly any failures that can be attributed to the displacement of spirit and oil enamel paints by the new products. In almost all instances where old products were discontinued or the output of them reduced, new products were simultaneously added to the firm's production program.

Oils, Soft Soap, Soap, Perfumes, and Cosmetics

By the end of World War I, handicraft methods had by and large disappeared in the production of *oils, soft soap, soap, and soap flakes*. Advances in mechanization had made it advantageous to operate on a considerably larger scale than previously and had already caused many of the old soapworks to close down. At the same time, however, the advent of caustic soda as a raw material had offered greater opportunities for smaller industrial firms from the point of view of production techniques, since they no longer needed to produce their own lye. Also, transport costs for soft soap, with its low ratio of value to weight, still was a disadvantage of operations on a very large scale.[92] While the firm structure of the branch had thus shifted toward larger production units, this had by no means led to complete dominance by big businesses. In 1919, 30 percent of the firms accounted for three fourths of the work force. At this time, the concentration of the industry in the cities was also pronounced—the main reason being that this branch, like the paints and varnishes branch, to a large degree had its origin in urban commerce.

The incidence of failures among the firms in existence in 1918 was very high, especially during the 1920's ($\gamma_{23} = 37$). A very large number of smaller businesses disappeared. To a considerable extent, it was a question of firms that had emerged in the dislocated economy of World War I. Many of them had manufactured substitute products and, in addition, lost their working capital on inventories of such goods. There were few if any disappearances due to the displacement of old product lines by completely new products. When an old product suffered too much in competition with a new one, it was easy to try something else, if the finances of the firm permitted. In this industry, process innovations, particularly within the older, big firms, were a more important cause of failures at this time, as had also been the case previously. Many plants were also closed down in connection with mergers. The mergers led

---

[92] Cf. Hj. Heimbürger, "Några drag ur tvättmedelsindustriens utveckling och samma industris ställning i vårt land, *Teknisk Tidskrift* (1925), K 25.

to increased specialization and concentration and undoubtedly to reduced competition as well. For much the same reasons as in the chocolate and candy industry, production could easily be discontinued. Plants were simple and were often operated in conjunction with a commercial business that was the backbone of the firm. Mortality was high, also, among the new firms that emerged in the interwar period. In order to understand the reasons for this, one must first study the nature of entry and the market conditions.

Despite the general prevalence of unused capacity among producers of soft soap, soap, and soap flakes during the 1920's, the rate of entry was rather high ($\alpha_{23} = 25$, cosmetics included).[93] A few new firms even entered the soft soap branch, which gradually became dominated by the quota cartel organized by the larger firms. The initial investment needed to start a firm was small, both in the soap-products branch and in the younger *cosmetics branch*. The latter experienced a high rate of entry, mostly because it dealt in new products for which demand grew more rapidly than the output of the pioneering firms. Except in the soft soap branch, it was in the nature of this industry that competition concerned qualities and product types more than prices. Firms were often tempted to gamble on some more or less apocryphal "new" product, especially since the market with its very numerous retail outlets could be counted on to grow almost continuously. It is precisely in branches where this type of competition obtains that unutilized capacity of existing firms will not discourage entry.

Having failed in attempts to acquire certain Swedish firms, the British Sunlight trust in 1925 began operations on a large scale in Nyköping. The plant had been purchased from a ball bearing firm which had never begun production. The entry of the Sunlight group was partly motivated by the desire to circumvent import duties and meant increased competition on the Swedish market.

In general, the new firms remained stationary (Appendix 8 in Swedish edition). Except for the Sunlight products, and a few others, the soap and cosmetics products of new firms could not be very extensively advertised. Consequently, only a few were able to establish a nationwide market, and still fewer, an international market. New firms generally began with equipment which was technically inferior to that of older firms, and not many managed to catch up later. Given the existing industry structure, entry was easy, especially since the productive apparatus was inexpensive. But expansion was difficult, not only because large-scale production in itself required relatively much more capital, but also be-

---

[93] In part, however, the excess capacity of this industry was a transitory phenomenon in that it was a consequence of the ongoing struggle between old and new methods to a greater extent than, for example, in the joinery industries or the leather-shoe industry.

cause distribution on the corresponding scale necessarily involved expensive and sustained advertising, requiring much capital.[94]

For the branch as a whole, the development was clearly of the demand-pull type. The supply-push contributed by specific, advertised brand-name products did not in general benefit other, similar products. The lively, and also quantitatively important, entry which, together with numerous progressive firms, was otherwise typical of branches developing on the basis of new, supply-push products, was therefore lacking. It is also significant that one of the new firms, Sunlight, alone accounted for more than one fourth of the medium-sized 1939 entry share. With respect to soft soap, there is also the additional factor that the new producers found it difficult to expand outside the cartel of the larger enterprises. Most of the new firms had to be satisfied with a local market in the shadow of the cartel.[95] Since so many of the larger and older firms grew rapidly, the industry structure gradually became more concentrated. In 1939, just 16 percent of the firms accounted for 75 percent of the industry work force.

This discussion of entry also explains the high mortality of new firms. If attempts to capture a large market failed, the operation would often turn out to be not very profitable in the long run, and it was then natural to discontinue. The great majority of new firms also emerged in the largest cities. They were most often started by merchants and/or grew in conjunction with some commercial enterprise (Appendices 10 and 14), as had typically been the case before World War I. The most common association was with an import firm, a type of origin explained mainly by the fact that most of the raw materials for all three branches were still imported.

Due to its historical background, the light chemicals industry is unique in that, in contrast to most other industries, it did not exhibit any locational shift toward smaller urban and rural communities. As in most branches where entry was inexpensive but workers did not play much of a role as entrepreneurs, firms generally showed little tendency to survive stubbornly under adverse market conditions.

---

[94] The increasing concentration on brand-name products and the intensified advertizing associated herewith has gradually made it more and more difficult for the smallest firms that cannot afford to advertise to manage—the nationally advertized and therefore more demanded products have simply crowded their products off the shelves of retailers. Toward the end of the 1940's in contrast to earlier periods. these firms seem to have had their best customers among the barber shops. Developments in the 1940's followed trends already clearly established in the two earlier decades.

[95] Cf. *SOU* (1940, No. 35), p. 74.

13 Analysis of Industries with Little Entry

All of the industries analyzed in Chapter 12 had a high rate of entry. In most cases, new entry accounted for a considerable proportion of the growth in work force and in output. The classification was schematic, however, in that within these industries there were some branches where entry was of little significance. Chapter 13 is based on a similarly schematic classification since some branches have shown lively and quantitatively significant entry. Furthermore, it should be noted that there was even considerable entry within some of the industries to be analyzed in this chapter (i.e., if "new firm" is strictly defined, in accord with our main rule as "new plant-location"). The reason for including such industries here is that in contrast to those dealt with in Chapter 12, it was usually not a question of the formation of new firms in the financial sense. Many of the new firms in the lumber mill industry, for example, represented a peculiar type of "firm" which cannot be compared with others. In the pulp industry, on the other hand, while there were many new plants, these were, with few exceptions, started by older firms.

Iron and Steel Mills

Several steel mills were started just before or during World War I in order to utilize new electrical processes or to meet the growing demand for commercial iron. Thus several mills for the production of electric steel and steel alloys were constructed, particularly in Trollhättan. A newly formed company built Halmstads Järnverk for the production of commercial iron. Two new mills introduced innovations— the sponge iron mill in Höganäs, built by Höganäs-Billesholms AB, and the coke-burning pig iron mill constructed during the war by Oxelösunds Järnverks AB, a company formed for this purpose.

During the interwar period, in contrast, no new mills were built. The new sponge-iron hearth at the old Söderfors Bruks AB should be mentioned, however, since it was constructed for a new production process and turned out to be an innovation of great significance. After World War I, no primary product innovations occurred which were of great importance relative to the entire stock of old products. Those new products that did emerge could be produced most advantageously in, or in direct conjunction with, the old plants. This was to an even greater degree the case with the secondary product innovations. The development of the steel industry was above all influenced by process innovations. These, however, were seldom entirely novel. The new processes seldom differed in principle from the old to such an extent that the advantages of tying them to existing plants did not become decisive. Nor did the industry enjoy significant demand-pull during the 1920's. In the 1930's, demand-pull was no stronger than could as a rule be met by existing firms, even without any expansion of capacity.

But the old firms would certainly have dominated the industry's development completely whatever the conditions. Even if many primary product innovations had emerged, the possibilities of entering into competition were almost nonexistent for a newly established firm. The construction of a new steel mill was an extremely costly venture, and it was the more risky because the basic capital investments of the old firms had to such a large extent been made in a period when costs were incomparably lower than in the interwar period. In this respect, the only exceptions were a few mills which were either newly established or were very much expanded during World War I, for example, Gimo-Österby Bruks AB and Halmstads Järnverk AB. Typically, these remained at a serious disadvantage in competition with other firms over a long period. Once the financial reconstructions following World War I had been carried out, most other steel mills were characterized by the low book values at which not only plants and equipment but also their forest and land properties were carried. This proved a favorable point of departure for undertaking the process innovations which, beginning in the late 1920's and continuing through the 1930's, played a prominent role in extricating the industry from its crisis. Under these conditions, the building of new steel mills was hardly to be contemplated. Furthermore, entry would have required not only a costly steel mill but also a sales organization in markets where the older firms were already well-established.

In the 1920's, Sandvikens Jernverks AB, which had been the innovator with respect to marketing organization, had the most modern cold-rolling mills among the producers of quality steel. The plants of Uddeholms AB were also among the most modern. The latter firm, together with

Avesta Jernverks AB, had made innovations in the field of stainless and acidproof steel which were pioneering contributions from an international standpoint. Other firms with contributions of the same caliber were the S.K.F.-owned Hofors Bruk and Fagersta Bruks AB—the former was a pioneer with new sintering processes and high-grade roller bearing steels, the latter particularly with new carbides.

It is no coincidence that these firms were so much in the vanguard. Having pursued a cautious policy during the inflationary war boom, they were either less burdened with debt and hence more liquid than most others or else better able to obtain the support of strong financial interests. Only when they had demonstrated the advantages of the new methods, and other firms began to experience demand-pull and an easier money market, was their example more generally followed.

Domnarfvets Järnverk, which like Söderfors belonged to Stora Kopparbergs Bergslags AB, led the way in the modernization efforts and demonstrated the feasibility of operating at full capacity even in the face of extremely low prices. These policies, which to an unusual extent were the contribution of a single individual, were generally adopted by other commercial iron producers in the 1930's.

All of the large innovating firms belonged to the group showing the earliest and most rapid growth during the interwar period. In this group one also finds those smaller firms in which management paid special attention to heavy manufacturing divisions and sales organizations. On the other hand, those firms which only operated blast furnaces, and perhaps some small rolling mill or manufacturing division, were as a rule stationary. This was also the case, of course, with firms which partly, or completely, still relied on the Lancashire process. Firms that were unable to devote much capital and effort to their sales organizations also fell behind as a rule. It was, however, the dissemination of innovations that dominated the industry's development during the 1930's. As in so many other industries, the difference between firms in efficiency and profitability was by 1939 considerably smaller than in 1929.

Specialization, concentration of production, and expansion of manufacturing were among the major motives in several financial reconstructions. The so-called "Brukskoncern" is of primary interest in this context. The formation of this group of companies was supervised by AB Svenska Handelsbanken, which had been forced to take over a number of weak firms, among them the previously mentioned Gimo-Österby Bruks AB. Prior to this time, plans for a larger merger of a still greater number of producers of both commercial iron and quality steels had been drawn up under government supervision. This giant merger, however, was to remain on paper only.[1] The Bruks group was originally intended to comprise a subset of the firms that were to be merged according to the

---

[1] Cf. Affärsvärlden (1925), pp. 437 ff.

government plan. When the Handelsbank drew up the initial plans for the Bruks group, the intention was to concentrate all production at Fagersta. This would have involved closing down, among others, the big mill in Kloster. The Kloster firm's finances had been seriously weakened following its involvement in the liquidation of a number of strategic malinvestments and unsound ventures in the roller bearing industry. Although such radical concentration then seemed the most rational alternative, this part of the plan was never put into effect simply because the investments sunk in Kloster and some other mills were too large. Subsequent developments in the 1930's and 1940's were also to demonstrate that even apart from these sunk costs, the projected concentration would hardly have been to advantage. The labor shortage and the housing problem had become steadily more serious, and the economic advantages of such large-scale operations were apparently considerably smaller than had at one time been assumed in the plan.

The Hellefors group, also engaged in the pulp industry, is another interesting and typical illustration. This group, with Hellefors Bruks AB as the core company, had to struggle far into the 1930's with the consequences of the both acute and chronic difficulties that the industry had encountered during the 1920's. The problems were especially serious for the Hellefors enterprises because of a processing capacity that was inadequate in relation to the group's forest and land holdings, among other things. The group gradually moved toward increased specialization and expansion of its manufacturing activities—a policy exemplified by its special plant for cold-rolled, high-quality steel products in Bångbro. Large investments, partly financed by the Swedish government, were made in more efficient plant and equipment. These policies proved to be the way to lasting success in this case also.

In summary, the generalization seems warranted that during the 1930's the Swedish steel industry saw the completion of an unusual number of technoeconomic development blocks. In principle, this development resembled the events of the 1880's and 1890's. Troublesome structural tensions characterized the 1920's, as they had the 1870's. By the late 1920's, furthermore, a few firms were far ahead of the others, while by the end of the next decade, most firms had caught up with the pioneering enterprises. Finally, it should be pointed out that both of the last-mentioned groups of companies are good examples of the generalization made earlier, namely, that the interwar renaissance of the Swedish steel industry—the third thoroughgoing transformation of this industry in the course of a hundred years—basically presupposed an initial situation in which plants and equipment were carried at low book values. It may be, however, that this also retarded to some extent the adoption of some completely new technologies, such as the sponge-iron processes innovated by Höganäs-Billesholms AB and the Söderfors mill of Stora Kopparbergs

Bergslags AB. These processes could, of course, not be utilized on the basis of existing equipment.

In studying interwar firm disappearances ($\gamma_{23} = 15$), one predictably encounters the majority of the steel mills initially mentioned as having been built during World War I. Thus, most of the electro-steel and steel-alloy mills were clearly revealed as malinvestments. This was not only because they had been constructed during a period of high prices, but also because of technical failures. These firms expected the new processes to replace older ones and perhaps even to lead to the renovation of the entire Swedish steel industry. This optimism was replaced with a pessimism so complete that the firms in question were in most cases not even reconstructed but simply discontinued.

The other new firms, as well as those older firms that had expanded particularly rapidly, were, by and large, based on methods of proven worth. These firms underwent financial reconstruction, even though the difficulties were considerable and large losses were involved. In some instances, these cases should have been recorded as "disappearances" in accord with our main definition, but they fell under the exceptions to this rule discussed in Chapter 10. Through the intervention of the banks, which were their creditors, these firms continued to operate, at least at first, along largely unchanged lines, even if on a reduced scale.

Negative transformation effects, however, form the dominant pattern in the mortality picture. If the relevant firms were generally rather small, their number was that much greater. First and foremost there were some 30 blast furnaces, with or without related dressing and sintering plants, which were unable to survive in competition with the more modern furnaces. In the depression of the 1930's, the last remainders of this clearly obsolete type of enterprise disappeared. This was true of the Lancashire works as well. When the last few of the latter disappeared, exactly 100 years had passed since they had saved the Swedish iron industry in its first great crisis. Most of the 10 or so Lancashire furnaces remaining at the end of the interwar period were part of modern blooming mills. In these mills they served certain very special functions but were quantitatively of little importance.[2]

Disappearances in this category were only in exceptional cases asso-

---

[2] In certain firms the Lancashire process had played a very large role as late as the end of World War I. The problems which firms using this method had to face in competing with the steadily more efficient new blooming processes and the need for them to engage in further manufacturing of their product in order to survive under these conditions emerge especially clearly from the interwar history of Boxholms AB. The history of this company, incidentally, provides good illustrations of the negative development component also in other areas, e.g., the struggle between coke and charcoal in the production of pig iron, or between wire nails and cut nails. Cf. E. Wettergren, *Boxholms AB 1872–1947* (Uppsala, 1947).

ciated with the financial failure of the firm. It was, in other words, mainly plants belonging to larger units that were closed down. When furnaces shut down, there was often a corresponding increase in the capacity of other, more modern furnaces. There were, however, still some 10 cases or so in which the discontinuation of plant also meant the definitive disappearance of the firm.

The delaying retreat which the Lancashire works fought over a long period before finally succumbing did not in general affect the competitive situation of other steel mills to any significant extent. They were not able to engage in any "dumping" based on consumption of their old real capital. This, however, was to some extent possible in the case of the old-fashioned blast furnaces. Their product was basically of the same type as that produced by the modern furnaces. In this respect, their situation vis-à-vis the blooming mills differed from that of the Lancashire works. That the "death struggle" of these older, obsolete furnaces could result in some dumping was undoubtedly due to the fact that many of the modern blast furnaces had been constructed at high cost during World War I. After the early 1930's, the market was no longer affected by this form of competitive dumping. The last furnaces of the old type had by then been blown for the last time, and most of them had been torn down. The steel industry at that point had achieved a highly stable firm structure.

The Cement Industry

By the end of World War I, the cement industry consisted of few production units. Entry ($\alpha_{23} = 12$) added three new plants: the cement factory built in 1924 by AB Gullhögens Bruk in Skövde; a small factory built in 1931 by K.F. at Lanna, in the county of Örebro; and the big plant in Köping that the largest firm, Skånska Cement AB, began to construct in 1939. Skånska Cement held a dominant position in the Swedish market. When the K.F. plant proved to be unprofitable and therefore was rented to Cementa (a marketing corporation organized by Skånska Cement), and when two other firms were also merged with Cementa (1925 and 1932), AB Gullhögens Bruk was the only competitor remaining. This predominant position had been built up over several decades. The cement industry, together with Skånska Cementgjuteriet, a large construction company founded by Skånska Cement,[3] formed a development block which after 1925 could not be dislodged by any new entrant. Construction costs for a new cement factory were very high, and in addition, the old firm underwent an exceptionally rapid, and effective, modernization process during the interwar period. Its efficiency is indi-

---

[3] Cf. Chap. 5, p. 65.

cated by the fact that K.F., which attempted entry, could not compete in the cement industry.[4] Thus the process innovations carried out by existing firms blocked the path for more lively entry.[5]

The modernization efforts involved, among other things, the concentration of operations through the closing down of a number of factories along with strong expansion of others into very large plants. Thus, in the interwar period, the factory in Maltesholm was purchased and closed down in 1928, and a plant in Klagshamn, rented by Cementa, was closed down in 1939. Also, preparations were made to discontinue operations at the factories in Visby, Ivö, and Rute; the latter factory had previously been converted to the manufacture of lightweight concrete. These three were closed in 1940–41. (γ_{23} was 26. If the plants discontinued in the very beginning of the forties are included, the result is $\gamma_{23} = 50$.)

Porcelain and Ceramics Industry

At the outset of the interwar period, the porcelain industry proper consisted of five firms. With respect to household china, in contrast to electrical and sanitary porcelain, the firms' output capacity was, by and large, sufficient to meet the needs of the Swedish market. But they were not well equipped to hold their own against the strong competition from imports of household china, and their chances of competing with imported electrical and sanitary porcelain hinged entirely on the raising of large sums of capital for thoroughgoing modernization, technological renovation, and capacity expansion. Primarily on account of the high costs of kilns, considerable capital was required in order to start a new, or modernize an old, porcelain factory. The history of the older factories was one of almost continuous financial problems and did not give cause for much optimism with regard to the profitability of porcelain production, even in the longer run. It is therefore not surprising that there was only a single case of entry into this branch, or that this firm—Hackefors Porslin AB—began its operation with decorating imported, finished household china. It may also be noted that AB Karlskrona Porslinsfabrik, built as late as 1918, in the beginning also operated to some extent along the lines later followed by Hackefors. Nor is it surprising that the interwar growth in capacity for the production of other types of porcelain was due to financially strong interests in the older firms injecting large sums of fresh capital and that this growth, therefore, came from the expansion of the old firms.

The evolution of firms is therefore more interesting than the formation of new firms. The renovation which especially the electric and sanitary

---

[4] Cf. Swedish Cooperative Union (KF), *Annual Report* (1933), p. 70.
[5] The relatively high (α_{23})-value should also be seen in the context of the labor-saving effects of these process innovations.

porcelain branch underwent took place primarily within the older firms—almost all of them quite ancient firms. The process began in the latter half of the 1920's but achieved full momentum only in the 1930's and 1940's. The electrical porcelain was introduced immediately after World War I by AB Iföverken, a company belonging to the Skånska Cement AB group. This firm expanded its capacity considerably in the 1930's and also took up the production of floor tiles (1930) and sanitary porcelain (1936) in the same period. AB Rörstrands Porslinsfabriker modernized its operations in connection with the closing down of its plant in Stockholm in 1926 and with the concentration of production to its Göteborg factory. Skånska Cement-Iföverken purchased Lidköpings Porslinsfabriks AB, which in turn bought Rörstrands. It subsequently closed down the Rörstrand plant in Göteborg in 1940 and built a new factory at its old plant in Lidköping.

AB Gustavsbergs Fabriks Intressenter pioneered with the electric kilns as early as in the 1920's, but in other respects it was not in a good position. For one thing, its financial weakness prevented innovations. After K.F. had bought the company in 1937, production, especially of sanitary porcelain, was increased in connection with important process innovations. The plant also began to produce electrical porcelain at this time. Finally, Upsala-Ekeby AB formed a concern by buying AB Gefle Porslinsfabrik in the late 1930's and AB Karlskrona Porslinsfabrik in the 1940's. At the same time, the company pursued intensive modernization programs. Its previously important production of stove tiles was more and more replaced by wall tiles, and so forth. To some extent this involved product innovations of at least a secondary nature. In contrast to the others, this firm also produced considerable quantities of earthenware.

While this renovation within older firms—which became still more pronounced in the 1940's—created certain advantages over foreign competitors, and at the same time discouraged entry, it did not cause any disappearances. All of the factories in existence at the end of World War I were involved in this renovation. None fell seriously behind. The closing of Rörstrand Company's Stockholm plant, and subsequently of its plant in Göteborg, has already been touched on as an exceptional event due to a planned policy of concentration of operations. The closing of the Stockholm factory accounts completely for the exit share of 1919 firms ($\gamma_{23} = 33$).

Apart from the porcelain industry proper, the *stove-tile branch* presents a ceramic industry in which disappearances completely dominated ($\gamma_{23} = 71$). The category "other ceramic industry" covers the production of flower pots, sundry earthenware, faience, ornamental ceramic goods, and so forth. Some small new producers of ornamental ceramics emerged, but they were quantitatively of little significance

(α_{23} = 10). The mortality rate in this category was rather normal and unremarkable (γ^{23} = 21). Production could be managed on a small scale.

Ceramic stove tile, which was frequently produced with methods bordering on handicraft, was a product that started to disappear with the advent of central heating. At the beginning of the interwar period, this branch already had a record of some 15 years of firm mortality. Practically all the remaining producers disappeared during the interwar period, although a few turned to the production of other ceramic products or some related activity. Disappearances must certainly have been far more numerous than can be judged from the *IS* data, since many of the firms in existence by the end of World War I were too small to be registered. All of the old producers of ceramic stove tiles were stationary or regressive until their disappearance. Many of them operated only intermittently. Tenacious resistance was, in general, out of the question. Either a firm had some behind-the-times customers or it lacked a market entirely. In the latter case, there was no point in reducing prices, or in trying in some other way to fight a delaying struggle in the manner characteristic of many other industries in which older firms were dislodged by process innovations (e.g., in the tanning industry), or in which the outcome of the struggle between new and old products was not from the very outset such a foregone conclusion as in the stove-tile branch (e.g., in the joinery industry). Nor was there any possibility in such a rapidly shrinking, obsolete industry to form a cartel which would be able to keep the firms alive.

The Glassworks

The *plate glass industry* cannot be counted among the industries with lively entry, even though it had an α_{23} of 60. Only three new plants were added, and one of these was started by an old firm in another branch of the industry. By the end of World War I, there were 10 plate glass works operating on handicraft methods. The last glasswork operating on handicraft lines was built in 1920. Förenade Fönsterglasbrukens AB, an association established in 1917–18 in an effort to concentrate production and curtail competition caused the closing down of several works. This cartel failed, however, during the first postwar crisis, both because of the general deflation and because of forceful foreign competition. It was reconstructed under the name of Fönsterglasbrukens AB. In this connection, plate glass production was discontinued at four more works, of which two some years later converted to the production of household glass. Attempts to keep small firms operating through production quotas were doomed to failure because of the foreign competition.

The mechanized plate glass process was a revolutionary innovation.

It was introduced in Sweden by Glafva Glasbruk and by Oxelösunds Järnverks AB, which constructed an entirely new machine glass plant, partly in order to find a use for the blast-furnace glass from its pig iron mill. The mechanized process immediately caused the disappearance of four of the older plate glass works. To some extent, these four were already engaged in an uneven struggle with foreign machine glass firms. One firm, Ramnåsa, was able to hold on for a few years mainly because of its large forests and peat bogs. Another, AB Emmaboda Glasverk, converted to mechanized production in the early 1930's. Glafva Glasbruk, one of the innovators, was discontinued in 1939. Due to a bad location, as well as for other reasons, it could not compete. Thus by the end of the interwar period, there were only two plate glass works, both new. During the 1940's, Årnäs Bruk, a glass bottle works, also took up mechanized plate glass production. The process, with its striking entry and exit shares, is a perfect example of an industry development based on innovations and a resulting dramatic mortality among firms.

The mechanization of a number of *glass container works* ($\alpha_{23} = 0$; $\gamma_{23} = 37$), which had already begun before and during World War I, had roughly the same consequences as the mechanization of plate glass production.[6] But the struggle between the positive and negative development components dragged on for a longer time. The impact of the innovations was somewhat less in this area, particularly since certain special products could still be made by hand.

Two rather large works operating with handicraft methods (namely, Sunds Glasbruks AB and AB Arboga Glasbruk) were bought and closed down by AB Surte-Liljedahl in 1928. Several other firms were either discontinued or were converted to the production of household glass when they were unable to compete with the increasingly mechanized works. The next to last handicraft producer among the glassworks concentrating on glass containers was AB Österviks Glasbruk. This mill was closed down entirely in 1935. The last one, Borensbergs Glasbruk, was still in operation by 1949. On the other hand, a cartel agreement undoubtedly made it possible to continue operations at several other firms which also produced household glass.

There was no entry worth mentioning in the *glass container branch*. The necessity of working with expensive machinery meant that great amounts of capital were required, and since several older glassworks had achieved a considerable lead in technical and economic development, the inducement to start new firms was small. Nor were there any supply-push products to stimulate entry. There is only one new firm to record,

---

[6] Only those firms for which large-size glass containers were the main product line have been classed under "container glassworks." A very large part of the total output of container glass was contributed by the "household glass" works, i.e., primarily small bottles, etc., for various technical purposes.

namely, a small plant making glass vats and small beer jugs, which was started in 1930 in Arboga by workers from the large glassworks which closed. But some producers of household glass, for example, Reijmyre, converted partly or completely to glass container production on a rather large scale. Some of these firms, however, left this branch after a short period.

The interwar history of the *household glass branch*[7] ($\alpha_{23} = 12$; $\gamma_{23} = 4$) is less dramatic than that of the plate glass and glass container branches, mostly because no revolutionary innovations occurred. It still has several aspects of interest, however. There were undoubtedly many firms whose financial restructuring bordered on failure, and rates of return were as a rule unsatisfactory. Limited process innovations, resulting from weak liquidity and little interest in the branch on the part of outside financial interests, were not the cause of many outright failures, although competition was both free and sharp during the whole period. Färe was the only major glassworks to disappear once and for all. This disappearance, however, was largely due to the fact that a strongly progressive engineering firm, AB Färe Armaturfabrik, needed the premises and therefore bought the glassworks and discontinued its operation. Otherwise, the tenacity with which a number of unprofitable firms in the household glass branch survived was considerable. There were numerous cases in which production was stopped temporarily, but, as a rule, it was resumed after an interval of time. The firms in question were located exclusively in minor towns. They operated with great technical skill—but not in a very businesslike fashion. Their capital equipment was old, and the handicraft techniques in use required little costly reinvestment.

It was most characteristic of this branch, however, that several new firms emerged even though the existing firms had unutilized capacity. Only a few of these entrants were new to the glass industry, but as already noted, several plate glass and glass container works converted to the production of household glass. The most noteworthy examples are Gullaskrufs Glasbruks AB, which discontinued its plate glass production in 1921 but started producing household glass in 1926, and AB Flygsfors Glasbruk, for which the corresponding dates were 1920 and 1930. This kind of conversion, which had already been common prior to World War I, was due to the even harder competition in the plate glass and glass container branches. It was not very costly to undertake, especially since the process innovations of older firms were so insignificant. To convert to mechanized production, on the other hand, was a much more expensive undertaking, and it was not very tempting once

---

[7] Apart from firms concentrating on "household glass" in the strict sense, producers of smaller sizes of technical container glass and similar items have also been included in this category.

the pioneers had gone ahead and, together, achieved a capacity more than sufficient for the country's needs. In this situation producers who were unable or unwilling to mechanize saw no alternatives other than to shut down altogether or to convert to household glass. The household glass branch typically showed a low degree of concentration of production.

The Brickyards

The brick industry had neither lively entry nor high firm mortality. Conditions in this industry were, however, quite out of the ordinary, resembling to some extent those in the woodworking industries. The number of bankruptcies and changes in ownership was undoubtedly large, but operations were almost always continued without interruption, in the same manner and with the same product line as before. Only a few of these bankruptcies and changes of ownership have therefore been recorded as exit-cum-entry in the present work. In addition, many of the changes in ownership were caused by underlying financial situations that should really be equated with bankruptcies, even when this did not take place formally.

Thus the entry recorded here refers almost exclusively to new plants ($\alpha_{23} = 6$). Of some 30 new firms which, according to this definition, appeared in the interwar period, only a handful were of any major significance, and several of these were started as subsidiaries. The remaining entrants were very small and were, as was also the case with four fifths of the "continuing" firms, stationary or regressive. This category was probably more numerous than apparent in *IS*—and thus in the present work. In general, these firms were started to meet a local demand for bricks, especially for chimneys. They were, therefore, particularly numerous in Norrland. A further noteworthy feature of the formation of new firms in the brick industry is that only very seldom was a new firm started by workers in an older brickyard. Neither did the workers continue operations in connection with all the bankruptcies and ownership changes, other than in a few exceptional instances. The primary reason for this lies in the seasonal nature of employment in the brickyards. To a substantial extent, the industry gave employment to vagrants who had neither the interest nor the ability to manage operations.

Porous, light brick was a very important innovation in the late twenties. This product was not introduced by a new firm but by the old Sala Tegelbruks AB. It met rather strong resistance from other brickyards who saw it as a mortal threat to the brick industry (cf., the concrete products and lightweight concrete industry), and who initially tried to have the municipal construction codes forbid the use of the new products. Yards which due to weak liquidity and difficulties in borrowing money saw few possibilities of acquiring new machinery felt especially threatened. But the resistance was of short duration. By 1930, practically all the brickyards in northern and mid-Sweden had converted to the new brick types. In southern Sweden, such conversion was not considered at the time, since the milder climate permitted the production of smaller-size bricks without first making the mix porous.

The other great process innovation of the period was forced drying and year-long operation. This was also introduced by Sala Tegelbruk. This mode of operation, however, became the general rule only during the 1940's. The innovations in the production of roof tiles did not originate with a new firm either. Until well into the 1920's, roof tiles did not really represent a distinct branch from the wall brick and facing brick branches. In this case, the brickyards in Heby were the ones to direct developments into new channels by specializing in the mass production of roof tiles. Production of roof tile at most other yards was gradually discontinued. While at the beginning of the interwar period the great majority of brickyards produced roof tiles, the output of this product was rather strongly concentrated by the end of the period. The considerable demand-pull which made itself felt during this time did, however, lead to the establishment of a couple of new yards, which specialized from the start.

Firm disappearances in the form of definitive cessation of operations were not very common during the interwar period ($\gamma_{23} = 10$). As indicated above, however, reconstruction following bankruptcies and ownership changes were frequent, but these have not been recorded as "disappearances," in contrast to the procedure followed with regard to most other industries. Most of the discontinuations occurred among the very small brickyards. These had been operating primarily with small open-air kilns, and they represented the last remainder of a type of enterprise which had previously been very common but was now largely obsolete. Of the brickyards of this old type which remained by the end of World War I, the majority disappeared during the 1920's. Apart from these disappearances, there were also a number of instances of larger brickworks, operating with annular kilns, which were closed down forever. These cases were of less importance in the total picture. For the most part, such disappearances were due to the exhaustion of usable clay deposits. The incidence of firm disappearance of this type was also highest during the 1920's. It was less common in the 1930's, mainly because of improvements in transportation technology. As long as the brickyards operated only with horses, they were dependent on having clay deposits in the immediate vicinity. The use of trucks and motor-powered locomotives severed this dependence.

The emergence of an effective cartel policy should be viewed in connection with the intensive price competition of the mid-1920's. Prices were obviously depressed to such an extent that variable costs were just barely covered. In addition, many brickyards were very dependent on wholesalers who financed production and inventory holdings, and who frequently were able to exploit their position to depress prices. The numerous bankruptcies mentioned above are ample evidence of the situation. The different brickyards were often played one against the other, and the owners, who usually did not operate in a very businesslike manner, had little knowledge of the prices accepted by their competitors. It is indicative of the weak market situation that while the older brickyards gradually made themselves independent of the wholesalers, this did not induce the latter to start their own yards, as in several analogous cases in other industries. The branch was far from attractive. In the late 1920's, cartels managed to achieve a certain stabilization of prices and limitation of sales to certain districts. This undoubtedly saved many brickyards from being closed down forever. Without the cartels, the majority of the yards, at least in mid-Sweden, would probably have disappeared. These firms were helped directly in that their operations could earn a tolerable return, and indirectly in that the profits made possible some modernization of plant. In the 1920's, very little progress had been made with the modernization, mainly because of the low rates of return, insufficient liquidity, and almost total lack of credit worthiness vis-à-vis the banks.

One precondition for the success of cartel pricing was the introduction of the porous, lightweight brick. Without this product innovation, it would surely have been impossible to improve the situation through collusive pricing, etc. The competitive pressure from the concrete products and lightweight concrete industry would have been simply overwhelming. It is significant that an earlier cartel arrangement had broken down in 1926. Thus it was new product development, together with renewed cooperation between the firms, which laid the foundation for the industry's development in the 1930's. The high level of construction activity that followed the labor-management conflict of 1933 obviously was a contributing factor also. But it is still clear that the changes made in the late 1920's were the decisive factors. The construction boom could very well have left the brickyards largely unaffected since the concrete products and lightweight concrete industry had gradually achieved a very strong position.

Although the firm structure of the industry was very unstable at the end of the 1920's, it remained largely unchanged through the 1930's due to innovations and cartelization. By the end of the decade, it was relatively stable. Variations in the efficiency or financial strength of different brickyards were not of such a magnitude that firms in any particular category were doomed to disappear. Nor were there many strongly progressive firms. By the late 1940's, however, the structure had again become unstable. A few of the older firms had by then introduced a number of technical novelties which were of far more significance than the innovations of the interwar period; simultaneously, the concrete products and lightweight concrete industry had grown stronger than ever. Thus, a revolution in the firm structure of the brick industry could be anticipated—or, in any case, a considerable change, through the dissemination of innovations and through the disappearance of numerous small brickyards.

The Forest Industries

The Lumber Mills. In the lumber milling industry the interwar period found a large number of new firms utilizing the so-called "circular saws." But these saws were usually mobile and very small,[8] and they were normally operated only during part of the year. Consequently, these "firms" did not give full-time employment to the entrepreneurs. Thus it has been impossible to study statistically the formation of firms in a manner that would give a satisfactory basis for comparison with other industries. Indeed, the concept of "formation of a firm," interpreted in the strict sense used in this work, is hardly applicable in this context.

One should note, however, that the total number of lumber mills, according to *IS*, increased from 1,410 in 1919 to 1,469 in 1935 and to 1,727 by 1939. Although this increase must in part be attributed to increasingly comprehensive statistical coverage, it undoubtedly reflects a lively "formation of firms" in the form of a growing number of small circular saws.[9] This interpretation seems particularly warranted since the industry also showed a considerable number of disappearances during the same period (see below). This conclusion seems unavoidable in view of the fact that only a modest proportion of the circular saws are reported in *IS*. Those reported are almost exclusively the stationary ones, but not even all these have been registered.[10]

Some of the new circular saws were stationary, but the mobile ones

---

[8] Cf. S. Grundström, "Cirkelsågningen i Norrbottens län," *Svensk Geografisk Årsbok* (1949). Grundström provides a fairly detailed description of "circular saw" activity in recent years and also discusses the relevant historical background.

[9] Cf. *Utredning med synpunkter på sågverksdriften i Norrland*, SOU (1947, No. 32); and E. Ruist and I. Svennilson, *Den norrländska skognäringens konjunkturkänslighet under mellankrigsperioden* (Stockholm, 1948), p. 18.

[10] We get an indication of this from a comparison of the 1931 census of firms with *IS* for the same year. Although the census cannot have included all sawmills and least of all every mobile saw, it reported a national total of well over 3,000 while the *IS* figure is 1,337. A special study covering only Noorland found

were far more common. Almost all of these enterprises remained small. In upper Norrland, firms of this type were a novelty in the interwar period, while they were an established phenomenon in the rest of the country. But they became increasingly common everywhere from the early 1920's on. In the southern parts of the country, their emergence was originally due mainly to the absence of floating ways. This made it advantageous from the standpoint of transport cost to move lumber that was already sawn.[11]

In Norrland, the emergence of the new sawmills was primarily connected with the spread of truck transportation. Usually, these firms were started by small farmers or their sons, by workers, merchants, truck owners, contractors, and so forth. The alternative modes of transport which had existed earlier had generally been too costly for the long distances in this part of the country. Typically, the new saws were mostly located far from the floating ways also.[12] Considerable advances in sawing techniques also played a significant role in the formation of "firms" in Norrland, particularly during the 1930's, following the pioneering contributions made in the 1920's. For example, it became possible to saw as straight as with frame saws, and the price obtainable on the lumber produced with circular saws improved relative to that on frame-saw products. Other factors of great importance were the rapid expansion of the road network and the great advances in the areas of motive power and transport technology, as exemplified by improved motors, truck trailers, and so forth. The new small saws could not as a rule utilize scrap lumber and sawdust as well as the stationary frame saws did. In spite of this, their costs were very low in many cases, at least in relation to those of the many obsolete frame saws. Their fixed costs were modest, and firms could often obtain labor more cheaply than the larger, and usually unionized, mills.[13] Many individuals who lacked the resources to build a frame saw were therefore induced to acquire circular saws.

The great increase in the number of circular saws was due also to demand-pull. Lively construction activity in various parts of Norrland in the interwar period led to strongly increasing local demands for lumber products. The stationary export mills on the coast with their frame-saw equipment were not always able to deliver these lumber products to the growing communities in the interior. The new circular saws stepped in to serve these markets, and at the same time they bought timber

---

an average for the two years 1938 and 1939 of no less than 1,389 sawmills *in excess* of the 321 reported in *IS* for 1938. In this case, a large number of mobile circular saws were included. Cf. *SOU* (1947, No. 32), pp. 120–21.

[11] *Betänkande angående nåvaruförsörjning, produktion och arbetarantal m. m. vid skogsindustrierna*, SOU (1935, No. 36), p. 123.

[12] Grundström, *op. cit.*

[13] *SOU* (1935, No. 36), p. 123.

which, at least in several cases, would otherwise have been purchased by the larger lumber mills. The mobile circular-saw mills benefited strongly from the increasing demand for lumber for various everyday purposes which followed the growth of Norrland communities. Thus their products were sold mainly on the domestic market. At intervals—with the exception of those located in the interior—there were also considerable exports from the circular-saw mills. In such instances, these new firms competed directly with the frame-saw mills. But, in general, the output of the circular saws did not compete seriously with that of the frame saws.[14] It is clear, on the other hand, that the new type of firms increased the competition that many of the old mills had to face in obtaining inputs. The new mills' needs were met in part by using stands of trees that either were of too low quality to meet the requirements of the larger lumber mills or so located that they could not be utilized by the larger mills at a reasonable price. Nevertheless these firms often purchased timber which the larger mills could well have used.

This type of competition from the new "firms" undoubtedly contributed to the disappearances which particularly characterized the latter half of the interwar period. It can, however, by no means be regarded as the most important factor. Other types of firm formation (e.g., new high-capacity frame saws) did not create sharper competition in either raw material markets or output markets. Firms of this type apparently were started in only a few exceptional cases. Important unexploited forest areas no longer existed, and for reasons to be elaborated later, a new lumber mill relying on purchases from farm forests could have little expectation of success. In addition, most of the old mills operated with plant and forest holdings that were carried at very low book values. These firms were not able to earn a normal return on net worth even when carrying their assets far below replacement costs. Thus, the prospects for new firms of the same type were far from bright, especially since the new firms could not enter as innovators. In this respect, the situation was similar to that in the iron and steel industry. At the beginning of the interwar period, both these industries had left behind them a relatively long successful period in which it had been possible to acquire new plants at relatively low costs and to write them off rapidly.

Strangely enough, we have as yet no general statistical study of lumber mill disappearances covering the major part of the country. The Report of the Rationalization Committee (*R.U.*) includes data on the number

---

[14] Some estimates of the exports of lumber by the circular saw firms in the early 1930's have been made by the Swedish Forestry Service (Domänstyrelsen). Thus this export was calculated as amounting to 13 percent of the total export of sawn lumber in 1934 as compared to 5 percent in 1933. Cf. *SOU* (1935, No. 36), pp. 122–23, and *Utredning rörande skogsnäringens ekonomiska läge, SOU* (1938, No. 53). Also Grundström, *op. cit.*

of discontinuations in the lumber mill industry in the 1922–36 period. Unfortunately, firms with less than 10 employees were not considered, and the report's definition of "discontinuation" does not altogether correspond to the definition of "disappearance" used in the present work. But the report does give a general impression of considerable mortality among lumber mills. Most of its 78 cases of discontinuation certainly represent disappearances in the sense used here. The data collected by the Committee would probably have been useful for a closer study of disappearances in this industry, But since the entire primary material, without any attempt at differentiation, was declared secret until 1957, it was, unfortunately, impossible to utilize it.[15] The printed report was, of course, not primarily historical in approach, and it contains only meager commentary and analysis.

In the Official Report (*SOU*, 1947, No. 32), one finds that about 40 lumber mills were closed down in the Sundsvall and Härnösand districts during the interwar period. This report also estimates a reduction by one-half in the aggregate capacity of Norrland lumber mills during the same period. Everything indicates that the new circular saws were not taken into account in this estimate. Even apart from this, it seems to exaggerate the decline in capacity.

Despite the emergence of many new circular saws, the interwar stagnation of the lumber mill industry was considerably more accentuated in Norrland than in the rest of Sweden. In order to obtain a reasonably accurate estimate of lumber mill disappearances, at least for Norrland, a rough calculation from the *IS* raw data was made.[16] Thus data were extracted on the number of workers and administrative staff at each individual lumber mill, in 1919, 1929, and 1939. The approximate number of definitive disappearances was then estimated with the help both of notations found in the primary material and of the Swedish Commercial Directory (*HK*). The results of this investigation cannot, however, be compared with the results of our studies of disappearances in other industries, which were more systematically conducted and, in part, followed different principles. The results for the lumber mill industry have, therefore, not been reported in the Appendices but only in the survey given in Table 16. The table shows that, when the new circular saws are disregarded, the closing down of lumber mills reduced employment in the industry by approximately one third.

Since the extent of lumber mill disappearances has not been the subject of an overall statistical survey covering the entire country, we do not

---

[15] Cf. Chap. 6, p. 117, n. 19.

[16] Concerning the decline in employment in the lumber mills of the different Norrland counties, cf. esp. *Utredning angående Norrlands näringsliv, förberedande undersökning verkställd av 1940 års Norrlandsutredning*, SOU (1943, No. 39), p. 120.

TABLE 16
Mortality of Lumber Mills in Norrland

Firms in Existence in 1919	Number of Firms	Number of Workers (in 1919)
Total number..............................	381	20,488
Known to have disappeared before 1940......	136	6,064
Probably disappeared before 1940............	50	1,497
Possibly disappeared before 1940.............	19	265

γ_{11} = max. 38, min. 30.

have any general work analyzing the cause of these disappearances in detail and putting them in a larger perspective. Passing references to the causes are, however, to be found in many different sources, particularly in a number of official reports.[17]

The immediate cause of the high mortality of lumber mills in the interwar period, and especially in 1931–33, as well as of a number of more or less lengthy interruptions of operations, was a decline in earnings combined with weakened liquidity. Developments both in the lumber market and on the cost side brought this about. Since the former have already been discussed in Chapter 9, in which we concluded that strong negative development effects during the interwar period resulted in declining prices of lumber products and in output stagnation, we will confine the discussion here to developments on the cost side.

Raw material costs constitute a very large proportion of total costs in the lumber mill industry. Consequently, the almost continuous rise in timber prices that took place between the wars created a serious problem. The primary reason for the price rise was the increasing scarcity of timber—the consequence, on the one hand, of problems connected with the transition from exploitative to regenerative forestry practice and, on the other hand, of the increased raw material demands by the rapidly expanding pulp industry. In this connection, one should note also that the expansion of the pulp industry contributed to the rise in wages in the lumber mill industry as well. In certain areas of Norrland especially, the operations of the circular saw also contributed to the increasing raw material scarcity, as did the fact that opportunities for importing timber from Finland gradually approached the vanishing point as a result of restrictions imposed by that country.

---

[17] Cf. e.g., *Rationaliseringsutredningen*, Vol. II, *SOU* (1939, No. 14), as well as *SOU* (1935, No. 36), and *SOU* (1938, No. 53). The most detailed and systematic survey is the unpublished paper, written for the research seminar at the University of Stockholm, by T. Kahlin, "Något om orsakerna till sågverksdöden" (available from the author at Sveriges Industriförbund, Stockholm).

Some of the factors listed as contributing to increasing scarcity had begun to be felt in certain areas even prior to the interwar period. At that time, however, the difficulties could usually be surmounted by relying on supplies from areas of Norrland with a surplus of timber. When this was no longer possible, the scarcity became more general. Similar difficulties concerned the supply of logs of different dimensions. The pulp industry was, of course, a competitor primarily for the more slender logs, and this was where the increasing scarcity was first felt. In many cases this led to a conversion to more rapid timber rotations, while the lumber mills, at the same time, converted to sawing larger dimensions as far as this was possible. In this manner the scarcity of lumber gradually came to apply to most dimensions, and especially to the larger ones. The difficulties of finding lumber at reasonable cost in relation to finished goods prices were compounded by the increasing necessity of relying on timber from less accessible stands. To the extent that the mills had to buy more from farmer-owned forests, the increasing scarcity was felt more quickly, since such forests seldom contained primeval stands of large dimension timber.

The depression of the early 1930's brought drastic price declines on lumber products. Initially, this had a serious impact on many firms that were already hard pressed, since timber purchases had to be made far in advance. While timber prices subsequently fell even faster than final good prices, demand by that time had declined to such an extent that this no longer brought decisive relief. With this as background, it is understandable that the situation became especially difficult for those mills that did not own forests, particularly since this usually put greater demands on their liquidity. In the interwar period, lumber mills could only acquire timber stands in exceptional cases due to the obstacles created by the 1906 legislation. A particularly large number of firms without forests of their own were, therefore, forced to discontinue operations. Those firms which combined lumber milling with pulp production, and which, in addition, owned forests, managed considerably better. Their rates of return and liquidity were better, and fewer lumber mills were closed down in this category. It is evident, on the other hand, that in some cases the combination of lumber mills, pulp, and owned forests only led to postponement of discontinuations that eventually became necessary in any case.

In summary, the lumber mill disappearances clearly were the result of negative development effects. The causes may well be called "structural"—on the basis of any of the definitions of "structure" used in the scientific or popular literature so far, the description fits. One should not be misled by the fact that disappearances did not become especially numerous until the depression of the 1930's. Most of them undoubtedly would have become unavoidable later in the decade, even if the purely cyclical decline in the demand for lumber products had not occurred in the early 1930's. The depression acted as an accelerating or triggering factor. It should also be remembered that many of the lumber mills that were closed down in the early 1930's had languished for a rather long time, had covered only their variable costs or else had been able to continue operations only because of a combination with a more profitable pulp production. Many of them had been erected during the lumber mill industry's most rapid expansion with a view to operating over some 50 years on the basis of exploitative forestry practices.

In the late 1920's and early 1930's, a few lumber mills had also begun a thoroughgoing modernization. Most of these were large, well-situated mills built on the basis of long-term planning. In many cases, this modernization was based on the concentration of production in large plants which became the reason for a number of lumber mill disappearances in the 1920's. The innovations introduced in this way by a relatively small number of old firms were often undertaken in conjunction with expansion of prefabricated house factories, joineries, or wallboard mills, etc., and led to progressive development of these firms, while making the situation still more serious for those firms that had been hardest hit by cost developments. This intensification of competition which came about at the beginning of the 1930's would undoubtedly have caused increasing difficulties for the firms in question and many definitive disappearances even if the decline in demand, associated with the economic transformation process, had not been intensified by the depression originating abroad. The difficulties increased, on the other hand, not only because of the cyclical decline in the demand for sawed and planed products, but also because of the transitory and typically cyclical difficulties that the lumbermill-supporting pulp industry simultaneously encountered.

Finally, it should be noted that the high mortality of lumber mills in the 1930's gradually relieved the situation of surviving firms. The discontinued mills had previously engaged in the delaying tactic characteristic of industrial dynamism, and the dumping which had been typical for the entire decade of the 1920's and for the early 1930's, now ceased. At the same time, competition for the increasingly scarce raw material was reduced. This contributed to improved returns in the lumber mill industry as a whole in the latter half of the 1930's, which in turn led to a generally more tranquil development of individual firms. Another important factor involved the dissemination of the innovations pioneered in the 1920's, a process that was facilitated by the devaluation and by the easier credit conditions.

The Pulp Industry. In studying the development of the pulp industry from the point of view of the individual firms, the treatment should be somewhat different from that given other industries. The reasons are the same as those applying to the lumber mills and the paper and cardboard industry (see below). If each plant is regarded as a "firm" in accordance with our main rule, the data show a high rate of entry into the sulphate branch ($\alpha_{23} = 44$). It is noteworthy that the majority of the new factories were built in Norrland. In the great majority of cases the new plants were, however, constructed by older pulp companies.[18] New firms, in the financial sense, were formed only in a few, exceptional cases of little significance. When the great lumber mill and steel manufacturing company AB Ytterstfors-Munksund was dissolved in 1926, the newly formed Munksunds AB immediately began to erect a big sulphate mill. In this instance there was a raw material base to build on. In other cases, the difficulty of acquiring such a base was one of the most decisive obstacles to the establishment of entirely new firms (in the financial sense). Corporations were not allowed to acquire forests, and to establish a new company depending entirely on purchased raw material was judged to be too risky. On the other hand, the phenomenon of older firms carrying their plants at low book values—which was an important deterrent to entry in the steel industry, for example—was of little importance here. The pulp producers did not need to rely on old assets in order to earn a return on their capital.

The industry had, moreover, by and large passed the stage of development that characterized the situation before World War I, when, in the 1880's, the hard-pressed steel industry—and later on, when the expansion of the lumber market had passed its peak, also the lumber mill industry—invaded the pulp business. Apart from the case already mentioned, a couple of typical instances of this occurred even after 1918, but they were not of much significance. The old, small steel mills were not as suitable as a basis for ventures into the pulp industry as they had been in an earlier period when small-scale pulp mills could still be profitable. Those lumber mills which had resources on the scale required to build a pulp factory had, as a rule, already entered the field by the beginning of the interwar period. This was also the case with the paper mills.[19]

At the same time that so many sulphate mills were built from scratch

---

[18] It should be noted that the different types of pulp mills and the paper mills have been kept separate throughout this study even when, as is frequently the case, such a separation cannot be made on the basis of the *IS* raw data. As previously noted, this study has drawn on the information in *Nordisk Papperskalender*, published by Hugo Brusewitz AB, for data on the individual plants and on their respective capacity (in tons of "dry" pulp). These capacity figures, however, represent maximum output rates. In general, the mills could operate at 100 percent of this capacity only for a short period. To get an idea of their respective actual capacity per annum over a longer interval of time, the figures should be reduced by some 10 or 15 percent. This has not been done here, however.

[19] There were, however, not a few instances of integration backward from paper to pulp between the wars. But integration forward was also common (cf. below concerning the paper mills).

by older companies in the 1920's, almost all existing plants were rebuilt, modernized, and expanded. In many instances, output capacity was doubled or tripled. The driving force in this development was the demand-pull stemming from the growing use of paper-packaging materials, which in turn was due to innovations in the paper and cardboard processing industry, both at home and abroad. In addition, the raw material base of many forest industry firms was not uniformly utilized. While the lumber mills mainly used the larger logs, and the sulphite mills used spruce almost exclusively, sulphate production could utilize both spruce and pine as well as lumber mill shavings. Furthermore, the distress of the lumber mills was undoubtedly another driving force. Many of the companies that built sulphate mills had previously operated lumber mills in addition to their production of sulphate and mechanical pulp. The product innovation which the new bleaching processes for sulphate involved did not lead to the establishment of any new sulphate plants, however. The pioneers, Stora Kopparbergs Bergslags AB, Kopparberg & Hofors Sågverks AB (subsequently Kopparfors AB), and Uddeholms AB, based their production of bleached sulphate with the new methods on their existing plants in Skutskär, Norrsundet, and Skoghall, respectively. The Norrsundet mill, however, was constructed as late as 1923, and this plant together with Munksund and Långrörs AB (see below) represents the foremost examples of the development from lumber milling to pulp production during the interwar period.

The pioneering contributions to the innovations on which the new high-grade sulphate cellulose was based were made in 1933 by Uddeholms AB at its Skoghall factory. The biggest and best-known of the new sulphate factories was the one built at Östrand in 1929–30. This plant, which introduced a number of important process innovations in the production of strong sulphate, was built by Svenska Cellulosa AB, the great lumber mill, cellulose, and mechanical pulp group newly formed under the direction of Ivar Kreuger. The Östrand mill has often been called Sweden's last new pulp factory. By Swedish standards it was constructed on a very large scale—a planned capacity of 100,000 tons strong sulphate per year. One reason for its construction was the new company's surplus of sulphate wood in the Sundsvall district.[20] Prior to the construction of the Ostrand mill, the three largest plants were those belonging to Wifstavarfs AB, Mo & Domsjö AB, and Långrörs AB, each of which

---

[20] It may be noted, however, that the output of this plant never reached even the 85 percent line, usually referred to as "full capacity," during the 1930's. Although the area initially had a surplus of sulphate wood, it was not large enough to feed an annual capacity of 100,000 tons. In the 1940's, however, it became possible to utilize birchwood as raw material also. In addition, the plant was then able to draw on sulphate wood which had become available following the discontinuation of the Frånö sulphate mill.

had a maximum annual capacity of 50,000 to 60,000 tons. The Långrörs plant was built from scratch a few years prior to the construction of Östrand, while the other two were older plants which had been expanded. By the end of the interwar period, the capacity spread between the different sulphate factories was relatively large despite the fact, already mentioned, that small and medium-sized plants also had been expanded. This can be seen from Figure 21 in which the corresponding capacity spread as of 1919 is also indicated.

FIGURE 21
Capacity of Sulphate Pulp Mills in 1919 and 1939

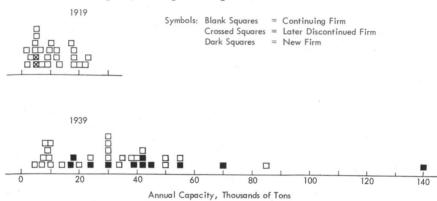

Annual Capacity, Thousands of Tons

SOURCE: *Nordisk papperskalender.*

The sulphite branch shows only two new "firms" ($\alpha_{23} = 2$)—the Åsen plant of Håfreströms AB, built in 1926 in conjunction with an already existing paper mill, and the viscous pulp plant in Jössefors, built in 1929 by Billeruds AB. The Jössefors plant, which complemented the Billeruds factory in Kyrkebyn, where the first viscose had been produced some 10 years earlier, cemented the leading position which this corporation had gained from the very start in this new and profitable field. As was the case with the older sulphate mills, most of the existing sulphite factories were also expanded by adding bleaching plants, and so forth. In general, additions to capacity were on a relatively more modest scale in this branch. The sulphite mills were as a rule smaller than the sulphate factories even at the beginning of the interwar period. In 1939, the largest plant belonged to Mo & Domsjö, closely followed by the Fagervik plant of Wifstavarfs AB and the Kramfors AB plant in Kramfors. In each, capacity was on the order of 70,000 to 80,000 tons per year. The factories were operated in conjunction with wood alcohol plants and, in Mo & Domsjö, with a bleaching plant. Later on the production of chemicals was also added at Mo & Domsjö, a field which Uddeholms AB had been the first to enter. Uddeholm also pioneered with the high-grade sulphite cellulose in the mid-1930's. All three of the plants just mentioned were greatly expanded during the interwar period. In 1919, the only factory with a capacity in excess of 35,000 tons was that in Fagervik, which at that time counted on 50,000 tons per year, an exceedingly large figure for the Swedish sulphite industry of the period. Figure 22 shows that in 1919 factories with a capacity of only 10,000 tons or so dominated in the industry.

The interwar history of the mechanical pulp branch records 10 or so entirely new plants, a couple of which were new firms in the financial

FIGURE 22
Capacity of Sulphite Pulp Mills in 1919 and 1939

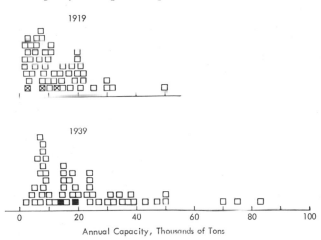

Annual Capacity, Thousands of Tons

SOURCE: *Nordisk papperskalender.*

sense ($\alpha_{23} = 18$). The most interesting case is that of the new mechanical pulp plant erected in 1926–27 by Tollare Pappersbruks AB. The company's paper mill had been constructed a few years previously by a wallpaper manufacturer. Initially, the new mechanical pulp plant produced exclusively for the firm's own paper mill. The paper company had been started outside the paper cartel and had in the beginning relied on wastepaper from Stockholm. In the long run, however, this arrangement proved to be less than perfect, whereupon the pulp mill was constructed. Most of the other new mechanical pulp mills were built by older firms. The biggest was the one constructed in 1927 by AB Scharins Söner in Sofiehem. This plant, which in its first stage had a capacity of almost 40,000 tons, was among the country's largest right from the start. For almost the entire interwar period, however, the largest plants in the branch were the two owned by Holmens Bruks & Fabriks AB in Norrköping and in Hallsta, both of which had been greatly expanded. These two plants were the basis for two of Sweden's largest newsprint mills. By 1939, each had a capacity of around 70,000 tons. In comparison with traditional capacity levels of Swedish mechanical pulp factories, this was an exceptionally large figure, exceeded only by the Kvarnsveden plant of Stora Kopparbergs Bergslags AB. The capacity figures for the mechanical pulp mills show very wide dispersion (see Figure 23). There will be reason to recall this fact in discussing firm disappearances in the industry.

FIGURE 23
Capacity of Mechanical Pulp Mills
in 1919 and 1939

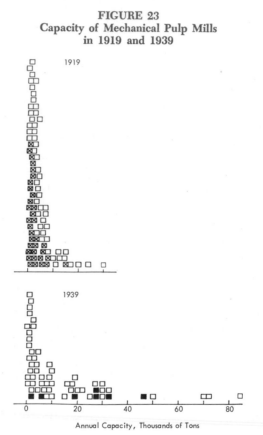

Annual Capacity, Thousands of Tons

Source: *Nordisk papperskalender.* For symbols used, cf. Fig. 21.

Two sulphate mills disappeared between the wars ($\gamma_{23} = 4$). One, which belonged to Forsmarks Bruk in the county of Stockholm, was destroyed by a fire. The other, the Stömne plant of Billeruds AB, was closed down in 1939 when the company decided to concentrate on its specialities—sulphite pulp, viscose, kraft-paper, and greaseproof paper. The sulphite industry had three disappearances ($\gamma_{23} = 3$). Two of these occurred in connection with deliberate consolidation efforts: in 1921 Fiskeby Fabriks AB closed down a small plant in Ljusfors, with a capacity of about 3,000 tons, and concentrated production to its Skärblacka plant; in the 1930's AB Mölnbacka-Trysil closed the considerably larger Klarafors factory and concentrated operations in its plant in Forshaga. The third case was that of a plant owned by Lilla Edets Pappersbruks AB which was discontinued in the 1920's.

The high mortality of mechanical pulp plants in the interwar period ($\gamma_{23} = 24$) represents, as with so many other industries, the last, or next to last, stage of a transformation process that had begun in the second and third phases of the industrialization of Sweden. As in the steel industry as well as in the tanneries, it was a question of large-scale production units, based on great process innovations, beginning to force the older, smaller plants out of business. For the mechanical pulp mills, this transformation process commenced just after the turn of the century, when Kvarnsveden introduced a decisive innovation—a hot-grinding plant on a completely different scale from that of the previously common cold-grinding pulp mill. This new plant created great problems for the majority of mechanical pulp mills around the country and particularly for those in the province of Värmland, the industry's traditional center. Most of the old plants were based on rather small water mills with insufficient power for the larger grinding mills. This often prevented imitation of the pioneering firm, even when the financial resources to do so were available. These firms, therefore, had no alternative but to gradually give up the struggle and close down, in many cases after recovering only variable costs for a period of time.

At the outset of the interwar period, the majority of the old plants had been discontinued and their water mills converted to supply local electric power. In certain cases, however, a successful conversion to hot-grinding was accomplished. But to the extent that expansion to large-scale production was not feasible, hot-grinding alone did not prove profitable in the long run, especially since subsequent technological developments particularly favored the large plants. By the end of World War I, some 40 cold-grinding mills remained—almost all of them were small, having an annual capacity of a few thousand tons each. In addition, there were about 10 small hot-grinding mills. Some 30 of the former and a half-dozen of the latter were to disappear. Only a couple out of almost a score larger hot-grinding mills, on the other hand, were closed down. Apart from those disappearances that were due to negative development effects, there were a couple of cases motivated by a desire to concentrate operations and/or economize on raw materials. The largest mechanical pulp mill to be closed down for such reasons was the Jössefors plant of Billeruds AB, which had a capacity between 15,000 and 20,000 tons when it was discontinued in 1931. The discontinuation in this instance was prompted by the effort to concentrate operations, managerial energies, and raw materials.

Although most of the discontinued mechanical pulp mills belonged to companies that did not simultaneously disappear, there were cases in which the closing of a plant was connected with the disappearance of a firm in the financial sense. These were of little significance, however. Two such mills had been started during the 1920's, one (oddly enough, a cold-grinding mill) by farmers, the other by a firm in the engineering industry.

The Paper and Cardboard Industry. The firms in the paper and cardboard branch cannot be grouped into homogeneous subbranches. While it is possible to isolate a number of fine-paper mills, as has been done in the present work, fine-grade paper was also produced by quite a number of firms that were at the same time engaged in the production of one or more other kinds of paper. A large number of firms were simultaneously producing newsprint, packaging paper, and other types of paper and card-

FIGURE 24
Capacity of Paper and Cardboard Mills in 1919 and 1939

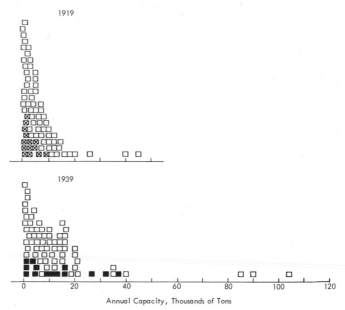

Annual Capacity, Thousands of Tons

Source: *Nordisk papperskalender*. For symbols used, cf. Fig. 21.

board. In these cases, the firm's main product line would often change from one year to the next.

Except for fine-grade paper, most of the different types of paper were found in the production program of the firms that entered the industry during the interwar period ($\alpha_{23} = 16$). One mill, which had previously produced newsprint and sundry other types of paper, did, however, begin production of fine-grade paper in 1938. This was the Långed plant of

AB Billingsfors-Långed, which at the same time discontinued its news-print production.[21] Since most of the older fine-paper mills increased their capacity considerably, it may be inferred that the strong cartel in this branch, together with its collaborating wholesalers, deterred entry. The absence of significant product innovations meant that the possibilities were limited for new firms to gain a foothold in this market.[22] The construction of a pulp mill and the acquisition of a raw material base in order to gain entry—even where possible—was hardly a tempting prospect.

It was less difficult to gain entry into the other, more rapidly growing, paper markets, where, for that matter, the cartels were somewhat less effective. A firm that already operated a pulp mill would, therefore, find it natural to avoid fine-grade paper in integrating forward. Tullare Pappersbruk[23] has already been mentioned as a new entrant that defied the cartel in the newsprint branch in the early 1920's. When in the early 1930's the situation in the newsprint market became especially difficult, however, this firm changed over to producing mainly packaging paper, a conversion which was also common in other quarters. In 1920, Billeruds AB built a newsprint and packaging paper mill in Jössefors, where newsprint production was eventually dropped in 1931. In 1919, Skönviks AB built a big newsprint mill in Matfors based on the firm's own mechanical pulp. No other new newsprint mills were started. Thus, in only one of the four cases—and typically enough, that of the smallest mill—was the firm new in the financial sense.

The growing market for packaging paper attracted two new, rather big, plants which were constructed to utilize both sulphite and sulphate pulp. Only one of the two was a new firm in the financial sense, namely, AB Laxå Pappersbruk which had developed out of a paper wholesale business. Its plant was built in 1938. Several paper mills converted to kraft-paper, in some cases in connection with the construction of sulphate plants. The most important one was Ljusfors, which began producing kraft-paper on a large scale in 1926. The Laxå mill was very small compared to the other, completely new plants—Uddeholms' Skoghall plant, built in 1929; the already mentioned Billerud AB plant for newsprint and sulphite packaging paper in Jössefors; the new mill for sulphite packaging paper built in 1924 by Korsnäs Sågverks AB; the Billingfors-Långed AB kraft-paper mill in Billingsfors (1924); and, finally, the Bil-

---

[21] This plant has been removed from the continuing "other paper and cardboard mills" and reclassified as continuing "fine paper mill" in all tables and appendices. This is the reason for the discrepancy between the number of continuing firms in 1919 and in 1939 in the branches affected.

[22] Cf. *SOU* (1940, No. 35), pp. 131 ff.

[23] This plant was built by a wallpaper manufacturer who had previously owned the pulp and paper mill in Ljusfors but had sold it to Fiskeby Fabriks AB.

leruds kraft paper mill in Gruvön (1930). The Gruvön mill was later expanded for the production of paper sacks. The greaseproof paper mill built by Billeruds AB in 1922, which was a large plant from the beginning, should also be mentioned in this connection. Although greaseproof paper had been produced at a couple of mills previously, the whole conception of this venture gave it the character of an important innovation. Significantly, this plant was erected in the middle of the depression.

With only two exceptions the remainder of the new mills built in the interwar period concentrated on cardboard production on the basis of pulp produced by the same firms. The two exceptions were also new firms in the financial sense. Both, however, were very small with an annual capacity of less than 1,000 tons.

Thus, with the exception of Tollare, all the cases of formation of firms that were of any quantitative significance bordered on firm development. The traditional integration from pulp to paper continued to some extent during the interwar period. At the same time, integration in the opposite direction also took place. As a consequence, only about 15, mostly small, paper and cardboard factories lacked their own pulp mills by the end of the period, while close to 60 had such mills.[24] The new paper mills were usually built by pulp companies which, in entering the paper field, largely ceased selling pulp in the markets that they supplied with paper. Taking the interests of the pulp customers into account, it was generally regarded as unwise to try to sell paper and pulp in the same market.[25] With regard to the development of different firms, the distribution of capacity increments was remarkably even. The dominating positions of Kvarnsveden and of Holmens Bruk in the newsprint branch was, however, accentuated. The only category of firms which generally remained stationary was that of those, often independent, cardboard mills that were small at the beginning of the period.

Plant disappearances in the paper and cardboard industry ($\gamma_{23} = 7$) involved the disappearance of the corresponding company in a number of cases. Some relatively old, small, obsolete and unspecialized producers without facilities for producing pulp closed down, as did a number of small firms started during World War I. A few large paper mills with their own pulp supplies also disappeared.[26] In most cases, production

---

[24] "Firm" is here used in the financial sense of the term, which is the one relevant in the present context.

[25] Still there remained about a dozen firms selling both pulp and paper at the end of the interwar period. As a rule, this was probably not done in the same markets, however.

[26] Corresponding to the common conversion to kraft-paper and in a couple of instances to other types of paper, there were also several instances in which the production of newsprint and magazine paper was discontinued. The mills in Långed, Tollare, and Ljusfors have already been mentioned as examples. The production of newsprint had become less profitable, particularly following the construction of some very large and efficient plants by certain companies.

was discontinued permanently. When pulp companies closed down their paper mills, the reasons were the disadvantages of marketing both pulp and paper, mentioned above, and/or the advantages of concentrating operations. Examples of this were the discontinuation of paper production at Billerud's Brättne-plant in 1936, of cardboard production at Kolsäter in 1937 (the plant was not rebuilt after a fire), and in the early 1920's, of paper and cardboard production at three plants in Norrland —Ortviken belonging to Skönvik, Essvik belonging to Sundsvalls Cellulosa AB, and Torpshammars AB. It is difficult to point to any strategic malinvestments. Only one of the plants constructed during the interwar period was closed down. In no case was the disappearance preceded by sizable expansion or modernization. One cannot exclude the possibility that the incidence of disappearances would have been higher in the absence of the cartels.

Cotton and Woolen Manufacture

Cotton and woolen manufacturing are good illustrations of how development processes dominated by process innovations leave little scope for new entry with respect to either number or size of entrants ($\alpha_{23} = 3$ and 2, respectively). The firms in existence at the beginning of the interwar period were usually many decades old and continued to dominate the markets. They were able to do so primarily as a result of their long and well-established relationships with wholesalers, and because of the technological and organizational advantage which old firms usually have over potential entrants in those branches where process innovations constitute the primary basis of industry development. There were, on the other hand, no organized attempts at restricting entry. Formation of a new firm required considerable amounts of capital, at least in spinning since not only spinning frames but many other kinds of machines had to be acquired. To build a cotton weaving mill required relatively less capital since looms were by and large the only equipment needed. Significantly, hardly any of the new firms that were established entered the spinning branch. Only one wholly new and important (cotton) spinning mill was started during the interwar period, namely, AB Svenska Textilverken (1937) in Genevad immediately south of Halmstad. Other isolated cases of entry were not of much importance either in terms of the total expansion of the industry or in terms of their innovational contributions.[27]

The number of new cloth mills was, on the other hand, not completely insignificant. But neither were they of much quantitative importance for the textile industries as a whole. Most of them fell into one of three categories—mills producing "novelty" fabrics, those weaving fabrics in traditional folk patterns, and finally, those engaged in producing drapery

---

[27] One new firm was, however, the first to introduce chenille yarn—a very specialized semifinished product for the textile industry—to Sweden in 1934.

and furniture fabrics, and so forth. Firms in the first category could gain a foothold in the market mainly because the older firms generally had little interest in the strongly fashion-oriented, small-volume specialties that "novelties" generally represented. In the 1930's especially, these firms attempted to standardize their output more in order to get longer production runs, following the example set by a few pioneers in the 1920's. Also, where big firms did not confine themselves to the large-volume items, small firms often had a chance to operate in their shadow by quickly imitating their fashionable novelties and living on their advertising.[28] The second category of entrants is also explained by these same policies of the older firms in conjunction with the development of fashions and the growth of national income. The third category, finally, represented a typical response to demand-pull. The big increase in the rate of household formation and the rapid growth in the production of "textile intensive" upholstered furniture brought such a rapid increase in the demand for furniture and drapery fabrics that the old enterprises were forced to let new firms take care of part of it.

This demand-pull led to lively, and quantitatively rather significant, entry also in another area of the cotton manufacturing industry. Many new firms were formed to produce wadding for bed quilts, and so forth. Characteristically, the entry shares in "other cotton manufacture" and "other woolen manufacture" were large ($\alpha_{23} = 25$ and 42, respectively).

At least in the first two of these categories, the nature of the new firms is clearly revealed by the fact that with few exceptions they were started on a small scale and remained small. As a rule, the older firms grew to the extent that they did not disappear (Appendix 8 in Swedish edition). The structure of the cotton manufacturing industry shows a shift of the center of gravity toward the large-size classes between 1919 and 1939 without any decrease in the total number of firms in the small-size classes. This was, however, not the case in woolen manufacturing.

A study of the nature of the firms indicates that in both cases the industry structure may be regarded as fairly stable by the end of the interwar period, except for a continuing tendency, in cotton manufacturing at least, toward expansion among large and medium-size firms. Any general tendency for the small businesses to grow into the medium or large classes cannot be observed. Competition between large and small firms was not intensive. Competition was more within, than between, the two categories, which to a certain extent complemented each other. The picture is thus completely different from that in the ready-made clothing and hosiery industries.

---

[28] In the main these firms seem to have exploited the growth in demand resulting from advertising which the advertising firms found it difficult to meet simply because they could not always be represented in every location or every retail establishment.

The mortality of cotton weaving mills was high ($\gamma_{23} = 31$) but was without much significance in other branches. In the late 1920's and early 1930's particularly, several large cotton textile mills disappeared. There was no cartel in this field to keep weak firms alive. But neither were any mills closed down in connection with deliberate concentration efforts. By the early or mid-1930's, the weakest firms had either disappeared or been merged into, and modernized by, other, healthier companies. In this respect the transformation which began with the many innovations introduced following the end of World War I was completed. The typical competitive struggle between strong pioneer firms and weak firms threatened with "creative destruction" was therefore much less in evidence in the 1930's than it had been in the 1920's. One of the bankruptcies and discontinuations that caused the most attention was that of Wiskabergs Fabriker AB in Borås in 1930. One brief comment on this case explains most of the discontinuations in cotton manufacturing:

> The reason for this bankruptcy is to be found in the difficulties with which the textile industry at present has to cope, but also in the fact that the products which this factory has been specially equipped to produce, namely, high-quality cotton fabrics, have not in the last few years met a demand sufficient to make it possible to continue operations profitably. The reason for this is probably the change in fashions which has led to increased use both of printed fabrics and of thinner and lighter woolen fabrics. These woolens are as a rule imported and their prices, following the decline of wool prices in the last few years, are on a par with, or even below, those of cotton fabrics.[29]

It was, in other words, a question of firm failures closely connected with negative development effects.

For the most part, disappearances in woolen manufacturing were of the same type and are by and large explained by the transformation of the industry's product-mix discussed in Chapter 7. A contributing factor in both cotton and woolen manufacturing, particularly toward the end of the 1920's, was the increasing competition created by the determined modernization efforts of the leading, financially strong companies. In both branches, on the other hand, strategic malinvestments were of little importance in either old or new firms. No firm was strongly progressive, and there is nothing to indicate that major investments were undertaken. Market conditions, at least during the 1920's, certainly did not invite new entry into parallel competition, or for that matter any other extensive investment. Neither did the woolen manufacturing branch have a cartel which could have influenced firm mortality.

The cyclical variations in entry offer little of interest except that the high rates of entry in the depression years shown by so many other

---

[29] *Svenska Dagbladet*, Feb. 13, 1930.

industries are missing in the present case. This was undoubtedly connected with the fact that founders of new enterprises seldom came from the ranks of employees. As was indicated above, the start of a new firm in these branches usually required such a large amount of equity that unemployment, or the risk of unemployment, could not act as a stimulating factor.

Firm disappearances show no important temporal variation. It should be noted, however, that they did not increase in the first postwar crisis as they did in most other industries. The main explanation for this is probably that the textile industry did not belong to those industries which expanded rapidly during the war and the immediate postwar years. The reason for this, in turn, was primarily the scarcity of raw material which it faced in those years.

The Tanneries

Few industries were as characterized by firm disappearances as was the tannery industry. Although the exit share was not overwhelming ($\gamma_{23} = 32$), the number of firms discontinued was that much larger. Of the 209 tanneries in existence in 1919, no less than 151 were closed down between the wars. In contrast to several other industries with a high incidence of disappearances, however, this was hardly a result of deliberate concentration efforts. The gap in size and in technology between the innovating firms and the small businesses was so large that the former seldom had cause to fear the competition of the latter. Neither did they have other reasons to be interested in buying them out. As indicated earlier, the fundamental causes for this high firm mortality had made their appearance already in the late 1880's, one of them being the revolutionary process innovation which quick-tanning involved. By the beginning of the interwar period, firm disappearances had marked the industry for more than a generation.[30] The number of small and medium-size tanneries utilizing methods bordering on handicraft in the technical sense which remained by 1919 was very small relative to the number 50 years earlier, and most of them had no chance of surviving in the long run. The majority could not compete with the larger tanneries of the modern type.[31]

Their high mortality during the whole interwar period and in all areas of the country is, therefore, not hard to explain. The question,

---

[30] Cf. W. Smith, "Garveriidustriens produktionsförhållanden," *Tull- och Traktat-kommittens utredningar och betänkanden*, Vol. XX, SOU (1923, No. 23).

[31] While the large tanneries made the whole large mass of small tanneries obsolete by adopting the quick-tanning process with its large capital requirements, it may be noted that no large tannery was founded in order to exploit this new process from the very beginning. The large firms had themselves developed from small craft-type tanneries which had begun to modernize already at an early stage.

instead, is why they survived as tenaciously as they did. Even though three quarters of the 209 firms in existence in 1919 had disappeared before 1940, there were still about a score of the very smallest shops remaining. Although their output was small and production often only intermittent, their equipment had been rather well maintained. One important reason was simply the tenacity of the individual entrepreneur. Transfer to another occupation was frequently almost out of the question, particularly when the tanner was well along in years. If the tannery did not yield much of a profit margin, it still offered a livelihood, although with small compensation for the labor put into it. Replacement of the productive equipment was no concern. The old equipment was utilized as long as it held together.

Another reason was the fact that many small tanneries were an integral part of a shoe or glove manufacturing firm or a leather business.[32] The owner would then frequently regard his business as one operation and would find advantages of one kind or another in the integration that would make him reluctant to close down the tannery. Presumably, cost calculations were not always too precise in such cases. Some costs which ought to have been imputed to the tannery were undoubtedly allocated to other activities. A third reason for the survival of some small tanneries over most or even all of the interwar period is that it sometimes was possible to continue operating along with the large tanneries by concentrating on very specialized products, often for a local market. Consequently, many of the surviving small tanneries worked with moose hides, sheepskins, and so forth, which were tanned for special purposes. A number of skin tanneries in Malung, tanneries making vegetable-tanned, oiled leather, particularly in Norrland, and harness tanneries scattered in rural areas, could thus survive and, in singular cases, even flourish.

But expansion was out of the question. The products were too specialized and the outlets too local. For much the same reasons, the obsolete firms were unable to engage in any general and serious dumping in the manner characteristic of the struggle between the new and the old in many other industries. But that a certain amount of dumping, albeit not on a very serious scale, made itself felt intermittently in certain areas during the 1920's cannot be disputed. In the 1930's, so few of the obsolete firms remained that it practically ceased.

---

[32] Apart from these cases, integration between tanneries and shoe factories was quite uncommon, primarily because a tannery capable of supplying a sizable shoe factory with leather and hides would have had to be large and to provide an unprofitably large assortment. From the standpoint of the tanneries, reluctance to compete with their own customers strongly inhibited integration. Characteristically, instances of integration are by and large found only among a couple of very large and among a number of very small firms. In the latter cases, both the tannery and the shoe factory of the firms involved produced highly specialized products.

The specialized production opportunities discussed above induced the formation of a few small firms. Four of the eight new firms still in existence by 1940 were, typically enough, located in Norrland. On the whole it is characteristic that by the end of the interwar period a large part of the industry was located in this part of the country. Of 66 tanneries in operation in 1939, 22 were in Norrland. That almost all of them were small, however, is evident from the fact that more than 90 percent of the industry's labor force worked in Svealand and Götaland.

14 The Financing of New Enterprises

A. Problems and Data

Firms started during the interwar period in all probability account for a relatively small share of the period's total industrial investment activity. While it is not possible to measure this directly or exactly, one can indirectly obtain a very rough estimate of their share in gross investment. If it is assumed, as a first approximation, that this share in a certain industry can be measured in terms of the long-term labor force increment due to new firms relative to that due to old firms, we obtain the "entry quotients" (β_{23}) for the various industries which were computed in Chapter 10. This, then, is an estimate of the new firms' share in total gross investment in each individual industry.[1] In order to obtain subsequently a corresponding estimate for manufacturing in general, it is necessary to take into account the fact that the different industries require different amounts of real capital per worker. To this end, one may weigh the contributions of the individual industries to this aggregate entry quotient by using data on fire insurance values per worker at normal employment levels.[2] The resulting investment quotient for all

---

[1] For the pulp, paper, and wallboard industries, the quotient has been calculated in terms of output capacity rather than in terms of size of work force. In the present context, this is an advantage. In aggregating over different industries (cf. below) it causes a complication, however, which it has been possible to circumvent only by using fictitious work-force figures in the calculations. In aggregating, increases in capacity have thus been recalculated into corresponding percentage increases in work force.

[2] Data on fire insurance values have been obtained from a 1946 study undertaken by Kommerskollegium. No earlier studies of this kind are available, but since

of the industries covered by the present work is 0.38. This would mean that new firms accounted for 38 percent of total gross investment. This percentage is lower than the unweighted entry quotient based on labor force figures (0.45) since the formation of new firms was most intensive in industries requiring relatively little real capital per worker.

It is evident, however, that the investment per additional worker was sometimes larger in the new firms than in the old ones. The new firms sometimes had to make relatively large capital outlays initially and during the following few years. But this was not always true since facilities and/or machinery were as a rule either rented to begin with or taken over from earlier firms. Old firms could frequently increase employment without investment. It should be remembered that there were more industries working with unutilized capacity in 1919 than in 1939.

On the other hand, investments were frequently undertaken without any corresponding increase in work force. Reinvestments were made in order to maintain plant and equipment, for one thing. The motive was often to replace labor, for another. Obviously, both types of investment, particularly the first one, were far more important in old than in new firms, since the former usually had older plant and equipment. A good basis for judging the influence of these factors on the average investment per worker added in old and in new firms, respectively, is lacking. As it turns out, however, the choice of assumptions with regard to the net effect of these counteracting tendencies is not a very important issue because it has been impossible to investigate the financing of the relevant portion of manufacturing investment in its entirety. But the attempt has been made to get at least an approximate grasp of how funds were obtained to *start* the new enterprises; with regard to the financing of the development of firms, it has only been possible to offer a few suggestions, based, among other things, on a special investigation of the incorporated firms. Thus, the main study deals with a relatively small portion of the total gross investment undertaken by new firms up to 1939. Even if the margin of error around the figure of 38 percent given above were very large, we could nonetheless conclude that this investigation deals only with a small part of the total gross investment in manufacturing between the wars—presumably 10 percent at most and probably considerably less. It is still evident, however, that it deals with an important part of the financing of the industrial sector's expansion.

---

it is a question of finding reasonably consistent weights for the various industries in computing an overall value per worker, the lack of such studies could hardly invalidate a calculation which is only to yield an approximation. That changes in real capital requirements per worker between the interwar period and 1946 may have varied between the different industries is, of course, a possible source of error.

Responses regarding the financing of the formation of firms were obtained on a total of 1,500 of the 2,969 questionnaires submitted to firms in the industries encompassed by our special investigation B (see Appendix 1 in Swedish edition). Unfortunately, the answers obtained on the questionnaire reproduced in Appendix 1 could not be quantitatively precise.[3] Although in many cases numerical information was obtained in the course of the interviews, the results of the investigation can still only be summarized in the form used in Tables 17 through 20. Thus, it has been possible to report (*a*) on the various methods of financing used, (*b*) on the cases in which only one such method was used, and (*c*) on the cases in which one particular method of financing stands out as the most "important" one.[4] Whereas these results could be cross-tabulated with any and all of the other data on individual firms reported in this work, only a few of these combinations yield information of much interest. In the tables, the results of the financing study have therefore been tabulated with the individual firms classified not only according to industry and/or major branch, but also according to their geographic location, their size at the start, and the previous occupation of the entrepreneur.

B. Results and Analysis

During the interwar period, *initial capital*, including capital for the years immediately following the start, was only to a very small extent obtained through *share issues*. As Table 17 shows, this form of financing was used, altogether, in somewhat less than 11 percent of the cases for which data on the financing of the new firms have been obtained. Since the smaller firms are underrepresented in the study and very rarely were financed by issuing shares, this figure undoubtedly sets an upper limit. In a very large number of cases, furthermore, it was a question of formation of subsidiaries so that the shares would not be subscribed to by individual investors. In a few other instances, practically all of the stock was in the name of the entrepreneur himself, in which case the financing is regarded as "financing with own funds" (see below). Everything indicates that only a few percent of the total number of new firms were financed by several individual investors contributing capital. Most corporations were formed long after the start of the firm and not with the intention of raising additional capital in connection with the incorporation. A contributing factor to the insignificant role of stock issues in

---

[3] Concerning methodological questions relevant to an appraisal of the questionnaire responses, cf. Appendix 1 of the Swedish edition. It should be noted, for example, that returns could be obtained almost exclusively from firms that were still in operation in 1946. A priori, it is not impossible that this may have introduced some systematic bias, but the risk seems small enough so that one dares disregard it.

[4] Cf. Appendix 1 of the Swedish edition.

establishing new firms has undoubtedly been the fact that the banks in this period were less able than previously to accept the risk of underwriting new issues for subsequent sale to the public.

Most commonly, the *entrepreneur invested funds* which he had either saved, obtained through his wife, or inherited.[5] In more than 80 percent of all cases where information on financing has been obtained, "own funds" contributed a part of the initial capital (Table 17). In almost one-third, or 28 percent, of all cases in which "own funds" were at all involved, this was the only method of financing (Table 18). In somewhat more than 25 percent of those cases where such funds were used

TABLE 17
The Financing of Firm-formation. Survey of All Sources Used

Industry Group*	Location†	Number of Firms	Number for Which Sources of Funds are Known	Number of Firms Utilizing Source						
				Own Funds	Issue of Shares	Jobbers	Loans from Relatives or Friends	Bank Loans	Credit from Suppliers	Other
1......	A	431	253	205	13	13	61	125	43	6
1......	B	475	309	248	44	28	66	82	46	11
3......	A	1 039	372	310	16	10	96	250	87	10
3......	B	244	95	78	9	3	24	32	19	2
4......	A	62	30	21	5	1	8	20	5	2
4......	B	75	30	27	2	3	4	9	3	3
5......	A	267	168	140	20	15	39	82	28	3
5......	B	256	186	152	36	12	42	60	28	6
7......	A	15	6	6	—	1	1	3	—	—
7......	B	105	51	44	15	4	14	11	5	—
All....	A	1 814	829	682	54	40	205	480	163	21
All....	B	1 155	671	549	106	50	150	194	101	22
Total...	A and B	2 969	1 500	1 231	160	90	355	674	264	43

* 1 = heavy industry; 3 = millwork, cardboard and paper; 4 = food processing; 5 = textiles and clothing; 7 = chemicals.
† A = rural areas and small towns (<10,000 pop. 1929). B = large towns (>10,000 pop. 1929).

in combination with other forms of financing, most of the capital consisted of "own funds." This means that own funds were either the only, or the most important, source at the start of more than 40 percent of all the new firms.

It is impossible, unfortunately, to say what proportion of the total

---

[5] As mentioned in the methodological discussion in Appendix 1 [Swedish edition], this source of funds hides some loans obtained by the founder immediately in advance of starting the firm. Own funds are, on the other hand, often hidden under "share issues." In neither case is it plausible that gross error is involved.

TABLE 18
**The Financing of Firm-formation. Number of Firms
with Only a Single Source of Funds**

Initial Size*	Source of Funds	Industry											
		13	14	15	31	35	41	43	54	55	71	72	Total
1–7	Own funds.........	76	45	27	51	13	11	2	13	38	7	13	296
	Issue of shares......	1	1	—	1	—	—	—	—	1	1	1	6
	Loans from relatives or friends......	9	2	1	10	—	3	1	1	1	—	2	30
	Bank loans.........	12	8	—	19	—	2	—	—	6	—	—	47
	Subtotal.....	98	56	28	81	13	16	3	14	46	8	16	379
8–19	Own funds.........	13	10	10	14	2	2	2	9	24	—	1	87
	Issue of shares......,	1	1	1	1	—	—	—	—	3	—	—	7
	Loans from relatives or friends.. ..	2	2	—	1	—	—	—	1	—	—	—	6
	Bank loans.........	1	1	1	1	—	—	—	1	3	1	—	9
	Subtotal.....	17	14	12	17	2	2	2	11	30	1	1	109
20–99	Own funds.........	—	1	1	1	1	—	1	—	14	—	—	19
	Issue of shares......	—	—	—	—	—	—	—	—	—	—	—	—
	Loans from relatives or friends......	—	—	—	—	—	—	—	—	—	—	—	—
	Bank loans.........	—	—	—	—	—	—	—	—	2	—	—	2
	Subtotal.....	—	1	1	1	1	—	1	—	16	—	—	21
100+	Own funds.........	—	1	1	2	—	—	—	—	13	—	—	17
	Issue of shares......	1	—	—	—	—	—	—	—	1	—	—	2
	Loans from relatives or friends......	—	—	—	—	—	—	—	1	—	—	—	1
	Bank loans.........	—	—	—	—	—	—	—	—	—	—	—	—
	Subtotal.....	1	1	1	2	—	—	—	1	14	—	—	20
All sizes	Own funds.........	89	57	39	68	16	13	5	22	89	7	14	419
	Issue of shares......	3	2	1	?	—	—	—	—	5	1	1	15
	Loans from relatives or friends.. ..	11	4	1	11	—	3	1	3	1	—	2	37
	Bank loans.........	13	9	1	20	—	2	—	1	11	1	—	58
	Total....	116	72	42	101	16	18	6	26	106	9	17	529

* Number of workers.

initial capital required for the formation of new firms between the wars consisted of own funds. The results of the financing study just reported give only the number of cases in which own funds were involved, not the amounts. But a reasonable guess would be that no other source of funds can be compared in quantitative importance to that of the entre-preneurs' own contributions. This conclusion seems all the more war-ranted since an investigation focusing on cash positions and supplier credit (see below) really reveals only part of the truth concerning the entre-preneur's own contribution in a wider and in many ways more relevant sense. The fact is that the entrepreneur's *contribution of services in combination with small withdrawals for his own consumption* represented a very considerable source of savings invested in his firm in exceptionally many cases. Were it not for the entrepreneur's overtime labor, and often that of his wife and sometimes of his children as well, and were it not for the exceedingly small cash withdrawals from the firm for support of his household, very many new firms would never have gotten off the ground. Neither the cash put in by the entrepreneur nor the borrowed funds would have sufficed. The entrepreneur's own resources, therefore, were far more important than the tables indicate. This conclusion stands firm, even when account is taken of the fact that the figures given in the tables in all probability give a somewhat low estimate of borrowed funds (as shown in detail below).

Statements like the following, chosen as illustrations, were frequently made in the returned questionnaires:

The most important means of financing was that the partners, during the first few years, took as little remuneration as it was possible to live on in the 1937–41 period—maybe kr. 60 per week each.

The most important source of funds for the development of the firm was that all the partners invested the better part of their labor earnings in the firm to develop it as fast as possible.

The firm was started in 1931 with the purchase of a machine for a price of kr. 200, which was the only capital we had; the start began in a carriage entrance, and I went around on a bike selling since total sales in the first year amounted to kr. 250 total sales, which increased steadily to some one hundred thousand crowns.

With regard to the financing, I can report that I had kr. 500 in my own money and kr. 3,500 through a cosigned loan; for the rest you had to get by on promissory notes and by working 15 to 16 hours a day.

When my workers got kr. 100 a week, I myself got 50 for twice as long a workweek.

The business was started by investing both a loan and accumulated savings, and the later expansion of the business came about through the owner's wages where you would also have to count a fantastic amount of overtime put into the firm every year.

The following statement from an entrepreneur, who quit farming to start a small mechanical shop which he had developed until it employed some 30 workers, is typical of the reluctance to borrow expressed by many:

Would only other people agree that you get more satisfaction from the results of your own creativity, initiative, and thriftiness. . . . The setbacks were unbelievable. . . . Only my determination and stubbornness helped me to succeed in time.

This entrepreneur built on his own idea for feed elevators for farms.

The fear of loans is also expressed by another entrepreneur, who regarded it as most essential

. . . not to get into more debt than that you would be sure to have funds available when goods and wages were to be paid.

The new firm has grown almost exclusively on retained earnings. Since it became law, the right to accelerated depreciation has influenced the development of the business a good deal.

In March of 1923 the owners of the firm, four in number, agreed to build a factory for producing chairs as our specialty. The factory was built by ourselves on overtime after the day's work for another firm in the community. . . .

The development of the business was completely determined by the possibilities for self-financing.

Since I myself could go on working to 12 at night, the most productive machine could be kept going 16 hours a day.

One entrepreneur, who worked a very small business up to a clothing factory with 80 employees, writes:

Through enormous thriftiness, self-denial, and small demands on life it was possible to build up savings during the years before the war which have constituted 90 percent of the capital. In 1924, 1925, and 1926 the personal account shows kr. 1300, 1400, and 1500 in withdrawals to the then newly married family and the kr. 400 rent for a small attic apartment was met by the wife's work with alterations for the store.

The financing was conducted such that if we earned kr. 25, kr. 20 was used privately and kr. 5 was left in the business.

This firm today has several hundred employees.

Besides own funds, *bank loans* against cosignatures or collateral have, as shown by Table 17, also played an important role as a source of funds. Evidently such loans constituted some proportion of the initial capital in almost half of all cases. When bank loans entered as one of the several sources of funds, they were conspicuously often the most important (Table 19). It is worth noting that loans were "most important" in approximately as many cases as were own funds. Obviously it has been fairly common to obtain the main part of the initial capital through the banks with own funds complementing the bank loans. The investment of equity funds was often a prerequisite for obtaining loans. The collateral offered, and especially the cosignatures, which as a rule were made by relatives, were not regarded as sufficient. The cosignatures could often not be obtained if the borrower did not have at least some capital of his own to invest. The entrepreneur's own money per se, naturally, was not primarily important as formal collateral. But lenders and cosigners saw a certain real "insurance" in the fact that the borrower risked his own money. Above all, however, even a very modest sum of own funds, particularly if it came out of savings, was regarded as evidence of an economic bent and solid character. The well-known fact that loans were hard to obtain in the absence of simultaneous investment of own funds is reflected in the rare instances in which bank loans and loans from relatives and acquaintances appear as the only form of financing. Although bank loans, for example, were present in altogether 45 percent of all cases and, in addition, accounted for most of the capital in 13 percent of the cases, they were the single source of funds in only a very small percentage of cases.

TABLE 19
The Financing of Firm Formation. Survey of Most Important
Sources for Firms Utilizing More than One

			Number of Firms Utilizing Source*					
Industry	Own Funds	Issue of Shares	Jobber	Loans from Relatives or Friends	Bank Loans	Credit from Suppliers	Other	Total
13.......	28	3	2	10	24	14	1	82
14.......	24	4	6	12	28	14	4	92
15.......	10	1	2	8	12	—	—	33
Subtotal.......	62	8	10	30	64	28	5	207
31.......	56	5	—	15	72	19	1	168
35.......	10	2	—	3	5	1	—	21
Subtotal.......	66	7	—	18	77	20	1	189
4.......	8	2	—	—	6	3	3	22
54.......	12	8	—	9	11	5	1	46
55.......	43	6	5	18	32	8	2	114
Subtotal.......	55	14	5	27	43	13	3	160
7.......	11	3	1	2	4	1	—	22
Total..........	202	34	16	77	194	65	12	600

* Only firms indicating a single source as the most important one have been included. Some 60 firms have given two or more sources as the "most important." The most common combination has been one of various kinds of loans. The table, consequently, somewhat understates the number of cases in which loans have been the most important source.

A separate question, which the data do not answer, concerns the type of bank loans which predominated. Short-term promissory notes certainly account for a considerable part of "bank loans on cosignatures, mortgages, or other collateral." Apparently the promissory note has been underestimated as a source of funds, however. Thus it was ascertained in some of the interviews that such notes had not always been included in the entrepreneur's rough calculations concerning financing. This may have been partly due to the formulation of the questionnaires. But the main reason seems to have been that in responding the entrepreneurs were thinking mostly of relatively long-term loans and trade credit, and thus

TABLE 20

The Financing of Firm Formation. Survey of Only Source or Most Important
Source of Funds, Grouped according to Previous Occupation of Founder.*

	Number of Firms Utilizing Source				
Previous Occupation of Founder	*Own Funds*	*Issue of Shares*	*Loans from Relatives and Friends*	*Bank Loans*	*Total*
Workers, foremen, etc	268	8	81	179	536
Other	313	34	44	96	487
Not known	37	4	2	13	56
Total	618	46	127	288	1 079

* Firms indicating several sources as equally important, as well as firms not responding to question of most important sources, are not included.

forgot about promissory notes. But this affects the conclusions concerning the sources of initial capital relatively little. Promissory notes were most important as a source of short-term working capital in sales and distribution.[6]

Among the long-term sources of borrowed funds, *loans from relatives or acquaintances* were second in importance only to bank loans.[7] It may still be possible, albeit improbable, that *credits from raw material and equipment suppliers* were equally important.[8] This latter source of funds, reported in barely 18 percent of the cases, was most important in about 4 percent of the cases, and the only source in 1 percent or so of all cases; while the corresponding figures for loans from relatives and acquaintances, were 24 percent, about 5 percent, and 2 percent. But one gets the distinct impression that supplier credits have been forgotten in some instances, and that, therefore, their role has been underestimated. Such forgetfulness is not hard to explain—these loans were not in the

[6] Cf. A. Iveroth, *Småindustri och hantverk i Sverige*, IUI (Stockholm, 1943).

[7] Information concerning the economic situation of the relatives and friends from whom funds were borrowed was obtained in a large number of the interviews. There was surprisingly little reluctance to respond to these questions. The sporadic and, of course, frequently also uncertain character of the results does not permit very firm conclusions. One striking impression, however, was that as a rule the number of such creditors was small in each individual case. Only very infrequently did the founder make a sweep of the entire clan and circle of friends for potential creditors. Undoubtedly the most common arrangement was one in which only a single, well-off individual was approached (usually the founder's father, or one of his aunts, but only rarely a male relative).

[8] The cases in which equipment was rented have not been treated as comparable with loan contracts. Renting of machinery was common above all in the shoe industry, but this industry is not included in the study of financing. The rental system has naturally reduced initial capital requirements considerably where it has been used.

form of cash. But this source of error can hardly be so serious as to bias the overall picture of financing. Everything indicates that this source of funds was of limited importance, if for no other reason than that many entrepreneurs feared becoming dependent on the suppliers, as could easily happen.

Financing through jobbers is an arrangement related to that of supplier credit. The difference is that the jobber not only supplies the firm with inputs but also markets its outputs. This form of financing apparently did not play a major role between the wars. It was most important in the textile industry, more specifically in ready-made clothing and hosiery. The garment contractors in the clothing industry worked with precisely this kind of jobber financing but it also existed elsewhere. It was most prevalent in Borås and the Sjuhärads area where putting-out arrangements were traditional. Except for this part of the country, financing through jobber credit was of relatively little importance.

The category "other sources of financing" covers a multitude of ways of raising funds. The major role here was probably played by government lending for the encouragement of private enterprise, but lending by municipalities was also of some importance. But these two forms of lending still did not add up to any major proportion of total initial capital.[9] Municipal lending probably increased somewhat in importance during the 1940's, when municipalities engaged in more determined policies of attracting new industry. In this period, the lending of various manufacturers' associations also became of some significance.[10]

Further study of Table 17 reveals that investments of own cash were made with the same relative frequency in rural areas and small towns as in the larger urbanized areas, while bank loans, in particular, were far more common outside the cities. Among the founders of new firms, former workers were especially dependent on bank loans and on loans from relatives and acquaintances (Table 20). That the new firms in the relatively larger urban areas were less dependent on borrowed funds was primarily due to the fact that these manufacturing firms more frequently grew out of commercial establishments. Loans are relatively seldom observed among the new urban firms in the ready-made clothing and light chemicals industries, where this pattern of development was common. In such cases, the commercial enterprise usually possessed sufficient resources for financing the manufacturing activity without recourse

---

[9] The lending of the national government became important mainly after 1933. The total sum of such credits, however, did not amount to more than some tens of millions of Swedish crowns during the thirties. Most of this went to supporting older firms. Concerning the nature and extent of these support measures, cf. *Betänkande med förslag till ordnande av kreditgivnings- och rådgivningsverksamhet för hantverk och småindustri samt bildande av företagsnämnder, SOU* (1946, No. 22).

[10] Cf. Chap. 15, p. 368.

to significant borrowing. As a rule, the many worker-entrepreneurs had more limited resources. The woodworking industries, in which this category of entrepreneurs played the major role, is the industry in which the new firms showed the greatest reliance on bank loans. The lack of own funds was, as already mentioned, compensated for as far as possible through the entrepreneurs' investments of their own labor.

It is unfortunately quite impossible to throw much light on the financing of the further *development of firms*. A comparative, and quantitatively reasonably accurate, study of this problem would require an extraordinary amount of work and constitute a separate research task. This tempting research problem has been touched upon here only to the extent of investigating the flotation of new shares issued to natural individuals in the 1921–39 period.[11] New issues which were not of this type have been subtracted on the basis of summaries of the National Patent and Registration Office's data on the manufacturing sector. Thus many new issues connected with mergers or the formation of subsidiaries have been eliminated; neither have new issues connected with financial reconstructions been included when they involved just the conversion of outside capital to equity. The data which have been utilized were obtained from the Swedish Shareowner's Handbook (*AU*) and from the archives of the National Patent and Registration Office. Information on individual cases was also obtained in different ways. The estimates are obviously subject to a considerable margin of error, but since subtractions have been made only in cases which were certain, the final figures are without doubt on the high side. Funds added to the capital of firms in connection with their incorporation, on the other hand, have not been included, although, to some extent, it may have been a question of additions contributed by outside individuals.[12]

With respect to new issues by existing corporations, the total sum obtained from natural individuals for the 1921–39 period is estimated at about kr. 500 millions. This estimate gives, then, a figure on the high side. Approximately 80 percent of the total refers to the 1921–31 period, while only 20 percent, or kr. 100 million, was raised in this way in the 1932–39 period. The importance of new issues of this type declined drastically in 1932, and the low figures continued even through the boom of the later 1930's. Of the kr. 400 million of new issues floated between 1921 and 1931, a few large firms in the engineering industries, and Svenska Tändsticksaktiebolaget (Swedish Match Co.), were responsible for more than 50 percent. To a large extent these shares were floated abroad,

---

[11] Thus the inflationary years of 1919 and 1920 have been excluded because the significance of the issues during these years is very hard to determine in the individual instances. Fraudulent schemes were common, for example.

[12] Much the greater part of the value of such new issues, however, surely did not constitute an injection of new capital.

and the issues were often obtained for the expansion of Swedish manufacturing firms in foreign countries. It has unfortunately not been possible
to obtain a reliable estimate of the amounts which in this manner were
neither raised in Sweden nor used for the development of the firms in
Sweden. But even a very rough calculation suffices to show that the
amounts must have been large. Thus the amounts subscribed to by natural
individuals in Sweden, and used for the domestic development of Swedish
corporations, apparently cannot have averaged more than some 10 million
crowns per year from 1921–31 and much less than that from 1932 on.

Obviously, these funds amounted to an insignificant proportion of the
total capital invested in the development of firms. Study of the primary
data also shows clearly that the firms newly established in the interwar
period financed a particularly small part of their development in this
way. The data also show that the forest industries were responsible for
the major part of these issues, with the engineering industries being
second in importance. Remaining industries, including textiles where
family firms were the rule, raised only very small sums through issues
of shares to private individuals for the financing of their development
within Sweden. It was, moreover, primarily the older, large firms, which
were quoted on the Stock Exchange, that could attract development
capital in this way. This was even more true of bond issues, where the
cooperation of the banks was of decisive importance.

As noted in previous chapters, most firms started on a small scale
and grew hardly at all, or only rather slowly. A closer study yields
the strong impression that the pace of expansion for these firms seldom
was allowed to become faster than what could be largely financed
through retained earnings or temporary loans, i.e., without significantly
increasing long-term debt or watering equity. As a rule, expansion was
limited to that which allowed the firm to count on reducing debt incurred
for that purpose to the rather low level regarded as "safe" within a
few years. It is easily established that entrepreneurial behavior frequently
was determined by this aversion to large indebtedness and, in family-
owned firms, to flotation of shares to outsiders, though it is very difficult
to distinguish such cases from those in which it was impossible to obtain
loans or subscriptions of equity capital on reasonable terms. The experiences of the crisis in the early 1920's in particular had contributed to
increased caution toward indebtedness. It is evident, however, that
formally short-term, but regularly renewed, bank loans were of extraordinary importance, especially in the 1930's, although firms seldom
would finance a very rapid expansion entirely in this way. The most
important forms of bank loans in this connection were the so-called account credits against cosignatures, real estate mortgages, and loans on
collateral in inventory.

The recruitment of entrepreneurs in all probability played a part in
this aversion toward financing expansion to any greater extent through

shares or large loans. In many cases, of course, the opportunity of doing so did not present itself. As noted in previous chapters, workers and persons of similar background frequently started and operated their businesses on the "livelihood principle." In many such cases, the entrepreneur simply did not desire any great expansion of the firm and, consequently, had no need to raise large amounts of funds, either through loans or sale of shares. But among the many who were not averse to expansion per se, the workers particularly did not want to borrow too much money. Their attitude was often more that of skilled craftsmen than of businessmen in their dislike of becoming dependent on outsiders, in this or any other way. Thus, these entrepreneurs preferred a stationary business or one growing at whatever rate could be attained by largely plowing back earnings. In other instances, however, it was undoubtedly more difficult for a relatively impecunious worker than for others to finance a large and/or rapidly growing enterprise, since he could not offer lenders the security that, for example, a commercial establishment, a salaried position, or even just a known name might provide. As indicated above, it was evidently not too difficult to borrow small sums to start a new firm, but it was usually harder to obtain larger amounts for expansion.

The fact that the great majority of the progressive firms showed remarkably continuous expansion is a strong indication of the major role of self-financing in combination with relatively modest account credits, short-term borrowing on notes and bills, and so forth. A survey of the data on the entire population of firms shows that approximately 80 percent of the moderately or strongly porgressive firms increased their work forces at a very steady pace. Only a small percentage had such a pronounced "stepwise" development that financing through retained earnings and relatively short-term and/or small loans seems out of the question.

Starts on a large scale—with the intention of immediately or shortly employing at least 100 workers—were relatively few. It should be emphasized that almost all of these were cases of subsidiaries started by existing firms, and that the rather few cases of new firms growing to considerable size were largely financed by plowing back earnings.[13] It is a striking fact that those large-scale starts and/or cases of rapid expansion which were not financed in this manner were as a rule financed by one individual or a very few persons. In other words, only infrequently was a firm started on a large scale and/or expanded rapidly by numerous investors contributing capital. Furthermore, the number of firms which started on a large scale and/or grew rapidly was small in comparison with the period before World War I. These observations raise the question of whether the *distribution of income* had shifted so as to make it more difficult than previously to raise capital.

---

[13] Formation of new firms through the creation of subsidiaries and through rapid expansion of acquired firms could in many instances just as well be labeled "firm development," financed by plowing back retained earnings.

FIGURE 25
Number of Persons in Each Income Class in 1912,
1920, and 1930. 1912 Crowns

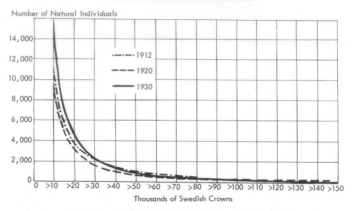

SOURCES: *Folkräkningen* (1920): V, p .94. *Folkräkningen* I (1930): VIII, p. 84.

In trying to form an opinion on this question, one immediately runs into severe problems. The picture that can be obtained of such shifts is only a rough approximation. The results of the calculations attempted for the years 1912, 1920, and 1930 are shown in Figures 25 and 26. Figure 26 indicates the aggregate amounts earned by all persons with income exceeding the indicated figures. Figure 25 shows the number of persons earning such incomes.

FIGURE 26
Total Incomes in Each Income Class in 1912,
1920, and 1930. 1912 Crowns

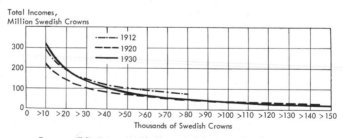

SOURCES: *Folkräkningen*(1920): V, p. 94; *Folkräkningen*(1930): VIII, p. 84.

The income-distribution figures for 1912, 1920 and 1930 have been taken from the 1920 and 1930 census data. The 1920 census includes a series calculated on the basis of the tax returns for 1913 and adjusted for the ⅟₆₀th of net worth there included.[14] Apart from the problem of taking changes

---

[14] Cf. the population census for 1920, *Folkräkningen 1920*, Vol. V., p. 95.

in the purchasing power of the *krona* into account (see below), the main problem with these data is the insufficient comparability of the data on the distribution of low incomes. Since such data have not been included in Figures 25 and 26, however, this source of error is of no concern here. It should also be noted that municipal taxes were deductible in all these years. Since taxes other than the municipal ones have not been subtracted, and state taxes were raised and made considerably more progressive between 1912 and 1930, the "after tax" figures for the upper income groups are too high relative to those for lower income groups, particularly in the 1920 and 1930 series. In the present context, adjustment for all taxes ought, of course, to have been made, but the immensely complicated calculations required for this purpose would have yielded only illusory accuracy and they have therefore been omitted. Actually, the neglect of these adjustments is of little significance since they undoubtedly would only serve to strengthen the conclusions which the figures permit us to draw (see below).

The data for 1920 and 1930 have been recalculated in terms of 1912 prices in order to remove the most important cause of insufficient comparability in the data as they appear in the census.[15] The census figures have been deflated with the help of the data on the development of living costs to be found in *Cost of Living in Sweden* (Stockholm Economic Studies, Vol. 2, p. 189). The margin of error involved is, of course, considerable, but it is still reduced relative to that of the unadjusted figures. The figures for 1920 are the most suspect, since the cost-of-living index rose strongly in that year but reflected very uneven price developments which were not equally relevant to all income groups. Discretion dictates, therefore, that weight be given only to the 1912-versus-1930 comparison. With respect to those two years, there is nothing to indicate that the increase in the index exaggerates the rise in living costs of lower income groups relative to that of higher income groups to such an extent that the comparison becomes seriously biased. Actually, there is little to indicate that the bias is necessarily in this direction. Some calculations, reported below, have nonetheless been made in order to show how large the margin of error in the index series may be without significantly changing the main conclusions of the investigation. The curve connecting the points calculated in the figures have been drawn freehand, a procedure which cannot have introduced any significant error.

It appears that, between 1912 and 1930, the number of persons with incomes in excess of kr. 35,000 in 1912 Sw. crowns declined somewhat even before all other taxes than the municipal ones.[16] The 1930 curve showing the sum of all incomes in excess of each indicated amount dips below the corresponding curve for 1912 already before the kr. 25,000

---

[15] Since the data on the distribution of wealth cover a very diverse spectrum of stores of value differing in their sensitivity to changes in the money price level, it is impossible to deflate the available time series, and a comparative study of the wealth distribution has therefore been out of the question.

[16] It is naturally the absolute number of large incomes and the aggregate total of incomes in the upper brackets that are relevant to the question as formulated.

point is reached. In order to be sure not to exaggerate, one may calculate with an error of some 20 units in the cost-of-living index. While this leads to a reduction in the number of persons only at very high income figures, the reduction in the sum of their incomes sets in at about kr. 40,000–45,000.[17] Again, only municipal taxes have been deducted. *There is a rather evident decline, therefore, in the funds at the disposal of persons in high income brackets, i.e., among those persons best able to invest large amounts in the formation or rapid expansion of firms.* This is really remarkable in view of the rapid growth of national income during the period in question. The causes behind this development will not be discussed here since it would lead us too far afield. It should only be noted that, aside from economic developments in general, one circumstance which probably played a part was that large wealth owners divided up their assets (e.g., among relatives) for tax purposes.

All this does not by itself mean that the difficulties of raising large amounts of capital among private individuals with high incomes actually increased. It only means that the changes in income distribution apparently acted in this direction. It is possible that the *propensity* to supply large firms with start or development capital may have increased so as to compensate wholly or partly for the reduced ability to do so. In all probability, however, the case was just the opposite.

During the greater part of the 1920's, short planning horizons and a rather dark pessimism characterized the business world. This was true in part in the absolute sense that one despaired of any recovery at all for several important industries following the serious crisis at the beginning of the decade. The future, particularly, of the iron and steel industry and of the lumber mill industry was regarded as dark. More importantly, however, pessimism was pervasive in the more relative sense that businessmen perceived comparatively few opportunities for quick and large returns to industrial enterpreneurship in general. One must remember that the decades from the late 19th century up to the outbreak of World War I, as well as the war years, had been spectacular times, offering very large profit opportunities in executing large industrial projects and in completing economic development blocks. Large fortunes were made in iron and steel, in lumber milling, and in the pulp industry.

There is not the least doubt that the situation in the 1920's appeared quite different. It evidently took some time before entrepreneurs and investors could adjust their expectations to the narrower profit margins. These narrower profit margins were not just the result of negative development effects, and so forth, which characterized the situation, but were also due to the fact that cartels had not as yet been organized nor had

---

[17] Cf. E. Browaldh, "Det riskvilliga kapitalet," i *Företagande, ekonomi, och teknik* (Stockholm, 1949).

other measures been taken that could improve returns, at least in the short run. It was only in the 1930's that profit margins were improved in some areas, partly as a consequence of greater success with such organizations than previously.[18] The mood which one finds expressed in organs most representative of the groups under discussion, such as *Affärsvärlden* (*The Business World*) and the larger daily newspapers, leaves no room for doubt on this point. Nor was this mood occasioned just by the acute business difficulties. The world situation, and above all the domestic political situation, were other influences. The unsettled world political situation and the problems in Germany were dampening factors. The eight-hour day was the subject of many dark reflections. How great the difficulties which this reform brought in its train actually were, is irrelevant here. In principle, one should look at the competition due mostly to German dumping in the same light. There is no doubt that foreign competition was fierce, but the significant fact for this study is simply that the business world perceived it as a serious threat to the Swedish economy in general and to the manufacturing sector in particular.

It thus seems evident that the acute difficulties and the pessimistic mood which characterized both decades must have dampened any willingness to invest large sums in starting or developing new firms. At the same time, the ability to undertake such investments was also reduced, to judge from the calculations reported above. In addition, the 1920's offered more opportunities for less risky placement of funds than had been available earlier in the industrialized era. The bond market had grown and become well organized. The effective yield on government bonds never fell below 4.5 percent in the 1920's, nor did bank deposit rates go below 4 percent. The larger corporations which were quoted on the stock exchange also, as a rule, came to offer a fairly high and certain return. There was for that matter a growing range of new investment opportunities outside the manufacturing sector proper as, for example, in sundry service activities, bus transportation, and the entertainment industry.

In summary, it is quite conceivable that increasing scarcity of capital for the formation of large enterprises or the rapid expansion of firms has been an important factor in the picture of firm formation and development outlined in earlier chapters. One can at least state with a good deal of confidence that the above observations with regard to shifts in the distribution of income, of changing profit opportunities, and so forth, are not inconsistent with such a possibility. There is, on the other hand, nothing to indicate that these shifts in income distribution limited the opportunities for starting and relatively slowly developing small businesses. Nor can business taxes have been very significant in the interwar

---

[18] Cf. *SOU* (1940, No. 35).

period. The tax laws did not particularly favor the formation of new, stationary, small firms, nor did they impede the rapid development of enterprises.

While it is conceivable that the changes in income distribution contributed to the emergence of the typical interwar picture of firm formation and development, this does not necessarily mean that they were the decisive factor. A continuing theme emerging from the analysis of previous chapters has been the presence of strong forces acting in this direction *quite apart from any effect that the income distributional changes may have had*. For one industry after another it has been possible to show that, apart from the financing problem, the opportunities for starting new, large firms were relatively limited for several reasons, which varied from case to case. It was also shown that conditions favored stationary, small firms and high rates of entry of such firms. At the same time, the basis for the recruitment of entrepreneurs was more and more extended to population groups with somewhat different attitudes toward entrepreneurial activity from those prevailing in the groups from which entrepreneurs had primarily been recruited. These attitudes were such that the demand for large financial resources, concentrated in a few hands, for the formation or development of firms was not particularly evident among enterprise founders belonging to this new group.

Thus, one must conclude that several different factors appear to have acted together in creating the industrial entrepreneurial activity which characterized the interwar period. It is impossible, unfortunately, to determine the relative importance of these factors. With regard to financing opportunities, one can state quite confidently that "the ceiling was lower" after World War I than it had been before. This was because the banks were unable to assume such large risks in financing industry as they had previously and because of the decline in the number of people in high-income brackets and in the aggregate after-tax income of such people. The question is whether "height of the ceiling" actually was a limiting factor or whether it was merely a factor that might have been important had the circumstances been different. This question cannot be conclusively answered. It would be difficult to answer even if a considerably more detailed study of the period had been made.

15 The Geographical Aspects: Some Brief Remarks

A. The Questions and the Data

As background for a survey of the geographical distribution of the formation, development, and disappearance of firms, a statistical picture of changes in population agglomerations in the interwar period is desirable. There are great difficulties, however, in obtaining the statistics needed for a detailed analysis and which, at the same time, would be appropriate in terms of the plan of the present work. The easily available statistics on the distribution of the population between rural areas and cities are unsatisfactory, even when adjusted as far as possible for the changes in administrative procedures and boundaries which took place during the period studied. To arrive at a more detailed analysis, one must first substitute the concept "(urban) agglomeration" for the concept "city." But this concept must be defined and differentiated in a different way from that of the official demographic statistics, which contain certain data with regard to "agglomerations" for 1930 and 1935, and to some extent also for 1920.[1] The questions to which the data are to be applied

[1] There are, furthermore, many sources of error hidden in the published figures, particularly for 1920. The statistics on population agglomerations contained in the official censuses and the "agglomeration register" assembled by the Department of Geography at the Stockholm School of Commerce (available, for example, from Industriens Produktionsråd, Stockholm) do distinguish between population agglomerations even within the same municipality, but a more thorough analysis would still require further special processing of the basic data. Borderlines for the agglomerations have been rather arbitrarily drawn in many cases. This has caused some problems, particularly since the automobile and bicycle have served to disperse the population geographically without causing corresponding weakening

should also be made more explicit with less concentration on mere numbers of residents.[2]

Thus the more explicit statement of the questions and the special adaptation of the statistical primary material should start from a definition and differentiation of the concept of "an agglomeration" in its geographic, economic, and social contexts. One can then raise the question of the extent to which the population movements between the wars led to the growth of those agglomerations of different types and sizes which were in existence at the beginning of the period, and to what extent they gave rise to new agglomerations or, perhaps, dissolved old ones. An investigation of this kind should, of course, be combined with an analysis of changes in the occupational distribution of the population. For the present work, the next step would be to relate this to the analysis of the formation, development, and disappearance of firms. The geographical aspects of these problems should then be studied statistically in an analogous manner, i.e., without regard for administrative boundaries. This would make feasible an analysis of the relationships between population movements and the development of agglomerations, taking into account the changes in their economic-geographic structure, on the one hand, and the formation, development, and disappearance of firms, with all the forces underlying these processes, on the other. This could lead further than an analysis relying on the published IS data, which only give the number of firms at various points in time.

But an investigation along these lines must remain outside the purview of the present work. It would involve too large a research task, primarily because it would require extensive scrutiny and special processing of the raw data underlying the available demographic statistics. Thus it becomes necessary to simplify drastically both the questions and the empirical task. Although this naturally makes the value of the investigation rather limited, it still seems possible to draw attention to some rather important development trends.

As a point of departure, one can state that population movements

---

of economic ties. Cf. M. Overton, "Sveriges icke-administrativa agglomererade orter," *Svensk Geografisk Årsbok* (1937), pp. 146 ff. and *idem*, "De svenska tätorternas hittillsvarande och framtida utveckling," *Svensk Geografisk Årsbok* (1941), pp. 169 ff. Also W. William-Olsson, *Stockholms framtida utveckling*, monographs publ. by the city government of Stockholm (Stockholm, 1941). Overton and William-Olsson provide a good survey of the weaknesses of the data and of the statistical problems involved.

[2] Considerable progress has been made in recent years through concentrating the study of demographic migrations on intensive analyses of the *moves* of households. So far, however, such studies have only been made for certain limited areas. Cf. J. Wallander, *Flykten från skogsbygden*, IUI (Stockholm, 1948); T. Hägerstrand, "En landsbygdsbefolknings flyttningsrörelser," *Svensk Geografisk Årsbok* (1947); and *idem*, "Flyttningarna till och från Simrishamn under 1900-talet," in *Simrishamn med omland* (Lund, 1949).

during the interwar period led to increased geographic concentration in the sense that the population, and particularly the productive population, decreased in most of the areas that can be labeled as "purely rural," while that of agglomerations increased.[3] Taken in a different sense, however, the proposition is not true, since the pattern of settlement in many agglomerations became more dispersed than previously.[4] Even though, for reasons already given, those investigations that have so far been published and deal with more than certain limited areas give but a very schematic picture of developments, the conclusions formulated in these very general terms are undoubtedly valid.

In order to obtain a better basis for comparisons with the results of our study of the formation, development, and disappearance of firms, some reworking, albeit very rough, of the demographic statistics has been done. The objective has been to trace the development of total population, and of the number of people employed in industry and crafts, in different categories of communities. The communities have been grouped according to their population in 1928–29. The categories are: rural areas and small communities with a population of less than 10,000; communities with 10,000–20,000 people; with 20,000–100,000 people; and with more than 100,000.[5] Towns with 10,000–20,000 people are referred to as "medium size" in what follows, and those with 20,000–100,000 are classed as "large." Towns with a population in excess of 100,000 are referred to as "very large," "largest," or "large cities," and so forth. The term "major towns" is used to include all communities with more than 10,000 people.

To the extent that administrative boundaries were changed, the data have been adjusted so as to refer to the boundaries in effect in 1940.[6]

---

[3] Cf. W. William-Olsson, *op. cit.*, and *idem*, "Utvecklingen av tätorter och landsbygd i Sverlge," *Ymer* (1938).

[4] Cf. Overton, *op. cit.*, *Svensk Geografisk Årsbok* (1941).

[5] The previously mentioned potential errors, which may have arisen through the dispersion of the population beyond administrative boundaries, are probably of relatively minor significance for agglomerations with a population in excess of 10,000. The investigation has taken into account the incorporations which took place prior to 1940 (see below). To a large extent, these incorporations concerned exactly "outskirts" of the type that had grown up due, among other things, to the automobile and the bicycle. The only outlying areas that have not been thus incorporated have always been of rather little importance to the municipalities in question.

[6] In some instances, only parts of an earlier administrative area were incorporated. This has caused considerable difficulties since population figures are available only for the earlier administrative areas as units. Population growth rates in these parts up to the date of incorporation have then been assumed to be the same as in the community into which they were absorbed. This assumption is probably unrealistic but is apt to be less so than the alternative assumption i.e., that population growth had been the same as for the entire administrative area from which these parts were absorbed. The chosen alternative will however make for little error in the overall result since the incorporated areas have been insignificant in relation

The next step has been to study the distribution of the formation, development, and disappearance of firms over the corresponding areas. In so doing, the statistics on the number of "continuing," "new," and "discontinued" firms, as of the end of 1918 and of 1939, had to be estimated in a rather rough manner. Thus some firms which were located in the immediate vicinity of a major town, but in a rural area in the administrative sense, have been reported as located in rural areas or small towns, even though from every basic economic point of view they belonged to the larger town and perhaps the majority of their employees were living within the boundaries of the town. In the same way, firms that operated within the administrative boundaries of a large town, but from an economic-geographic standpoint rather far from the area of dense settlement, have been recorded as located in large towns. But this cannot cause any great error in the results of the investigation, given the circumstances that actually prevailed. This is evident from a study of the primary data. Finally, it should be emphasized that the statistical data and the analysis pertain only to the industries included in our two sample studies.

B. Results and Analysis

According to the special reworking of the demographic statistics, *total population* expanded most in the largest towns, not only in absolute but also in relative terms. The larger the towns were at the beginning of the interwar period, the more they grew. Actually, the smallest agglomerations—for which it has not been possible to get specific data—probably grew at a higher rate than the larger ones.[7] The labor-force data behave in much the same way. The results of this reworking of the demographic statistics are shown in Table 21.

Entry into the industries covered in this work was, on the other hand, highest in rural areas and small towns, not only in relation to the number of firms in existence by the end of 1918 but also in absolute terms. The only outstanding exception to this general tendency toward a greater number of new firms relative to the initial number in small rather than

---

to the population of the units doing the incorporating. The same holds for the necessary guesses about the occupational distribution in the areas incorporated. These guesses consist of the assumption that the occupational structure has developed in the same way as in the incorporating unit. For the 1920–30 period, it has been necessary to use this assumption also where an entire municipality was incorporated, since occupational data for 1920 exist only for towns and "hundreds" (*härader*). Since the particular administrative form—"town," "municipality," etc.—is of no significance in context, it has not been necessary to adjust for changes in these forms. In the calculations concerning the Stockholm and Gothenburg "metropolitan areas," the areas "added" to Stockholm or Gothenburg proper (except for the Stockholm suburbs of Lindingö och Djursholm) have been treated as if incorporated.

[7] Cf. Overton, *op. cit., Svensk Geografisk Årsbok* (1937).

TABLE 21
Total Population and Employment in Industry and Crafts, 1920, 1930, and 1940

Rural and Urban Areas according to 1929 Population	Population of Communities (Using 1940 Boundaries) as of December 31			Employed in Industry and Crafts		
	1920	*1930*	*1940*	*1920*	*1930*	*1940*
Total number:						
Under 10 000...	4 371 722	4 419 065	4 377 600	469 199	532 384	597 993
10 000— 20 000...	265 812	284 141	315 001	54 418	56 172	64 766
20 000—100 000...	461 682	497 226	577 152	108 999	120 993	146 412
Over 100 000...	805 273	941 759	1 101 679	175 625	217 450	241 182
Total.........	*5 904 489*	*6 142 191*	*6 371 432*	*808 241*	*926 999*	*1 050 353*
Index 1920 = 100:						
Under 10 000...	100	101	100	100	113	127
10 000— 20 000...	100	107	119	100	103	119
20 000 -100 000...	100	108	125	100	111	134
Over 100 000...	100	117	137	100	124	137
Total.........	*100*	*104*	*108*	*100*	*115*	*130*

in large towns is the capital goods industry. A more detailed study reveals a very high rate of firm formation in many towns. It is evident, on the other hand, that older manufacturing firms in the existing large towns and cities expanded greatly, while commerce, services, administration, and so forth, also grew particularly rapidly in these communities. Among both new and old firms a relatively greater number were progressive in the major towns than in small towns and rural areas, although the difference was not great. Finally, it should be noted that the new firms of the smallest initial size were, as a rule, not started in major towns (see Appendix 8 in Swedish edition).

Certain parts of the country show particularly lively firm formation. This is especially noticeable for large parts of the provinces of Småland and Västergötland. The Götaland provinces generally were foremost in this respect. Firm formation in Norrland, on the other hand, was relatively insignificant during almost the entire interwar period. Norrland's share of the population of firms declined between 1919 and 1939.[8] The new firms that appeared were typically formed to meet local demands almost exclusively, while the older firms concentrated on exports. For that matter, many of the new firms were located in the county of Kopparberg—for example, in Malung—which is not generally considered part of Norrland. But there are also areas in other parts of Norrland with small-scale industries, sometimes of old origin, where numerous firms were started in the latter half of the 1930's. This was true especially

---

[8] Had the circular saws been included, however, the picture might well have been different.

of the areas around the northern trunk line of the state railways. Many of these firms remained so small, however, that they were not reported in *IS* and consequently are not included in our data. The small business areas of Norrland do not compare in importance with the industry concentrations in Götaland. In the 1940's, however, there was a rather remarkable rise in the formation rate of small firms, partly as a consequence of the financing and other support activities provided by the manufacturers' associations which were established from the late 1930's onward. This very lively formation of new firms has been of great importance to the solution of the employment problems typical of Norrland and for the economic and social life of the communities involved.[9]

Firm formation in these areas deserves a detailed study. Such a study would not just add local color but would contribute to our general understanding of many of the novel trends in the formation of new firms in the Swedish interwar period. But to the extent that such an intensive investigation has not been offered in Chapters 12 through 14—and the special geographical aspects were ignored there—it must be regarded as outside the purview of this work. The main objective here has been to survey the industrial transformation and the formation, development, and disappearance of firms in the country as a whole. The discussion must therefore be limited to a few observations concerning some particularly characteristic development features in certain industries.

In general, old centers retained their positions even when the industry in question spread to all parts of the country between the wars. This does not mean that the locational patterns of many industries did not undergo significant changes.

In *iron, steel, and metals manufacturing*, numerous new firms appeared, relatively evenly dispersed outside the industry's old centers. The lively and important formation of new firms along the western trunk line in the counties of Älvsborg and Skaraborg is particularly noteworthy, since previously the number of firms in these areas was not especially large. But the old centers—particularly Eskilstuna, the Stockholm metropolitan area, Malmö, and the Västbo district of Jönköping county—continued to experience considerable entry throughout the entire interwar period. In Göteborg, on the other hand, there were few new firms of any importance. It is remarkable how few of the new Eskilstuna firms grew into the larger size classes. Since the large and medium-sized old firms generally expanded vigorously, the entry share for Eskilstuna was conspicuously small. It was considerably higher in the other centers of iron, steel, and metals manufacturing, as, for example, the Stockholm metropolitan area.

The old center which grew most rapidly in terms of both labor force

---

[9] E. Lindberg, "Västerbotten lever upp," *Industria* (1946), No. 7.

and number of firms was the Västbo district, with its two population agglomerations in Gnosjö and Anderstorp. This district exhibited an almost unique concentration of lively entry. Many of these firms were too small to be reported in *IS* and, consequently, to be included here. They were almost always started by employees of older firms in the area or by sons, often young, of small farmers. The start was always on a very small scale, and most often under primitive conditions. While they remained small, many of these firms nonetheless developed into highly mechanized and specialized operations producing sundry minor iron and metals manufactures, often on a subcontracting basis.[10] In general, these small businesses were very sound, primarily because of their extraordinary flexibility in adjusting to changing market conditions and cycles and because of the tenacity typical of worker-owned firms in general. This rather remarkable example of small-scale entrepreneurial activity lacked almost completely any elements of agreements in restraint of trade. Over a whole range of products, it undoubtedly meant fierce competition for segments of the older iron, steel, and metals manufacturing industry, both at home and abroad. It conquered the better part of the Swedish market for certain products while sometimes also working for export.

In contrast to this industry, the *mechanical engineering industry* did not have any large or otherwise noteworthy centers outside the larger towns and the cities. Nor has this been changed by the appearance of many, mostly small, new firms. Many of the entrants were, however, dispersed over large parts of the country, which meant a certain change in the locational pattern. It was not common for old firms in small or medium-sized towns to spawn a number of small firms through "desertions" among their engineers, supervisors, foremen, or workers. This was probably due, at least in part, to the progressiveness of the majority of the big firms. The opportunities for advancement offered by these firms were relatively good, so their employees had less reason to start on their own than those in more stationary companies. During the 1940's,

---

[10] The historical preconditions in early times for the industrialization of this district have been investigated in C. Härenstam, "Järn- och metallmanufakturer i västra Småland," *Svensk Geografisk Årsbok* (1942). The remarkable thing is that it is impossible to point to any particular natural advantages. That opportunities for profitable farming were lacking has indeed contributed to this development, but such opportunities were, after all, missing in many other areas as well. Originally, however, this industry developed out of craft-organized production for the firearms factory in Jönköping and out of wire-drawing which became increasingly important as the manufacture of guns declined and was industrialized in Huskvarna. When, in a later period, wire-drawing also became industrialized within large firms, the Västbo manufacturers gradually converted to the production of sundry, small items in which wire was used as an essential semimanufactured input. The present character of the Västbo district has been studied also by A. Iveroth in his *Småindustri och hantverk i Sverige* (Stockholm, 1943).

on the other hand, it appears that the lengthy inflation in many areas did cause such desertions from the big companies outside the major towns and cities, since inflationary conditions, particularly in certain periods, led to relatively severe shortages of certain products that were well suited to small businesses.

In the two main branches of the *woodworking industries*, furniture and construction joinery, desertion of this kind was common between the wars. The firms deserted were often stationary or regressive ones located outside the major towns, so the concentration of the industry to the old "rural centers" became even more pronounced than it had been at the end of World War I, while at the same time new such centers emerged. On the other hand, the number of furniture manufacturers in major towns declined. Thus, the shift of the industry from larger to smaller towns and to rural areas which had begun toward the end of the 19th century continued in the interwar period.[11] The three counties of Småland and particularly the county of Jönköping became steadily more prominent, even though there was very lively entry in most other parts of the country as well. Even in Norrland, a relatively large number of new joineries were started, particularly along the northern trunk line. This fact should be seen in the context of the otherwise rather modest number of new firms in Norrland in the interwar period, if one ignores the many small, mobile circular saws, and the many firms in the concrete products, brick, and soft drink industries which often were so small that they have not been included either in *IS* or here. These Norrland firms, however, were mostly construction joineries which grew up in connection with lively local or regional construction activity and often produced some furniture on the side.

While, by the end of the interwar period, the locational pattern of construction joineries shows a center in Småland which did not exist 25 years earlier, in general the firms in this branch became even more widely dispersed over most of the country than was the case with the furniture factories (see Maps pp. 371–372). The construction joineries relied on a local or regional market more often than did the furniture factories. In both branches, there emerged some more modern firms which expanded rapidly and which, in contrast to the majority of firms in earlier periods, spread their products over large areas and even the entire country. It is also characteristic of the construction joineries that in competing with these modern firms they managed to survive in the major towns for a longer time than did the furniture factories. The concentration of small businesses found in the parish of Kyrkefalla in Skaraborg county, with its center at Tibro, is characteristic of the furniture industry and is without counterpart in the construction joinery branch. In many

---

[11] Cf. Chap. 5.

MAP 1
The Furniture Industry in 1939

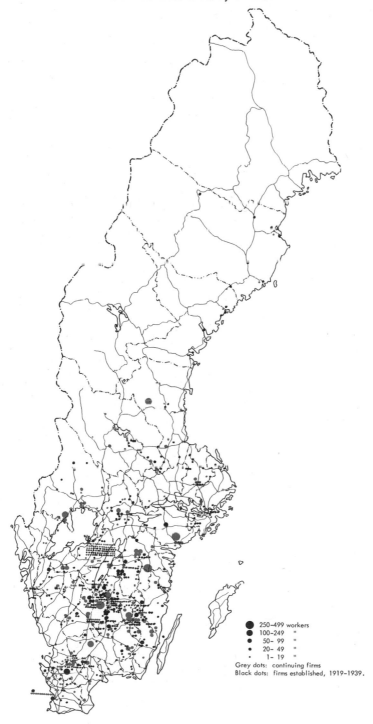

250–499 workers
100–249   "
50– 99   "
20– 49   "
1– 19   "

Grey dots: continuing firms
Black dots: firms established, 1919–1939.

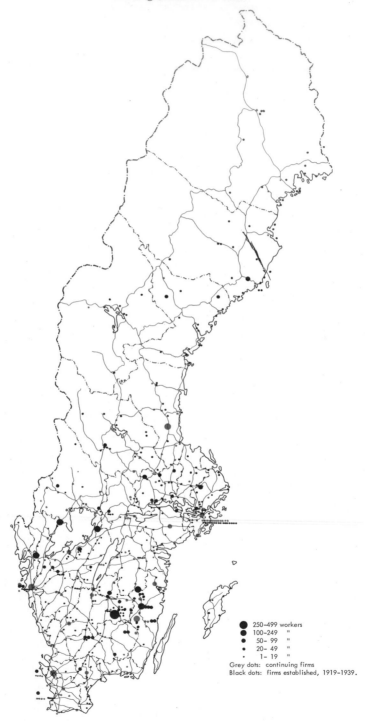

MAP 2
Building Joineries in 1939

● 250–499 workers
● 100–249 "
● 50– 99 "
• 20– 49 "
· 1– 19 "
Grey dots: continuing firms
Black dots: firms established, 1919–1939.

respects, Kyrkefalla parish presents a remarkable analogy to the iron, steel, and metals manufacturing district of Västbo in the county of Jönköping. Both specialization and mechanization were often carried rather far. But most of the firms were still small and stationary in terms of number of employees.[12]

A still more noteworthy shift in the locational pattern occurred in the *ready-made clothing industry*. For reasons explained in Chapter 12, this industry was concentrated in the three major cities of Stockholm, Göteborg, and Malmö—in that order   and in Borås when World War I ended. During the interwar period, a very large number of new clothing manufacturing firms were started, not just in these cities but also all over the country, with the exception of Norrland. The exceptionally large number of new firms in the Sjuhärads district around Borås is most conspicuous in this connection. These were frequently started in small agglomerations or in purely rural areas. Here the formation of firms meant the industrialization of a cottage industry, in the sense that production in the home disappeared and was replaced by small industrial shops. To a large extent, these firms began as garment contractors, but gradually many of them achieved a more independent status, sometimes doing some contracting on the side. The reasons for this industrialization, which took place mainly in the 1930's, have been analyzed in Chapter 12.[13] In those other parts of the country where new firms emerged, this industrialization of an existing cottage industry generally did not occur. Consequently, the new firms did not show the same pattern of clustering as in the Sjuhärads district. In the 1940's, this dispersal of new firms over rural areas and small towns, which is so characteristic of the ready-made clothing industry, has continued unabated. In this period a new factor has become important—the branch systems of established firms created in response to shortages of labor in the old locations. Besides the branch systems and some other new elements in the process, the formation of new firms has proceeded very much along the same lines as in the interwar period.

The *hosiery industry* shows a shift in its locational pattern resembling that in the ready-made clothing and garment industry. While there was relatively less entry in the cities, the dispersion over rural areas and small towns was much the same. The Sjuhärads district was prominent but not to the same extent as in the case of the clothing industry.

The *paper processing industry* had the rather pronounced character of a big-city industry both at the beginning of the interwar period and at its close. So many new small businesses were, however, started in

---

[12] Cf. Ålund, "Möbel industrins uppkomst och första utveckling i Virserum och Tibro," *Möbelvärlden* (1946), p. 44 ff.

[13] Cf. B. Sterner, *Sjuhäradsbygden*, publ. by Industriens Upplysningstjänst (Stockholm, 1949).

towns that previously lacked a paper processing plant that there was a rather conspicuous shift in the industry's overall locational pattern. As was pointed out in Chapter 12, this is explained mainly by the fact that many of its more or less novel products could not be economically transported over long distances.

Unfortunately, it has not been possible to study closely the location patterns of the *concrete products industry* and of the *soft drinks and mineral water industry*. There is no doubt, however, that for the same reasons as in the paper processing industry these industries also show a similar dispersion to areas that previously lacked such firms.[14]

Among the industries with a more or less drastically altered locational pattern, the *tanneries* should be mentioned. In this case, the industry became less dispersed than it had been previously. Most of the firms in small towns around the country disappeared, while a limited number of big firms in major towns, but not in the big cities, not only survived but also grew. There was little entry into this industry, and the formation of new firms did not play a significant role in changing the pattern.

In contrast to the industries discussed thus far, the traditional patterns of the *confectionery, light chemicals,* and *canning* industries changed relatively little between the wars, despite lively entry into all three. The first two largely maintained their concentration in major towns. This was particularly true of the light chemicals industry, in which the manufacturing firms had developed out of commercial establishments to such a high degree. The confectionery industry, however, still shows a significant number of new firms in communities that previously lacked such firms. The canning industry retained its traditional concentration in Göteborg and Bohuslän to a particularly high degree. The decisive factor was proximity to the raw material and the industry's link to the fisheries.

A survey of discontinued enterprises shows that firm *mortality* was highest in medium-size and large towns and in the big cities. Of 2,318 firms in rural areas or small towns at the end of 1918, 638, or 29 percent, had disappeared by 1940. In the rest of the country the corresponding figures were 647 out of 1,793, or 36 percent. If the tanning industry, where the mortality of small tanneries in small towns was particularly high, is excluded, this tendency becomes more pronounced. Some branches show exceedingly high firm mortality in the urban centers. As noted above, examples of this are the furniture industry and the clothing industry. The reasons for this were made clear in Chapter 12. The mortality rate for the new firms started during the interwar period was highest in major towns also.[15]

---

[14] Concerning the concrete products industry, cf. L. Bjerning. *Skanes jord- och stenindustri* (Hälsingborg, 1947).

[15] Cf., however, p. 379n.

In summary, the data on the number of firms in different localities show a certain shift away from major towns toward smaller communities. This tendency becomes particularly marked if the tanneries are excluded. The increase in the number of very large firms in rural areas and small towns which took place between the wars is particularly significant. By 1939, there were no less than 48 big firms with more than 500 employees in relatively small communities and only 22 in the three biggest cities. The formation of industrial enterprises did not, however, give rise to any significant number of entirely new population agglomerations during this period. Localization in literally rural areas was all in all a rather rare phenomenon, something which does not appear to have changed during the 1940's. In the typical case, the formation of industrial enterprises apparently led to a considerable acceleration of population growth in small communities that already existed and had begun to grow as the result of other causes.

The data are summarized in Tables 22(*a*) and (*b*), 23(*a*) and (*b*),

TABLE 22*a*
Number of Firms in 1919 Grouped According to Geographical Location and Size of Work Force

Rural and Urban Areas According to 1929 Population	Firms in 1919 According to Size of Work Force in That Year					Unknown but		Total
	1–7	8–19	20–99	100–499	500+	under 100	over 100	
	Number of Firms							
Under 10 000...	896	498	574	242	23	84	1	2 318
10 000— 20 000...	90	63	61	24	4	9	—	251
20 000—100 000..	210	157	189	57	9	27	—	649
Over 100 000...	347	215	212	65	13	41	—	893
Total.......	1 543	933	1 036	388	49	161	1	4 111
	Percentage of Firms							
Under 10 000...	58	53	55	62	47	52	100	56
10 000—100 000...	6	7	6	6	8	6	—	6
20 000—100 000...	14	17	18	15	18	17	—	16
Over 100 000...	22	23	20	17	27	25	—	22
Total.......	100	100	100	100	100	100	100	100

and 24. For a more detailed picture, the reader is referred to the maps (pp. 371–72) and to Appendices 7, 8, 10, and 11 of the Swedish edition.

The question of the relative importance of the different causes underlying this shift with regard to the number of firms from major towns to smaller communities poses problems which we cannot undertake to solve here. We will only note a number of different factors that were

TABLE 22b
Mortality between 1919 and 1939 among Firms in Operation in 1919 Grouped According to Geographical Location and Size of Work Force

Rural and Urban Areas According to 1929 Population	Discontinued Firms, as a Percentage of the Number of Firms in 1919, Grouped According to Size of Work Force in that Year							
						Unknown but		
	1–7	8–19	20–99	100–499	500+	under 100	over 100	Total
Under 10 000	31	36	30	9	—	36	—	29
10 000— 20 000	39	56	39	29	—	44	—	42
20 000—100 000	31	36	33	16	—	44	—	32
Over 100 000	35	48	35	23	23	46	—	38
Total	32	40	32	14	6	40	—	32

of obvious importance. Most of these are well-known and have been emphasized in studies that take up the problem of the location of manufacturing industries.[16]

It should be recalled, to begin with, that the unusually large number of big firms outside the major towns represents an old pattern, typical

TABLE 23a
Number of Enterprises Newly Established 1919–39 Grouped by Geographical Location and Size of Work Force

Rural and Urban Areas According to 1929 Population	New Firms 1919–39 Grouped by Size of Work Force at Date of Entry							
	1–7	8–19	20–99	100–499	500+	Unknown but under 100	Unknown	Total
			Number of Firms					
Under 10 000	1 566	410	147	23	—	154	3	2 303
10 000— 20 000	107	32	20	4	—	7	—	170
20 000—100 000	306	96	38	1	—	36	—	477
Over 100 000	622	190	73	7	—	75	4	971
Total	2 601	728	278	35	—	272	7	3 921
			Percentage of Firms					
Under 10 000	60	56	53	66	—	57	43	59
10 000— 20 000	4	4	7	11	—	2	—	4
20 000—100 000	12	13	14	3	—	13	—	12
Over 100 000	24	26	26	20	—	28	57	25
Total	100	100	100	100	—	100	100	100

[16] Cf. H. Nelson, "Industrialisering och stadsbygdsbildning," *Svensk Geografisk Årsbok* (1947). Also *Betänkande angående hantverkets och småindustriens befrämjande SOU* (1946, No. 40).

TABLE 23b

Mortality of Enterprises Established 1919–39, Grouped by Geographical
Location and Size of Work Force

Rural and Urban Areas According to 1929 Population	Discontinued Firms as a Percentage of Total Formed in 1919–39 by Size of Work Force at Date of Entry							
	1–7	8–19	20–99	100–499	500+	Unknown but under 100	Unknown	Total
Under 10 000.....	11	17	16	—	—	37	33	*14*
10 000— 20 000.....	17	22	20		—	57		*19*
20 000—100 000.....	17	23	32	—	—	47	—	*22*
Over 100 000.....	21	21	26	43	—	57	—	*25*
Total..........	*14*	*19*	*21*	*9*		*44*	*14*	*18*

of Sweden, which is due to the strong raw material and energy-source
orientation of two of the dominating industry groups—the iron and steel
and the forest industries. In the interwar period, however, such orientation
was not an important factor in the formation of new firms. One must,
therefore, look for other causes in order to explain the continued localization in small communities.

Location in major towns became less advantageous than previously
for those industries that were not tied to raw material or energy sources
in the manner indicated above. The more rapid rise of wages and real

TABLE 24

Number of Firms in 1939 Grouped According to Geographical
Location and Size of Work Force

Rural and Urban Areas According to 1929 Population	Firms in 1939 According to Size of Work Force in That Year							
	1–7	8–19	20–49	50–99	100–249	250–499	500+	Total
	Number of Firms							
Under 10 000....	1 419	1 005	555	292	219	84	48	*3 622*
10 000— 20 000....	97	80	43	25	23	12	6	*286*
20 000—100 000....	304	196	136	73	64	25	18	*816*
Over 100 000....	507	351	213	86	70	39	22	*1 288*
Total........	*2 327*	*1 632*	*947*	*476*	*376*	*160*	*94*	*6 012*
	Percentage of Firms							
Under 10 000....	61	62	59	61	58	53	51	*60*
10 000— 20 000....	4	5	5	5	6	8	6	*5*
20 000—100 000....	13	12	14	15	17	16	19	*14*
Over 100 000....	22	22	22	18	19	24	23	*21*
Total........	*100*	*100*	*100*	*100*	*100*	*100*	*100*	*100*

estate values in the major towns, together with more restrictive fire ordinances, etc., are factors to note. Labor shortages, on the other hand, did not play a significant role in the interwar period.[17] In this respect, circumstances changed in the 1940's, when many firms created branch systems in response to labor shortages in their original locations.[18] Other factors, which evidently were of great importance, reduced or even eliminated the disadvantages of locating in small towns and rural areas. The automobile and improved communications in general made many firms less dependent on proximity to their markets than previously. The electrification of rural areas and small towns and the expansion of telephone and telegraph facilities were also important.

These factors which improved the opportunities for small firms outside urban centers at the same time contributed to the interwar shift in the recruitment of enterprise founders. Earlier periods show strong historical development relationships between the formation of new manufacturing enterprises and city-centered commerce. These became less dominant when the rural areas and small towns, where commerce was less well developed, began to offer improved opportunities for new firms. At the same time, however, it is evident that other circumstances also contributed to the shift in the recruitment of entrepreneurs and thus, in turn, to the change in location patterns. The commercialization of rural areas and small towns and the rise in the level of educational attainment closer to that of urban centers were undoubtedly important. It should also be recalled that the tendency in many areas for employees of older firms to start their own manufacturing businesses was most prevalent outside the major towns. For a worker dissatisfied with his place of employment, the major towns offered more opportunities of moving to other employers than were found in rural areas and small towns. Dissatisfaction with job conditions would not necessarily be the only inducement. Often the limited opportunities for advancement within a stationary, or only slowly growing, firm would be the decisive factor. When such a firm was located in a large town, the dissatisfied employee found it easier to leave the firm and obtain a new job than when the firm was located in a small town or rural area. In the latter case, the alternative would be to start a new firm, to the extent that the person in question did not prefer to move to another community. While, for obvious reasons, these motives are most frequently observed among administrators, engineers, foremen,

---

[17] New firms would, on the other hand, often be particularly attracted to certain districts with a good supply of skilled labor and with a strong local occupational tradition in the relevant skills. Districts, such as Borås with surrounding areas, that were typically clothing and hosiery industry districts at the beginning of the interwar period remained as typically so by its close. Another factor, to which we will have occasion to refer, contributed to this, however.

[18] Cf. p. 373.

and so forth, they were not unusual among ordinary workers. In many cases, a firm would have been started by several partners, but when its expansion did not proceed rapidly enough to give several persons opportunities for executive positions in the long run, the result would often be desertions and the formation of new firms. Here and there in the country, and particularly in certain industries, one may thus observe some small communities with a somewhat older "mother firm" and several "offspring."[19]

Finally, as already mentioned, certain new products meant a dispersion of the formation of firms to areas previously little industrialized. For some of these new items—such as concrete products and soft drinks— long-distance transport was not economically feasible; hence the pioneering firms could not plan on covering any major part of the Swedish market.

A closer study of location patterns reveals not only the "desertion tendency" and the spread of industry into new areas in connection with product innovations, but also, between the wars, a conspicuous concentration of new firms in railroad communities. Evidently the greatly improved possibilities for economical distribution through truck transport did not give rise to a strong tendency toward locating firms at greater distances from rail connections. But this does not really demonstrate conclusively the all-dominating importance of rail transport. Probably new firms were simply attracted to the many small towns, while access to the railroads, along which these communities had originally sprung up a generation or so earlier, was at most incidental. We have already noted that industry generally tended to locate at population agglomerations which were already in existence. There is, for that matter, no lack of examples of communities without railroads but with good highway connections attracting new industry. This, of course, is not to deny that rail connections frequently were of decisive importance.

The relatively low mortality of firms in rural areas and small towns is a phenomenon worth attention for several reasons. It should first be emphasized that a great proportion of interwar firm disappearances concerned particular categories of enterprises, representing activities that were definitely obsolete. As noted in the discussion in Chapter 12 of the engineering and ready-made clothing industries, for example, these firms were located mainly in the old and major towns. The only im-

---

[19] The factors here enumerated have all tended to induce localization in rural areas or small towns. At the same time, however, they have in some instances contributed to a concentration of industrial agglomeration. Trucks and automobiles, for example, have made it possible for certain firms to market their products over a larger area and this has sometimes led to the elimination of other firms serving a purely local market. This tendency, however, cannot be seen in Tables 20 to 22 but only in the raw data.

portant exception here is that of the tanneries. But this greater tenacity of firms in rural areas and small towns should not, on the other hand, be regarded as conclusive evidence of their superior financial strength. As repeatedly indicated, the picture of low firm mortality is in some ways deceptive. Externally, these firms certainly did show greater continuity than was the case in the larger towns. In Chapter 12, however, the frequency of "concealed" discontinuations was pointed out: In small towns and rural areas, firms would undergo a change of ownership and then continue to operate in much the same and often, in the long run, just as unprofitable, manner as before; whereas in a major town, but under otherwise identical circumstances, the firm would be discontinued or in one way or another reconstructed.

This was not just a matter of more tenacious entrepreneurs tightening their belts and forever increasing their own inputs of labor. There was also a steady stream of new entrepreneurs who, partly out of sheer necessity, stepped in when a predecessor finally, albeit in many cases without bankruptcy, had to give up.[20] This compulsion to continue usually resulted from a recognition of the difficult local unemployment situation which would arise if operations at the distressed plant were discontinued. Community loyalties often provided the main reason for continuing. Problems of this kind were usually far less pressing in the major towns, where alternative employment opportunities generally existed. In rural areas, social prestige also proved an attraction for many people to become manufacturers.

The shift in the recruitment of entrepreneurs should also be mentioned here. Small blue-collar enterprises were more common outside major towns, and they struggled more tenaciously for their continued existence than other categories of firms. In general, these firms operated on a smaller scale and with less outside financing, but these were not the only reasons. The owner's entire attitude toward the enterprise was often the decisive factor. The frequently all-dominating importance of the "livelihood principle" is very conspicuous in this context. The blue-collar enterprises often operated under conditions rather different from those of other firms, not only from a purely geographic standpoint but also with regard to the entrepreneur's ability to contribute his labor to the firm in much the same manner as an ordinary worker.

The preceding discussion has already made it apparent that the formation of new firms in Sweden between the wars was, to a considerable extent and in a special sense, "constrained" in regard to its localization. Most of the new firms started in this period did not have their location

---

[20] It should be recalled that the present study does not count a change of ownership as a case of exit-cum-entry when it is not associated with bankruptcy and closing down of the plant. Cf. Chap. 10.

determined as a result of a calculation of the economic advantages and disadvantages of several, distinct alternatives. In very many cases, all alternatives but one were, for all practical purposes, excluded. In contrast to what was often the case earlier, however, it was not natural resources, the proximity of raw materials, and energy sources that constrained the choice of location. Nor was the distance to major output markets as important a constraint for the new interwar firms as it had been for new firms in earlier times, as already explained. But in a great many cases, the "human factor" may be said to have had the same effect.

No less than 80 percent of the new firms for which this information has been obtained were established in the home town of the founder or of one of the founders. Evidently circumstances were usually such that the formation of a new firm would never have been undertaken if an opportunity had not offered itself in that very community.[21] One important factor in this connection was that the opportunities to borrow from banks or from individuals usually were better for members of the community than for outsiders. As a rule, lenders also preferred to have the firm established in the same community, both because of local loyalties and because this made it easier to follow the management of the firm closely. Another conspicuous feature for which, however, no statistics can be provided was the great number of cases in which the firm was started in a locality that turned out to be the community where either the entrepreneur or his wife spent their childhood and where their parents often were still living. In one way or another, therefore, the human factor generally was *the* determinant of the location of new firms in the interwar period.

---

[21] In this connection it should also be emphasized that the formation of some of the new firms was predicated on assistance of one form or another from local governments (loans, cheap land, etc.). Localization in this way become "tied" at least to the extent that other location-determinants, as was often true, exerted only a minor influence. But it is above all during the 1940's that such local government measures have come to assume an important role.

Part IV

Conclusions

16 Systematic Summary and Concluding Remarks

A. Systematic Summary

The Interwar Period—An Era of Industrial Metamorphosis. It is no exaggeration to say that Swedish industry underwent a metamorphosis between the wars. One cannot, it is true, point to any completely revolutionary, entirely new, lines of development to compare with those that emerged during the last decades of the 19th century. But the economy proceeded so rapidly along the path it had entered upon that this alone would have drastically altered the character of industry and, thereby, of society in general. When the emergence of the many new, exceedingly important, and previously more or less unknown, lines of development is also taken into account, one has ample reason to use the term "metamorphosis."

The development of a whole range of industries was based on products that were either completely novel or were of insignificant importance at the end of World War I. This was true in part of the steel industry, and of large segments of the engineering industries, where consumer durables played a particularly conspicuous role. It was also the case with most construction materials industries. The output of the furniture industry was of an essentially different character, too. Although old products still constituted the major part of the pulp industry's output, new products were of very great importance. This was also the situation among the paper mills. At the outbreak of World War II, an almost completely new packaging industry had come into existence. By this time, several food-processing industries were also characterized by new development trends. Perhaps no other industries had changed their character to the same extent as had the ready-made clothing and hosiery industries. The light chemicals industries, finally, were in many respects unrecognizable from a few decades previously.

Illustrations of the great metamorphosis are also found outside the manufacturing sector proper. Automobiles, buses, and radio brought a development of communications almost as revolutionary as that of the railroad construction era. These developments, together with electrification, entirely changed the face of large areas of rural Sweden. The significance of the "commercialization" of rural areas through improved communications can hardly be overemphasized.

There is no purpose in trying to single out one factor as the driving force behind this metamorphosis. In reality, the progress of events reflected the complex interaction of a large number of different factors. One might claim, perhaps, that progress was based on the exceptional advances in technology realized through entrepreneurial activity. But such a general statement is not only rather empty of content, it also gives too one-sided a picture of the process. In order really to understand the development process, one must pose more well-defined questions and attempt to study the events from different points of view. Where to begin then becomes a rather subjective matter. Whatever the point of departure, one will gradually have to take up the whole array of important driving forces. Since the period studied here begins immediately following World War I, it seemed rather natural to begin by considering the consequences of that worldwide political cataclysm. The political process then emerged not just as a factor giving certain impulses to an economic process, based on essentially different determinants, but as a strong, driving force in the industrial development process.

Consequences of World War I and Impulses from the United States. In the context of the issues with which the present work is generally concerned, the transitory changes in industrial employment, dependent on the exchange and monetary policies pursued, belong in the background. For the moment we may also disregard the strategic malinvestments which took place during the war. Instead, one may begin by reemphasizing the extent to which large sectors of industry were affected by the changed conditions in agriculture. In addition, the important changes in the strategic competitive position of a whole range of industries vis-à-vis foreign industry should be stressed. Above all, however, the war gave rise in various ways to a great number of innovations, i.e., new products, new production and distribution methods, new organizational forms, etc. Conversely, it caused many products and methods to become obsolete.

Following the end of the war, Swedish farmers were hard pressed in competition with the agricultural sectors in overseas countries which had been modernized and expanded under the special circumstances of the war years. As was the case also during the 1870's and 1880's, the purchasing power of Swedish farmers evidently grew rather slowly through the 1920's. For industries particularly dependent on the demand of the rural population, this meant very limited demand-pull. On the other hand, the conditions in agriculture contributed to the increasing attraction of urban industries and communities.

In the area of industry itself, one should recall that the war had caused more rapid expansion of the heavy manufacturing sectors of many countries than would otherwise have taken place. In the process, new products and new methods had also emerged. Both these factors contributed to the difficulties which Swedish heavy manufacturing industries faced. The iron and steel industry was particularly affected and had to struggle through its third great structural crisis. The difficulties of the heavy chemicals industry should also be mentioned in this context. This industry had to cope with the keener competition of foreign industries expanded and modernized during the war. Finally, the strong inflation of the war years should be recalled. By reducing the tariff protection afforded by specific import duties the inflation had lasting effects on many domestic industries. These effects were serious not only for the industries mentioned but also for many others.

In turning to the processes on the positive side of the industrial transformation in Sweden, which in one way or another had their origin in World War I, the following typical examples may be stressed.

First, it should be pointed out that systematic and scientific technological research achieved considerable momentum during the years of the war blockade. Several research institutes were created, frequently in rather close association with industry.[1] The institutes gave an entirely new continuity to this work. Good results were in many cases already achieved during the war, but the real fruits of this development were above all harvested in the interwar period.

In considering the important events in industry, which in part had their origin in the new research laboratories, one should focus first on the greatest achievement of Swedish industry since the outbreak of World War I—the mining industry in the province of Västerbotten. Since it does not belong to manufacturing proper, this industry was not discussed in the preceding chapters. The severe wartime metal shortages caused strong financial interests closely associated with Skandinaviska Banken to initiate systematic ore-prospecting, utilizing electrical methods. The first great discoveries of rich ore deposits worth mining came in 1924.

---

[1] Cf., e.g., K. Modin, "Teknisk-vetenskaplig forskning," *Svensk ingenjörskonst och storindustri* (Stockholm, 1935), p. 177.

Subsequently, two different firms began a succession of large capital investments. Later, in 1930, the two were merged to form Bolidens Gruv AB. By that time a good foundation had been laid and the mines were supplemented with, among other things, the large Rönnskär smelter, a plant which introduced several innovations of importance. The company's production eventually had a much broader basis than originally expected. The major products were copper, gold, and silver, but the firm also produced a number of other metals, iron pyrites, and arsenic.

A number of product innovations, many of which originated during the war in the armaments-oriented steel industry at home and abroad, came to have great importance as they gradually were adopted in Sweden. The process innovations, too, frequently had their roots in the special circumstances of the war years, also in those cases when they were not just another aspect of a product innovation. The new lightweight metals, particularly aluminum, should be mentioned in this connection. Except for the demands of the war, they would certainly never have achieved such a rapid breakthrough, either in Sweden or abroad. In different ways these lightweight metals in turn gave rise to many new products in the engineering industries. Generally, these industries give innumerable examples of the decisive effects of World War I in both the product and process areas. In the beginning, this was particularly true, of course, in the belligerent countries, but the Swedish engineering firms also accumulated their own experiences and, most important, received impulses from abroad. Here the automotive and radio industries should be mentioned first of all, but it is easy to find a great number of other illustrative examples, for example, in the electrical engineering industry. The latter was stimulated greatly by the accelerated electrification undertaken in response to the wartime kerosene shortages. The new lines of modern office equipment deserve special emphasis because of their strategic importance to industrial production and distribution.

With regard to process innovations, by far the most important development was the impetus given to the "rationalization" of production. The principles for this modernization in Sweden, summarized in the concept of "Taylorism," had already been laid down before the war, but they were brought very much to the fore by the wartime demands for mass production. Taylor's works were disseminated in Swedish translations. His ideas also reached Sweden through other channels, and they attracted great interest because, among other things, of the legislation on the eight-hour day passed immediately following the end of the war. This legislation, in turn, must be viewed in the light of the acceleration of progress toward political democracy brought about by wartime conditions. The Swedish Manufacturers' Association, and its subsidiary organizations, adopted Taylor's ideas, as well as many other American innovations, and were very active in promoting their dissemination. The innovative impulses, which had originated in the experiences with wartime production abroad, and which in this way reached Sweden, were very apparent, not only in production processes and organization but also in the product area. They were very important in the different branches of the engineering industries, and especially in the textile industries. Several construction material industries, and even the furniture industry, were similarly affected. This was true of the rubber industry and of the various chemical industries also.

Thus the wartime demands on industrial production gave rise, on the one hand, to the difficulties initially discussed, and on the other hand, to the abovementioned development-stimulating innovations. But these were not the only effects. Indirectly, wartime demands also caused an acceleration of developments in many areas after the war. On the one hand, this concerned a variety of needs that were neglected during the war. The most typical example of this were the textile products whose production was restricted by import difficulties. This type of problem is of limited interest, however, in the present context since it does not concern those products that forced old products out of the market or in any other way lent drama to the transformation process. On the other hand, however, it was also a matter of the war holding back the dissemination of innovations which had emerged before the war but had not yet achieved a great breakthrough. Central heating of apartment houses is a typical example. During the war, material shortages reduced the rate at which central heating plants were installed below what would otherwise have been the case. When, after the war, central heating came into general demand, this had profound effects in many different areas. Habits of dress changed, for example, and this in turn affected the textile industry. Although of less importance, the fully preserved canned foods are another typical example. During the war, their dissemination was held back by the lack of tinplate. When the war ended, the output of these products increased dramatically.

In other areas, the wartime shortages of many products speeded up, rather than held back, the transition to new lines of development which had begun to emerge before the war. Electrification has already been mentioned, and the various industries yield numerous examples of similar processes, each of minor significance in itself but *in toto* of great importance.

It may naturally be asked whether these innovations, discussed in more detail in the previous chapters, would not have emerged even if the war had not come along. In most cases the answer would certainly be in the affirmative. The significant point, however, is that the war in various ways gave the innovation processes a strong impetus *concentrated within a brief period of time*. This caused the development to be of a different nature in many aspects than would have been the case with a more time-consuming process. Taken together, the innovations were so great that their simultaneous emergence lent drama to both sides of the development process. The tension between the new and the old became so strong that the old activities often had to be liquidated in a more painful manner than usual. New activities normally emerge rather cautiously and hesitantly and at a pace that is frequently affected by concern for old products, and for investments that have already been made within the framework of old processes. Under such circumstances, the need to liquidate is often revealed simply by the way in which old plants are allowed to deteriorate. Strong, dynamic tensions often necessitate a more dramatic liquidation process since the variable costs of old plants can only barely be covered under such circumstances. Consequently, an even, "harmonic" development process could not have re-emerged immediately after the war even if monetary and exchange conditions in the world had promptly returned to normal.

The interwar transformation of Swedish industry, however, was characterized not only by the great number of innovations which the war brought to fruition within such a short span of time, but also by the great extent to which the impulses were derived from the United States. With the end of the blockade westward, the way was open for the impulses to be felt from that country, which stood as the victor of the war and whose economy had developed extremely rapidly, particularly during the war, along both old and completely new lines. At the same time, Germany was vanquished—the country with which Sweden previously, as well as during the war years, had had its most well-established contacts, and not only in the industrial area. The German economy was in disarray, and postwar inflation made the situation worse.

This shift of power had strong psychological effects and gave rise to particularly strong impulses in the economic field. These impulses were transmitted by Swedish businessmen and industry executives; by scientists in the natural sciences, in engineering, and in the social sciences who now made the United States the destination for their study trips much more than before; by invited American experts in engineering and business administration; and by American fiction and professional literature that had been relatively little read in Sweden before the war. It is significant, for example, that from 1919 to 1939, of 214 fellowships recipients at the Stockholm School of Business, 101 traveled to the United States and only 34 to Germany, while in the period 1911–13, 6 out of 12 had gone to Germany and none to the United States. With regard to students from the Stockholm School of Engineering, the United States became at least as popular a destination in the 1920's as Germany. In the 1930's, however, Germany again attracted the greatest number of fellows, but this was, in part, due to a new policy of giving a greater number of smaller stipends. Furthermore, the quantitative breakthrough of Swedish pulp on the American market was of the greatest importance throughout the interwar period for establishing and maintaining closer contacts with the United States. To a large extent this development was due to paper-consuming and cardboard-consuming innovations in packaging and distribution methods in that country (cf. below, p. 392). The possibilities for importing from the United States improved, and the Swedish pulp exports contributed also in many other ways to new contacts with the United States. In 1913, the United States accounted for only 9.2 percent of the volume of Swedish imports. In the 1921–25 period, the U.S. share averaged 16.4 percent.

Thus the economic transformation of Sweden in the 1920's received its distinct characteristics through influences emanating primarily from the United States. This was not only a question of technological and organizational impulses of the type exemplified above, which had originated in wartime industrial experiences. Throughout this decade, a very large number of new methods, which were novel to Sweden but were not directly of wartime origin although they were distinctly American in nature, were introduced. The assembly-line techniques developed by American industry should be particularly emphasized in this context. These methods became known in Sweden in the late 1920's and subsequently became exceedingly important. In the pulp industry, the previously dominating German influence was succeeded by American influence, and this was true with many other industries, also. It is difficult, too, to disregard the strong impression that American living habits, demonstrated especially through the movies, stimulated many wholly or partly novel product developments. Therefore, even if the wartime industrial experiences had been absent, and the resulting new tendencies or strongly accelerated developments had not been present, this new westward orientation would undoubtedly still have emerged as an important source of impulses to the transformation of industrial production in Sweden. Some examples chosen from the previous analysis may be mentioned here in passing.

First and foremost, American industry at the beginning of the interwar period was relatively more engaged in the production of consumer durables—such as automobiles and household appliances—than was Swedish industry. This must primarily be regarded as a reflection of the higher living standard which the greater economic strength of the United States permitted its people to maintain, but it may perhaps be attributed in part also to consumption habits relatively independent of living standards. It can hardly be disputed that the especially rapid advance of consumer durables in Sweden must be considered against this background. It is true, of course, that a development in this direction undoubtedly would have taken place under any circumstances. Apart from the attraction of the consumer durables in themselves, demographic structural changes—particularly the high rate of household formation—together with the growth in national income based on other industries worked in this direction. But it is obvious that American influences speeded up this development through the very rapid pace at which American consumption habits were transplanted into Swedish standards of living. Among other relevant factors was the role played by the consumer credit practices which were common in the United States and spread to Sweden.

In addition to consumer durables, it should be remembered that the transformation of Swedish industrial output, and thereby the rise in Swedish standards of living, was based in large part on the development of the clothing and hosiery industries. American influences were of decisive importance here: they had an impact not only on production methods but also on fashions. Something similar was true also of paper and cardboard processing and printing. The impulses to the development of the hard corrugated cardboard box, which revolutionized packaging techniques, also emanated from the United States, as did the interest in lightweight concrete technology, which became one of the greatest innovations of the interwar period in the area of construction materials.

Last but not least, the revolutionary new principles employed in distribution should be emphasized. The increasing discrepancy between manufacturing, where costs had successively been dramatically reduced, and distribution, which long remained labor-intensive and costly, led to a revolution in the United States. American producers increasingly began to package their own products, a practice which represented another aspect of the innovation implied by the emergence of a specialized packaging industry. Simultaneously with, and as an integral part of, this development came the breakthrough of the brand-name system which led, in turn, to strongly intensified advertising. In part, this development presumed the short and fast hauls which trucks and automobiles made possible, but it was also, in itself, a contributing factor in the revolution in transportation. As the analysis of a whole group of industries has shown, this development had very strong economic repercussions. By way of summary, one of the consequences should be particularly emphasized, namely, that the majority of small firms in many industries simply could not become progressive under the new conditions. For one thing, the prepackaged brand-name products, and the independence from wholesalers which they often implied, required expensive advertising. Another integral part of this development involved the entirely new appearance of retail stores with regard to interior layout, window dressing, and so forth. This, in turn, led to the alteration of most commercial buildings in the cities. All this, which in a rather fascinating way illustrates a thoroughgoing transformation process, emerged with great force and on a broad front in the United States during and following World War I, and then gradually reached Sweden.

Finally, it may be concluded that the driving force in the development inherent in these strong American influences to a large extent compensated for the weakening of the purely domestic driving forces in the technical-economic area, which became evident particularly in the 1930's. The progress achieved by Swedish entrepreneurial activity from the last few decades of the 19th century up to World War I is probably without counterpart in its exceptional speed and in the degree to which the advances made were based on the contributions of so relatively few individuals. Although some other countries did develop at a comparable rate, among small countries, Sweden's performance must be regarded as singular, in that so many internationally epoch making innovations of purely domestic origin, especially in the engineering industries, were so decisive. This judgment is not changed by the fact that Sweden's development was based also on unusually favorable natural resource endowments—primarily ore deposits and forests. Against this background, the weakening of the interwar period is not surprising. A technological and economic development of this speed and nature must be regarded as exceptional and, in itself, as far more remarkable than the subsequent weakening of those driving forces which were of purely Swedish origin.

The First Stage of the Industrial Transformation. The first act of the transformation which the Swedish economy underwent during the interwar period took place during the 1920's. Before we summarize its distinctive features, however, the prelude—i.e., the first postwar crisis—should be discussed.

This may be done briefly since the crisis and depression of the early 1920's did not bear a strong imprint of the struggle between the new and the old. It therefore falls outside our main sphere of interest. Strongly negative development effects certainly did contribute to the great difficulties of the heavy manufacturing industries and, therefore, to the extreme severity of the depression. But it cannot be argued that difficulties of this kind were decisive. Strategic malinvestments undoubtedly played a considerably more important role; however, it was less a question of malinvestments in the formation and development of firms, in the sense that "firm" has been defined here, than of financial constructions and mergers in a more formal sense, which, when revealed, contributed to a crisis of confidence. One very characteristic feature was the very large number of peculiar "enterprises" started in the final phase of the war, often based on quite stillborn "inventions" which never got to the point of producing any output. In addition, the most remarkable combinations of various descriptions were undertaken, and all kinds of people without experience in industrial activities participated with great abandon in this "enterprise formation." These ill-conceived creations would not have survived long even had no crisis developed for other reasons. As it was, they contributed to the severity of the depression. But in this respect, the price movements due to international market developments and to Swedish exchange and monetary policies were undoubtedly the most important factor. They caused large losses on inventories which, in part, had been speculatively accumulated. In this connection one notes that in both commerce and industry the majority even of the older, honest firms had thoughtlessly adopted frivolous accounting principles for the valuation of all kinds of assets. This undoubtedly had very severe, depression-amplifying effects.

Once the acute crisis passed, the 1920's were characterized by pioneering contributions in a great many fields. To a great extent, these derived from war industry experiences in the United States, but there were also a large number of pioneering contributions unrelated to wartime experiences. In this decade, they were all promoted and realized by a relatively small number of usually older firms. The positive aspect of the transformation process which they represented simultaneously had its evident counterpart in "creative destruction." Although to a considerable extent the innovation process was the foundation for an export offensive in new fields, and this did not give rise to a struggle between new and old within Sweden, such a struggle still emerged—for example, in certain branches of the engineering industries, among the brickyards and tanneries, in the leather shoe industry, and in the textile and clothing industries.

Changes in Sweden's strategic position within the world economy, often due to great innovations in foreign countries, also had negative development effects which, in the 1920's in particular, put strong pressure on the iron and steel industry, the lumber mills, the glass industry, the porcelain and ceramics industry, and the chemical industry. One should also point out that the pioneering enterprises often had to wait rather long for the profits from their innovations. In the short run, the old methods and products which they sought to displace frequently fought a successful delaying action by calculating merely with variable costs, thus consuming the existing capital stock. In many industries, delaying actions of this type were particularly characteristic of the 1920's. Outside of manufacturing, finally, one can point to the competition between automobiles and railroads as a new development in the 1920's. During the latter half of the decade, many railroad companies suffered greatly from this competition.

Actually, therefore, the latter half of the decade was not such a period of general industrial boom as a superficial inspection of certain aggregative cyclical indicators might make one believe. The dazzling success of a relatively few industrial sectors undoubtedly already dominated the contemporary, but especially the later, popular view of the period in a somewhat misleading manner. Attention was primarily attracted by the pulp industry and by a number of engineering industry companies enjoying great success, especially in export markets. More than anything else, however, the emergence of the match industry's gigantic, systematically constructed, international power position, together with Ivar Kreuger's activities in other areas, gave such a strong impression of splendid business conditions that other conflicting impressions were discounted. To some extent, the speculative boom on the New York Stock Exchange in the late 1920's may also have been a contributing factor.

One interesting note in this context is that, in a whole range of Swedish industries, the firms generally reported profits considerably in excess of contemporary taxable income in the late 1920's, while the reverse was the case during the prosperity of the 1930's. In the 1920's, firms apparently did not want to report profit estimates "on the low side" in the same way as in the following decade. This was the temper of the times and does not necessarily mean that balance sheets were "dressed up." But the fact remains that official balance sheets of the late 1920's give too favorable an impression of profits in comparison with those of the late 1930's. This is true despite the fact that the rates of return officially reported during the boom of the 1920's were lower than those of the late 1930's.

With regard to the engineering industries, another significant piece of evidence is found in the unpublished statistics of the Manufacturers' Association which reports the number of workers who quit on their own initiative. The voluntary separations figure for the boom of the 1930's exceeds that for the boom of the 1920's by more than one-third. This cannot be misinterpreted. That it was not a question of a longer run trend, relatively independent of business fluctuations, is evident, for example, in the fact that labor mobility was higher during World War I than during World War II. Furthermore, one notes that the number of discontinued firms for every 1,000 in existence was somewhat higher during the boom of the 1920's than during the depression of the 1930's, and far higher than during the prosperity of the latter decade. The total number of annual bankruptcies in the boom years 1927–29 is listed as between 3,000 and 3,200. By 1934, the number had declined below 3,000, and in the late 1930's, it was only half as high as in the late 1920's. Data on the number of protested bills of exchange and on their total value show a similar picture.[2] Both these observations are even more remarkable in view of the fact that gross national product was far greater in the late 1930's than in the late 1920's.

Nor were the 1920's a period primarily characterized by what, in the present work, has been called demand-pull. First, it should be recalled

---

[2] Cf. the economic surveys for 1929 and 1939 in *Kommersiella Meddelanden*.

that the number of births declined greatly throughout the decade, while at the same time the age groups of younger adolescents became smaller each year. Second, the number of new marriages declined through 1924, and the subsequent increase was small. The figure for 1929 is below that for 1920.[3] It is more difficult to find data on the formation of households, but evidently the rate of formation increased through the greater part of the decade. In comparison with later developments, however, this increase appears to have been of rather modest proportions. Third, the very rapidly expanding export enterprises in the engineering industries based their success for the most part on supply-push due to new or young products. By and large, only the pulp industry enjoyed strong demand-pull.

To the extent that they were not greatly affected by the lively construction activity, or were protected from imports by high transport costs, the home-market branches generally could not depend on such "effortless" demand-pull expansion. Apart from the pressure of negative development effects domestically, this situation was mostly due to the competition from imports. The pressure of foreign competition was felt also in product areas where foreign innovations were not of decisive importance. In many broad product groups, the Swedish market was open and received little or no protection through government intervention by means of tariffs, subsidies, or other measures, or through international cartel arrangements. Effective cartel agreements negating competition within the country existed only in exceptional cases. The cartels remaining from the period before World War I had frequently been disbanded or had lost their effectiveness during the often chaotic conditions of the war and immediate postwar period. In several other cases, cartels had been rendered ineffective by the entry into the market of the Cooperative Union (KF). In the industrial expansion, which was achieved during the 1920's side-by-side with stagnation and regression in numerous areas, the driving forces lay *within* industry to a remarkably high degree—much more so than during the next decade.

In taking up the struggle with old products and old processes, the pioneering innovators and their immediate successors laid down the guidelines for the subsequent development and prepared the way for great advances on a broad front. But certain other conditions essential to the realization of these advances were not yet at hand in the 1920's. Mining of the new Västerbotten ore deposits began in earnest in the late 1920's, at which time the great Rönnskär smelter was also completed. This new mining industry was about to enter a period of revolutionary development. As the steel industry entered the 1930's, its pioneers had broken new ground, but most of the steel mills had not yet had time, or been

---

[3] Cf. *Statistiska undersökningar kring befolkningsfrågan, SOU* (1945, No. 53).

able, to follow their example. The situation was much the same in the engineering industries. An unusual discrepancy prevailed between the relatively small number of firms which had already been modernized and the majority of firms. This is true also when comparison is made between firms in the same size class. In the concrete products and light-weight concrete industry, the decisive innovations had been realized, while the brickyards had just found a successful way of defending them-selves. Here, however, the full consequences only became apparent during the 1930's. Among the plate glass works, mechanization had just been introduced. In the lumber mill industry, a few firms were conspicuously far ahead of the great majority of mills which, for the most part, struggled with financial difficulties. The small circular-saw mills had also begun to appear in upper and mid-Norrland at this time. But they were not yet of quantitative importance. In the building joinery industry, prefab-ricated frame houses and interior fittings had just begun to achieve a breakthrough, but these innovations were as yet far from generally known in the country. In the furniture industry, the new developments, which were to predominate in the 1930's, were only introduced in the late 1920's. In 1930 the innovations had just been realized by a few firms, but a general breakthrough had not yet been achieved. The pioneering contributions of the 1920's, both in this and in many other fields of industrial activity, were demonstrated at the 1930 Stockholm Exposition. Many of them were to be trend setters in the 1930's.[4] In both cotton and woolen manufacturing, a few large firms had successfully converted to new processes and new products, but the majority still struggled along with their old systems of operation. In the ready-made clothing industry, the pioneering contributions that set the stage for the subsequent excep-tionally rapid development had just been made in both the product and the process areas. This was also the case in the rayon hosiery industry. The fur products manufacturers had begun the production of long fur coats in earnest but had not yet found a sizable market for them. The paints and varnishes industry had entered the new field of cellulose enamels, but the oil enamel paints still predominated since the new prod-ucts were not yet generally known and accepted.

One development which the majority of industries had in common should be emphasized, namely, the new trends emerging in distribution. Here industry in general really stood on the threshold of a revolution. It is no coincidence that Sweden's—and at the same time, Europe's—first packaging industry of the American type began just as the 1920's ended.

One extremely significant development remains to be pointed out—

---

[4] One gets a good picture of the conflict between "traditionalism and "functional-ism" in many areas at this time in G. Johansson, "Konstindustrien på Stockholms-utställningen," *Ord och Bild* (1930), p. 485 ff.

technological research systematically conducted either within, or in close association with, industry. This trend had become fully apparent by the end of the 1920's, but the development of organized industrial research was still in its first stage in most of the pioneering industries, and it had hardly begun to emerge at all in the rest. But in all essentials, the modern counterpart of the lonely inventor-genius tinkering in his backyard shed had arrived in the form of the research staff with great resources of various kinds at its disposal. This new trend became exceedingly important to the nature of innovations and technological progress only in succeeding decades. But, as already mentioned, serious industry interest in organized research had been awakened during World War I and had steadily spread into more numerous areas of industrial activity in the 1920's. This was the decisive factor. By the end of the decade, it was only the financial resources and the sometimes necessary cooperation between individual firms that was still lacking.

Closer study of the situation prevailing at the end of the 1920's reveals that many *development blocks in the different industries* had been started. Frequently a relatively small number of firms were far ahead of the rest of the industry while other firms had, so far, been prevented from following their example due to the weak liquidity and tight credit conditions characteristic of the 1920's. In addition, it is evident that numerous strong technological and economic *structural tensions existed within the individual firms* in the sense that certain links in the productive and/or distributive chain had progressed far more rapidly than others. Innovations made in certain departments, for example, awaited their utilization in other departments where they might be just as applicable. Or the advances made at one stage increased the need for improvements in other stages where the innovations were not directly applicable. In these cases, especially, one inhibiting factor, aside from liquidity problems and "dear money," would be of purely human nature. The step from a pioneering contribution to the general dissemination of the innovation would often require a new generation taking over in management and in supervisory positions. Frequently it might also require a changed attitude on the part of the workers. During the 1920's, the dissemination of process innovations proceeded rather slowly in many areas because of the time required for a new generation to take over and achieve this more understanding attitude toward "rationalization," time-and-motion studies, and so forth. That the structural tensions within firms were so very much in evidence in the late 1920's was due to the great number of innovations which had begun to emerge immediately following the end of the war.

Toward the close of the 1920's, however, there had occurred considerable improvement in the conditions needed for the general dissemination of innovations and a more balanced development. To begin with, the pioneering contributions had only by then become more generally known even if they had been made earlier. The inducement to imitate these contributions was clear and strong. Furthermore, a long series of extensive financial reconstructions had liquidated the burden of heavy indebtedness for the firms involved. This had often been combined with mergers and specialization efforts. The purely financial after-effects of the first postwar crisis, with its deflation, had usually been surmounted. The banks, many of which had also been reconstructed, had created improved financial opportunities for manufacturing firms. To a far greater extent than had previously been common, bank executives had gained industry experience and insight into industrial problems. They no longer acted merely as guardians of bank claims. Cooperation between industrialists and bankers therefore was smoother than previously. Furthermore, many banks had converted their claims into shares. In some instances they had also been able to place these shares with the public. The capital-owning segments of society, in both the upper class and the upper-middle class, had begun to overcome the aftermath of the 1920–21 crisis which had caused them large losses. Their ability to purchase shares as well as to contribute to the financing of firms in other ways had improved.

Finally, it should be recalled that the electrical engineering industry, which was of exceptional importance to the interwar industrial expansion, had laid the foundation for new, large development blocks of a special type. In 1929, both ASEA and L. M. Ericsson started specialized contractor subsidiaries in order to create a wider market for the products of the manufacturing company. To achieve increased sales over the long run, it was not sufficient merely to supply first-class products at competitive prices and to provide an efficient sales organization. It was also necessary to create a market for the firm through wholly owned subsidiaries which contracted for electrification projects and for extensions of telephone networks. The necessity of operating in this manner had long been evident, and the companies had begun to do so at an early stage.[5] But by the late 1920's, the situation was regarded as requiring a bold new step in this direction.

The evidence set forth above has been analyzed in more detail in previous chapters. It all points to the same conclusion. *By the end of the 1920's, the Swedish manufacturing industry stood at the beginning of a strong, general expansion. In one area after another, the conditions necessary for such an expansion had either been created or were just being created.* In some cases, this was apparent, while in others, the emerging lines of development were not clearly perceived. The areas in which the end of a period of expansion had just been reached, in the sense that the achievement of a structural balance had temporarily weakened the dynamic forces, were very few. For the moment, no

---

[5] Cf. Chap. 5, p. 65.

further innovations were needed to continue the expansion. The dynamic force of those already realized was far from exhausted. On the contrary, their effects had just begun to be fully felt. Nor were many industries at the end of a period of development, in the sense that their markets had become more "saturated" than in previous years. In fact, the mechanical pulp industry and the newsprint mills were about the only examples of this. Nor had the preceding period been characterized by such sluggishness of the creative destruction associated with development that one had to look forward to a period of concentrated liquidation and adjustment. The end of the boom, on the contrary, more or less coincided with the conclusion of just such a period of liquidation and adjustment. During the entire decade, obsolete products, processes, and firms had been in process of liquidation, and most of this was finished and done with by 1930. The delaying actions, and the characteristic dumping associated with such liquidation, were also coming to an end.

It should also be strongly emphasized how conspicuously few and insignificant were the malinvestments made during the 1920's. The prosperity of this decade was in many respects characterized by the caution induced by the lessons of the first postwar crisis. Thus malinvestments were seldom made, even in the sense of building plants with some initial excess capacity "to grow into" which could create a danger, in the short run, of a critical situation arising from a temporary recession. The incomplete development blocks did, however, cause some difficulties when the depression, and its consequent economic myopia, arrived. But there will be occasion to discuss this in section B, below.

The investments carried out during the 1920's were seldom based on grossly mistaken calculations. The formation and development of firms has been investigated on a systematic, industry-by-industry basis, with reference to the developments which followed during the depression of the 1930's. Very few examples were found in which an acute crisis and financial reconstruction could be avoided only because a relatively long view was maintained, and because of the faith in the future which the late 1920's had induced. The economic problems encountered in the first few years of the 1930's were far more often due to underinvestment than to overinvestment during the preceding decade.

When the perspective is widened to take in the relationships between the different industries, another series of conspicuous structural tensions and incomplete development blocks demand attention. Thus certain industries had progressed rather far along the lines of development characteristic of the 1920's. This was true, for example, with regard to both productive and distributive organization and machinery and equipment. Other industries lagged behind simply because the application of the pioneering contributions made in the first-mentioned industries as a rule required special adaptation and sometimes secondary innovations. Another reason was that certain industries suffered from particularly low profits and impaired liquidity and credit worthiness. These industries, of which the brickyards and the ceramics industry are examples, could not afford the required investments. Negative development effects often put strong pressure on them, and they did not benefit from any demand-pull.

Turning to the economy and society as a whole, one again encounters a number of conditions at the end of the 1920's which clearly indicate that industry had not, even temporarily, reached the end of a growth period. There is, in fact, far more reason to say that an unusually rapid and general expansion was just about to begin, or was even fully underway. In part, these conditions had their origin in the manufacturing sector of the economy. At the same time, they also affected it. The areas which primarily deserve our attention in this context are, first, communications in the broadest sense and, second, construction activity.

In a most conspicuous way, the 1920's represented the adolescence of motor traffic and the bus system. These largely new modes of transportation had begun to spin their first wide-meshed net over the Swedish countryside. Their quantitative significance for the general economic development of the 1920's, must, however, not be exaggerated. Not even by the end of the decade had they achieved a significance at all commensurate with the role which they were to play in the 1930's. The very important shift toward heavier trucks, for example, had only begun, while at the same time the basic advances in the use of diesel engines had just been made. The fact that the Swedish automotive industry was entering a new stage was of great importance. The experimental stage had passed. In the years around 1930, producers were well aware of the lines of development that they subsequently were to follow. At this time, General Motors had also just completed its first large assembly plant in Sweden. Finally, one should note that the competition between trucks and buses, on the one hand, and the railroads, on the other, which had characterized the 1920's, began to be replaced by a period in which the two means of transport largely complemented each other. The railroads had adopted a new, more differentiated rate structure. They had also begun to modernize operations and to acquire their own trucks and buses; however, in 1930, this was still an incomplete development block. Despite the exceptional development of motor transport, due among other things to the diesel engine and long-haul trucking, which took place during the 1930's, the period following the depression years was by and large one of lessening competition. This was by no means simply a cyclical phenomenon, but the result of the completion of this development block.

The electrification of railroads was another area in which, by the end of the 1920's, one could look back on the first successful experiments. But the electrification of a few railroads here and there could be only one stage in the construction of a development block. The coordination of steam and electric traffic caused such severe technical and economic difficulties that the "mixed" system could only be regarded as a necessary, transitory phenomenon. By the end of the 1920's, this exceedingly important development block had just begun to emerge and was as yet far from complete.[6]

If, finally, one includes radio in the communication system, a rather similar situation is found to have prevailed here also. Swedish broadcasting began in 1925, but it was still in its infancy by 1929. Crystal receivers were prevalent everywhere. The built-in speaker, which was to displace the crystal receiver completely in the 1930's, had been introduced, however, and its dissemination was merely a question of time.

While the end of the boom of the 1920's signaled the beginning of a period of expansion in the area of communications, the outlines of which could be clearly foreseen, construction activity was already in the middle of such a period. Here it was not a question of being in the beginning stages in the same way as in the areas inside and outside manufacturing illustrated above. Nor, on the other hand, did the peak of a "building cycle" occur at this time. The successive changes in demographic structure, and the associated increases in the frequency of marriages and household formation, were fairly independent of business fluctuations; they had been going on for many years and were still continuing. Construction activity had been brisk since 1923, but the continuing rise in the frequency of marriages led to a steadily growing demand. Hence, demand at the prevailing level of rents continued unsatisfied, and a stagnation in construction was not in prospect. The small modern apartments, equipped in a manner very much influenced by the new consumer durables that the industry introduced during the 1920's, were especially in demand. There is little reason to consider the question of whether, by the end of the 1920's, "neglected needs" in one sense or other still remained in this area. It has been argued[7] that they did and that this, in part, was the result of the reduction in the capacity of the construction industry which took place during the limited building of the war years. To the extent that these arguments are warranted, therefore, we may point to this area also as one in which the consequences of the war were still discernible by the end of the 1920's.

In addition to the remaining tension in the relation between demographic development and residential construction, there was also a noticeable, although certainly less significant, lack of balance between industrial

---

[6] Concerning the pace at which the railroads converted to electricity, cf., e.g., F. Hjulström, "Sveriges elektrifiering," Geographica, No. 8 (Uppsala, 1940).

[7] Cf. Slutbetänkande avgivet av Bostadssociala utredningen, Part I, SOU (1945, No. 63), p. 66 ff.

expansion, on the one hand, and residential construction and community development in general, on the other. Everything indicates that industrial expansion in many areas had run ahead of residential construction and community development. In this connection, one should note particularly the penetration of industry in smaller towns and rural areas. Here, industrial firms often moved into communities in which the entire scale and structure of settlement was different from that required in the longer run, even for a small industrial community. New manufacturing firms in such communities would with the passage of time create a need for new apartment buildings, commercial structures, meeting facilities, etc., and at the same time a latent need for other complementary industrial firms. When studying the nature of these agglomerations at the end of the 1920's, one gets the impression that this process of adaptation within the communities frequently had barely begun in earnest. Only the first steps toward this economic-geographic development block had been taken.

At the end of the 1920's, a general industrial depression was about to begin. In summarizing the Swedish situation at this time, one may assert that there was very little that predisposed the Swedish economy toward a severe crisis and depression. On the contrary, strong dynamic forces, leading toward a rapid, general expansion, had accumulated within the manufacturing sector itself and in the economy and society in general. A period characterized by strongly conflicting tendencies in the economy had, in fact, just been concluded. Numerous new and young products had begun to expand their markets without as yet having achieved a quantitative breakthrough on a broad front. In many areas, the "rationalization" had made substantial progress and had led to a considerable saving of labor. But a tremendous amount remained to be done even if we only consider the opportunities that were then generally known. At the same time, there had been an extensive struggle between the new and the old. All of this contributes to an explanation of the lingering unemployment throughout the 1920's and of the relatively low profits in many areas during the decade.

The Second Phase of the Industrial Transformation. The summary of the situation by the end of the 1920's given in the preceding section makes it evident that the unemployment crisis which hit Sweden in the early 1930's did not originate in conditions internal to the country. There were no weak spots in the Swedish economy of such a nature that they could play an active role in the process. Nor can the decline in the demand for Swedish export products, which initiated the crisis, be explained by reference to negative development effects affecting these products. The depression of the early 190's had to some extent been caused by Swedish products being rendered incompetitive by foreign innovations and industrial expansion abroad. But this was not now true. The only exceptions of major importance would be the lumber mills and quarries. For the rest, the decline in demand fell on products which, from a long-run perspective of the industrial transformation, were strongly progressive. This, of course, does not mean that the temporary decline in demand caused by the international recession cannot be put in the larger context of the international economic transformation and thus be explained from a more global perspective with reference to the struggle between new and old in other areas, lags on the negative side of the development process, and so forth.[8] At present it is sufficient just to emphasize the conclusion that the Swedish crisis and depression were neither manifestations of the struggle between old and new within Sweden nor reflections of a deterioration in Sweden's strategic position in the world economy. Nor can they be regarded as a consequence of the immediately preceding Swedish boom. To the extent that the proposition found in business cycle theory that "the only cause of depression lies in the boom" is not just a truism, it is obviously false with regard to the present case. This must be remembered if one wishes to understand the developments of the 1930's.

More than anything else, the new phase in the industrial transformation of Sweden that had been initiated in the last years of the 1920's put its imprint on economic development during the better part of the 1930's. This decade brought the second act of the interwar revolution. In most of the important sectors of industry, the dissemination on a broad front of the innovations introduced by a small number of pioneers as well as the completion of the important development blocks, which had been begun, were developments which can easily be traced through the entire decade. A closer study of developments in those industries and areas of the economy for which the situation at the onset of the crisis was described above leaves no doubt of the nature of the process.[9] From this point of view, the depression appears as an interlude between the two acts of the transformation process. The first glimmer of better prospects in the markets for Sweden's big export products set free the whole array of strong expansionary forces, which subsequently were to be strongly reinforced by favorable export conditions, especially for the pulp industry. We will have reason to return to this below. The

---

[8] Cf. also Chap. 3, p. 35 and below p. 421n.

[9] One of several interesting indicators is the revenue of the Organization Department of AB Industribyran, a company owned by Industriförbundet (the Swedish Manufacturers' Association). The main activity of this department is consulting on the organization of production processes ("rationalization"). Following a modest start right after World War I, revenues reached an annual average of Sw. Cr. 62,000 for 1926–29. The average for the next four years, which included the depression, was Sw. Cr. 95,000 and for 1934–39 the figure reached was 140,000. This growth mainly reflects the increasing number of consultations.

improved export prospects thus created a more favorable atmosphere for a continuation of the transformation process, the first act of which had taken place during the 1920's, while its second act had been temporarily postponed by the crisis and depression at the onset of the 1930's. Although the first increase in exports primarily drew on previously accumulated inventories, and thus generated little income, it improved the liquidity of firms and caused increased confidence in the future.

The devaluation of the Swedish krona and the associated new policy of low interest rates may be regarded in much the same light. The exchange policy gave increased protection to home-market industries, raised export revenues, and improved export opportunities. The earlier policy of tight money had mainly contributed to impeding and arresting the continuation of the development of the 1920's and, thereby, to the interlude of the early 1930's. The changed character of monetary policy was one of the impulses to the recovery of 1932 and 1933, and made it easier to resume the earlier lines of development. This was true also of other general economic policies. The public works projects, financed through a deficit budget, were the most important of a number of unemployment policy measures which undoubtedly contributed toward a certain demand-pull for the manufacturing sector in these years, even though demand-pull did not play an important part until 1934. To some extent, therefore, these measures aided in removing some of the obstacles to a continuation of the expansion of the 1920's which the spread to Sweden of the international depression had created.

The new policy for agriculture was more than just a stimulus toward cyclical improvement. The strong structural tensions in the development of the manufacturing sector, and in the economy in general, during the 1920's were lacking here. Instead, Sweden's entire agricultural sector was under severe pressure from negative development effects. From the beginning of the 1930's, the policies pursued in support of agriculture were of a more active nature than was the case with economic policies generally. To the extent that this policy, by way of the improved situation in agriculture, created some demand-pull for industry, it can be regarded as giving an impetus to industrial recovery.

In turning from the beginning of the recovery to the subsequent course of development, it should first be pointed out that the dissemination of innovations did not, in the prevailing situation, necessarily lead to increased competition between firms. The adoption of the new methods and new products of the innovators by the great majority of firms did not always narrow the profit margins of the pioneering firms.[10] That

---

[10] It should be evident that both this and the following arguments rest on the realistic assumption that the situation was not one of "pure competition" in the sense of classical theory.

rates of return generally were higher in the 1930's than in the 1920's does not contradict the thesis of a general dissemination of innovations, even if one disregards the fact that negative development effects were much more in evidence in the 1920's than in the 1930's. It is undoubtedly true that profit margins in certain industries were compressed due to the dissemination of innovations. But the more conspicuous fact is that this usually was not the case. Nor are there any theoretical reasons to expect that such a narrowing of profit margins should always take place. This is made clear by considering the type of development process which was characteristic of the 1930's.

First and foremost, then, the spread of innovations did not necessarily mean hardening competition for the firms, simply because it was often a matter of dissemination of process innovations among firms with different product lines or separate output markets. In the latter case, for example, the products involved might be of a type that could not economically be transported over long distances. Even where process innovations were disseminated among firms with overlapping product lines and markets, a narrowing of profit margins was by no means inevitable. Often the dissemination process actually led to an expansion of the market, through the relative or absolute price reductions or quality improvements which the innovations made possible. This was the case, for example, in several export industries, particularly steel, paper, and pulp, where relatively long-established relationships between suppliers and customers were common.

Second, there were few instances in the 1930's of severe dumping competition by firms able to conduct a delaying action through calculating only with variable costs—and sometimes not even all of those. Although the dissemination of innovations during the 1930's narrowed the profit margins of the best firms more than would otherwise have been the case, they were still not as narrow as in the 1920's when dumping of this kind was much more common. It should also be emphasized here that both this transitory, and the more chronic, dumping characteristic of some industries frequently was brought to an end by cartel agreements. Thus such agreements contributed to a general improvement in the rates of return of the affected industries in the 1930's. During the 1920's, the situation was one of drastic disturbances in old relations between firms and associations, innumerable changes of ownership, financial reconstructions, and so forth. The 1930's offered more favorable conditions for cartels, and such arrangements even contributed to improved earnings in some industries which were not affected by dumping. How significant this was it is impossible to say, but there is nothing to indicate that it was the prime reason for the improved returns of the 1930's.

Third, it must be kept in mind that during the 1930's whole sectors and branches of industry enjoyed demand-pull to an extent not experienced in the 1920's. Numerous industries experienced a growing demand for their products which had little connection with developments internal to the branches in question. A further discussion of this point may, more than anything else, contribute to an understanding of the most fundamental features of economic development in the 1930's.

To begin with, one should point to demographic developments. The number of births increased strongly in the latter half of the 1930's. In several different ways, this created a demand-pull for the manufacturing sector to which there had been no counterpart in the 1920's. Furthermore, the number of marriages began to rise as early as in 1933, and the increase continued very strongly through the rest of the decade. While the figure for 1929 was below that of 1920, the average for the 1935–39 period was no less than 34 percent higher than the 1929 figure. At the same time, the formation of households undoubtedly increased at an even more rapid rate.[11]

One of the factors that made the strong demand-pull of the 1930's possible has already been indicated in connection with our discussion of the 1932–33 recovery phase—namely, the increased protection against foreign competition enjoyed in many areas. In addition, there was less of an incentive to compete on the part of some foreign exporters simply because the domestic markets of the countries in question put greater demands on their output. Gradually these growing demands became more and more closely connected with the arms race preceding World War II and also a source of strong demand-pull for large segments of the Swedish export sector, to which there had been no counterpart in the 1920's.

The exchange and monetary policies introduced in the early 1930's were important also in other ways to the cumulative development process, and hence to the overall demand-pull as well. While the 1920's had been a period of "dear money," credit conditions were easy in the 1930's. In the aftermath of the first postwar crisis, and while its lessons were still fresh in memory, lending was characterized by great, sometimes enforced, sometimes voluntary, caution. This was no longer the case in the 1930's. Credit on a contractually or *de facto* long-term basis became more easily available than during the 1920's, even though lenders and investors engaged in risky projects only to a limited extent and even less in speculations of the type common during World War I and especially during the immediate postwar years. Two factors joined in bringing this about. For one thing, the extremely difficult years of the early 1920's were now simply bygones—despite the Kreuger crash, the losses suffered in the crisis of the 1930's were obviously much less severe. For an-

---

[11] *SOU* (1945, No. 63), p. 153.

other, the opportunities inherent in the new lines of development, which the pioneers of the 1920's demonstrated, were much more clearly perceived.

In addition, the exchange policy was not only of importance in making easier credit conditions possible. It also had the direct effect of improving the opportunities for self-financing of the modernization of industry, i.e., the dissemination of innovations. Following the devaluation and the pegging of the exchange rate vis-à-vis the pound, net revenues from exports improved in terms of Swedish crowns. Directly, this enabled the export industries to look after their own houses better than previously; indirectly, it also helped other industries which, through various channels, benefited from the growth in export revenues. Furthermore, the dissemination of innovations in itself introduced a cumulative element. It meant improved profits and liquidity for a steadily growing number of firms, and this, in turn, meant increased opportunities to complete the modernization. During the 1930's, this also contributed toward making Swedish industry self-financing to an extent not previously experienced.[12]

In a way, this self-financing involved a form of "forced saving" from the point of view of the economy as a whole. Compared to the 1920's, profits were high. To what extent this was due to the self-evident and quite natural circumstance that the situation in most industries in this period of increasing export revenues and strong demand-pull had little or no resemblance to the "pure competition" case of classical theory, or was due to the *organized* curtailment of competition, is not the question here. The point is that the higher earnings were not used to raise dividends to any significant extent, and consequently, a relatively large proportion of national income was used for the modernization of industry.

The completion of the development blocks, which had been initiated in the 1920's, created strong demand-pull for a number of industries. This process played an increasingly important role as the 1930's progressed. The demand-pull was generated both by the large investments directly involved and by the kind of feedbacks, through increased incomes for raw material suppliers, workers, distributing firms, and so forth, which are typical of all such cumulative processes. The expansionary effect of these development blocks was all the stronger because of the size of the geographical regions affected and since the areas involved were often almost virginal from an economic viewpoint. This applies both to development blocks within single industries and to those with wider coverage. Instances of the latter type are particularly worth atten-

---

[12] Cf. A. Ostlind, "Industriens finansiering 1924–1941," *Ekonomisk Revy* (1944), No. 1.

tion. Even in those areas where industry at one time has been the decisive driving force in initiating such a development block, it played a more passive role during the 1930's when the process acquired a momentum of its own. This was the case, for example, in the field of transportation, where innovations, especially in the automotive industry, had started the process off. The growth of bus, truck, and car traffic, with all its derivative phenomena, is indeed the best illustration. But one can also point to residential construction where, after all, the purely demographic developments were not exclusively the determining factors, but industrial innovations from the 1920's also played a role. From this standpoint, economic development during the 1930's appears as a cumulative continuation of that of the 1920's. There was not at all the same kind of continuity between the 1920's and the period before 1914.

In a general way, the interaction between the factors discussed above is readily seen. But it is useless to attempt a quantitative judgment of their relative importance in the absence of a more detailed analysis than it has been possible to undertake here. One question is so significant, however, that a tentative answer should at least be essayed. The issue is this: There are many things indicating that the situation of numerous other industrial countries at the end of the 1920's resembled, at least basically, that of Sweden. It should be recognized, of course, that conclusive judgments on this point would require a detailed analysis which, as in Sweden's case, could rely only on published sources and literature. But, *if* the situation was, in fact, similar, one wonders why the Swedish economy showed stronger expansionary characteristics in the 1930's than did the majority of other countries.

To begin with, the dynamic forces inherent in uncompleted development blocks probably were unusually strong in Sweden. Everything indicates that the impulses emanating from the United States affected Sweden with particular force. In addition, Sweden probably benefited from unusually forceful industrial entrepreneurship. In part, this entrepreneurial activity was based on a number of earlier, magnificent, and peculiarly Swedish inventions. Furthermore, Sweden had escaped the direct physical and financial ravages of war and had thereby gained a certain lead.

In all probability these general considerations largely explain the particularly favorable development of Sweden in the 1930's. But it is possible to be more specific. Everything indicates that the favorable position of the pulp industry, and its consequent rapid expansion was of great importance. The growth of this large export industry, with its rather dominant position in the Swedish economy, had two consequences—which more than the factors previously discussed served to make Sweden's position different from that of most other industrial countries. Through many different channels, the expansion of the pulp industry created demand-pull for other Swedish industries. At the same time, it led to a greater supply of foreign exchange, aiding the growth-stimulating import of both capital goods and consumer goods from the United States.

But this last point does not, of course, solve the problem of the relative importance, quantitatively, of the different factors. While the analysis should indicate that one cannot regard the role of exchange and monetary policy, for example, as of primary importance, this does not mean that a general, quantitative ranking of all factors has been achieved. There are, in fact, methodological reasons why such a ranking would pose an exceedingly difficult task. It is possible to say that the second act of the industrialization process, on which the present work has focused, would have proceeded more slowly if, for example, the new exchange and monetary policies had not been pursued. But how much the process would have been slowed down is extremely difficult to judge. Furthermore, one is undoubtedly fully justified in claiming that economic development would have proceeded far more slowly, even with a much more expansionary economic policy, if the unusually strong dynamic forces which characterized both the economy in general and industry in particular had not been present, i.e., had the transformation process been in a different phase. But here, again, it is impossible to arrive at more exact conclusions. Still, these questions are of evident interest to anyone who would devote himself to a more comprehensive causal analysis of economic development in the 1930's. But they do pose very great demands, both on theoretical model-building analysis and on empirical research, within the framework of a causal analysis of this type. The present study of the industrial transformation process has only pointed to one aspect which has received little attention but which should prove fruitful to pursue in connection with a more comprehensive research effort. We will shortly have occasion to return to this point in the concluding methodological discussion.

Characteristics of the Formation, Development, and Disappearance of Firms.   In this concluding chapter, the previous analysis of the formation, development, and disappearance of industrial enterprises has been referred to in a variety of contexts. It is also possible, however, to draw some general conclusions on the subject, particularly with respect to the nature and importance of the formation of new firms as seen from certain specific points of view.

In the decades before World War I, the formation of industrial firms was largely conditioned by the fact that the industrialization process still was in a relatively early phase. It was in high degree a matter of supply-push processes based on important primary product innovations that were of purely Swedish origin with conspicuous frequency. In part, firm formation also got its character from the exploitation of rich natural resources. It was affected, too, by the fact that development took place within a social and political structure which to a considerable extent still retained features characteristic of an earlier, less advanced stage of economic development. A relatively few and small social groups still retained positions of economic, social, cultural, and political prominence and power. This permitted them to shape the industrial development after their own design, so to speak, without encountering major obstacles either in the labor market or in the general political sphere. The world market, furthermore, was generally open. The barriers at political boundaries were easily surmounted. Although political tensions gradually grew, it was only at the outbreak of World War I that political obstacles to international intercourse really developed.

Under these conditions, entry was very lively in most industries, and in addition, a remarkably high proportion of the new firms typically expanded rather rapidly and strongly. In the various branches, the successive entrants were of much the same character as the somewhat older firms. Thus, new and old firms did not complement each other—through a subcontracting system, for example. While the new firms as a rule started on a relatively small scale, there were still numerous entrants of considerable size. Many of them rapidly created a large export market for themselves, based on product innovations. As a rule, the founders and/or financiers were either private individuals or syndicates, often closely associated with the banks. To a large extent, merchants, as well as the upper class and middle class in general, constituted the pool from which founders were recruited.

In the *interwar period*, the society and industry of Sweden entered a phase of development which in a number of different respects involved fundamental changes in the conditions for the formation and development of new enterprises. In part, this new phase was the natural continuation of the preceding one, but it also bore the imprint of new international and Swedish developments, particularly in the social and political spheres. The positions of the previously dominant social groups were undermined through the shift of economic, social, and cultural influence and, thereby, of political power which the industrial development originally engineered by these groups involved. In important respects, the new phase brought a weakening of the domestic driving forces, but in return, it also involved a decisive strengthening of the impulses received from abroad. This may be illustrated by a short recapitulation of the scope and character of the formation and development of firms during this period, as presented in earlier chapters.

In certain industries, such as iron, steel, pulp, and paper, entry was insignificant, in direct contrast to the situation in the decades prior to World War I. At most, a few subsidiaries were formed or a few new plants built. For various reasons, the old companies were so far ahead and occupied such strong positions that the opportunities left for newcomers were negligible. This was particularly true because of the greater difficulties during the interwar period of raising the large sums of start-and-development capital required for these industries. It is significant that very few firms were started with funds raised through the issue of shares to private individuals. Not only was the supply of risk capital smaller, the sums required were greater than previously. Large firms were already operating in these industries, and it was not advisable to enter into competition without being evenly matched with them in terms of plant and equipment, sales organization, etc., from the beginning. The cost of building a competitive sales organization often proved the decisive obstacle. The decreased supply of capital may in turn be regarded as due, among other things, to the reduction in the number of high-income recipients and in their combined after-tax income, as well as to the fact that a growing number of such individuals had, with time, become actively engaged or otherwise interested in existing enterprises. Finally, it should be pointed out that the banks were, practically speaking, prevented from absorbing new stock issues at their own risk during the interwar period.

In other very large and important industries, the rate of entry was very high between the wars—often far higher than during the prewar decades. This was especially true of many branches of the engineering industries. In contrast to this earlier period, the formation of subsidiaries by older firms became relatively common. But apart from such cases, the new firms were usually relatively small at the start. They also remained small much more frequently than previously, at least to the extent that they were not bought up by existing firms, which was not an uncommon occurrence.

Underlying this picture were, in part, the same conditions that applied to the industries previously discussed. But some significant circumstances were completely different. In these industries, the new firms were largely of a different character than the older enterprises which had been established during the first 50 years of the industrialization process. In stark contrast to such older firms, the new firms seldom concentrated on exports. New firms contributed little to the interwar growth of Swedish exports. In general, they concentrated on products which could be produced in relatively short series, or even to individual order only. In some cases they sought a nationwide market, but very often their markets were only local or regional. They thus complemented the older, larger enterprises which frequently were reluctant to accept orders that did not concern their standard series and/or brand-name products. Often this reluctance became increasingly pronounced as firms became more generally aware of the dangers of excessive diversification and inadequate cost calculations. The great role of the many new, small, and stationary firms in the interwar period was, consequently, to a large extent associated with a change in the production structure of the larger existing firms. In numerous cases, no actual change of policy on the part of the older firms took place—it was simply that many new products appeared—each insignificant separately but important in the aggregate—to which the larger firms were not inclined to divert their resources. This was especially true with many consumer durables. But the great importance of this development, particularly in the engineering industries, was also due to the fact that many production processes became so complicated that it appeared rational to buy a number of different parts from small outside businesses, which were well-suited for production of this kind. Hence many of the new firms became subcontractors. In many industries, furthermore, the structural change in distribution toward brand names and packaging in the factories meant that the small firms tended to remain small. It became more difficult to catch up gradually with older firms that had the advantage of well-established brand names and larger financial resources. Finally, the gradual shift in the recruitment of new entrepreneurs should be mentioned. But this is the subject of a separate discussion because it was of very great importance in several different ways to the development of industry in general.

In a third group of industries, finally, formation of firms was not only lively but also of great importance to the development process. The picture here was not significantly different from that which was typical of the period before 1914. This type of firm formation was prevalent mostly in industries in which development was based largely on new products. In such industries older firms seldom possessed the same advantages as they otherwise had, even though in the great majority of cases they were the ones to introduce the new products. Usually, the new products gave rise to such a rapid supply-push expansion of demand that neither the older firms nor the successive entrants were alone able, or willing, to meet it. In many industries, such as ready-made clothing and hosiery, this supply-push process embraced a nationwide market. In other industries, such as concrete products and soft drinks, it concerned limited geographical areas since the products could not be economically transported over great distances. In the latter type of cases, the entrants, for equally natural reasons, generally remained stationary, which thus did not prevent them from together accounting for a very considerable portion of the quantitative growth of the respective industries.

Those development processes which were based primarily on new supply-push products generally gave rise to a higher rate of entry and to quantitatively more important entry than those which were mainly of the demand-pull type. To some extent, this would seem to explain why in many industries the rate of entry in the boom of the 1930's did not exceed that of the boom of the 1920's, despite the fact that the former was much more intensive than the latter—to judge, for example, from capacity utilization, employment, and rates of return of continuing firms. Hence, quite apart from the fact that in the interwar period bad business conditions had given evidence of leading to lively firm formation, there is no general correlation between the intensity of booms and the rate of entry. The necessity in a causal analysis of differentiating the import of the various processes is evident here.

In many industries, finally, the new firms contributed to the maintenance of competition. In this respect, the new plants of the Cooperative Union were particularly important. But the new entrants cannot be assigned the most important role in this connection. In a great number of cases, especially in the 1930's, the new firms mostly complemented the existing ones and competed with each other, while the older firms competed among themselves to the extent that competition was not curtailed by cartels and similar arrangements. Everything indicates that the preservation of competition was just as much due to older firms and the emergence of foreign firms in Swedish markets as to new domestic firms. This may be explained with reference both to the difficulties of starting new firms in many industries and to the fact that cartel policies, where at all important, often were rather cautious—exactly because of the risk of new entry. There were also a number of instances in which new firms preferred to live in the "shadow" of a cartel and/or entering before long into cartel arrangements with existing firms. But it must be emphasized that it is impossible to provide a general answer to the question as to which of the two concepts is the more realistic—whether new firms play a decisive role in maintaining competition in a branch or whether their capacity for doing so is very narrowly circumscribed.[13] Circumstances obviously vary drastically from one time to another and from branch to branch, while the character of competition also is highly variable (e.g., from predominantly type competition and quality competition to rather pure price competition). The question also loses significance when one considers the fact that in the final analysis it always is the human factor which is decisive. The emergence of new firms, therefore, cannot without further ado be assigned the decisive role. It should, instead, be ascribed to the appearance of new entrepreneurs and new initiative. It is characteristic that the fiercest competition frequently took place between new and old products, and that the new firms of the interwar period were not particularly responsible for the introduction of new products, even though the majority produced such products.

The shift in the recruitment of enterprise founders was a conspicuous feature in the formation of manufacturing firms in the interwar period.

---

[13] Cf. Chap. 4, p. 53 f.

Before 1914, and especially in the earliest decades of the industrialization of Sweden, the new firms, particularly in certain industries, were both founded and financed by persons who either were active in commerce, especially in wholesaling, or else had many ties to commercial activity. Landowners and government officials are also frequently found among the enterprise founders of this period. Toward the end of the 19th century, the beginnings of a shift toward the working class could be perceived. This trend became marked in almost all industries during the interwar period. The majority of firms started between the wars had workers, or persons of similar status, as founders. About 80 percent of them were started in the community where the founder happened to have his residence. Had it been possible to include all new firms and not just those reported in *Industry Statistics* in the present work, one could no doubt have concluded that only a small fraction of them had been founded by persons other than workers and those of similar status or on a different location from that of the founder's residence.

This picture is very typical of the interwar period. It is explained both by the emerging need for small businesses and by the improvement in other conditions favoring small firms. In the latter connection, the progress of motor transport and electrification was most important, particularly in rural areas and smaller towns. These factors drastically lessen producer dependence on proximity both of output markets and of energy sources. A pronounced shift in the formation of new firms from larger to smaller agglomerations can be observed throughout the interwar period. The development of banking and financial intermediaries should also be noted. This facilitated the financing of new small businesses although, to a very large extent, reliance was still placed on small amounts of founders' own cash and great amounts of founders' labor. In addition, the rising educational level of the working class was a factor of great importance. The opportunities for acquiring an advanced technical education in occupational schools, technical schools, etc., had also improved. A richer background experience in industrial work was also the rule (it is worth noting that the founders of new firms generally were not particularly young), and the possibilities for accumulating start capital improved as well.

It is of considerable interest to note how many industries followed a distinct, two-stage pattern of development—first a great expansion through the formation of new firms started by individuals engaged in commerce and through the development of these firms, and then gradually, and after a few decades with full strength, a second stage in which numerous new firms were started by workers and other subordinate employees of the first-generation firms. The expansion of the second-generation firms gradually led to a further broadening of the recruitment-base for enterprise founders. No industry was built from scratch primarily by workers, simply because a pool of trained industrial workers did not exist. But when these industries had developed over some decades, the workers would begin to loom large among the founders of new firms.

At the same time that the steadily growing importance of such blue-collar enterprises was the consequence of the features of the industrial transformation process analyzed above and of the circumstances just mentioned, it also served to alter the pattern of the development of firms. The new worker firms were frequently started not with any thought of rapid growth but, rather, on what may be called the livelihood principle. This led to the complete disappearance of the cyclical variation in firm formation which had been very marked in the period before 1914. This is not to say that there were not a number of strongly progressive firms that were started by workers, but it should be noted that the most rapid expansion frequently came only when the firm had been sold to some larger, and usually older, company. Purchases by older firms of small, promising businesses were very common in the interwar period—particularly in the engineering industries—as was the formation of subsidiaries.

The broadening of the recruitment base to include the workers undoubtedly contributed to the increased ability of Swedish industry in the interwar period to supply the country with previously imported finished goods. Such goods, which sometimes had a relatively small market, were often particularly well-suited for small blue-collar enterprises and less suitable for the older and larger firms. Not infrequently, moreover, the latter had a tradition of concentrating on different lines. It is thus rather obvious that the change in the composition of Swedish imports, described in Chapter 3, was not just the result of the exchange-rate policy and other economic-political conditions. It was due also to a rather natural and, with time, increasing participation of workers in the formation of new manufacturing firms.

The *mortality* of manufacturing firms was considerable, especially in the twenties. On the average, 22 firms out of every 1,000 disappeared each year during the 1920's and 16 out of every 1,000 during the 1930's. In addition, there were numerous financial reconstructions, which in this work have not been registered as disappearances. Despite this, firm mortality cannot be regarded as the most important cause, quantitatively, of the unemployment problems which existed during certain periods. Only in the lumber mill industry did the closing down of plants lead to severe and persistent unemployment problems. That discontinuation of firms did not generally cause more severe difficulties is explained by the fact that the disappearance of one firm frequently was followed by the formation of a new enterprise based on its plant and equipment so that a larger or smaller proportion of its work force could be kept employed continuously. In addition, the work force typically gradually declined over many years until, finally, the firm ceased operating. This gradual decline, in turn, was but one symptom of the general process which preceded discontinuation in the majority of cases—the firms in question would gradually slide into steadily more stagnant waters, with their products or production processes becoming obsolete and their managements unable to strike out on new paths. Failure was seldom a matter of speculative mistakes in the formation and development of firms. The subordinate role of speculative mistakes, may, for that matter, be ascribed, in part, to the above-mentioned shift in recruitment. The change in the entire character of entrepreneurial activity, of conditions of financing, etc., with the consequent tendency toward less grandiose and capital-demanding projects, must in part be seen in the context of the proliferation of worker enterprises.

A summary of the extent and significance of the formation, development, and disappearance of firms provides a general picture of the *character of, and changes in, branch structures*. To begin with, it should be observed that the firm structures of some branches were relatively unstable already at the beginning of the interwar period. This was the case, for example, with the tanneries, the porcelain and ceramic tile industry, and the iron and steel industry. Many small firms lacked vitality and were destined to definitive disappearance before long. Most of them were eliminated during the 1920's. The innovations, which in the 1920's and 1930's were introduced in, and disseminated through, most fields of industry with or without concurrent entry of new firms, gradually made the firm structures of other branches also unstable. In some cases, such as the engineering industries and the ready-made clothing industry, this led to the elimination of certain categories of firms even before the outbreak of World War II. In other instances, the instability still remained at the end of the 1930's. The construction joineries are one example.

If the firm structures of the various branches, as of the end of the interwar period, are grouped into dynamic and static structures, the clothing industry, the hosiery industry, and the canning industry will be found to be examples of the former category. Each had numerous firms in the process of growth, and the "underbrush" of new firms on their way up among the larger firms was extensive. The majority of the remaining branches were not very dynamic at this time. Even where many new small businesses had been formed and were still being established, as in the chocolate and candy industry for example, it was not primarily a question of growing, new firms. While these branch structures might well present a changing appearance, therefore, they were not dynamic in the same way as in the clothing, hosiery, and canning industries.

As for the situation another 10 years later (i.e., by the end of the 1940's), no firm judgment can be made without a detailed analysis of the kind we have provided for the interwar period. But it may still be established that, from all indications, very few branch structures were dynamic, even though the rate of entry was exceptionally high in several industries—for example, engineering and clothing. It is hard to find any other example of a dynamic branch structure than that of the plastic products industry which was practically new to the 1940's. In other industries, the new firms have for the most part been of such a character that they probably will either remain stationary or be weeded out. One thus finds more examples of unstable branch structures than 10 years previously. While it is difficult to gain perspective on such a recent period, there is much to indicate that the postwar years of the 1940's have brought a phase in the industrial transformation process resembling that of the 1920's in that particularly important innovations have been pioneered by a limited number of enterprises. Among other things, this seems to presage a change in the firm structure of several branches. World War II undoubtedly played an important role in generating the relevant impulses. It is also worth noting that the United States was once again the origin of most of these impulses. At the same time, it may be observed that many new firms have been brought into being due to the inflationary conditions of the war and postwar years. To that extent, therefore, the structure appears unstable, for these firms will probably disappear. But, on the other hand, many of the new small businesses which appeared during the 1940's should last since they represent a type of firm which was proliferating already before World War II, e.g., in the engineering industries. This type of firm should be seen in the context not only of the successive structural changes within the older firms, but also of the continuing shift in the social structure of Sweden. One must not forget, in other words, that the formation of new firms during the 1940's represented, in part, a natural continuation of the interwar period. A closer analysis of the transformation of manufacturing output, and of the formation and development of firms during the 1940's, would be of considerable interest—particularly since the similarities with the 1920's are rather evident, while at the same time institutional conditions differ in significant respects and the entire economic-political structure is essentially different. Not only inflation but also price controls, investment controls, exchange controls, and so forth, as well as drastically higher taxes, have entirely changed the conditions under which entrepreneurial activity functions.

B. The Industrial Transformation and the Problem of Business Fluctuations. Some Methodological Comments and Conclusions in the Light of the Results of the Causal Analysis

The point of departure for the present work has been the judgment that research on economic development has been somewhat biased in favor of a particular approach. This was discussed from a number of different viewpoints in Chapter 1. The *cyclical* aspects of development, we pointed out, have been well clarified by both theoretical and empirical research. The century-long development of business cycle research has produced knowledge of exceptional importance about the dynamics of modern economies. This knowledge is generally shared—the frequently heard reference to a multiplicity of conflicting business cycle theories may be regarded as erroneous. At the same time, however, certain aspects of economic development have been relatively neglected. Chapter 1 gave some preliminary illustrations of these, and they were summarized under the heading of economic *transformation.*

With this view of economic research on development as a point of departure and with reference to the basic methodological principles of Johan Akerman, the following working hypothesis was posited—namely, that the study of transformation could best be approached through a causal analysis, that is an analysis of a specific, actual, process with the choice of data guided by explicit and systematically formulated questions. To the *critical premise*, i.e., the judgment that certain aspects of economic development have received insufficient attention, was thus conjoined the *constructive premise* that a rather detailed study of a limited period ought to be made. This study should be conducted with a somewhat larger kit of theoretical tools than has commonly been utilized in traditional economic historical research but without attempting to elaborate a complete, independent theoretical structure. The analytical tools should be selected with reference to their relevance to a study of the *industrial transformation process*. In this way, it should be possible to bridge to some extent the obvious gulf between business cycle research and economic-historical research. Sweden's development during the eventful period between World War I and World War II was chosen as the object of study. In Chapter 4, a series of questions were formulated and a number of analytical tools for the causal analysis of this period were forged along the lines suggested by Schumpeter's well-known, but little-utilized, approach. With this causal analysis now concluded, there is reason to examine its most important results (which were summarized above) in relation to the critical and constructive premises from which the study was initiated.

To judge the results of the analysis performed in the present work as a contribution to our historical knowledge is left entirely to the reader. As has been emphasized from the very beginning, anyone who so wishes is free to regard the results primarily in these terms. A discussion of the meaning of the results in relation to the problems of business cycle research should, however, be of some interest to those who wish to regard the results from a more theoretical angle. It is then appropriate to link this discussion to the question of the *relationship between industrial trans-*

formation and business cycles. It should be understood, however, that the discussion will deal primarily with some relatively limited aspects of these relationships—namely, the industrial tranformation and business cycles in Sweden—and that only some rather general and preliminary reflections can be attempted. To begin with, we will consider Schumpeter's hypotheses about the role of innovations. In earlier chapters, we have regarded these hypotheses primarily as an approach to the analysis of economic transformation, but here they should be conceived of as constituting a *business cycle theory*.

Schumpeter regards his "primary cycle" as the essential component of business fluctuations.[14] Variations in employment are the primary outward manifestation of this cycle. The "secondary cycle," caused by speculative excesses and cumulative processes of various kinds, will often be more conspicuous since it gives the impression of serious depression. But, in Schumpeter's view, it is always the innovations that fundamentally determine every cyclical process through their ability to render older products and processes obsolete, and through the processes in the money and capital markets which this sets in motion.[15] This view applies both to the short Kitchin cycles of three or four years' duration and to the "standard" seven to eleven year Juglar-cycles, and to a considerable extent, also, to the long Kondratieff cycles, i.e., the secular fluctuations in economic activity.[16] In Schumpeter's view, therefore, recessions reflect what has been called in this work "the negative side of economic development" and the processes related thereto, although the trough of the depression is not so regarded. In other words, cyclical fluctuations are synchronized with those stages in the transformation process which are primarily characterized by the struggle and victory of new activities over old. Within this conception, therefore, there is no problem in coordinating the cyclical analysis of economic development and the analysis of transformation. The relationship between progress and fluctuations is indeed conceived to be fundamental.

---

[14] Cf. Schumpeter, *Business Cycles*, Vol. 1 (New York, 1939), p. 130 ff.

[15] According to this view, the system will twice be momentarily in an "equilibrium neighborhood" in passing from peak to peak of the cycle. The "secondary process" will, however, move the system off the first of these equilibrium neighborhoods in a contractionary direction before endogenous forces turn it around in an expansionary direction so that it reaches the second equilibrium neighborhood. Schumpeter refers to the period between these two equilibrium neighborhoods as the "depression," while the contractionary phase of the primary cycle is called "recession." Having reached the second equilibrium neighborhood, the system will begin on another primary cycle caused by a new wave of innovations. Although at the outset of a new primary cycle there may still be present "unabsorbed" elements of a primary cycle of longer period, Schumpeter thus considers even the shorter fluctuation from the equilibrium neighborhood of one recession to the equilibrium neighborhood of the next as essentially related to transformation of the economy by innovations.

[16] Schumpeter, *op. cit.*, Vol. I, p. 172.

The question then is whether this can be regarded as realistic. Schumpeter's answer to this is, by and large, in the affirmative. He is, however, forced to emphasize a variety of "external" factors—such as political events, serious deficiencies in the organization of credit markets, and so forth—as "disturbances" which sometimes disrupt the synchronization in question. Since these "external" factors are often dependent on institutional conditions and political boundaries, the temporal pattern of the processes is sometimes found to vary among the large countries which he studied. Schumpeter did not discuss how the question should be answered with reference to those smaller countries for which foreign trade plays a very large role, and for which strong reasons exist to assume that cyclical variations in their employment in all circumstances primarily follow international economic fluctuations.[17] Sweden can be counted in this category of countries, at least from the turn of the century. With regard to the earlier economic development of Sweden, one cannot draw very firm conclusions. With some reservations, however, it was concluded in Chapter 5 that the depressions of the 1870's and 1880's probably should be regarded as synchronized with a typical "liquidation and adjustment phase" in the economic transformation process. For these depressions, it is at least possible to argue that their causes were basically to be found in the innovations of the preceding booms at home and abroad. With regard to other crises and depressions, however, this way of putting it would in all probability be misleading. Most of the evidence seems to indicate that they were not primarily characterized by the last struggle of old processes and products with new processes and products. As for the interwar period, it is evident that the negative

---

[17] We may note in passing that almost the entire business cycle literature has been in high degree "global" and that *international relationships have not been integrated into the theory.* Many business cycle theories leave unanswered the question of whether the analysis pertains to the "closed" economy of a particular country or, in some way that is not clearly explained, the entire world economy. To the extent that the international aspects of economic fluctuations are at all discussed, the problem has usually been regarded purely as one of the dissemination of cycles, a fact heavily underscored by J. Åkerman in connection with exposition of causal analysis in his *Ekonomisk teori,* Vol. II (Lund, 1944). Not even Schumpeter's exposition is quite clear on this point. In the context of his work it might otherwise be worthwhile to develop the hypothesis that the struggle between new products and processes in one country and the old in another country, in conjunction with the particular sluggishness in the liquidation of the obsolete—due to the use of tariffs, subsidies, etc.—frequently to be observed where political boundaries are involved, may at intervals create serious disruptions in the world economy. The result could then be crises and depressions even in cases where a struggle of this kind might not have such consequences had it taken place *within* each separate country. As indicated in Chap. 3, the depression of 1930–33 represents at least one example of a crisis and depression in which international economic relationships played a very large role. This, *nota bene,* was not just due to linkages via the money and capital markets but also to relationships between the transformation processes in the different countries that quite evidently hinged on political factors.

development effects made themselves strongly felt during the entire 1920's—also in the midst of "general" prosperity. The crisis and depression of the early 1930's, on the other hand, were only in small degree a direct—or via the "secondary process", an indirect—reflection of the negative component of the development process, i.e., of the struggle between new and old activities within Sweden, or between new foreign and old Swedish activities. On the contrary, the crisis appeared at the *end* of a period characterized by such a struggle. The prosperity of the 1930's, finally, was indeed "general" by almost any criterion, but in no way did it start from a situation which could be termed an "equilibrium neighborhood." It emerged instead from a situation dominated by unusually strong structural tensions.[18]

In summary, therefore, the Swedish economy was exposed to "disturbances" which always originated abroad. These initiated cumulative contraction processes, which were sometimes weak, sometimes strong, but usually short-lived. The nature of these disturbances has not been analyzed in detail in the present work, both because this has already been done in several earlier works by various authors and because the main objective of the present work has centered on an essentially different sphere. For the same reason, it has not been appropriate to enter into a detailed analysis of the directly associated cumulative processes. For our purpose, it is necessary only to emphasize that the latter cannot possibly be understood except by use of standard tools of business cycle research. Not only the crisis and depression, but also the prosperity of the 1930's, for example, can and must be reconstructed in the terms of standard business cycle theory. One must analyze the mutual relationships between changes in investment activity, the production of capital goods and consumer goods, and consumption and their connection with events, e.g., in the money and capital markets during the different phases of the cycle. But, quite apart from whether these cumulative cyclical processes are initiated and amplified by external disturbances or whether the transformation process is synchronized with the cycles in the way described above, the analysis of economic transformation may, on the one hand, give life and more tangible content to such a reconstruction and, on the other, provide insights into the special features of the cumula-

---

[18] Nor is it warranted to assume that the Swedish Juglar-cycle of the interwar period was superimposed on a declining Kondratieff in order to "explain" the "adjustment stage" of the twenties as part of the trough phase of the longer cycle. First and foremost, the negative side of the development component should still be particularly in evidence during the trough of the Juglar. But this was not the case in 1931–33. Furthermore, it is undeniably difficult to regard World War I as a turning point in the sense that the completion of the "absorption" of previous, very great innovations had consequences that, from this time onward, began to submerge the consequences of the first emergence of other, later innovations related to the Juglar-cycle.

tive processes associated with different periods of prosperity or depression. This type of analysis can, therefore, be of value apart from the picture of the transformation process which it provides and which is of interest independently of the general problem of business cycles. As an illustration, one may point to differences between the situations underlying the booms of the 1920's and those of the 1930's, even though certain relationships, e.g., between investment, employment, and income generation, remained similar from a "cyclical" standpoint. One could also point to the extent to which the formation of new firms, and its cyclical variation, was affected by shifts in the character of firms and in the recruitment of enterprise founders.

This causal analysis focusing on the transformation process does not, therefore, reveal the relationship between industrial transformation and economic crises as being strong in Sweden, in the sense that crises and general depressions were an unavoidable, organic part of its progress. But the relationship is, on the other hand, evident in the fact that the transformation process, especially during certain periods, has always created weak sections in the economy. The factors making the economy progressive have also made it sensitive to a variety of contractionary impulses, but of a type not directly related to the Swedish industrial transformation process. Instability has undeniably been inherent in the nature of the transformation, and the more new activities have emerged, the more old ones have come to appear as obsolete and ripe for liquidation. If the decline in exports which hit Sweden in the early 1930's had taken place in 1926, for example, the resulting depression would in all probability have been considerably more lengthy than was actually the case in 1931–33 since, from the present perspective, the economy undoubtedly was more sensitive at the earlier than at the later point in time.

The relationship between rapid transformation and severe depressions may also be viewed from another perspective to which business cycle research has also devoted far more attention. This perspective is indeed of central concern to those business cycle theorists who, in contrast to Schumpeter,[19] emphasize partial overinvestment and malinvestments due to mistaken forecasts of one kind or another.[20] With regard to Sweden, the causal analysis undertaken has only provided firm conclusions on

---

[19] It cannot be emphasized too strongly that Schumpeter's theory was *not* a malinvestment theory. Cf. Chap. I, p. 10, and Schumpeter, *op. cit.,* Vol. I, p. 140.

[20] We are not referring here to those theories which assume general overinvestment in a context of undersaving and regard this as the sole factor responsible for crises and depressions. Nor are we referring to the general underconsumption theory viewed as a monocausal business cycle theory. Too much has already been written on these theories during the century-long development of business cycle research. The results have been most discouraging, for the gap between theoretical hypotheses and empirical fact has been wide and deep throughout and very little attention has been given to the transformation aspects of economic development. Cf. Schumpeter, *op. cit.,* Vol. I, p. 141 ff.

this question for the interwar period. With reference to the first half-century of industrialization, we can point only to the crisis of 1873 as one which probably did have strong elements of such malinvestments, while any judgment on the other crises of this era must remain exceedingly uncertain, even though there is very little in the printed sources to indicate that malinvestments were of much significance.

These sources, in fact, do not even give much support to the thesis that revelation of malinvestments and possibly associated bankruptcies have served to trigger the crises in Sweden, whereas they apparently did play this role in several other countries where, it is significant to note, several crises have been named after the enterprises commonly regarded as having triggered them. With reference to the Swedish interwar period, there is some evidence of this relationship in the 1920–21 crisis, to the extent that the process was made more severe by the emergence during the 1914–20 period of a large number of strange, formal cases of firm formation and firm development, as previously explained, and by the use of frivolous principles for the valuation of plant and inventory. But it should then also be stressed that misconceived firm formation, in the sense of construction of new factories or expansion of older ones, did not play a dominant role either in triggering the crisis or in shaping the course of the depression. There can be no doubt, however, that these factors played a much more significant role than in the crisis and depression of the 1930's. In the latter case, they were by and large of no consequence. Nor is there anything to indicate that the boom of the 1920's was characterized by increased inventory holdings. Thus, with regard to malinvestments in general, in the sense intended here, it cannot be said that the Swedish economy was more sensitive to disturbances at the end than it had been in the midst of the prosperity of the 1920's. The formation of new firms, particularly, was of little significance. The Kreuger enterprises were by and large the only exceptions, but for the most part they did not involve the formation of new firms in the sense of new real capital being created.

There is also a third aspect to the relationship between transformation and cycles. It is evident that the existence of incomplete development blocks, particularly common when transformation is very rapid, usually involves a weakness in the economic system in the short run, while at the same time it means a strong dynamic force. When at a certain point in time, one or two segments of such a block that had required large capital investments were completed, weak liquidity, possibly as a consequence of revoked credits, could evidently lead to very severe financial difficulties for the entrepreneurs responsible for the construction of these segments. A development block, as a rule, requires good liquidity and a long planning perspective since the investments often will only earn a return when at least the major part of the block has been completed.

In certain periods of the industrialization of Sweden, this factor played a rather important role. This appears to have been particularly true in its earlier phases when some very capital-demanding development blocks were under construction, involving, for example, railroads and industry, industry and power stations, industry and construction contracting, sales organizations, etc., while the banking and financial intermediaries of the time left much to be wished for. Under such conditions, it was only natural that the economy would be rather sensitive to contractionary impulses which in various ways brought a shortening of planning perspectives and liquidity crisis. Whether voluntary or forced, this shortening of perspectives would make many investments appear as malinvestments. In the latter case, it was often a question of a conflict between the perspectives of financiers and those of entrepreneurs. As pointed out in connection with the analysis of the first half-century of the industrialization of Sweden, this often gave a rather dramatic flavor to the development process. We also noted that such crises very often led to different persons or groups from those initiating the development blocks completing them. Those who lacked the ability to perceive the development blocks or the funds to complete them had to leave the arena and frequently suffered great losses in the process, while the newcomers, who often could buy the first segments cheaply and then were able to complete the blocks, laid the foundations to large fortunes.

It must be emphasized, however, that this factor, relatively neglected in economic-development research, has been of varying significance in different periods, and that it hardly ever has been the dominant one in shaping the course of a depression. Undoubtedly, it has served more to sharpen the initial crisis than to make the depression more severe, particularly because of the strong dynamic forces inherent in it. As for the Swedish interwar period, it is evident that the incomplete development blocks played a very subordinate role from 1919 to 1922. We can also conclude that while there were an unusually large number of them by the end of the 1920's, they did not especially contribute to making the depression of the early 1930's more severe, even though tight monetary policy, and the shortening of the perspectives in the initial crisis and during the first stage of the depression, undoubtedly created difficulties for many enterprises. This was especially true of all those firms that had not as yet been able to follow the examples set by the pioneers and/or had expanded or modernized certain productive stages or departments in advance of others and, therefore, had a productive apparatus with a particularly bad structural balance. The reason for the moderate effect of the many incomplete development blocks is found in the fact that the banking and credit system was far more stable than during the first phase of industrialization; hence, in spite of everything, the credit crisis did not become as severe and above all not as long-lived.

The dynamic forces inherent in the development blocks could thus more easily and rapidly reassert themselves. The monetary policy pursued from 1931–32 onward also worked in the same direction. In addition, it appears that the expansion of firms was financed by plowing back profits to a larger extent than previously.

Finally, it should be noted that the interwar period showed no complete counterpart to the development blocks requiring exceptionally large amounts of capital and a very long time for their completion, as had been involved, for example, in the construction of the railroads and in the industrialization of surrounding areas in an earlier era. On this issue, however, a deeper analysis would be of particular interest. In this area, where the concern of economics and business administration overlap, it is impossible without a more detailed investigation to give a more precise account of the role played by the incomplete development blocks in the crisis and depression of the early 1930's. But there is no doubt that this factor, in contrast to those previously discussed, tended to make the economy more sensitive to external disturbances as the 1930's succeeded the 1920's than it had been in the mid-1920's.

A much more intensive and, above all, extensive analysis than has been feasible in the present work would evidently be required in order to reveal all the relevant aspects of the relationships between economic transformation and business fluctuations. The present work has, of course, dealt almost exclusively with a number of questions specifically restricted to the transformation of Swedish industry in the period between the wars. Still, there are a couple of methodological conclusions which may be drawn from the results summarized above.

First, if it is desired to arrive at a judgment on the relationship between economic transformation and business fluctuations, and on the related question of the tendency of booms gradually to make the economic system more sensitive to "disturbances" of various kinds, the need is clearly evident for an analysis differentiated with regard to time and place. We have shown that the brief boom immediately after World War I meant an increasing instability both because of the gradual intensification of the struggle between new and old activities and because of the malinvestments based on mistaken calculations of one sort or another that were made. But one cannot ascribe a very significant role to the development blocks which were begun during the boom but on which construction was interrupted in the crisis. With regard to the boom of the late 1920's and the crisis and depression that followed, on the other hand, such development blocks did play a certain, albeit far from predominant, role, while both the struggle between new and old activities within the country and malinvestments in the sense indicated receded into the background.

Second, there is reason to caution against generalization. Such a warning is, for that matter, implicit in what has been said about the necessity of differentiation. Not even with regard to Swedish experience alone is it possible to fit the business cycles and the industrial transformation processes into the framework of some general theory. The kind of results which are possible consist in demonstrating the evident similarity between certain aspects of different processes. But parallel occurrences and repetitive phenomena will emerge in quite different dress from one time to another, and in addition, they apply as a rule only to parts of the field being studied. In causal analysis, it is advantageous to draw attention to these repetitive phenomena by taking as one's tools of analysis, for example, the concepts of supply-push, demand-pull, development block, etc., which have been central to the present work, or the so-called acceleration principle of business cycle theory. But the *instrumental* character of these concepts must be stressed, and they must be complemented in various ways in any more extensive analysis. The criterion of their significance is their usefulness in helping to trace specific relationships in the data referring to a certain period and the extent to which they serve to systematize and order the historical description. But there is no compelling reason to strive to link together the results of the causal analysis into some general and universally valid theory of development and/or business cycles.

Third, we may conclude that there is no reason to assume a priori that the best approach to the study of the problems of economic progress will emerge through an analysis focusing on *business cycles*. Since in Sweden the impulses to a crisis have generally come from abroad, e.g., through the markets for exports and imports, and since experience shows that they always suffice to create a depression whenever they occur, to that extent there are hardly any reasons to tie the study of Swedish economic development to this particular chronology of ups and downs in the economy. Instead it would appear more fruitful to proceed somewhat independently of the business cycle issues and to focus, for example, on the *periodicity of the industrial transformation process*. It is hoped that the present work has shown that the periodicity evidenced in different areas in the struggle between new and old activities—in the completion of what has been termed "economic development blocks," in the relationship between supply-push and demand-pull growth processes, in the driving forces underlying the formation and development of enterprises, in the shifts in the firm structure of industries, and so forth—is not without significance. Increasing attention devoted to problems of this kind need not mean neglect of business fluctuations. It only means that they are approached in a roundabout fashion which may yet prove to be a shortcut to the understanding of their changing nature and character.

This conclusion leads, in turn, to the area of economic-political issues. Since these issues fall completely outside the purview of the present work, we will only take brief note of the fact that it evidently is of the greatest importance in formulating economic policies to make use of the insights into the development problem provided by the analysis

of economic transformation. One cannot very well claim that this somewhat banal truth has been entirely disregarded, say, in contemporary business cycle research. So-called "structural" changes in the economy have,
in particular, gradually received increasing attention, especially in
Sweden. But it still seems justified to argue that the subject has not yet
received its due. For the most part, the interest in structural change
has only meant that some account has been taken of certain such changes
which, while very important, are still of a rather general nature. It can
hardly be disputed that the stabilization policies of the different countries
have lacked sufficient foundation in a more many-faceted analysis of
their development, and that these policies, consequently, have been un-
duly influenced by theories which have originated, at best, in the experiences of some particular country, usually the United States. There is,
after all, every reason to expect quite different results from, for example,
a countercyclical financial policy or a drastic low-interest policy, depending upon whether one is in a stage of the transformation process characterized by unusually strong tensions between new and old activities
and by an unusual number of incomplete development blocks, etc.,
or whether the converse happens to be the case. This, of course, applies
equally to attempts to prevent a boom from going to excess by raising
the discount rate and by tightening monetary policy in general.

Finally, a more general methodological conclusion relating to the
premises outlined in Chapter 1 seems warranted. The exploratory, and
certainly flawed, attempt made in the present work indicates that a transformation analysis which avoids the direct approach through aggregative
business-cycle analysis and avoids giving its exclusive attention to the
problem of fluctuations will open up favorable opportunities for research
in the border areas between the different social sciences, as well as in
the insufficiently explored areas which the social sciences have in common
with the field of business administration. This work has, for example,
sought to point to certain intercyclical relationships in the industrial transformation, to shifts in the recruitment of enterprise founders and in the
character of new firms and their significance for the development process,
to changes in the motives underlying the formation of new firms, and
so forth—all developments which in varying degree are related to changes
in the social and political structure of the community as well as to changes
in the nature and origin of the driving forces in the technical-economic
area. This seems to open up a rewarding area for research which we
have only touched upon but which in principle falls within the framework of the approach of the present work. To some small extent, an
effort has also been made to tie together what has heretofore commonly
been regarded as purely socioeconomic issues with issues of geography
and business economics. This has been done, for example, by utilizing
the concepts of supply-push and development block, differentiated in
various ways in the analysis of specific issues.

Indexes

Index of Names

A

Åkerman, J., 7–8, 34 n, 36 n, 65 n, 77, 417, 421 n
Åkerman, R., 70 n
Althin, T., 85 n
Ålund, S., 138 n, 271 n, 373 n
Améen, W., 141 n, 142 n
Andreasson, G., 85 n
Åqvist, T., 302 n

B

Bagge, G., 14, 20
Bilde, T., 133 n
Bjerning, L., 81 n, 133 n, 374 n
Bohman, C., 164 n, 171 n
Bosaeus, E., 81 n, 83 n, 85 n, 87 n, 141 n, 142 n
Brodén, C. G., 129 n, 131 n, 160 n
Browaldh, E., 360 n

C

Carlsson, S., 52 n, 185 n
Cederschiöld, G., 81 n

D

Dahlgren, E., 26, 31, 62 n, 76
Dalén, G., 128
Danielson, N., 158 n
Darwin, C., 8
Dillner, G., 160 n

E

Eckermann, H. von, 160 n
Ekdahl, G., 31
Ekman, G., 70 n, 160 n
Elinder, R., 176 n, 177 n, 178 n, 302 n
Eriksson, A., 136 n

F

Feilitzen, E. von, 81 n
Forsell, B., 301 n
Forsstrand, C., 81 n

G

Gårlund, T., 14 n, 19 n, 63 n, 65 n, 66 n, 73 n, 83 n, 137 n
Gasslander, O., 67 n
Gemmel, H., 146 n
Gerhard, I., 41 n
Gillberg, 164 n, 171 n
Grenander-Nyberg, G., 289 n
Grundström, S., 174 n, 323 n, 324 n, 325 n
Gustavsson, J., 31

H

Haberler, G., 4
Hägerstrand, T., 364 n
Hagnell, H., 186 n
Hammarskjöld, D., 36 n
Härenstam, C., 369 n
Heckscher, E. F., 27 n, 33 n, 64 n, 73 n, 236 n

431

Heimbürger, H., 157 n, 306 n
Hellberg, K., 85 n
Hellberg, R., 143 n
Hjulström, F., 402 n

IJ

Iveroth, A., 353 n, 369 n
Johansson, C. E., 128
Johansson, G., 137 n, 397 n

K

Kahlin, T., 327 n
Key-Åberg, K., 19 n
Kjerrman, H., 129 n
Kock, K., 14, 26, 31, 41 n, 62 n, 65 n, 76
Kragh, B., 38 n
Kreuger, Ivar, 40, 331, 395, 407, 424
Kristensson, F., 105 n, 150 n, 151 n, 154 n, 166 n, 167 n, 292 n

L

deLaval, 128
Lindahl, E., 14, 26, 31, 62 n, 76
Lindberg, E., 368 n
Linder, E., 236 n, 259 n
Lindgren, G., 186 n
Linnaeus, C., 8
Ljung, E., 137 n
Lundberg, E., 14, 20, 34 n, 35, 36 n, 40 n, 41 n
Lundén, 18 n

M

Malcolm, A., 65 n
Mantoux, F., 72 n
Marshall, A., 8, 53
Mebius, A., 136 n
Miltopaeus, E., 137 n, 138 n
Modin, K., 387 n
Montgomery, A., 19 n, 27 n, 36 n, 40 n, 41 n, 64 n, 65 n, 73 n

NO

Nyströmer, C. B., 131 n
Odelberg, A. S. W., 163 n

Ohlin, B., 35 n, 125 n
Östlind, A., 27 n, 28 n, 29 n, 30 n, 408 n
Overton, M., 364 n, 365 n, 366 n
Oxenfeldt, A., 53 n, 221 n, 237 n, 238

PR

Palme, H., 74 n
Rausing, J., 143 n
Rausing, R., 278 n
Reinholds, J., 127 n
Ring, H. A., 81 n
Rosenberg, G., 167 n
Rowe, J. W. F., 35 n
Ruist, E., 37 n, 113 n, 143 n, 175 n, 323 n

S

Sahlin, C., 69 n
Sandström, G. E., 164 n
Schiller, E., 144 n, 145 n
Schumpeter, J. A., 7–12, 35 n, 40 n, 45 n, 53 n, 96 n, 97 n, 419, 420–21, 423
Sjögren, C., 81 n
Sjunnesson, L., 146 n
Smith, W., 342 n
Söderquist, R., 141 n
Stålberg, H., 271 n
Steindel, J., 53 n
Sterner, B., 373 n
Streyffert, Th., 132 n, 143 n, 175 n
Strömberg, C. A., 173 n
Strömberg, E., 81 n
Sundin, J. A., 174 n
Svennilsson, I., 14, 20, 33 n, 37 n, 41 n, 42, 43 n, 83 n, 113 n 132 n, 143 n, 175 n, 323 n

TV

Taylor, 388
Veblen, T., 7–8

W

Wallander, J., 364 n
Werner, P. E., 174 n
Wettergren, E., 313 n
William-Olsson, W., 364 n, 365 n
Wohlin, N., 19 n

Index of Firms

A

AB Åkerlund & Rausing, 278
Apotekarnes Mineralvattens AB, 288
AB Arboga Glasbruk, 318
Ärnäs Bruk, 318
ASEA, 65, 185 n, 399
AB Åtuidabergs Industrier, 270
Avesta Jernverks AB, 311

B

Banankompaniet, 277 n
Billerud AB, 332, 334 35, 337 39
AB Billingsfors-Långed, 337
Bolidens Gruv AB, 388
Borensbergs Glasbruk, 318
Boxholms AB, 313 n
AB Bröderna Ameln, 285

C

Cementa, 134, 314–15
Charles Westerberg & Co., 254
Chokladfabriken Standard, 281–82
AB Cykelfabriken Monark, 254 n

DE

Domnarfvets Järnverk, 311
AB Emmaboda Glasverk, 318

F

Fagersta Bruks AB, 311
AB Färe Armaturfabrik, 319

Färg-och Fernissfabriks AB Arvid Lind-
gren & Co., 304
Ferniss AB, 304, 306
AB Findus, 284
Fiskeby Fabriks AB, 334, 337
Flygsfors Glasbruk, 319
Fönsterglasbrukens AB, 317
Förenade Fönsterglasbrukens AB, 317
Forsmarks Bruk, 334
Forsså Bruks AB, 277
AB Furuplywood, 263

G

AB Gefle Porslinsfabrik, 316
General Motors, 235, 401
Gimo-Österby Bruks AB, 310 11
Glafva Glasbruk, 318
Gullaskrufs Glasbruks AB, 319
AB Gullhögens Bruk, 314
AB Gunnar Collijn, 293
AB Gustavsbergs Fabriks Intressenter,
316

H

Hackefors AB, 315
Håfreströms AB, 332
AB Hägglund & Söner, 254
Halmsteads Järnverk AB, 309–10
Hellefors Bruks AB, 312
Hofors Bruk, 311
Höganäs-Billesholms AB, 309, 312
Holmens Bruk, 333, 338

IJ

AB Iföverken, 316
Jonssons Fabriker AB (Jofa), 300

K

AB Karlskrona Porslinsfabrik, 315–16
KF (Swedish Cooperative Union), 171
243, 243 n, 280–81, 284, 296 n, 303,
314–15, 396, 414
AB Konservfabriken Sirius, 285
Kopparberg & Hofors Sågverks AB,
331
Kopparfors AB, 331
Korsnäs Sågverks AB, 337
AB Kraftbox, 277
Kramfors AB, 332

L

Långrörs AB, 331–32
AB Laxå Pappersbruk, 377
Lidköpings Porslinsfabriks AB, 316
Lilla Edets Pappersbruks AB, 335
L. M. Ericsson, 399

M

Malmö Handsk-och Glacéläderfabrik,
300
AB Malmö Strumpfabrik, 296
AB Marabou, 282, 284
Margarine Company, 280–81
Margarinfabrikernas Försäljnings AB,
280
Mo & Domsjö AB, 331–32
AB Mölnbacka-Trysil, 335
Munksunds AB, 330–31

NO

AB Nordmalings Ångsåg, 262
Oscaria Group, 303
AB Österviks Glasbruk, 318
Oxelösunds Järnverks AB, 310, 318

P

AB Pappenballage, 277

R

Ramnäsa, 318
Reijmyre, 319
AB Rörstrands Porslinsfabriker, 316

S

Sala Tegelbruks AB, 320–21
Sandvikens Jernverks AB, 161, 310
AB Scharins Söner, 333

Siporex, 261
Skandinaviska Banken, 387
Skånska Cement AB, 65, 261, 314, 316
Skånska Cementgjuteriet, 314
SKF, 231, 249 n, 256 n, 311
Skönviks AB, 337, 339
Skövde Gasbetong AB, 261
Skövde Mek. Stenhuggeri & Kalkbruks
AB, 261
Söderfors Bruks AB, 310–11
Stens Choklad- och Konfektfabrik AB,
282
AB Stockholms Bryggerier, 288
Stockholms Kartong och Litografiska
AB, 277
Stora Kopparbergs Berslags AB, 311–12,
331, 334
Strömstads Canning Co. AB, 285
Sunds Glasbruks AB, 318
Sundsvalls Cellulosa AB, 339
Sunlight Group, 307–8
AB Surte-Liljedahl, 318
Svenska Aeroplan AB (SAAB), 248
Svenska Cellulosa AB, 331
AB Svenska Handelsbanken, 311–12
Svenska Skoindustri AB, 303
Svenska Suchard AB, 281–82
Svenska Tändsticksaktiebolaget (Swedish
Match Co.), 355
AB Svenska Textilverken, 339
Svenska AB Vato, 287
AB Sveriges Förenade Konservfabriker,
285
AB Sveriges Litografiska Tryckerier
(SLT), 277, 279–80

T

Tollare Pappersbruks AB, 333, 337–38
Torpshammars AB, 339

U

Uddeholms AB, 310, 331–32
Upsala-Ekeby AB, 316

V

Värnamo Wellpappfabrik, 277
AB Volvo, 235, 249 n

W

Wifstavarfs AB, 331–32
AB Wilhelm Becker, 304, 306
Wiskabergs Fabrikers AB, 341

Y

AB Ytterstfors-Munksund, 330
Yxhults Stenhuggeri AB, 261

Index of Subjects

A

Acceleration principle, 427
  adjustment process, in the Schumpeterian system, 10
Advertising material, production of, 279
Agglomeration, concept of, 363–64
Agricultural sector, 13, 15–16, 24, 30, 33, 37, 43, 84, 86, 386–87, 405
Aktieägarnas uppslagsbok, 91, 355
Armaments, international armaments boom, 162
Asplund pulp, 141, 262
Assembly-line production, 127, 146, 152, 177, 258, 294, 297, 391
Austria, 30

B

Balance of payments, 37, 43
Balance of trade, 29
Banking and credit system, 13, 24, 64, 73, 161, 240, 257–58, 351–56, 381, 392, 399, 407, 412, 415, 425
Bar iron, 70
Belgium, 296
Bessemer process, 17, 69–70, 158–59
Board of Commerce; *see Kommerskollegium*
Bond market, 361
Branch structure, 417–18
Brand-name system, 143, 146, 152–53, 156, 277–78, 282, 292–93, 296, 308 n, 392, 412–13
Brickworks, 172–73, 320–23

Brukskoncern, 311
Building joineries, 135–39, 262–69, 370–73
Business cycle research, 3–7, 11
  and the transformation process, 50–52, 419–25
Business cycle theory, 3, 6–7, 11, 75, 404, 420–23
  and investment, 50–51, 423
  Schumpeter's theory, 9–10, 420–23

C

Canning industry, 149–50, 285–87, 374
Capital; *see also* Financing of new firms
  foreign, 63, 71, 83
Cardboard industry, 143–46, 336–39
Cardboard processing industry, 146–47, 277–80
Cartels, 16, 396, 406
  brickworks, 322
  engineering industries, 233, 242 n
  glassworks, 317–18
  lumber mills, 175
  margarine industry, 171
  paper and cardboard industry, 146, 277–78, 333
  soap industry, 308
  soft drinks industry, 149
Causal analysis
  description of, 6
  relation to choice-theoretical analysis, 8
Cement industry, 132–34, 172 n, 314–15
Ceramics industry, 163–65, 315–17

Chemicals industry
  heavy, 387
  light, 155–57, 304–8, 374
Clothing industry, 151–54, 168, 288–97, 373
Commerce, 13–14, 25
  and new firms, 62, 305, 378, 415
Commercial Directory; *see Handelsregistret*
Commercial iron, 158 n
Communications, 378, 386
  with foreign countries, 73
  motor transportation, 13, 24, 324, 379, 392, 394, 401, 409, 415
  railways, 13, 16–17, 24, 67–71, 85–86, 368, 379, 394, 401–2
Competition, curtailment of, 43, 54, 408; *see also* Cartels
  engineering industry, 253–55
  shoe industry, 302–3
Concrete industry, 134–35, 260–62, 322–23
Confectionary industry, 147–48, 281–85, 374
Constitutional reform of 1864, 64
Construction activity, 28, 31–33, 37, 42, 322, 402–3, 409
Cooperative Union; *see* KF
Cosmetics industry, 307
Cottage industry, 62, 289, 299, 373
Cotton industry, 150–51, 167, 339–42
Crafts
  ceramics industry, 317
  concept of, 61, 186
  confectionary industry, 281
  employment in, 13, 24, 62
  furniture industry, 271
  glassworks, 317–19
  and industrial activities, 186
  and the industrialization process, 61–62
  leather and fur industry 298–300
  ready-made clothing industry, 153
  shoe industry, 301
Credit system; *see* Banking and credit system
Cyclical process; *see also* Business cycle theory *and* Firm formation
  important features of, 4
Czechoslovakia, 296

D

Demand-pull process
  description of, 47
  and dissemination of innovation, 132 n
  measurement of, 117–20
  and rate of entry, 200, 202–3, 205
Demographic developments, 16, 32–33, 41–42, 132, 153, 391, 396, 402, 407,

Demographic developments—*Cont.*
  409; *see also* Population of Sweden
  and firm formation, 363–81
  statistics on, 363–65
Depression of the 1930's, 26, 34–39, 146, 221, 224–26, 296, 302, 313, 328–29, 405, 421 n, 424–25
Depression of the 1920's, 26, 30, 221, 224–26, 249, 393, 403–4, 424
Desertion tendency, 379; *see also* Firm formation
Devaluation of the Swedish *krona*, 38, 40, 43, 131, 151, 155, 157, 250, 296, 405, 408
Development balance, 65–69, 159–61
Development block, 65–66, 71–74, 86, 312, 314, 360, 398–400, 402, 404, 408–9, 424–28
Development types, classification of, 196–97
Disappearance of firms
  cyclical aspects, 224–27, 255–59
  defined, 189
  and demographic developments, 374–80
  determination of death dates, 190
  geographical aspects, 374–80
  source of data, 182–84
  summary analysis, 416–17
  systematic studies, 52 n
"Dumping"
  building joineries, 268–69
  chinaware industry, 164
  engineering industries, 255, 258–59
  furniture industry, 274–75
  lumber mills, 329
  in the 1930's, 406
  shoe industry, 304
  steel industry, 314
  tanneries, 343

E

Econometrics, 3–7
Economic historical research, 3, 5–7
Economic liberalism, 26, 64
Economic transformation process
  components of, 44
  description of, 4
  principles of analysis, 46–47, 419
  the study of, 6–7, 419–28
Eight-hour day, 28, 127, 361, 388
Electrification, 15, 33, 42, 65, 250, 265, 290, 378, 386–89, 401, 415
Emigration, 75 n, 83
Employment, 20–22, 37, 39, 403–5
  in entry size classes, 194–97
Engineering industries, 13, 15–17, 28, 30, 32, 129–32

Engineering industries—*Cont.*
  development block, 65, 399
  firm formation, 229–255
    curtailment of competition, 253–55
    cyclical variation, 249–250
    financing, 240–42, 247–48, 256–58
    geographical aspects, 368–70
    market orientation, 235–36
    new firms with product innovations, 232–34, 248–49
    parallel competition, 232–33, 239–48
    product specialization, 250–53
    size of firms, 229–30
    subcontracting, 231–32, 234–39
  firm mortality, 255–59
  and iron and steel works, 159–61
  new products, 127–31, 388
  recruitment of entrepreneurs, 73, 236–38, 240–42
Enterprise, defined, 184–85
Entrepreneurs
  recruitment of
    clothing and hosiery industry, 290–94
    and financing of new firms, 357, 362
    and firm location, 378–81
    lumber mills, 324
    mineral water and soft drinks industry, 287
    shoe industry, 301–2
    summary analysis, 414–16
    woodworking industries, 266–68, 273
    before World War I, 73, 411, 415
  Schumpeter's idea of, 8–9
Entry
  control of; *see* Competition, curtailment of
  rate of; *see* Firm formation
Entry quotient, defined, 193–94, 345
Entry shares, defined, 193–94
Entry size classes, 194–97
Eskilstuna manufacturers, 17, 62, 85
Excise taxes; *see* Taxes
Exit share, defined, 193–94
Export sector, 15, 27–28, 31–33, 36–37, 39, 41, 43, 163, 236, 404–5, 407–8, 412, 423

F

Farm policy, 43, 171, 405
Financial reconstruction, concept of, 188
Financing of new firms, 63–64, 347–62, 412, 415
  bank loans, 351–56
  credit from suppliers, 353–54
  and income distribution, 358–62
  jobber financing, 354
  loans from relatives and friends, 353–54

Financing of new firms—*Cont.*
  other sources, 354
  own funds, 348–51
  and recruitment of entrepreneurs, 357, 362
  share issues, 347–48, 355–56
Finland, 134, 327
Firm, defined, 184–85
Firm formation
  and business cycles, 77–82, 208–27, 249–50, 414
  and competition, 54–55, 414
  defined, 187–88
  and demographic developments, 363–81
  determination of birth date, 188–89
  financing; *see* Financing of new firms
  geographical aspects, 363–81
  international dependence, 82, 411
  source of data, 182–84
  summary analysis, 410–16
Firm mortality; *see* Disappearance of firms
Fiscal policy, 4, 37
Forest industry, 74, 323–39; *see also* Lumber industry; Pulp industry; Paper industry; *and* Cardboard industry
France, 39–40, 64
Fruit processing industries, 284–85
Fur products, 169–70, 297–301
Furniture industry, 136–39, 270–77, 370–73

G

Germany, 8, 30, 32, 39–41, 130, 136–37, 152, 154, 301, 361, 390–91
Glassworks industry, 165–66, 317–20
Gold standard, 31, 36–40
Great Britain, 32, 39, 41, 63, 71, 72 n, 168, 174, 307

H

Handelsregistret, 182 n, 184, 326
Handicraft; *see* Crafts
Hellefors group, 312
Hesselman auto diesel, 129
Historical school (in Germany), 8
Hollanders, 145
Hosiery industry, 154–55, 288–97, 373
H.S.B., 263–64

I

Imo-pump, 129
Income distribution, 358–62
Individual operation, defined, 127
Industrial development of Sweden, 1850–1914

Industrial development of Sweden—*Cont.*
    stages of, 15–16
    statistical data on, 19–23
Industry Statistics, on the formation and
    disappearance of firms, 182–84, 185 n,
    189, 221–25
Inflation, after World War I, 29, 223,
    387
Innovation
    effect of World War I, 386–90
    influences from the United States, 388,
        391–93
    and invention, 44–46, 96 n
    and limited markets, 65–68
    during the 1920's, 397–98
    primary innovation, defined, 97, 101
    process innovation
        defined, 44
        and rate of entry, 200–205
    product innovation
        defined, 97, 101
        and rate of entry, 200–205
    in the Schumpeterian system, 9, 53,
        420–21
    secondary innovation, defined, 97, 101
    and statistical measurement problems,
        105–17
    and supply-push processes, 48, 200–205
    and the wage level, 72–75
Installed horsepower, measurement of,
    116
Investment
    new firms' share of, 345–46
    and the transformation process, 50–51
Iron industry; *see* Steel industry
Iron ores, 70–71

J

Juglar cycles, 420, 422 n

K

KF, 171, 243, 280–81, 284, 296 n, 303,
    314–16, 396, 414
Kitchin cycles, 420
Kommerskollegium, 90, 182 n, 183, 345 n
Kommunaltekniska Föreningen, 260 n
Kondratieff cycles, 420, 422 n
Kreuger crash, 40, 407
Kreuger enterprises, 32, 424

L

Labor market, 16, 20–22, 37, 52, 76, 395,
    405; *see also* Unemployment
Lancashire iron, 70, 311, 313
Leather products, 169–70, 297–301, 343

Legislation
    economic, 64
    labor (eight-hour day), 28, 127, 361,
        388
    of 1906, 328
    temperance, 141
Livelihood principle, 238, 250, 266–67,
    269, 273, 293, 357, 380, 417
Ljungström turbine locomotive, 128
Lumber industry, 28, 30–31, 68, 173–75
    effect of economic legislation, 64
    firm formation, 323–29
    before 1914, 13, 15–18

M

Malinvestment
    and the analysis of transformation, 50
    and business cycles, 423–27
    canning industry, 286
    clothing and hosiery industry, 296
    concrete industry, 262
    confectionary industry, 284
    cotton and woolen industry, 431
    engineering industries, 66, 255–59
    and firm mortality, 206–7, 255–59
    furniture industry, 270
    iron and steel industry, 85, 161, 313
    leather and fur industry, 299, 301
    during the 1920's, 393–94, 400
    paper industry, 85
    relation to regressive processes, 49
    and Schumpeterian system, 10, 423
    shoe industry, 303–4
    before World War I, 85–87
Manufacturers' discount, 63
Margarine industry, 170–71, 280–81
"Market vacuum," 205
Masonite, 136, 262
Merchant marine, 32
Mineral water industry, 148–49, 287–88
Mining industry of Västerbotten, 387–96
Monetary policy, 29, 32, 37–38, 42–43,
    386–394, 405, 407–8, 410, 425–26, 428
Munich crisis, 40

N

Nationalization Committee, 92
National income of Sweden, 14, 36
National Patent and Registration Office,
    91, 355
New York Stock Exchange, 395

O

Output
    measurement of, 89–90

Output—*Cont.*
 source of data on market value, 182
Own capital, defined, 91

P

Paints and varnishes industry, 304–6; *see also* Chemical industry
Paper industry, 18, 28, 30, 85, 143–46, 336–39, 411–12
Paper processing industry, 146–47, 277–80, 373–74
Parallel competition, concept of, 232 n
Patent protection, 247
Pig iron, 70, 158
Plywood, 136, 263
Population of Sweden, 13–15, 24–25, 366; *see also* Demographic developments
Porcelain industry; *see* Ceramics industry
Price competition
 brickworks, 322
 engineering industries, 239
 furniture industry, 274
 margarine industry, 171
 paper and cardboard industry, 145
Primary cycle, 10, 420
Profitability
 effect on investment, 51
 measurement of, 90–93
 and rate of entry, 202–3
Progressive industries
 description of, 17–18, 89
 and rate of entry, 200–204
Puddeled iron, 17, 158
Pulp industry, 18, 28, 30, 32, 68, 140–43, 391, 409
 firm formation, 329–36, 411–12

R

Rates of return; *see* Profitability
Rationalization
 concept of, 31 n, 126 n
 organizational aspects, 127
Rationalization Committee, 117 n, 325–27
Rayon products, 140–41, 150–55, 166–68, 289–91, 294
Ready-made clothing; *see* Clothing industry
Recession of 1937–38, 41, 249
Regressive industry
 description of, 47–50, 89
 and rate of entry, 200–204
Rental system, 301
Representative firm, Marshall's notion of, 53

Research, industrial, 387, 398
Roller bearings, 101, 128–29, 255 n, 311–12
Russia, 129, 255 n

S

Sampling
 stratified, defined, 183
 use of, 183
School reform of 1846, 64
Schumpeterian system, 9–11, 420–21
Shoe industry, 76–78, 301–4, 343
Soft drinks industry, 148–49, 287–88
Sponge-iron, 309–12
Stagnating industry
 description of, 47–50
 and rate of entry, 200–204
Standardization of products
 clothing industry, 340
 engineering industry, 127
 paper industry, 144
 woodworking industry, 137, 263, 276
 woolen industry, 168
State tobacco monopoly, 277 n
Stationary circular flow, 9, 48, 49 n
Steam engine, introduction in Sweden, 16–17
Steel industry, 13, 15, 17, 28, 30, 70, 84, 158–63, 330, 387–88
 effect of economic legislation, 64
 firm formation, 309–14, 368–69, 411–12
 structural tensions, 69–70, 312
Stock exchange, 356, 361
Stockholm exhibition, 128 n, 138, 297
Structure
 economic-political, concept of, 51
 industry, concept of, 52, 55
 social, concept of, 51
Subcontracting
 definition of, 231
 engineering industry, 126 n, 231–32, 234, 239
 woodworking industries, 265–66, 273
Sunlight group, 307–8
Supply push
 description of, 47
 measurement of, 117–20
 and rate of entry, 200
Swedish Cement Association, 133
Swedish Cooperative Union; *see* KF
Swedish Furniture Manufacturers' Association, 270
Swedish Manufacturers' Association, 388, 395, 404 n
Swedish Patent Bureau; *see* National Patent and Registration Office
Switzerland, 281

T

Tanneries, 176–78, 342–44, 374
Tariffs, 38, 43, 85, 155, 157, 159, 164, 170, 233, 387, 396, 407
  increase in 1888, 15, 74 n, 82
  and rate of entry, 226
Tax laws, 362
Taxes
  excise, 148, 155, 171
  municipal, 359–60
  state, 359
Taylorism, 388
Time-and-motion studies, 127, 146, 167, 177, 398
Trade press, 28, 117

Turnover of firms, Marshall's theory of, 53

U

Unemployment, 37, 75 n, 83, 405
  and firm mortality, 416
United States, 32, 35–36, 39–41, 134–38, 151–52, 156, 390–94, 409, 428

W

Wage level, changes in, 28–31, 33, 43, 74–75
Woodworking industries, 135–40, 262–77, 370–73
Woolen industry, 166–69, 339–42

This book has been set in 10 and 9 point Janson, leaded 2 points. Part numbers and part titles are in 24 and 12 point Craw Modern. Chapter numbers and Chapter titles are in 24 and 14 point Craw Modern. The size of the type page is 27 by 45½ picas.